Research Matters

Research Matters
2nd edition

Editors:

Franzél du Plooy-Cilliers • Corné Davis • Rose-Marié Bezuidenhout

juta

Research Matters 2nd Edition

First Edition: 2014
Second Edition: 2021

Juta and Company Ltd
First Floor
Sunclare Building
21 Dreyer Street
Claremont
7708

ISBN: 978 1 48513 210 3
eISBN: 978 1 48513 211 0 (WebPDF)
       978 1 48513 212 7 (ePub)

Production Specialist: Valencia Wyngaard-Arenz
Editor: Rod Prodgers
Proofreader: Deidre du Preez
Typesetter: Wouter Reinders
Cover designer: Nicole de Swardt
Illustrator: James Berrangé
Indexer: Lexinfo

Typeset in 10.5 pt on 13 Adobe Caslon Pro

Contents

About the authors

About the editors

Dr Franzél du Plooy-Cilliers is the Executive Dean: Academic at the Da Vinci Institute of Technology: School of Business Leadership. Before she joined the Da Vinci Institute she was The Dean: Research and Postgraduate Studies at The Independent Institute of Education (The IIE). Franzél started her academic career as a lecturer in the Communication Department at the Rand Afrikaans University and then joined Monash South Africa where she was the Head of Section of Communication and Media Studies. She then joined The IIE as Head of Faculty of Humanities. She is a referee for accredited journals, an external moderator and examiner, a programme reviewer for the Council on Higher Education (CHE) and is a mentor for the Phakama's Women's Academy.

Prof Corné Davis is an associate professor in the Department of Strategic Communication at the University of Johannesburg. She lectures undergraduate and postgraduate modules in strategic communication and has won a Faculty of Humanities Teaching Excellence award in 2020. Her research focuses on gender-based violence (GBV) and gender inequality as global sustainability challenges. She collaborates with NGOs such as Shared Value Africa Initiative, Matla a Bana and TEARS Foundation and is a member of Pillar 6 in the presidency's National Strategic Plan.

Dr Rose-Marié Bezuidenhout is an independent lecturer, researcher and supervisor. She has been in the academic world for nearly four decades, specialising in lecturing research on both under- and postgraduate levels. She has supervised students in communication and related fields. Her research interests are varied and multi-disciplinary and include consciousness studies, interpersonal communication, and mythological media representations.

About the contributors

Dr Franci Cronje is a Research Associate of the IIE Vega School of Brand Leadership. She specialises in the mining and assemblage of knowledge across the fields of media studies, critical studies, and sociocultural issues. She supervises master's students in the humanities, and focuses much of her attention on Academic Development Editing and conducting workshops on academic writing and qualitative research methodologies. She has an MPhil in Fine Art, a PhD in Media Studies, and an MPhil in Teaching and Learning in Higher Education.

Johannes Cronje is a professor of e-learning and the former Dean of the Faculty of Informatics and Design at the Cape Peninsula University of Technology. He has supervised 60 or more doctoral students and authored or co-authored more than 50 academic journal papers as well as numerous book chapters and conference papers in the fields of instructional design and design research.

Dr Carla Enslin is Head of Postgraduate Studies & Research at Vega School, a brand of The Independent Institute of Education. Carla's interest and experience in brand building includes the design and implementation of brand identity systems, brand alignment and contact strategies. She lectures widely in Africa and abroad and conducts corporate training, consulting and coaching, is a course supervisor and trainer for the Master of Arts and the Doctorate in Brand Leadership at Vega, a Research Associate at the University of Stellenbosch Business School and teaching fellow at the University of Cape Town's Graduate School of Business.

Ghita-Michelli Howard has been lecturing various Communication Science, Research, Sociology, Marketing, Advertising and Media Studies modules on the Pietermaritzburg, Westville and Durban North campuses of Varsity College since 2003. She obtained her Bachelor of Arts degree in Communications and Sociology through Unisa at Varsity College, Pietermaritzburg. She later obtained her Honors in Organisational Communication. In 2019 she was the Durban North nominee and KZN finalist for the The Dr Freysen Teaching Excellence Award which is an acknowledgement of the dedicated and committed work that is happening in and out of the classroom to pursue academic excellence and successful student learning that contributes to socially responsible and employable graduates.

Prof Lorette Jacobs' academic career includes lecturing at a comprehensive online distance e-learning (CODeL) higher education institution in library and information technology, archives, and records management as well as research methodology. She supervises a number of master's and PhD students and is currently conducting extensive research in citizen science as well as gamification and ethics in artificial intelligence (AI) related to archives and records management. She holds a DLitt et Phil in information science from the University of Johannesburg and a MPhil in higher education from the University of Stellenbosch.

Ross Khan is an information security consultant based in Australia. He has qualifications in technology-oriented fields and utilises various quantitative and qualitative techniques to assess the performance of information security risk treatments for monitoring and decision support.

Dr Marla Koonin is the Executive Dean: Strategy and Stakeholder Management at The Da Vinci Institute. She began her working career in the Journalism and Public Relations sector and is a registered Chartered Public Relations Practitioner (CPRP). She has subsequently held various senior academic, institutional research, programme development and accreditation-orientated positions at various public and private higher education institutions. Marla is a supervisor, has served as a referee on academic journals, an external examiner for various higher education institutions, and a programme evaluator and site panellist for the Council on Higher Education (CHE). She has published articles for mainstream media, public relations projects, academic journals and online platforms, and is the author of various chapters in several textbooks.

Dr Marianne Louw is the deputy dean of faculty operations and quality assurance at Cornerstone Institute, with an academic specialisation in interpersonal leadership relations. In addition to stints in other industries, her academic career spans over 17 years, including periods at IIE MSA, the University of Johannesburg and the Vaal Triangle University of Technology. She is the coauthor of the first comprehensive South African textbook on interpersonal communication, *Let's talk about interpersonal communication*, which saw its fifth edition in 2019, and has contributed to other textbooks on strategic organisational communication and persuasive communication.

Dionne Morris holds a MPhil from Monash University and has worked in academia for over five years, lecturing and developing curricula in personality and social psychology, quantitative and qualitative research and psychological testing and assessment. She has supervised honours students and contributed to several publications in personality and social psychology textbooks. She has a particular interest in psychological research methods and social psychology.

Gerald Pascoe is head of the Faculty of Humanities and Social Science at the Independent Institute of Education (IIE), a subsidiary of AdvTech (Ltd). He has supervised honours students and contributed to textbooks with a communication focus. He is also a member of the Golden Key Society and has worked in the public relations industry. He holds a master's degree in communication from Unisa, and an honours and bachelor's degree from Monash South Africa in communication and media studies.

Nola Payne is a Senior Head of Programme in the Faculty of Information and Communications Technology at the Independent Institute of Education (IIE). She was previously a senior lecturer at the University of Johannesburg and also lectured on the George satellite campus of the Nelson Mandela Metropolitan University. She has published several articles in her academic fields, which include higher education and IT. She has a particular interest in student employability and the development of curricula to meet the needs of the IT industry. She has 36 years' experience as an academic in IT, specialising in computer programming, and has a master's degree in education with a focus on e-learning, from the University of Johannesburg.

Dr Annemi Strydom is the Head of the Faculty of Education at Lyceum College, where she provides academic support and operational guidance to both students and lecturers in the distance as well as online modalities. She lectures research methodology, has supervised numerous post-graduate students, and was invited to develop curricula at the University of Science and Technology in Beijing, where she resided for a year, after which she was the Project Manager for the Online Programmes at Wits University. She holds a PhD in Higher Education Studies from UFS.

Preface

As human beings we are naturally curious. We like to know, understand, and make sense of the world around us. Curiosity is the driving force behind research, and research is therefore something that is supposed to come to us naturally. Researchers, then, are people who never lost their curiosity and who continue to ask critical questions. Researchers' quest for answers, in turn, has the power to change the world and to open our minds.

Unfortunately though, students often experience great uncertainty and apprehension when it comes to research. One of the reasons for this is that most textbooks on the topic are written at an advanced level and include complex explanations of the intricate research process, contributing to and affirming students' anxiety. The unfamiliarity of the process and the multitude of terminology and techniques that students need to learn and understand tend to intimidate and overwhelm them. When students are then expected to choose from, understand and apply the paradigms, theoretical constructs, and myriad of methodologies in their first research endeavour, it is not surprising that they battle with it.

It is with this in mind that *Research Matters* has been written. Its main aim is to demystify the research process for the novice researcher using a basic, step-by-step explanation of its philosophical, theoretical, and pragmatic underpinnings. Examples are presented in a simplified form to assist students to build a solid foundation in research, which they can then expand on in future.

A further aim of this book is to convince students of the importance of research, why it matters and how it can be used to contribute to a better world for all. It is through the research efforts of dedicated scholars that the world has evolved into a place where we can increase human comfort and alleviate some of the suffering and problems humanity faces. Research helps us to solve complex problems and to enhance our knowledge and understanding of the world. Moreover, it assists us in making informed decisions that guide our actions and behaviour.

We hope that this second and updated edition of *Research Matters* will instil in students a love for research and the exciting process of discovery that it inherently entails. May all who engages with this book continue to be curios and ask critical questions.

The editors
Johannesburg
December 2021

CHAPTER 1

What is research?

Corné Davis

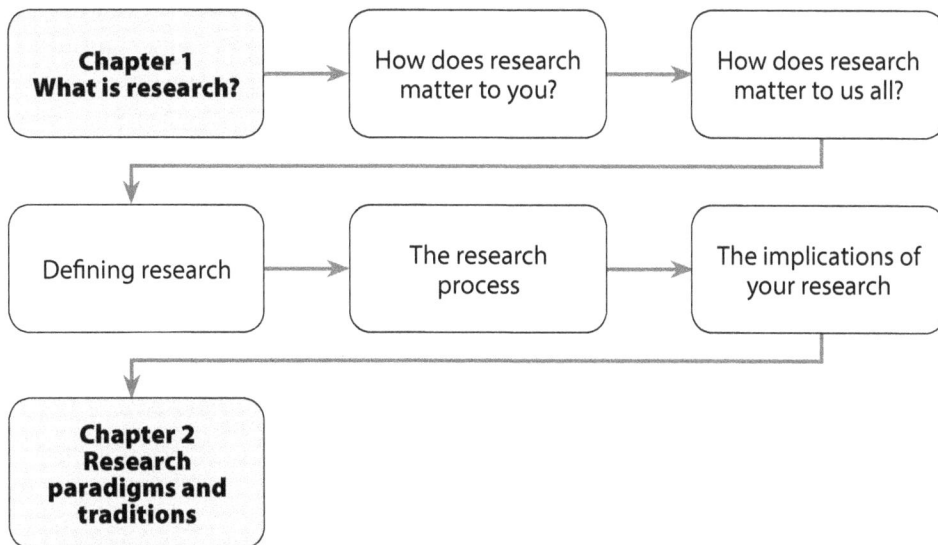

Overview

Research matters to all of us in so many important ways and it seems impossible not to notice it in every aspect and dimension of our daily lives. Yet, when it becomes a module or subject within tertiary education curricula, students generally appear to be apprehensive about it, probably because it seems complicated and difficult. The purpose of this chapter is to encourage you to change the way you look at research and to show you how you can do research that matters. While we became aware how much we depended on medical science and technology during the Covid-19 pandemic, it has also become increasingly clear how people's behaviour influenced the spread of the virus and impacted people's lives. We saw how both natural and social sciences had significant roles to play in addressing this global pandemic. If you are reading this book, you are probably a scholar in social sciences and you will likely be studying people and their behaviour for many different reasons. We will be introducing you to different kinds of research and some of the topics and decisions involved in the many different stages of the research process. There is so much to learn, indeed, but we hope to show you how exciting your research journey can be when you discover what you can do to change the world for the better in some way.

We start this chapter by reflecting with you on some of the research that you have done throughout your life, perhaps without realising it, and pointing out how this research matters to you. In terms of how research matters to us all, global sustainability has become a central theme across multiple disciplinary curricula. We are living in the information age and we are constantly presented with a cacophony of research on just about anything and everything. We have instant access to all kinds of information on the Internet at all times. Yet it seems that we never know enough. We may be on the cusp of ending the Covid-19 pandemic, but its long-term physical and social consequences are not yet clear. In simple terms, research can be described as asking questions and finding answers, but to find meaningful answers means that you need to learn how to ask meaningful questions first. We will be asking you some questions that you must answer for yourself and you will see that your answers lead to more questions. You will discover for yourself that research is dynamic and evolves constantly, meaning that there is never one right answer or one right way of doing things.

Each chapter in this book introduces you to different kinds of decisions you will make during different stages and processes of research. Think of these processes as different destinations on an exciting journey. We have created chapter flowcharts as maps which show you the specific lessons you should learn in each chapter to guide you along the way.

Objectives of this chapter

By the end of this chapter you should be able to demonstrate your understanding of the following:
- what research is;
- why and how research matters to you and to all of us;
- different kinds of research;
- the processes involved in research;
- some of the implications of research; and
- key concepts identified and discussed in this chapter.

How does research matter to you?

Understanding how research matters to you means that you have to take a closer look at yourself, your lifeworld, the things you do, the people you engage with, your beliefs, thoughts, values and many other things. In research we use the term '*observation*', and when you focus on yourself this would be called self-observation, or second-order observation. It is an interesting exercise to observe yourself while you are observing other people or objects. When you pay attention to how you observe you will see that objectivity is questionable because everybody observes differently. We will return to this point a bit later.

You don't exist in isolation and how you see your world depends on where you are coming from. We are typically born in family of relatives who live in a society with certain values, beliefs and ideas, speaking a certain language, and so forth. We grow up in specific ways that influence the way we see the world and the kinds of questions we ask. We can refer to these ways as culture, and we experience how culture can shape the way we communicate. For example, in some cultures there is a strong sense of hierarchy, meaning that there are expectations relating to how people speak to one another and what kinds of questions you may or may not ask. It may not be considered acceptable for a child to argue with an adult in some cultures for example.

You may recall that your first questions as a child primarily revolved around learning words to name people and things. If you think about it, your next level of inquiry probably involved how things worked. From there you would have progressed to learning skills, such as reading, writing, counting, drawing, and so forth. You can see that research, conceptualised as asking questions and finding answers, is something we do naturally and instinctively.

The kinds of questions you ask naturally changed as you got older and more knowledgeable and became more aware of what research mattered to you. In other words, you came to learn how you choose the kinds of information you pay attention to or not. For example, how much does information about health, fitness and diet matter to you and whose advice do you follow on these topics, if you do? Think about your frame of reference and the environment that shaped it. How do you choose what information is correct, relevant and important? When you think about the answers, you may come to see why research is so complicated, considering how many topics are relevant to you for so many different reasons and considering that there are so many (often contradictory) sources of information to choose from. Making right choices is difficult when there are so many options. The multitude of problems we have in society shows us the consequences of poor decisions that have been made and are still being made. Our lives are the outcomes of choices, whether these are good or bad. You need to consider that the past, present and future co-exist when you do research. The current challenges we face are the outcomes of past decisions, actions and phenomena and how we address these challenges now will determine future solutions and challenges.

From this perspective research as the skill of asking relevant questions and obtaining good and sound answers which can help you make good decisions can and does ultimately change your life. Whatever you decide and do changes the world in some way for you and the people in your life, and through learning how to do research you can consciously make decisions that make a difference to yourself and to others. This is why your in-depth understanding of research matters and why you need to learn so many terms and skills.

Let's start with an example that you can easily relate to so that you can look at your own informal research in more specific terms. Let's use the topic of how you decided what career to pursue, using Figure 1.1 below to guide your reflection.

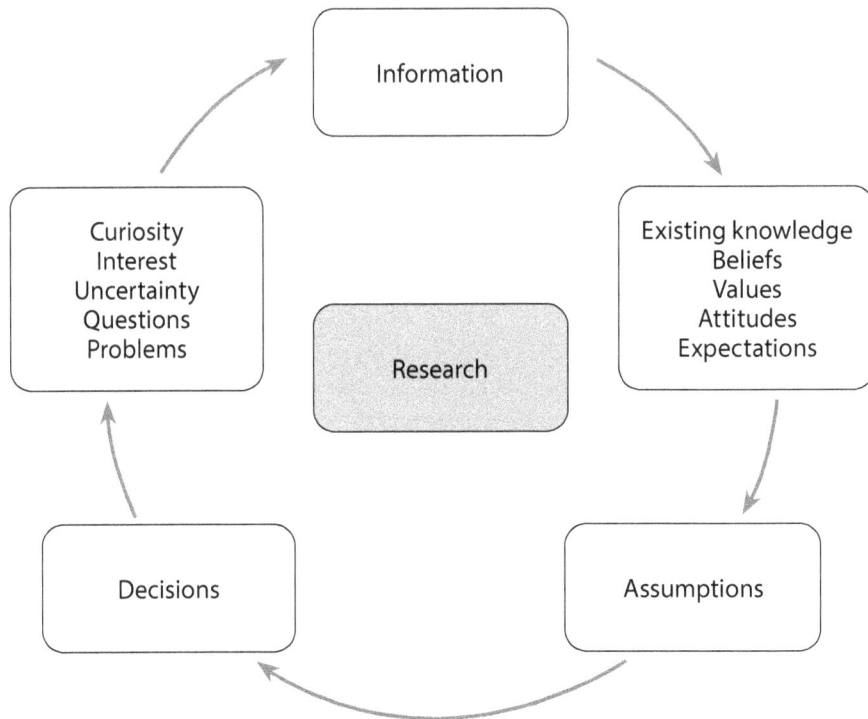

Figure 1.1 Research as a process of inquiry

The process of inquiry in this instance started with you deciding what you wanted to do after school. For some students this might have been an easy question, but for many it was not because there are typically so many things to consider. For many students, financial considerations play a significant role. Other factors include your high school examination results, access to universities and the approval and support of parents. So if you look at Figure 1.1 you would probably start with curiosity, interest, uncertainty, questions and problems that lead to the next step of finding information. However, as we alluded to earlier, it is never that simple because you need to distinguish good, relevant and useful information from bad, irrelevant and useless information. Making these decisions about information will depend on your existing knowledge, beliefs, values and expectations. For example, if you know what your desired career choice is and which college or university you want to study at, your decision still depends on your beliefs, values and expectations. If you believe that a tertiary education is important and your values include success and determination, you will expect to find the means to study, based on your assumptions. Assumptions are things you believe to be true, such as that hard work comes with rewards. Those assumptions determine the decisions you make and the things you do which lead back to further curiosity, interests, uncertainties and so forth. We go through these processes of informal research throughout our lives.

When the process of inquiry illustrated in Figure 1.1 involves other people, or society at large, we typically move to more formal research, which means that we ask different questions in different ways and for different reasons.

How does research matter to us all?

Let's look at systems-thinking for a moment to help us understand how things relate to each other. There are many different kinds of systems, including natural systems, such as ecosystems which you learned about in school. Then there are social systems, such as families, organisations, schools or even countries, for example. There are also economic, political, technological, legal and other systems. We will take a closer look at systems-thinking in Chapter 3, but for now the central understanding is that many different kinds of systems depend on each other. We say they are *interdependent*. This means that we cannot research things without considering their relations within the different systems we are working with. The Covid-19 pandemic demonstrates this clearly. While the medical scientists, such as doctors and epidemiologists, studied the virus, it was people's behaviours that influenced the spread of the virus. Thus, combatting the Covid-19 pandemic depends as much, if not more so, on studying people and their behaviour as it does on developing effective vaccines. This pandemic has led us to understand clearly how what we do affects others and, on a larger scale, how groups of individuals affect other individuals in both positive and negative ways. It presents fertile ground for many different kinds of research to make sense of the experience and to find solutions which can prevent the repetition of such a pandemic and its consequences.

Both natural and social sciences research are usually concerned with matters that affect many other people, processes and systems. Although all scientific research includes both quantitative and qualitative research methods, as we discuss in later chapters, you will find that some well-known sources, such as Denzin and Lincoln (2018) focus exclusively on qualitative research, while others, such as Babbie (2017), Walliman (2018) or Hall (2020), among many others, specifically write on research for social sciences. With reference to the social sciences, you may hear about the *narrative turn*, meaning that analysis of many different kinds of stories have come to feature prominently in social scientific research. You will notice, for example, that research methodology sources such as Babbie (2015) and Salganik (2018) tell their stories about how they became involved in research. Knowing the stories of the scholars in your field may add much value to your own research experience and what you believe about research. Do you believe that we can change the world and solve its problems? Do you believe that everybody is responsible to make this happen? I recall the day I read the paper by one of the most prolific social scientists (in my opinion of course) in the twentieth century, who introduced social systems theory based on his theory of social autopoiesis (self-creating systems) and he said the following in his paper on globalisation and world society:

> We have to come to terms, once and for all, with a society without human happiness and, of course, without taste, without solidarity, without similarity of living conditions. It makes no sense to insist on these aspirations, to revitalise or to supplement the list by renewing old names such as civil society or community. This can only mean dreaming up new utopias and generating new disappointments in the narrow span of political possibilities (Luhmann, 1998:69).

I recall the shock and horror I felt when I read these words, because as a social scientist I want to believe that we can make a difference and that we can solve some of the world's many problems if we work together. We do read many reports on successful research and we can see that there are concerted efforts to make social progress. Think of the developments in the field of gender identity and social inclusion that is currently positioned at the top of the global sustainability agenda.

Consider how the identification of multiple gender identities (that are still not recognised in many countries in the world) has implications for social scientific research. In previous research textbooks sources such as Babbie (2017:14) refer to attributes and variables, saying that a variable is 'a logical set of attributes', such as the variable sex being made up of male and female. This is no longer the case, as there are currently as many as 72 different gender identities recognised on social media platforms such as Facebook. Generally, we refer to lesbian, gay, bisexual, transsexual, queer, intersexual, asexual and other (LGBTQIA+), but many other gender identities are being recognised. Look at the United Nations web pages, for example. You will find a lot of information on this topic. Developments such as these need to be taken into account when we define attributes and variables.

The scope or extent of the matters that we address in research depends on the *perspective* we adopt. For example, the Covid-19 pandemic is a global pandemic which requires a global perspective. At the same time every country has very specific challenges that require national perspectives. There are specific factors at play in specific cities in a particular country that require a local perspective. You, personally, will have your own unique perspective, depending on whether you were sick with Covid or not or whether you lost a close friend or relative, and so forth. The perspective of your research is always an important consideration because it will determine how much time, effort or money it will require to do the research. The perspective of your research will determine the kind of questions you will ask to articulate and to achieve the purposes of your research. Figure 1.2 illustrates an example that enables us to make more sense of the process of asking questions in research.

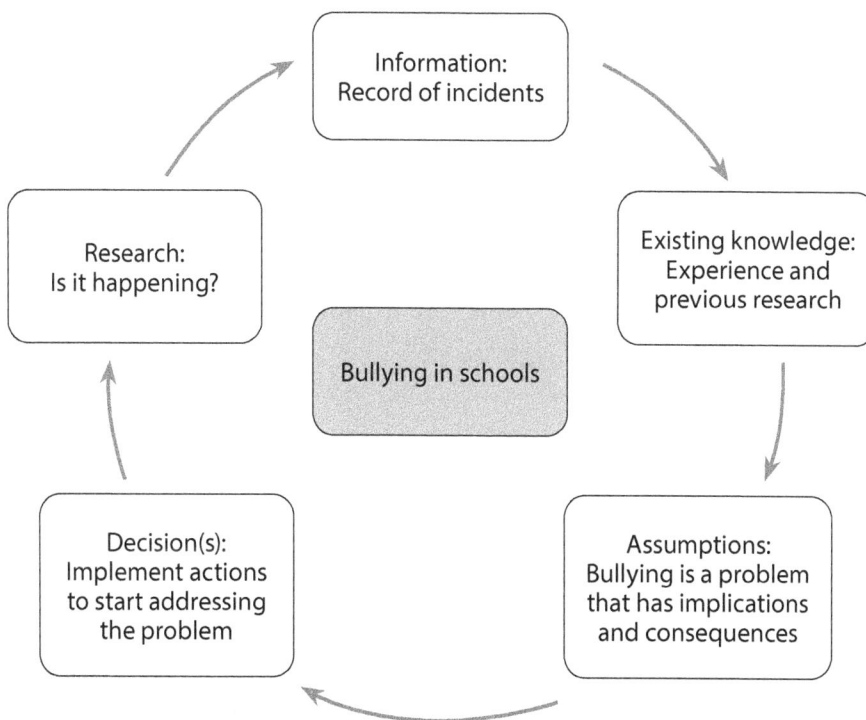

Figure 1.2 Bullying as a research problem

Some of you may be aware of a project called 'Anti-bullying Week', launched in some South African schools. Several incidents of bullying have been recorded in many schools, which led some researchers to ask questions about why this phenomenon is occurring. Teachers and parents wanted to find a solution, since it had, and still has, an impact on learners' well-being and inadvertently on their success rates. Since the identification of the high incidence of bullying in schools, the subject has been included in the Life Orientation curriculum for primary school learners. Children are being educated about their rights through all kinds of initiatives and activities. Plays, for example, are utilised to enact real-life situations that children can relate to and learn from. However, further research is required to gain greater understanding of the causes and extent of this phenomenon, the factors that contribute to the problem, the effectiveness of anti-bullying programmes, the identification of further solutions to the problem, and so forth. Thus, the phenomenon of 'bullying in schools' can be described as a research problem in need of solutions. Keep in mind that although we have a general understanding of what bullying means and what causes it, there will be different contributing factors or consequences to consider in different contexts. You should also note that when you do research involving people and their opinions, perceptions and behaviours, you require their consent as well as ethical clearance from your institution to ensure that your research causes no harm to others.

This example of bullying in schools highlights many important purposes and functions of research, including the following:
- identifying problems;
- addressing uncertainties;
- identifying relationships between things;
- finding solutions;
- testing theories;
- developing theories;
- planning for the future;
- predicting things;
- preventing undesired consequences;
- improving our lives;
- improving the lives of others;
- resolving conflicts;
- generating awareness and sensitivity;
- challenging and changing stereotypes;
- adding value and comfort to people's lives;
- contributing to the body of knowledge;
- overcoming challenges; and
- generating further research.

The more you learn about research in this book, the more functions and utilities of research you will be able to identify. Let's just pause for a moment and look at how we can define research more clearly, based on what we have learned so far.

Defining research

Considering how many functions research has and how it affects every aspect of our lives, it makes sense that there is much more to it than asking questions and finding answers. Some answers or solutions can be identified instantly, while others take more time, as we are experiencing with the Covid-19 pandemic, for example. Also, we often research processes and not just things or objects. Processes are typically invisible. For example, you cannot see how water evaporates or how another person thinks. As much as we can find out almost anything if we have technology and access to the Internet, we are aware that we do not know everything and some of the world's biggest problems remain unsolved in spite of everything we do know. Before we come up with a more comprehensive and expansive definition of research, let us look at a few more questions that may guide us:

- What is scientific observation?
- Can research be objective?
- What constitutes a fact?
- What is truth?
- How do we prove that information is correct?
- What is the relationship between research and knowledge?

You may have many more questions of your own and you may come up with different answers to the same questions. The reason for this difficulty is that we work with concepts in research. Concepts are abstract ideas that are associated with other ideas and that are created through language. We cannot see concepts, but we create an understanding of them through our experiences within many different contexts. Figure 1.3 illustrates some of the many concepts that can be related to research.

As you will see, research is an activity and process that follows certain logical steps. You will also become aware of the fact that we use many concepts and constructs when we do research. As we explain in Chapter 9, abstract concepts are referred to as constructs. Most *concepts* and *constructs* are not concrete objects we can see, touch, smell, hear or taste. This is part of the problem—most concepts and constructs are open to interpretation, and people experience the world in unique ways (Luhmann, 2012:15). For example, if you look at concepts such as 'facts', 'reality', 'truth', and so on, you may find that their meanings are relative to interpretation or *perception*, which is determined by our beliefs.

You may hear on the news, for example, that recent studies show that there is a decline in confidence in the global economy. Would that be a fact that you assume is true and that represents *reality* to you? You may require some more concepts to clarify your understanding, for example whether the comment is based on *objective* information or on someone's *subjective* opinion. These questions require further clarification and more concepts have to be employed to answer them. For example, what does 'objective' mean? Is it possible to be objective? Can you observe reality as if it is not you who are observing it? The same understanding applies to concepts such as 'relevance' and 'relationship', for

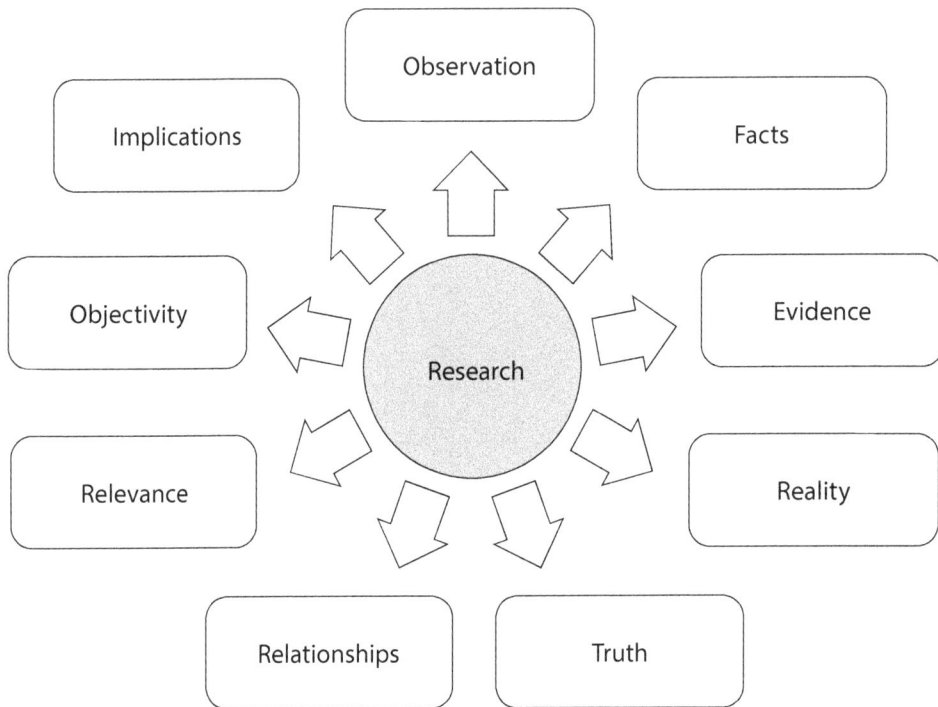

Figure 1.3 Concepts related to research

example. Who decides whether something is relevant or what the relationships between concepts are? The answer to that, if you are the researcher, is that *you* do.

Formal research will always depend on the information that is available, together with the existing knowledge, such as previous research, and new information that is collected through ongoing research projects. The decision of what kind of information to collect will depend on various *assumptions*. These assumptions will also determine the chains of decisions that will follow in the process of research. Our assumptions range from broad assumptions (beliefs) to narrow assumptions (actions), as illustrated in Figure 1.4.

Philosophical assumptions revolve around epistemology, ontology and axiology, as you will learn in the following chapter. Briefly, epistemology refers to your beliefs about knowledge. For example, do you believe knowledge is discovered or created? Ontology refers to reality; in other words, 'what is'. Axiology refers to our values, in other words whether we believe inquiry is value-free (objective) or value-bound (subjective). These kinds of assumptions often relate to the ethical considerations in a study; that is, whether anybody may be affected negatively in any way through the research that is being conducted.

Theoretical assumptions are related to the theoretical frameworks to which you subscribe as well as what is known as *metatheory*, or theories about the role

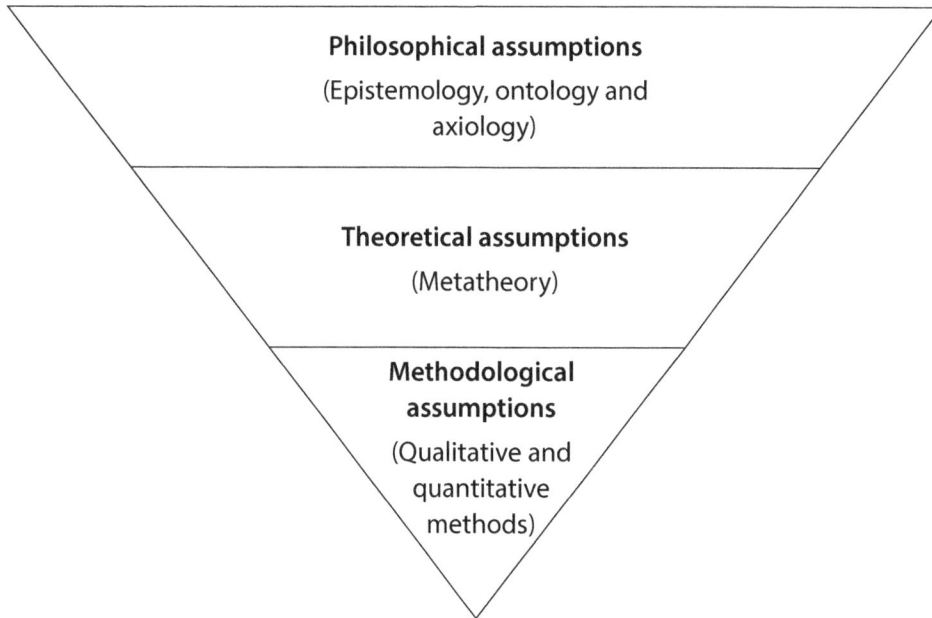

Figure 1.4 Hierarchy of assumptions in research

of theory in research. Theories are the result of research, and you will apply them for various purposes in your own research. We will discuss these different kinds of assumptions in more detail in Chapters 2 and 3.

Therefore, *what* we identify as a problem or question, the relevance of an issue, problem or question, the *methods* of obtaining information about the issue, problem or question, the *assumptions* about the issue, problem or question, and the *conclusions* or *solutions* you present at the end of your research will be based on the arguments and evidence you present to support your proposal for why your research should be done.

In formal research you need to find and present evidence that a problem exists and what knowledge about the problem exists currently. Fortunately, we are living in the information age, as we observed earlier, so the Internet can provide you with much of the information you need. Be aware, that all of the information you find online is not necessarily correct, so be sure to verify the credibility of your sources. The key consideration at all times is that research is a process involving many steps. Each step in the research process involves its own cycle of inquiry and justification, as portrayed in Figure 1.2 on page 7. Each step starts with questions and ends with questions in order to move to the next step. We can therefore make the following statements about research:
• Research begins with a question or a problem.
• It involves processes of inquiry—every answer leads to more questions.

- It requires a plan.
- You need to collect information that can be used as evidence to support your arguments.
- Research should be based on a sound theoretical foundation.
- It should arrive at valid conclusions.
- It should serve a specific purpose.
- It should generate relevant information.
- It should lead to further research.

We can therefore define research as a *process of inquiry* during which information is collected. It follows a plan that is based on previous research (a theoretical foundation) to gain understanding and to arrive at conclusions based on evidence which can be used to present solutions to particular problems, which in turn will generate further research questions. A process necessarily involves steps. The chapters that follow will take you through all of these steps. We describe them here briefly to give you a general overview of the research process.

The research process

We say that research is a 'recursive process' because it starts with a question, goes through the process of finding answers, and returns to answer the initial question, which then leads to further questions (even after finding answers or solutions). Figure 1.5 illustrates a formal research process.

The nine steps identified in Figure 1.5 and explained in the sections that follow should give you an overall picture of the research process. Bear in mind, however, that there is a lot more information required for each of these steps, as you will discover in the chapters that follow.

Identifying and analysing the question or problem

Students often find it difficult to identify and analyse a research question or problem, particularly when research is the subject they are studying. It is very important to think of a topic that interests you before you identify a research question or problem, considering that you will be investing a lot of time in your research project. You may, for example, be interested in gender or racial inequality or how the media promotes certain stereotypes. If you are not really interested in your research topic, you may find it difficult to engage with it or to remain motivated.

A good place to start looking for a research topic is to turn to existing literature on things that interest you. You can also come up with an interesting

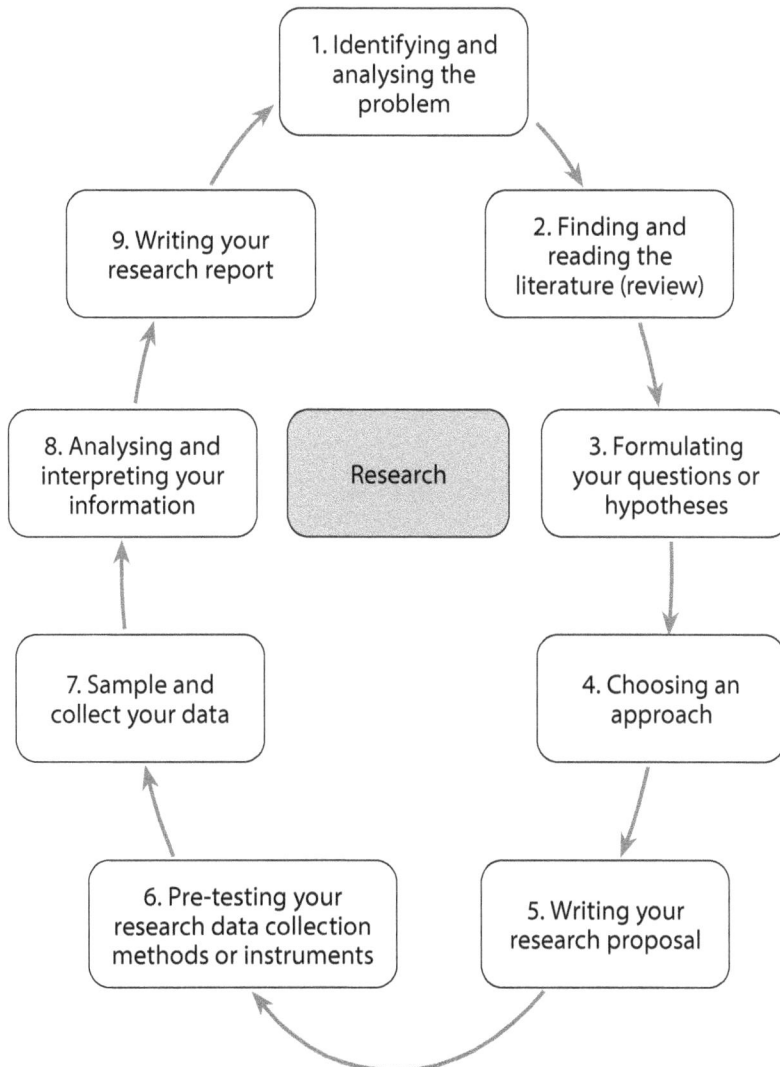

Figure 1.5 Research as a cyclical process

topic by being more observant and by reflecting on things happening around you. You may find information in your local newspaper or on the Internet. You may observe things happening in your immediate surroundings, or you may read something about other research findings.

Sometimes you will find that you are interested in learning more about a particular topic to gain more insight and understanding, such as in the example about stereotyping in the media. We refer to this type of research as basic or *pure research*. Conversely, we sometimes want to find a practical solution to a problem, such as finding a way to improve a particular system. This type of research is known as *applied research*. Research should also always have a purpose. In other words, it should make a contribution to a larger body of existing knowledge. Therefore, ask yourself who, besides you, will find your research valuable. Social media has become a valuable source of information on other people's views, opinions and questions on current topics. In fact, many students collect and analyse social media content in their research. This kind of research can be referred to as content analysis or documentation studies. Many students prefer this kind of research because it involves no engagement with participants (that can save time) and most often does not require ethical clearance because it analyses data that is publicly available on social media platforms such as Twitter. In terms of information available online, we have seen the introduction of the concept *big data* and 'freakonomics'. In simple terms, freakonomics was introduced by Levitt and Dubner in 2005, but it is probably not a concept you will work through as it 'explored associations within large sets of data, associations which were too easily mistaken for causality' (Hammond & Wellington, 2021). In other words, a lot of data does not necessarily mean something. On the other hand, the use of cookies and other instruments used to track consumer behaviour and to develop market intelligence is a contingent issue that we will not delve into at this point.

Research topics are usually grouped in three broad categories, namely exploratory, explanatory and descriptive research. These categories can guide you in determining the purposes and goals of your research.

- In *exploratory research* the aim is to gather new information about a topic that has not been researched before, for example: 'To what extent does the South African media represent the interests of the majority group within South Africa?'
- The aim of *explanatory research* is to find an explanation for a specific phenomenon. The explanation can be formulated as a research problem or a question, for example: 'Why is there such an alarming increase in child abuse in South Africa?'
- In *descriptive research* we aim to describe a phenomenon that is identified through the research conducted. This type of research is typically guided by a question, for example: 'What are the living conditions of South African women who have little or no access to education?'

We describe the different aims of research in more detail in Chapter 5. Once you have identified a topic, you can progress to the next step in the research process.

Conducting a literature review

During this step in the research process, you have to search for relevant literature relating to your topic which has been published before, preferably in accredited academic journals. This is not always an easy task, since you have to find this literature, which requires some skill. You have to be familiar with the databases in your library. The Internet is a useful resource, but not all sources on the Internet are valid and reliable academic sources. You may only refer to accredited sources and valid academic sources such as scholarly works and books. Google Scholar is very useful in this regard. However, a source such as Wikipedia, for example, is not a valid academic source because anyone can edit the content and it is therefore not possible to determine what information is accurate and what is not.

Students often underestimate the amount of time it takes to conduct a proper literature review and to find valid sources related to their topics. You may often find that published articles contain key words that at first seem to relate to your research topic, but then do not contain information that is relevant to your inquiry. Lecturers sometimes provide a list of sources related to a prescribed research topic, but you should still ensure that you are familiar with the requirements. Gathering information relating to your research topic will enable you to formulate your research question and problem more clearly. It will also provide you with information needed for your rationale.

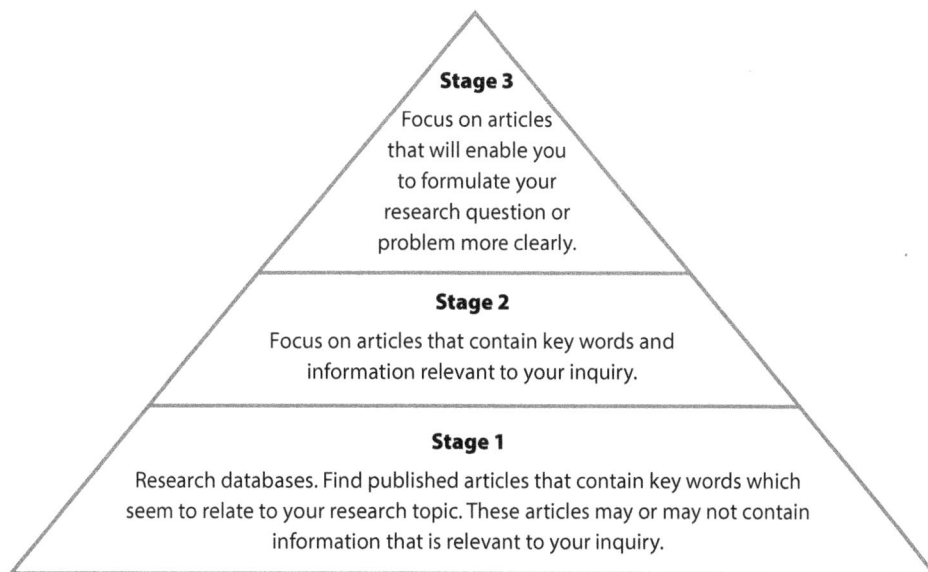

Stage 3
Focus on articles
that will enable you
to formulate your
research question or
problem more clearly.

Stage 2
Focus on articles that contain key words and
information relevant to your inquiry.

Stage 1
Research databases. Find published articles that contain key words which
seem to relate to your research topic. These articles may or may not contain
information that is relevant to your inquiry.

Figure 1.6 The literature review process

Figure 1.6 illustrates that the literature review also proceeds in stages. During these stages, you will formulate your research questions and, in some instances, hypotheses. In the first stage you have to find relevant publications that appear to be related to your topic. As you gain a deeper understanding of your own topic and questions, you will probably discover that many of the publications you collect are irrelevant. During stage two, your inquiry becomes more specific as you eliminate literature that does not apply to your investigation. When you reach stage three, you should have a clear understanding of your topic and should be able to decide which publications, or at least which kinds of publications, will be applicable to your specific study.

Formulating a research question

Asking a question or stating a hypothesis may sound like an easy task, but you have to consider the probability of finding answers to your questions and proving or disproving your hypotheses, where relevant. We refer to this as the feasibility of the research project. You also have to find out whether the same question has been asked before and what answers were found, including when, how and where they were found, and what the outcomes or implications of those answers were. Some questions may be simple, such as: 'How many students at College X go to nightclubs on a regular basis?' However, there has to be a reason for asking the question, so you always have to bear in mind what you want to accomplish with the answers. This will help you to make sure that your questions are relevant.

A hypothesis is a statement you will attempt to accept or reject at the end of your research. You may make a statement such as: 'Students at College X who frequent nightclubs are more likely to fail some of their modules.' You will then have to test this hypothesis. Again, you need to know what you want to accomplish with your findings, who wants to know, and how, when and where you are going to collect the information. Moreover, what will the implications be for your study if you find that students at College X who frequent nightclubs are actually more likely to pass all their modules, or if you find that some do and some do not? It is therefore crucial that you create a research design which will enable you to plan how you anticipate to collect your information.

Deciding on a research approach

When you arrive at this step in the research process, you should already have an idea of what or who you want to investigate. Your main consideration during this step will be whether you use a qualitative or quantitative approach, or even both, known as a mixed-methods approach. In brief, the distinction between quantitative and qualitative approaches rests on how you choose, collect, analyse and interpret the information that will serve as evidence. It also determines the data collection and analysis methods you will use. (See Chapters 12 and 13 for a discussion on quantitative and qualitative data collection.)

Quantitative methods present numerical or statistical data, while qualitative research presents interpretive data. The purpose, objective and aim of your research will provide you with some guidelines in this regard. If you want to predict and control future outcomes, explain the significance of quantities, degrees and relationships of quantities, or to generalise from a sample of people to a larger population, you will use quantitative methods such as surveys or experimental designs, for example. When your objective is to understand, explore or to describe people's behaviour; themes in behaviours, attitudes or trends, or relations between people's actions, for example, you will use qualitative methods such as participant observation, in-depth interviews or textual analysis. The key consideration during this step is that your research approach has to ensure the validity of your findings. As far as possible, you have to account for all the factors that may affect the outcome of your hypotheses or research questions.

Writing your research proposal

You may have gathered that this is one of the most crucial steps in the research process, because at this point you have to provide evidence of the work you have done so far and you have to unpack your thinking around how you are going to answer your research question and solve the research problem that you have identified. During this step in the research process, you are presenting your case, so to speak. You have to provide detailed answers to the following questions:

- What are you going to research?
- Why is your research worth doing?
- What is the feasibility of your research?
- How will you gain access to the participants or respondents, if you are working with people?
- How big is your population and what should the sample size be?
- What are the ethical implications of your research?
- How are you going to collect and analyse your data?
- Who is involved in your research project?
- Where will the study take place?
- When will the research take place?
- What kind of a contribution to the body of knowledge will your study make?
- What are some of the potential limitations of your study?

You have to provide clear and specific answers to all of these questions. It is therefore advisable that you pre-test your data collection methods or instruments. This is referred to as a pilot test, or a trial run.

Pre-testing data collection methods or instruments

You will find that a researcher spends a significant amount of time and effort in designing data collection instruments, such as questionnaires. It is therefore important to pre-test this instrument before data collection actually begins. In the case of a questionnaire, for example, you could test it on a small group of respondents to see whether they understand the questions, provide the kind of information you intend on gathering, follow the sequence of questioning, and so forth.

The purpose of a pilot test is to eliminate problems that you may not have foreseen when you designed the instrument. You will not use the data you collect during this step in your actual findings, but rather to find and correct any mistakes in your research instrument. Once you have completed the pilot test and corrected any errors, you will continue with the data collection process, as described in Step 6 in Figure 1.5. When you have collected all the data, you will proceed to the analysis and interpretation of your data.

Analysing and interpreting your data

The analysis and interpretation of your data form the basis of your findings, conclusions and recommendations. This step will determine whether your recommendations will be implemented in your study or what the recommendations for further research may be. During this step you will utilise your theoretical framework to interpret your findings. Your method of analysis will depend on the specific research method(s) you have chosen.

Writing your research report

Your research process is completed during this final step. A research report presents your findings, conclusions and recommendations. It summarises the entire process in a clear, logical and accurate manner. Lecturers usually prescribe a specific format for presenting your report. We will provide you with a recommended structure when we discuss the research report in more depth in Chapter 21.

The implications of your research

You must have gathered by now that everything related to research is very important; however, we want you to consider the implications of research before you progress any further. The primary reason for all the steps and processes we have introduced to you so far is to contribute to your understanding that research should be accompanied by a great deal of consideration and responsibility.

Earlier, we discussed the fact that objectivity is questionable, and that, at best, we can attempt to exclude bias. In other words, we should not manipulate information to prove our personal position relating to the research we conduct.

It is your responsibility to ensure that your research does not cause anybody emotional stress, physical discomfort, humiliation or even embarrassment. You may be collecting information from people who do not wish to be identified. For example, if you want to establish the incidence of child abuse or molestation in a particular community, your research may have catastrophic consequences for a child whose identity is not protected. You therefore have to obtain consent, or substitute consent, where children are involved, for example. There may also be legal considerations if, for example, people's privacy may be breached in any way. You have to consider that research has implications and that you, as a researcher, can be held accountable for the information you publicise.

On a more positive note, your research may find solutions to problems, so while you have to ensure that you consider the adverse implications of your research, potentially positive implications should motivate and steer your research process.

Summary

We have aimed to illustrate in this chapter how and why research matters to you and to other people. The simplest description of research is that it involves processes of asking questions and finding answers—which lead to further questions—that will help you to solve a particular problem. It can therefore be described as a recursive process.

Every research project should be directed and driven by specific aims and objectives based on certain philosophical orientations that co-determine the selection of theoretical and methodological orientations. Research also depends, to a large degree, on the selection of concepts that are identified and described for the particular purposes of the research project. It is therefore imperative that researchers familiarise themselves with the various concepts related to research in general and the research topic in particular.

Research is typically conducted by following steps. Each step may contain several other steps, as determined during the processes of research.

Research has and should have implications. While we anticipate positive implications, the possibility of negative implications should always remain a key consideration.

Review the chapter

Answer the questions and complete the tasks to assess whether you understand the content of this chapter:

1. Why does research matter to you and to others? Reflect on your personal experiences relating to research.
2. Describe the process of research and identify some of the questions involved in each step.
3. Discuss some of the implications of research by referring to a specific topic you can relate to.
4. List and describe the key concepts in this chapter and provide examples to demonstrate your understanding.

CHAPTER 2

Research paradigms and traditions

Franzél du Plooy-Cilliers

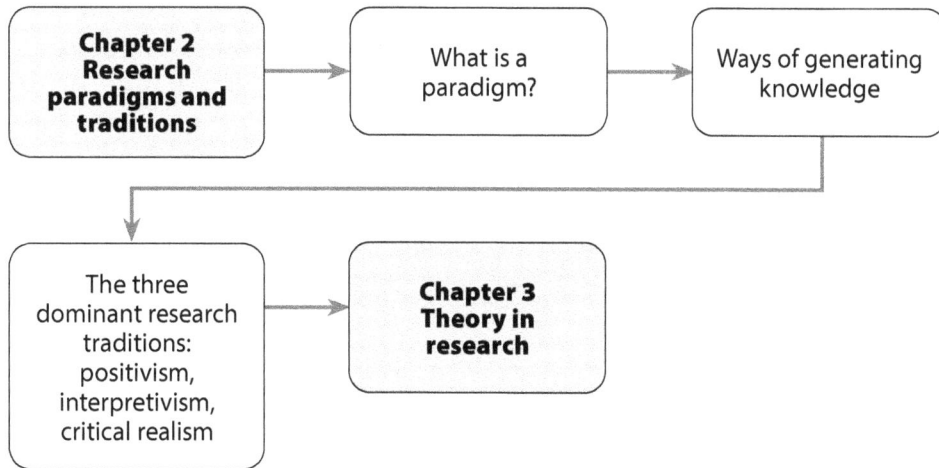

```
┌─────────────────┐      ┌─────────────────┐      ┌─────────────────┐
│   Chapter 2     │      │                 │      │                 │
│   Research      │ ───▶ │   What is a     │ ───▶ │ Ways of         │
│ paradigms and   │      │   paradigm?     │      │ generating      │
│  traditions     │      │                 │      │ knowledge       │
└─────────────────┘      └─────────────────┘      └─────────────────┘

┌─────────────────┐      ┌─────────────────┐
│   The three     │      │   Chapter 3     │
│ dominant research│ ──▶ │   Theory in     │
│  traditions:    │      │   research      │
│  positivism,    │      │                 │
│ interpretivism, │      │                 │
│ critical realism│      │                 │
└─────────────────┘      └─────────────────┘
```

Overview

If two people go to the same party, they will share many common experiences. However, if you ask them about the party, they will probably tell you different stories. One person may tell you about the decorations, the food and the excellent music that the DJ played. The other person may focus more on the people that attended the party, the clothes they were wearing and the delightful conversations they were having. Both of them went to exactly the same party, but they experienced it in different ways. Both stories are true, but they are told from different perspectives.

There is also the poem 'The blind men and the elephant' by John Godfrey Saxe (1873:135), which is based on an Indian legend that has been retold in different ways. The poem is about six blind men who heard about an elephant that had been brought to their town. They were very curious about this animal with whose form and shape they were not familiar. Each one of the blind men inspected a different part of the elephant through touch. The one who touched the trunk said: 'An elephant must be like a thick snake', while the one who touched the ears said: 'It must be like fan!' Another, who was touching the leg of the elephant, said it must be similar to a tree trunk and the one who was holding on to the tail said it must be like a rope. The fifth blind man touched the side of the elephant and said it is like a wall, while the sixth, touching the tusk, said it felt like a spear. Each one of these men was partially correct, but they were also all partially wrong.

Figure 2.1: Parable of the elephant

In many ways the same thing happens when different scientists or researchers look at the same phenomenon.

A phenomenon (singular), or phenomena (plural), is anything that happens in our world that can be experienced or observed. In fact, you will sometimes hear people refer to something or someone as 'phenomenal'. The word 'phenomenon' was introduced to modern philosophy by the philosopher Immanuel Kant. We often use it in research to refer to something that is worth investigating or that we would like to inquire into or learn more about. Crime, for example, is a phenomenon. It is something that affects and intrigues us and most people want to know more about it: what causes it, how it can be prevented, how it should be punished, and so on.

Thus, when researchers do research they investigate a particular phenomenon that they believe is worthy of further inquiry, try to find solutions to a particular problem, or try to answer a specific question. Yet, similar to the party example, different researchers will approach the same phenomenon or problem in different ways and, similar to the parable about the elephant, they may only focus on one aspect of a phenomenon. There are many reasons for this, one of the main ones being that researchers work from different paradigms.

In this chapter, we briefly overview three of the most common research paradigms and we look at how these paradigms impact on the way researchers conduct their research.

Objectives of this chapter

By the end of this chapter, you should be able to demonstrate your understanding of the following:

- the three key paradigms in terms of their epistemological, ontological, metatheoretical, methodological and axiological positions;
- the implications of choosing a specific paradigm for your research; and
- applying the conceptual model of ontological, epistemological, meta-theoretical, methodological and axiological assumptions to quantitative and qualitative approaches.

What is a paradigm?

The historian Thomas Kuhn is responsible for coining the term 'paradigm'. It describes 'a cluster of beliefs and dictates which for scientists in a particular discipline influence what should be studied, how research should be done, and how results should be interpreted' (Bryman, 2012:630).

The notion of a paradigm is most often used in the natural sciences. In the social sciences, paradigms are more likely to be referred to as research traditions or worldviews. However, what is important to understand is that, by following a particular paradigm or research tradition, researchers adopt a specific way of studying phenomena relevant to their field. Knowing what paradigm or tradition you as a researcher ascribe to is important because it determines what questions are considered worthy of investigation and what processes are required for the answers to these questions to be acceptable.

What is important to understand about a paradigm or tradition though, is that it is just that — a tradition, not a rule. Please have a look at the image below. What does it remind you of? When are those of us living in South Africa most likely to eat this kind of food?

Figure 2.2: Paradigm explained with a combination of foods

Most of you are likely to recognise this combination of food as breakfast, since it is a tradition to eat cereal, fruit, bacon and eggs, toast, etc for breakfast. We also normally serve coffee and fruit juice with breakfast. If you were invited to dinner at a friend's house and they served the above for dinner, you would be a bit puzzled or even confused because it deviates from the tradition. Similarly, if someone served breakfast with beer or wine, you would also be confused because, again, the tradition is not being followed.

But we want you to think about this carefully. Is there a rule or a law that says you cannot have the above food for dinner, or that you cannot serve wine or beer with breakfast? The answer is no, but if we deviate from the tradition, we confuse people and when people are confused they would like to have some kind of explanation. Research traditions are the same. If you do not follow the conventions of the tradition or paradigm, you are likely to confuse people, so it is always good to provide people with an explanation or justification if you deviate from the convention.

So Thomas Kuhn observed that when researchers adopt and follow certain methods and processes of doing research, they are inevitably faced with certain problems and inconsistencies. At some point, these inconsistencies lead to a crisis. If the crisis cannot be solved, a revolution tends to take place. A revolution can be described as a struggle that eventually leads to change. In research, such a change is referred to as a 'paradigm shift'. When a paradigm shift takes place in a discipline, the researchers take on new views, methods and beliefs and start conducting their research in a different way. However, the emergence of a new or different paradigm does not mean that the previous paradigms become obsolete and are disregarded. Some researchers will always continue to follow the paradigm which they are most familiar with; some simply refuse to see beyond their habitual model of thinking.

In this chapter, and for the purpose of this introductory book, we explore only the three dominant traditions in research, namely the positivist, interpretivist and critical realist traditions. Many more paradigms or traditions exist, and even the three dominant traditions are often referred to by different names. You can explore more of these traditions once you have familiarised yourself with the three basic traditions and their premises, or principles. First, however, it might be worth our while to look at some of the aims of research, since understanding the aims of research will likely help you distinguish more clearly between the different traditions.

Ways of generating knowledge

The word 'research' consists of two parts: the prefix 're-' and the stem (core part) '-search'. Let us look at the prefix first. What does it mean to say that something is, for example, re-usable? It means we can use it again and again. Thus, 're-' means 'again' or 'anew'. The prefix 're-' can also mean 'back'. For example, when somebody revisits something, they go back, and the same is true if someone reverses. As you know, the verb 'search' means 'to look for something'. If we put the two meanings together, 'research' means that we are looking for something again and again or we go back to look at something again. The question that arises now is what exactly we are looking for again when we conduct research. The answer is that we are looking for answers to questions, solutions to problems or simply for more knowledge or the 'truth'. (We have placed 'truth' in quotes because what exactly can be considered as true is highly debateable, an idea that you will become very familiar with as you work through this chapter.) Most of the time we use research to generate knowledge so that we can understand the world around us better than before conducting the research.

If you think of activities you engage in every day, you will find that a lot of them actually involve some form of research. Children, in particular, are very active 'researchers'. Children have an insatiable curiosity and try to make sense of their world and experiences by asking 'Why?' all the time. They are therefore looking for answers to questions so that they can gain knowledge and an understanding of how the world works. However, as you have seen in the previous chapter, there are different ways of generating knowledge and people find all kinds of ways of explaining reality to themselves. In the past, for example, in an attempt to explain the phenomenon of lightning, the Vikings attributed lightning and thunder to the mythical god Thor.

However, the knowledge generated through the process of research differs from the knowledge generated through our daily actions, in the sense that scientific research is characterised by rigorous investigations where we attempt to find evidence for our beliefs and where we go to great effort to verify our results. Conducting research is therefore, for the most part, a search for the 'truth', knowledge and understanding. This search takes the form of the critical and controlled investigation of a research problem through a systematic (step-by-step) process involving the collection and analysis of data in order to establish certain facts or principles.

The German critical theorist Jürgen Habermas offers a useful distinction between the various ways of generating knowledge. His distinctions rest on what he calls three different cognitive interests, namely technical (something you can learn from a book or theory), practical (learned through observation and doing) and emancipatory (learning to empower). The word 'cognitive' refers to the mental processes of knowing things; he therefore believes that there are three ways of knowing, depending on what you want to know. The three cognitive interests identified by Habermas correspond closely to the three most common research paradigms or traditions that are discussed in this chapter.

The three cognitive interests, or sciences, identified by Habermas are the following:

1. The *empirical–analytical* sciences are empirical and technical, and their aim is to find causal (cause-and-effect) relationships. This type of science is closely related to positivism.

2. The *historical–hermeneutic* (or hermeneutic–phenomenological) sciences are practical, and their aim is in-depth understanding of a phenomenon. This type of science is related to interpretivism.

3. The *critically oriented* sciences are emancipatory and related to critical realism. The aim here is to empower people through knowledge.

The cognitive interests of the researcher then determine:

- the aims or goals of research, or the reasons for doing research;
- what are considered worthwhile phenomena for research;
- what research methods should be used; and
- what is considered knowledge.

Empirical research is concerned with phenomena that are confirmable through observation and experience, as opposed to the application of theory or logic. In fact, the word 'empirical' is derived from the word 'experiment'. Thus, in the empirical–analytical sciences the primary interest of the researchers is to use controlled observations, such as experiments, in order to find causal relationships. These researchers are interested in what causes certain things and what effects certain things have, and they try to determine this through controlled observations. The reason why they want to determine the causes and effects of phenomena is so that they can use this knowledge to manipulate and gain as much control as possible over nature as well as human actions. We will explore this in greater depth when we look at positivism.

In contrast, the primary goal of the historical–hermeneutic sciences is to gain understanding. They are more interested in symbolism and the way in which people use symbols to create their own reality. Here, a *sharing of meaning*, or a mutual understanding, counts more than empirical observation when it comes to making knowledge claims. These researchers believe that social reality is comprised of meaningful actions, artefacts and events that need to be understood from different people's perspectives. The point of research in this context is not to gain control, but rather to establish harmony among people and between humanity and its environment. These sciences tend to use the interpretivist approach, which we will discuss later in this chapter.

The empirical–analytical and the historical–hermeneutic approaches gave rise to the debate around explaining (*erklären*) versus understanding (*verstehen*). We need to look at this debate in a bit more detail because, in a sense, it is the most important fundamental methodological debate. It is a debate between, on the one hand, thinkers who insist on a single, universal method which will provide objective knowledge, and, on the other hand, those who believe that finding a single method that can be universally applied is an impossible dream. It is also often described, in the broadest sense, as the difference between the natural sciences and the human sciences. Thus, phenomena found in the natural sciences can be explained through, for example, laws, but phenomena that form part of the human sciences can be understood from multiple perspectives and hardly ever has a single explanation. We also engage with human beings, which leads to understanding, where we can only observe phenomena in the natural sciences and, therefore, we can only explain it as opposed to understanding it.

- *Objective knowledge* is defined as knowledge that is non-subjective, in the sense that it is culture-free, value-free, universal and, therefore, absolutely certain. Empirical researchers want to ensure that the knowledge we gain via scientific means is based on facts alone, completely free from personal feelings or opinions. In other words, they want to use methods that will provide factual evidence as to why certain phenomena occur, evidence that is not influenced by people's personal feelings about the matter. For example, they would want to determine what the physical and factual causes of ill health are and would not be interested in opinions about why people get ill or understanding what people go through when they are ill.
- Some thinkers disagree that objective knowledge is possible. They argue that *subjective factors*—on the part of the researcher as well as the phenomenon itself, especially in the case of human beings, or both—unavoidably play a role in knowledge acquisition. Thus, they argue that subjective factors, such as the researcher's own interests and expectations, will influence what kind of questions she or he will ask and what kind of observations she or

he is likely to favour over others. This is particularly relevant in the social sciences, where the object of observation tends to be people. Consequently, these researchers argue that there are many kinds of knowledge and many different methods of knowledge acquisition.

The *erklären* versus *verstehen* debate also paved the way for the traditional distinction between quantitative research (objective and value-free) and qualitative research (subjective and value-sensitive), which you will learn more about in later chapters.

Another form of critical interest identified by Habermas is the critical sciences. The main aim of critical researchers is to free people from all forms of domination and oppression, and to use knowledge to empower people to do so. They believe that, ideally, researchers should use both quantitative and qualitative methodologies in their search for the 'truth'. They insist that knowledge should be used to sharpen people's critical thinking skills in every aspect so that they can become self-actualised (reach their full potential) and autonomous (free and self-governing).

Although this distinction between the different sciences is very useful, keep in mind that it cannot be maintained in a clear-cut way, since there is a great deal of interaction and overlap between the different approaches. Moreover, as we look at the three dominant paradigms or traditions, you should keep in mind that all frameworks are problematic. Most thinkers and research problems are more complex than a single framework allows for, and few thinkers can fit their ideas neatly into only one of them. Often, then, choosing a paradigm is a matter of where the emphasis in your thinking lies, the particular problem you want to solve, and several other aspects. Nonetheless, it is useful to understand the different traditions in science. Understanding the principles and positions of these traditions will guide your research, which can become rather complex and confusing if you do not have a clear idea of where you want to go with your research and what you would like to establish.

The three dominant research traditions

We will look at the three dominant traditions, namely positivism, interpretivism and critical realism. We will explore each of them in terms of the following positions:

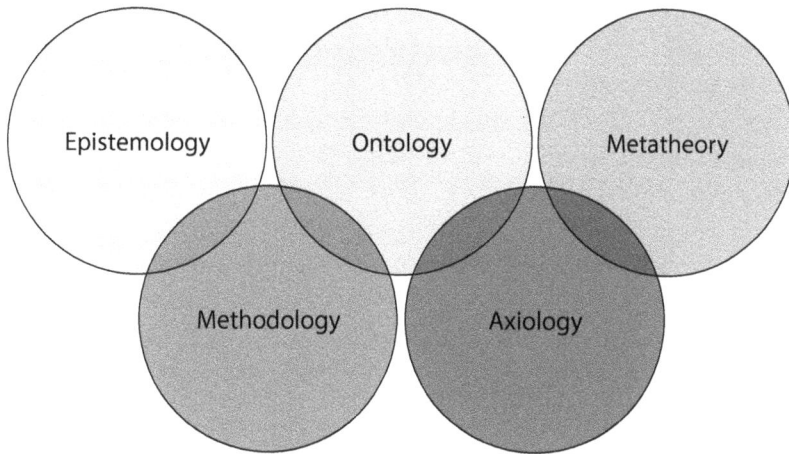

Figure 2.3: The dominant research positions

1. The *epistemological position*. 'Epistemology' is a compound word that has its roots in the Greek words '*episteme*', which means 'knowledge', and '*logos*' or '*logia*', which means 'the study, science or theory of'. Epistemology then literally means 'the study of knowledge'. Put differently, epistemology deals with the nature of knowledge and the different ways of knowing. All research is about knowledge, and each research study is expected to contribute to the body of existing knowledge. Epistemology thus deals with questions such as what counts as knowledge and what are the limits of knowledge.

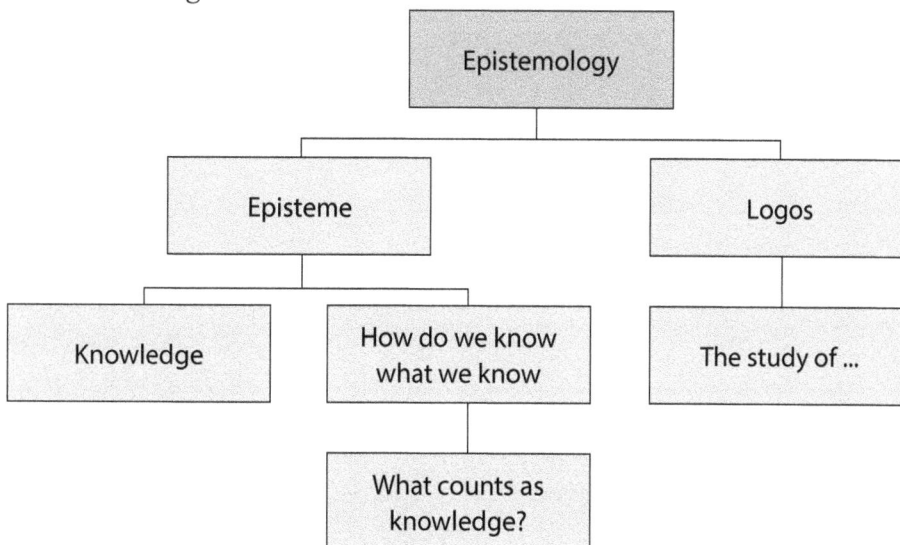

Figure 2.4: The Epistemological position

2.   The *ontological position*. 'Ontology' is also a compound word with its roots in Greek. '*Ontos*' means 'being, or that which is' and '*logos*', as we already said, means 'the study of'. Ontology then is the study of being, existence or reality, and includes the assumptions that are made about certain phenomena. The main questions that it deals with are what reality is and how we know what is real. Questions regarding what reality is, what truth is and whether such things as objective truth and reality exist, are very complex philosophical questions which cannot be explored in depth in this book. However, if you are interested in these debates, read more about it them. A good place to start, in order to grasp why philosophers question the nature of reality, is by reading up on Plato's analogy of the cave.

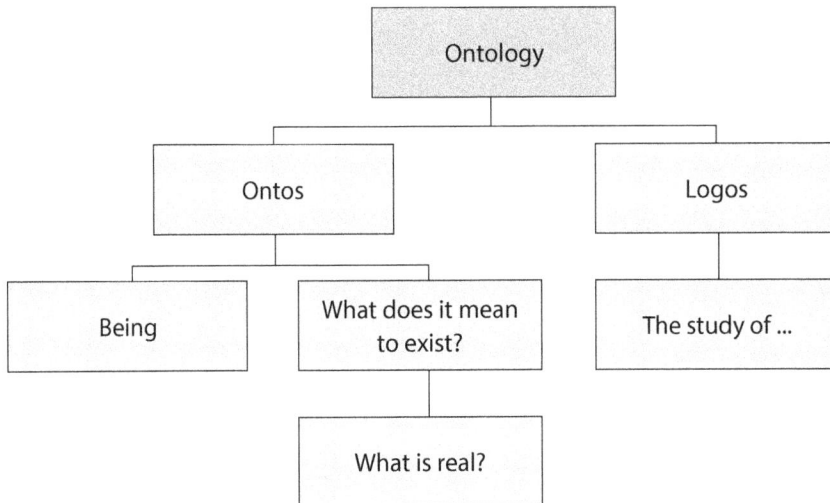

Figure 2.5: The Ontological position

3.   The *metatheoretical position*. The word '*meta*' means 'about'. Metatheory is thus, literally, 'theory about theory'. Metatheory refers to exploring the theoretical lenses that provide direction to the research in a particular field of study. We use lenses in cameras and binoculars, for example, to create a clearer image of an object. Similarly, theories are 'lenses' that we use to provide us with a clearer perspective on a particular phenomenon. As you will see later in this book, theory is inseparable from research, and a good research study is usually built on a solid theoretical foundation. We use theory for several purposes, such as describing and explaining certain phenomena. Metatheory helps us to look at the underlying assumptions and implications of particular theories, and it helps us to refine our thinking so that we can come up with more sophisticated ways of describing and explaining phenomena.

4. The *methodological position*. 'Methodology' is a guiding system for solving problems. Although it is not synonymous with methods, it does include the research methods that are deemed most appropriate for collecting and analysing data in order to generate knowledge about the phenomenon being studied. It usually refers to a qualitative, quantitative or mixed-methods approach to research.

5. The *axiological position*. 'Axiology' is another compound word, derived from the Greek *'axios'*, meaning 'worthy', and *'logos'*. Axiology then refers to the study of values and value judgements. In the widest sense of the term, it deals with the question of the role of values in research and it gives us insight into what is valued within a particular paradigm or tradition. It asks the important question of whether values can be suspended in order to understand, or whether values mediate and shape what is understood.

Positivism

Positivism can be defined broadly as the approach of the natural sciences. Positivists advocate the application of natural sciences' methods to study certain phenomena, including social phenomena. If you look at the words 'positivism' and 'positivist', you will see that the stem is 'positive'. This is because the early positivists had a very positive view of science — they believed that science could enlighten people and, in the process, make the world a better place to live in. In other words, they believed that humans could improve their own world and become better people through educating themselves.

The Enlightenment, which began in England in the 17th century and flourished in France in the years after that, encouraged people to think for themselves, to challenge societal norms and to move away from believing in and using myth and superstition to explain natural and social phenomena. Positivism therefore encapsulates the spirit of the Enlightenment, or the Age of Reason, as thinkers in this era insisted that only objective, observable and verifiable facts should be considered when we attempt to understand and explain natural and social phenomena.

The epistemological position of positivism

You will recall that epistemology is concerned with what is regarded as valid knowledge. We have also mentioned that positivists believe that valid knowledge can only be gained from objective, observable (empirical) evidence. Therefore, in their view, only knowledge confirmed by the senses can genuinely be considered as knowledge. Keep in mind that the main aim of these researchers is to discover causal relationships so that they can predict and control the natural and social world. Thus, they want to learn how the world works in order to predict and control events. If we are able to predict something, we can take action. For example, science can help us to predict the weather, and we can take action by dressing warmly when we know it is going to be a cold day. Similarly, if we know the causes of heart disease, we can take action by avoiding certain foods, for example, to try to reduce our chances of having a heart attack.

Positivists believe that knowledge is the result of empirical observation only, and they therefore see a clear separation between science and non-science. They obtain knowledge through careful and meticulous observation and the testing of assumptions (called hypotheses) against the real world (we will discuss their view of reality when we explore their ontological position). Positivist researchers must therefore find evidence to either support or reject these hypotheses.

Moreover, in order to test hypotheses — to be sure which A is indeed causing B and that nothing else is the cause of B — the researcher must isolate the variables that she or he is interested in from other factors that may interfere or influence the outcome. This is best done under controlled conditions. Positivists therefore rely heavily on experiments, utilising control groups and experimental groups. For example, if researchers want to establish a relationship (called a positive correlation) between the reading speed of a student and her or his academic performance, they will have to control for variables such as IQ, substance abuse, number of hours spent studying, number of hours' sleep, and so on, to ensure that it is indeed the student's reading speed that is influencing academic performance, and nothing else.

The ontological position of positivism

When we look at the positivistic perspective on reality, we see that positivists hold the view that there is a single, objective and stable social and physical external reality that is governed by laws. Positivists believe that this reality can be observed and measured — and therefore known or at least knowable — and that the duty of the researcher is to discover the laws that govern reality. For positivists, reality has order and regularity. For example, through observation and experience we know that the sun rises every morning (it happens regularly) and therefore we can predict that the sun will rise tomorrow morning. Because of regularity, we can identify patterns that help us to also predict the different seasons of the year, the cycles of the moon and the weather, the tides, and so forth. Likewise, we can predict outcomes of human behaviour. For example, studying hard for a test will lead to good results, so we can predict that somebody who puts in many hours of studying will do well in a test.

Moreover, the positivists are of the opinion that a given cause has the same effect on all people. They therefore do not consider the effect that the social, psychological, historical or cultural context can have on behaviour. Since they believe in the existence of an external reality, they are not interested in examining the unobservable internal motivations of an individual's behaviour. They consequently ascribe to what is known as objectivism.

The metatheoretical position of positivism

According to the positivists, the overall aim of scientific inquiry is to develop generalisations about the causal relationship between variables. Positivists maintain that theories must be universally valid or true, regardless of culture or history, and must therefore be universally applicable. Positivists thus place emphasis on objective and value-free research, where theories are often tested by using hypotheses. Once these hypotheses have been tested for validity and reliability (see Chapter 17), a theory, which is likely to explain complex phenomena in terms of causal relationships, is postulated.

Positivists assert that, by establishing causal relationships and by meeting the conditions of the cause, certain predictions can be made in terms of the effect. For example, a researcher could hypothesise that if developing countries are provided with technology, this will automatically lead to benefits such as economic development or democracy. In other words, positivists argue that, given the right conditions or cause (technology), the effect (development) will follow naturally. Other examples of causal relationships are the hypotheses that the breakdown of traditional moral order causes an increase in the rate of criminal behaviour or that rising unemployment is associated with increased child abuse.

The methodological position of positivism

As we explained earlier, the methodological position of a tradition must not be confused with research methods, although the research methods employed in a study form an important part of the methodology. First and foremost, positivists maintain that science must be based on empirical data produced by direct observation. Since the aim of positivistic research is to find valid and reliable causal relationships and to further objectivity and precision, positivists favour recording 'facts' in terms of quantities, or numbers, that can be processed by using statistical techniques. Quantitative research can thus be seen as a research strategy that emphasises quantification in the collection and analysis of data.

Methods are the techniques a researcher applies when conducting research. For positivists, methods must be devised in such a way as to study reality objectively. They therefore favour methods such as direct observation, measurement and experiments in laboratory conditions, where the researcher can control the conditions or variables. They further prefer methods that make reliability possible—methods that can be repeated in order to verify the results of previous studies. For example, in order to claim that IQ tests are reliable, people need to get the same score, or a closely related score, every time they take the test. Since positivist researchers aim to test and verify theories and hypotheses, they support a deductive (theory testing) as opposed to an inductive (theory building) approach to research (see also Chapters 3, 6 and 10).

The axiological position of positivism

The positivist paradigm has an objectivist axiology that is integral to the paradigm. Thus, positivists value objective and value-free research that is not tainted by personal bias. Positivist research therefore values honesty and personal integrity more than anything else, as these values have the function of creating trust. Positivists want to be able to trust that the findings of a research study are an accurate reflection or representation of an objective reality. Remember that their ultimate aim is to investigate an objective reality, with the expectation that they will obtain an understanding of that reality that can be used to predict and control nature, people and events. Anything that threatens this understanding of reality is considered malevolent.

Positivist researchers insist on an honest representation of facts. In the case of an experiment, for example, the results would have to be described exactly, without any distortion. Positivist researchers also value preciseness because they believe that the more precise the measurement, the more accurate it will be as a reflection of reality. Rigorous logic is also highly valued.

Interpretivism

Interpretivism developed as a reaction to the shortcomings and limitations of positivism, specifically in its application to the social sciences. The main idea on which this paradigm rests is that people are fundamentally different from objects. Consequently, we cannot study human beings in the same way that we study objects in the natural sciences because, unlike objects, human beings change all the time and the environment in which they find themselves constantly influences them. Interpretivists, for example, argue that it does not make sense to study people in laboratory settings, as people do not live in laboratories and are always influenced by the things that are happening in their environment.

Interpretivism has been influenced by several intellectual traditions, among which the dominant ones are hermeneutics, phenomenology and symbolic interactionism:

* *Hermeneutics* is concerned with the 'theory and method of the interpretation of human action' (Bryman, 2012:28).
* *Phenomenology* looks at the way in which individuals make sense of the world around them. Phenomenologists maintain that human action is meaningful and that people therefore ascribe meaning both to their own

and other people's actions. For phenomenologists, the task of the researcher is to interpret and gain an understanding of human actions and then to describe them from the point of view of the person or group being studied.

- *Symbolic interactionists* see reality as highly symbolic and constructed. We will return to this point when we look at the ontological position of interpretivism. In brief, symbolic interactionists argue that human action has little inherent meaning, but that humans have the ability to read meaning into one another's actions because they share a meaning system such as language. Shared meaning systems permit us to interpret signs or actions and give meaning to them. For example, if someone winks at you, you need to have learnt what a wink means in order to understand this action. The meaning of the wink will also depend on the situation. Someone can be winking at you because she or he is flirting with you or because she or he is joking with you.

In short, interpretivists assert that, in the social sciences in particular, researchers should study and describe meaningful social action. Therefore, unlike the positivists, who want to discover and explain causal relationships in an attempt to predict and control nature and the behaviour of humans and animals alike, interpretivists merely want to understand human behaviour. For example, instead of wanting to be able to provide statistics on how many prostitutes work in a certain area and how much on average they earn per month, interpretivists want to gain an empathetic, in-depth understanding of what it is like to live the life of a prostitute. They therefore want to see the world through the eyes of the person they are studying.

Because the aim of interpretivist research is to gain in-depth understanding, it often requires the researcher to spend many hours in direct contact with those being studied in order to be able to appreciate how they experience daily life and to get an understanding of what is meaningful and relevant to them.

The epistemological position of interpretivism

Positivists see scientific knowledge as the only valid form of knowledge, and totally disregard common sense as a form of knowledge. Interpretivists challenge this view and argue that common sense guides people in daily living. Therefore if you want to understand human behaviour, you need to grasp what people view as common sense. For interpretivists, this is an essential source of information for understanding people.

More importantly, interpretivists challenge the idea of objective knowledge and objective truth. Interpretivists see facts as fluid and embedded within a meaning system. For example, many centuries ago people believed that the Earth was flat and that it was the centre of the universe. These beliefs were seen as facts. Today, however, we know that this is not true—what is seen as factual has therefore changed. According to interpretivists, facts are not objective and neutral, especially in the social sciences. Instead, what is factual depends heavily on the context and people's interpretation of information. Thus, people can only assign appropriate meaning to an act if they take into account the social context in which the act occurs. For example, in cultures where polygamy is acceptable, having more than one wife is not frowned upon and is seen as normal. However, in most Western cultures, having more than one wife is unacceptable, and even illegal in some countries. What this implies is that views and facts about polygamy will vary vastly depending on the particular cultural background in which it occurs.

Because interpretivists believe that truth is dependent on people's interpretation of facts, they are not interested in generalising their results and do not expect their results to be universally applicable. As a result, the research methodologies they use are sensitive to the specific context and never generalised beyond the context in which the study was conducted. Thus, if they did an in-depth study about the lived lives of prostitutes in the Western Cape, they would not attempt to generalise this knowledge to all prostitutes living in South Africa, even though some of their experiences may be similar.

The ontological position of interpretivism

Interpretivists do not believe in an objective, external reality that is experienced in the same way by everyone. They believe that reality is a social construction and that it is dependent on the meanings that people ascribe to their own experiences and interactions with others. According to interpretivists, the social world is what people perceive it to be. It is fluid and fragile and changes as people's perceptions change. For example, suppose you are madly in love with your partner and that, in your reality, your lover is perfect. If you find out that your lover has been unfaithful to you, your perception of her or him changes dramatically and suddenly. Thus, the reality you constructed around your relationship also changes. This implies that people possess an internally experienced sense of reality. The interpretivists believe that, depending on circumstances, culture, experiences, and so on, people may or may not experience reality in the same way. Moreover, they believe the way in which we experience reality today may change over time. A very good example of a reality-altering event is the global pandemic of the coronavirus disease 2019 (Covid-19). Most people experienced the world in a different way before the virus, so for most people reality changed dramatically since people became aware of the virus and certain measures were put in place worldwide to stop the spread of the disease.

The metatheoretical position of interpretivism

Many early interpretivists experienced great disappointment when they tried to publish their research findings because their work was improperly evaluated and treated unfairly, using criteria attuned to positivism rather than interpretivism. Unlike positivistic research—characterised by theories based on hypotheses that are tested for reliability and validity, and that are described in terms of correlations and causal relationships—interpretivist theory tells a story. It describes and interprets how people living in a particular context conduct their daily lives. Instead of abstract statistics that serves as evidence, and objective, formal language to describe relationships between variables, interpretivist research is rich in detailed description and direct quotes from participants. It aims to reveal the meanings and values of the people studied because researchers want to help us understand people directly involved in a particular phenomenon. The writing style is also more informal, subjective and rich in quotes in order to give the reader a feel for another person's social reality. By making use of the stories (called narratives) of a group of poor people living in a particular township, for example, interpretivists will describe how these people subjectively experience poverty and township life.

Replication (reliability) is important to positivists. They only consider something as true if different researchers are able to replicate a study and get the same results. Interpretivists, on the contrary, propose criteria such as credibility, transferability, dependability and confirmability when evaluating knowledge claims (see Chapter 17). They do not see it as necessary that others agree with the claims that the researcher is making; others should, however, be willing to concede that the researcher's conclusions are plausible. The knowledge claims made by the researcher should also be defensible. Thus, for interpretivists, theories should help us understand the experiences and lived realities of others through what is known as 'thick descriptions'.

Interpretivists are also more likely to use inductive approaches to theory formulation. In other words, instead of first formulating a theory and then testing hypotheses to test the theory against reality, interpretivists prefer to collect information, analyse it, and then formulate a theory based on the information and analysis.

The methodological position of interpretivism

As you will have gathered by now, interpretivism embodies the view that social reality is in a constant state of flux and dependent on the way in which individuals experience reality internally. Since the aim of interpretivists is to gain an in-depth understanding of multiple realities, they depend on qualitative research. Qualitative research can be described as a research strategy that emphasises words rather than numbers (quantification) in the collection and analysis of data. Interpretivist researchers aim to study reality subjectively and, as a result, they use methods that are sensitive to the context and that will help them to gain an in-depth understanding. These methods include focus groups, in-depth interviews, ethnography and narrative inquiry.

Unlike the positivists, interpretivists do not try to do value-free research. In fact, they attempt to empathise with and share in the social values of those they are studying. They further insist that researchers should consider their own personal points of view and feelings as part of the process of studying others. Moreover, in qualitative research the researcher becomes the primary research instrument and participants 'teach' the researcher about their lives.

The axiological position of interpretivism

Interpretivists value the complex understanding of unique realities. They do not attempt to conduct value-free research. Instead, they openly discuss the values that shape their research, including their own interpretations and those of participants.

Critical realism

Critical realism has its origins in Germany. It was born out of a frustration with positivism's non-humanistic and narrow focus and its emphasis on the causal nature of universal laws. Moreover, there was also frustration with interpretivism's passive, contextual, subjective and relativist view. As a result, critical realism took aspects from both traditions and combined it in a unique way. Critical realism holds that real structures exist independent of human consciousness, a view similar to that of the positivists, who believe that a single objective reality exists. However, the critical realists propose that our knowledge of reality is a result of social conditioning. In other words, they support the view that knowledge is a social construct, which is similar to what the interpretivists believe (Saunders, Lewis & Thornhill, 2019).

On the one hand, in line with the interpretivist position, critical realism recognises that the natural and social sciences are different, and that the way in which reality is experienced is based on how people perceive reality. On the other hand, in line with the positivists, they insist that science must be rational and based on evidence. However, instead of trying to discover causal relationships, critical realists try to understand and explain rather than predict. Both positivists and critical realists aim to generalise their results.

Critical realists maintain that researchers have a responsibility to transform social relations by exposing, critiquing and changing any unjust practices in society. The main aim of their research is therefore, by exposing myths, to transform society and free people from all forms of oppression, and to empower people to build a better world for themselves in the process. Because the aim is to empower people, critical realists often take dramatic action and are likely to be activists. Feminist researchers are a good example of critical realists.

The epistemological position of critical realism

Unlike the positivists, critical realists do not see knowledge as permanent, but as something that should be considered within its historical and social context. They consequently propose that the knowledge that a researcher produces will always be clouded by the values of the researcher. They further insist that everything put forward as knowledge should be questioned and scrutinised. Critical realists therefore acknowledge that they will never be able to provide permanent answers, but they do not believe that this should be the aim of research in the first place.

Critical realists do not aim to merely accumulate knowledge for the sake of knowing or understanding. For them, knowledge should be geared towards action and should therefore have practical value. They prefer to focus their research on social issues that stand in the way of social change towards a society without domination. Although they believe that complete knowledge about the outside world may not always be possible and may often be imperfect, they nevertheless insist that it can, in principle, be acquired and that the outside world is essentially different from the abstract world of our minds.

The ontological position of critical realism

Critical realists propose that there are certain institutions (such as schools, churches, the family, and so on), practices (religious practices such as weddings, cultural practices such as rites of passage, and so on) and ideologies (dominant ideas, such as capitalism) to which members of a society ascribe due to socialisation and indoctrination. These institutions, practices and ideologies empower certain people and constrain others, and they influence people's realities. For critical realists, certain aspects of reality are seen as real and existing independently of human interpretation. For example, oppression and forms of domination are seen as real and it is acknowledged that the consequences of oppression are very real for those who are being oppressed, mistreated and/or exploited. Thus, for example, the oppression of women, people of colour or the poor deprives these people of certain opportunities, especially opportunities to better their own lives.

Critical realists point out that domination and oppression are often the result of dominant ideologies based on illusions, distortions and myths about how society operates. These illusions then empower some groups to exploit others. For example, the myth that women are inferior to men enabled men to exploit and oppress women for a very long time.

Critical realists also argue that social reality has multiple layers and that what we observe and experience is often merely a surface reality, which is only partial and sometimes even false. We often do not see the deep structures on which the myths and illusions by which social reality operates are built. These deep structures are difficult to uncover because some myths and distortions are so completely internalised that we accept them as the norm without questioning them. In fact, people who are oppressed often cannot see how change is possible and thus lose their independence, freedom and control over their own lives. For critical realists, the role of the researcher is to uncover these deep structures, expose and criticise them, and empower people to free themselves from all forms of oppression and exploitation.

The metatheoretical position of critical realism

A core belief of critical realists is that the material, cultural and historical conditions in which people find themselves may hold them back. For example, a poor, illiterate black woman who grew up during the apartheid era in South Africa would have had very few opportunities and would have experienced oppression and exploitation due to her racial, gender, educational and material status. Thus, the world people live in limits their options and shapes their beliefs and behaviour. For example, in the past, due to indoctrination, most women also believed that they were inferior to men and, as a result, accepted domination and oppression as the norm. Women in most societies were also denied certain opportunities, such as the opportunity to get a good education, which limited their options. The same is true for many black South Africans who grew up during apartheid.

Because of critical realists' emphasis on change, they maintain that theory should be practical and include a plan for change. Critical theory therefore seeks to provide people with a resource that will help them understand, question and change their world.

The methodological position of critical realism

The critical realists' idea of a multi-faceted reality that can be investigated from different angles informs their belief that no single method can provide definite results about any given object of research. They therefore tend to use what is known as mixed-methods research. Mixed-methods research combines methods associated with both quantitative and qualitative research, where the aim is for quantitative and qualitative methods to supplement each other. The reason why critical realists use multiple sources of data collection is that it increases the validity and reliability of a study.

Critical researchers tend to start their research with a critical analysis of existing knowledge on the subject because of their belief that knowledge itself should be questioned. They further consider it important to look at structural relationships, for example the relationship between the media and government, in order to uncover hidden and deep structures.

The axiological position of critical realism

Critical realists accept a degree of subjectivism in their research and support the idea that it is almost impossible to do value-free research, as even the choice of a research topic is often value-laden. They therefore accept their own bias. More importantly, they value equality and human freedom and consequently have an orientation towards emancipation.

Summary

All the dominant traditions discussed in this chapter have one thing in common: they agree that research is a systematic process whereby data are collected and analysed through applying appropriate data collection and analysis methods. They differ from one another in terms of the aims of research, what counts as knowledge and what methods of data collection and analysis are used to produce knowledge seen as valuable.

While we should understand the differences between the different paradigms or traditions, we should not allow these differences to divide us, since each paradigm makes a unique contribution to the body of knowledge and our understanding of the world. It is highly unlikely that we will ever be able to understand any person, event or phenomenon from every vantage point simultaneously.

Table 2.1 Summary of the dominant research traditions

	Positivism	Interpretivism	Critical realism
Reasons for research	To discover causal relationships in order to predict and control events.	To understand and describe meaningful social action and experiences.	To expose myths and empower people to transform society radically.
Ontology	Reality is external and objective and the laws that govern it can be discovered.	Reality is fluid and subjective and is created by human interaction.	Reality changes over time and is governed by underlying structures.
Epistemology	The only valid knowledge is knowledge produced via empirical observation.	Something is seen as knowledge when it feels right to those being studied. Common sense is an important source of knowledge.	Knowledge should supply people with the tools needed to change their own world.
Metatheory	By establishing causal relationships we can predict effects and therefore take action to manipulate or control phenomena. Often uses deductive reasoning.	Theory should tell a story in order to create an in-depth understanding of other people's realities. Often uses inductive reasoning.	Theory should be a critique which reveals true social conditions and that helps people to see the way to a better world. Often uses abductive reasoning.
Methodology	Reliability is important. Objective, quantitative research is used.	Subjective, qualitative methods are used.	Mixed methods are used: quantitative and qualitative methods are combined.
Axiology	Objective research, truth and reason are valued.	Uniqueness is valued.	Freedom, equality and emancipation are valued.

Review the chapter

Answer the questions and complete the tasks to assess whether you understand the content of this chapter:

1. What is meant by 'paradigm'?
2. What is meant by 'paradigm shift'?
3. Which of the three research traditions discussed in this chapter appeals to you most? Explain why.
4. Dr Thabalala believes that research cannot be neutral and value free and that a worthwhile study is one whose results can be put into action in order to change society and free people from all forms of oppression. Which paradigm does Dr Thabalala ascribe to?
5. In which approach is theory used to critique the status quo, showing how people are being misled, and to suggest action plans to promote social change? Compare this to the other two traditions' use of theory and explain how they differ from one another.
6. The German critical theorist Jürgen Habermas offers a useful distinction between the various ways of generating knowledge. List and explain the three cognitive interests as posited by Habermas. Link each of them to one of the three paradigms discussed in this chapter.
7. In table format, compare positivism, interpretivism and critical realism in terms of their epistemological, ontological, metatheoretical, methodological and axiological positions.

CHAPTER 3

Theory in research

Rose-Marié Bezuidenhout

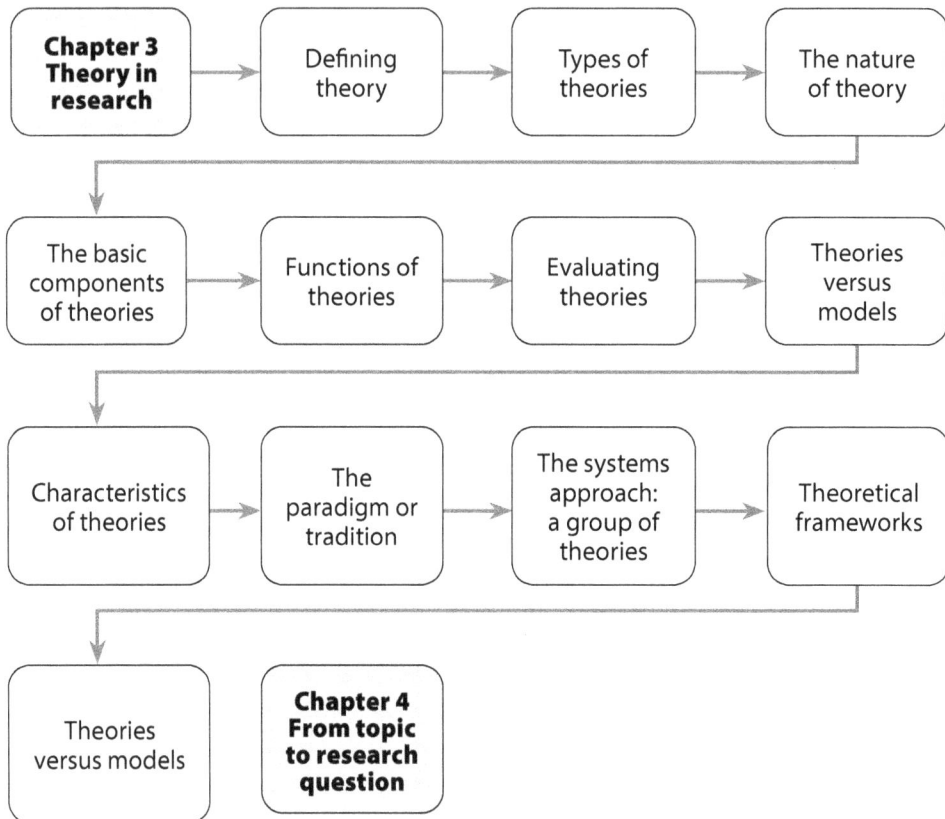

```
┌─────────────┐   ┌─────────────┐   ┌─────────────┐   ┌─────────────┐
│ Chapter 3   │→  │ Defining    │→  │ Types of    │→  │ The nature  │
│ Theory in   │   │ theory      │   │ theories    │   │ of theory   │
│ research    │   │             │   │             │   │             │
└─────────────┘   └─────────────┘   └─────────────┘   └─────────────┘

┌─────────────┐   ┌─────────────┐   ┌─────────────┐   ┌─────────────┐
│ The basic   │→  │ Functions of│→  │ Evaluating  │→  │ Theories    │
│ components  │   │ theories    │   │ theories    │   │ versus      │
│ of theories │   │             │   │             │   │ models      │
└─────────────┘   └─────────────┘   └─────────────┘   └─────────────┘

┌─────────────┐   ┌─────────────┐   ┌─────────────┐   ┌─────────────┐
│Characteristics│→ │ The         │→  │ The systems │→  │ Theoretical │
│ of theories │   │ paradigm or │   │ approach:   │   │ frameworks  │
│             │   │ tradition   │   │ a group of  │   │             │
│             │   │             │   │ theories    │   │             │
└─────────────┘   └─────────────┘   └─────────────┘   └─────────────┘

┌─────────────┐   ┌─────────────┐
│ Theories    │   │ Chapter 4   │
│ versus models│  │ From topic  │
│             │   │ to research │
│             │   │ question    │
└─────────────┘   └─────────────┘
```

Overview

When one mentions the terms 'theory' or 'theoretical', people outwardly respond either convincingly negatively or slightly positively. Some complain that theories are idealistic, since they are too abstract and far removed from practice. Others compare theory to being in a labyrinth or maze where there is no escape from the overwhelmingly unfamiliar ideas presented. However, we need to understand that theories establish and embrace most of what we know and experience, whether we recognise it or not. We use and assess theories in our interaction with others and our subjective experiences in different contexts.

Theory and practice are the two sides of the same coin; they cannot, and should not, be separated. The same inseparability characterises research and theory. Theory is vital in most research studies.

In the well-known fairy tale *Hansel and Gretel* by the Brothers Grimm, two small children use a trail of breadcrumbs to find their way out of the woods and back home. This is a powerful metaphor to describe the importance of theory in research. Theoretical concepts and constructs are the breadcrumbs we use to help us crisscross the research journey. A theoretical framework frames the analysis and interpretation of data, and the findings of a research study. It is the roadmap we use in our expedition of finding patterns in answering research questions and finding solutions to research problems.

In this chapter, we define and describe what theory is and explain its assumptions, concepts and functions. We discuss different types of theory. We further explore what theoretical frameworks are and how to use them in a research study.

Objectives of this chapter

By the end of this chapter, you should be able to demonstrate your understanding of the following:
- the definition of theory;
- different types of theories;
- the nature of theory;
- the basic components of theories;
- the functions of theories;
- the criteria used for evaluating a theory;
- theories versus models;
- the characteristics of theories;
- deductive and inductive theorising;
- the levels of analysing a theory;
- what a theoretical framework entails;
- the functions of a theoretical framework; and
- the strategies that can be used to develop a theoretical framework.

Defining theory

Theories can be compared to binoculars through which we can view distant objects in the fields of interest around us. Binoculars magnify and bring images closer and into focus. In the same way, theory enables a focused and closer or deeper understanding of a phenomenon. Broadly speaking, a theory is a systematic (logical, or step-by-step) description of the concepts, constructs, assumptions and relationships of specific processes or phenomena in a discipline. A theory is thus also a statement of how and why specific concepts are related. Theories form the academic foundation of every discipline and allow the transformation of information into knowledge (Littlejohn, Foss & Oetzel, 2017). Specifically, a theory may be defined as a body or an organised set of assumptions, concepts, principles and relationships we use to explain a phenomenon or some aspect of human experience (Leedy & Ormrod, 2019; Littlejohn et al, 2017).

Theory is the grounding in which a research study is rooted. It forms the conceptual and theoretical framework within which data is collected, interpreted and understood. The theoretical foundation thus provides the frame or outline by which we organise what we know about a phenomenon. A theory represents the current 'reality' of what is known about a phenomenon, but may also grow or change, because further research findings may confirm a theory and build on it. A theory thus often provides suggestions for further research.

Types of theories

Theories can be grouped together in terms of the similarities and characteristics they share and the level of abstraction or concreteness they represent. Dainton and Zelley (2019) identify three types of theories: commonsense theories, working theories and scholarly theories:

- A *commonsense theory* is created through, for example, an individual's personal experiences or what he or she has learnt about a phenomenon through his or her group and cultural membership. Thus, it is an understanding about a phenomenon that a group of people share, an understanding that developed over time and that the group members accept as being true. It is also referred to as theory-in-use. For example, you may have a theory that lending money to a friend will ruin your friendship. Although commonsense theories are interesting to consider and discuss, they are not used in the theoretical framework of a scientific research study because they are based on opinions and beliefs and are not backed by research.

- *Working theories* apply to business practices and professions where there are agreed-upon ways of carrying out a specific task. They are general ideas about activities and are more precise than commonsense theories. Using a particular method to write a business report, a business and marketing plan or a news release, because it is the generally accepted way of executing the task, are examples of the use of working theories. Like commonsense theories, working theories are not based on evidence gathered from scientific research studies. They are therefore not used in the theoretical frameworks of scholarly studies.

- *Scholarly theories* are the focus of this chapter. A scholarly theory is a theory that has been constructed based on evidence collected through a thorough and systematic (step-by-step) research process. A scholarly theory provides an in-depth, precise and abstract description of interconnected concepts related to a studied phenomenon. A scholarly theory also identifies and explains the relationships between concepts and constructs. It is thus perceived as more complex and difficult to understand. Researchers select different scholarly theories for their respective studies based on which theories best suit their research problems and questions.

The nature of theory

Some people believe that what they perceive to be real is the only explanation for their experiences. However, by reading news articles and following comments on social media platforms, for example, we realise that most of the conflict in the world is due to the different beliefs people have about some phenomenon or practice. We gain a sense of security from thinking about and believing in something in the same way as others do. However, as scholars and researchers, we are curious about these beliefs and experiences. As researchers we thus use theories to explain the regularity of patterns of behaviour over time (Babbie, 2021:13). We cannot afford to be content that there is only one explanation for a phenomenon and therefore we ask questions and keep mining for more and different answers. We also come to realise that none of the explanations we find are permanent and final.

The same principle applies when we define a theory as a conceptual representation or explanation of a phenomenon. We need to remember that theories are abstract concepts and constructions of a phenomenon and that they are constantly refined and changed based on new research studies. As theories are based on theoretical assumptions and are abstract constructions of a phenomenon, we seldom refer to 'facts' when we talk about theories.

Theories are abstractions

Theories are abstractions and, hence, partial and incomplete explanations or descriptions of a phenomenon. They can be positioned on a continuum of abstraction varying from general or grand theories as high abstraction theories with a wide scope of application to lower-level abstraction theories with a narrow focus explaining a limited set of phenomena (Nilsen, 2015). A particular theory is an abstract or intangible description of a particular phenomenon viewed from a particular point of view. Remember the poem 'The blind men and the elephant' by John Godfrey Saxe (1873:135), that we referred to in Chapter 2? Similar to paradigms, it also illustrates that different theories may describe different aspects of a phenomenon, but none of them can describe the entire phenomenon.

In the same way that each man in the poem describes the elephant from a different angle, each theory describes a phenomenon from a particular angle. A theory can never embody and express the totality of a phenomenon—especially not human experience. Human experience is too complex and multi-layered to be captured completely in the theories we construct. Once you start searching for a theory that fits your study, you will notice how many theories there are to explain one single phenomenon. We are barely skimming the surface of the depth of possibilities of human understanding. In a way, this is exciting because it means there is still so much that we can discover, explore and theorise about.

Theories are constructions

Theories are constructions created by people. They provide ways to view a phenomenon. However, as in the poem of the six blind men that we described earlier, these constructions merely describe aspects of the phenomenon and do not describe it completely. Constructions can change as more evidence is gathered. Therefore, all theories are subject to refutation and reformulation.

Sometimes, the reformulation of a theory may be far-reaching and revolutionary. Consider, for example, the fate of Galileo Galilei, the 16th-century Italian physicist, mathematician, astronomer and philosopher who played a major role in the scientific revolution. He supported the theory postulated by Nicolaus Copernicus, the Renaissance mathematician and astronomer, namely that the Earth circles the Sun, and not the other way around as was theorised at the time. Galileo's writings and arguments were investigated by the Roman Inquisition in 1632–1633 and he was charged with heresy. Heresy is any belief or theory that is different from established beliefs or customs. He was therefore accused of going against the dogmatic belief of the time. Fortunately, modern theorists and researchers are not forced to renounce and deny their theories and are not placed under house arrest as Galileo was. However, they do sometimes attract severe criticism from other theorists if they challenge existing constructs and theories or propose new theories to explain the phenomenon under investigation.

The basic components of theories

The basic components of theories are the essential elements used in describing a theory and are fundamental in all scholarly theories. They represent the 'language' of theory and are universally used by researchers, theorists and scholars in all disciplines working from different traditions.

A thought-provoking symbolic way of understanding the basic elements of theories and their increasing levels of complexity is by comparing them to Russian, or *matryoshka*, dolls. These dolls consist of a set of five to eight wooden dolls of different sizes placed one inside the other. When you remove an outer doll, there is a smaller doll nested inside, with a smaller one nested inside that doll, and so on. In the same way, theories represent different levels of abstractness, yet they all share some similarities, characteristics and components. A theory also frequently embodies and reveals more levels of complexity as you probe its nature. According to Littlejohn et al (2017), one theory cannot reveal the absolute truth and does not include all possible concepts or explanations of a topic under investigation. This means that, as with the Russian dolls, there are more and deeper levels of a phenomenon that a certain theory does not and cannot include.

Figure 3.1 Russian dolls illustrate the increasing levels of abstractness and complexity of the concepts of a theory

The importance of some components will vary according to the research paradigm or tradition used by a researcher. For example, in a qualitative study you will not have a hypothesis because the purpose of your research is not to predict the outcome of your study. You also do not identify any dependent and independent variables. In this chapter, we describe the most commonly shared elements of a theory, namely:
- assumptions;
- concepts and constructs;
- relationships; and
- prediction and explanation.

Assumptions

Assumptions are theoretical statements or assertions that cannot be confirmed by direct observation, about a phenomenon, issues and the nature of humanity. An assumption may be defined as an unconfirmed initial statement about the nature of human existence, phenomena and a theory or a belief in a theory. Assumptions are fundamental in theoretical frameworks, since we use them as points of departure in understanding, explaining and testing theories (Kivunja, 2018:45; Littlejohn et al, 2017:8).

Theoretical assumptions are embedded in paradigms, or the essential frames of reference researchers use as frameworks to develop theories. Theories include assumptions about epistemology, ontology and axiology, thus assumptions about the nature, source and value of knowledge and reality (Babbie, 2021; Littlejohn et al, 2017). See Chapter 2 for an explanation of the philosophical assumptions which underpin various paradigms and traditions.

Concepts and constructs

Concepts are notions and ideas about a phenomenon and, when articulated and labelled, become the most basic components or parts of a theory. They are considered as the key elements and building blocks of a theory consisting of two dimensions, namely a label (or symbol) and a definition. Labelling a concept means giving it a name—a verbal symbol — and defining it provides a description of the meaning of the concept. Concepts and their definitions are inseparable. The process of framing and defining a concept, referred to as its conceptualisation, is vital to avoid the elusiveness of some concepts that may result in their misapplication in a research study (DeCarlo, 2018; Onen, 2016). Consider the terms 'Netflix effect', 'binge-watching' and 'marathoning', for example. Although you may have an idea of what these terms might mean, as a researcher you would need to conceptualise these concepts for a study on the viewing and streaming behaviour of Generation Next, which is receiving increasing scholarly attention in various disciplines.

Certain concepts that were used in previous research studies become popular cultural terms and phrases we use in everyday life. The term 'ego' is an example of a concept that forms part of a theory and model of the human psyche constructed by Austrian neurologist and psychoanalyst Sigmund Freud. The way the term is used in everyday conversation nowadays is often far removed from the original definition of the concept used by Freud. It thus becomes necessary in a research study to describe the exact operational and theoretical meaning of a concept. This is exactly the purpose of conceptualisation, which is discussed in Chapter 9. By conceptualising the theoretical aspects of a study, we define concepts and constructs in terms of their theoretical meaning, to help us organise our thoughts and hence also our studies.

Concepts have different levels of abstraction and vary from direct, concrete, observable aspects to abstract mental constructs or creations that are difficult to explain and measure. 'Observational terms' are concepts that are easily verified since they are more concrete, whereas constructs are often neither directly nor indirectly observable, but when defined may become observable and measurable (Kaplan cited in DeCarlo, 2018). For example, the construct 'wokeness' is defined as 'critical consciousness to intersecting systems of oppression' (Ashlee, Zamora & Karikari, 2017:90). However, the construct may have multiple dimensions and would need more explanation and mutual agreement by researchers on its contextual meaning to shift it from a mental notion to an observable and measurable concept.

Conceptual analysis is indispensable for any theory. However, a range of concepts does not constitute a theory. A theory makes use of several concepts and explains the relationship between them, as discussed below.

Relationships

Theories describe the relationships between concepts by explaining their basic associations. For example, a theory of learning explains how information is understood and remembered during the learning process. It explains, for example, how the process of learning is influenced by emotional and environmental factors and previous experience. In explaining learning, the theory points to basic relationships or associations between understanding and remembering information and our prior experience and mental ability, and the environment in which we find ourselves. Concepts about learning are thus not presented in isolation, but are described in terms of relationships and interrelated clusters of concepts.

When two or more concepts are related, a theoretical statement, or proposition, is used to describe the relationship. Propositions, when logically interrelated, constitute a theory. A proposition must be based on precisely defined and consistent concepts. Using the learning theory as an example, we can make a proposition that there is a relationship between learning and a learner's environment. However, we have to explain precisely what we mean by the concepts 'learning' and 'environment'.

When a proposition can be tested using empirical data, it is called a hypothesis. For example, stating that learning (the dependent variable) increases with the improvement of a learner's environment (an independent variable) is a proposition that can be tested, and is thus a hypothesis which can be tested. A hypothesis is therefore an explanation or statement about the underlying relationships between concepts in terms of dependent and independent variables. See Chapter 6 for a thorough explanation of hypotheses and variables.

Explanation and prediction

Prediction and explanation (Fried, 2020) are two components of certain theories, such as those used in quantitative studies.

- A *prediction* is a statement that an event or outcome of a research study will occur. A hypothesis, for example, is a predictive statement about the desired outcomes of a quantitative study. A hypothesis makes a specific prediction about a specified set of circumstances. It is necessary to test theories through, for example, observational or experimental designs to determine whether they fit the phenomena observed and to derive predictions from them.

- An *explanation* can either be ordinary or theoretical. An ordinary explanation describes aspects of everyday life to make them more understandable. An explanation of the voting process of a country is an example of an ordinary explanation. A theoretical explanation includes a logical argument or position (a thesis) and explains the concepts and underlying principles that establish the argument. Theories should assist in understanding phenomena and aspects of our world through explanation and description that will endure refutation.

A theory usually explains interrelations between ranges of concepts and variables. A theoretical explanation has three potential forms, namely causal, structural and interpretive. A causal explanation explains the cause of a phenomenon, such as the causes of poverty in a society. A structural explanation allows us to place an event or phenomenon within a broader framework or structure. Lastly, an interpretive explanation is an attempt to promote the understanding of an event, social relationship or cultural tradition.

Functions of theories

You may be wondering why theories are significant and indispensable in a research study; in other words, what purposes they serve and what functions they perform. Theories perform a host of functions, the most important of which are the following:

- We use theories to organise a range of experiences into smaller categories. Thus, theories help us to organise and make sense of our experiences and different aspects of a phenomenon.
- Theories help us to identify and select what concepts or key areas of a phenomenon to study.
- In quantitative studies, theories allow us to predict and control aspects of a phenomenon (for example, the more you study, the higher your grades will be).
- In order to challenge the status quo we use critical theories to ask questions about aspects of the human condition. Theories thus allow us to contest social and cultural practices so that we can generate novel ways of thinking and experiencing (think of the feminists in this regard).
- Theories may promote a previously insignificant concept and may help us to see things we have not observed before, or in ways we have not considered before.

- A theory explains the relationships among a set of concepts.
- In quantitative studies a theory assists us to identify variables that could be used to test a hypothesis. A theory also explains the relationship between independent and dependent variables, for example whether an increase in exposure to television violence (the independent variable) will lead to an increase in aggressive behaviour (the dependent variable) in children.

Evaluating theories

Researchers and theorists evaluate theories by comparing one theory with another. Several criteria have been proposed by Littlejohn et al (2017) to assess the usefulness of a theory, including theoretical scope, appropriateness, heuristic value, validity, parsimony and openness. We now discuss these concepts in a bit more depth, based on the work of Littlejohn et al (2017:14–16).

The theoretical scope

The theoretical scope of a theory refers to how broadly and generally it explains a single phenomenon or a whole range of phenomena. On the one hand, a theory should be applicable to a broad field, but, on the other hand, its applicability should not be too broad and superficial.

Assumptions made about a single instance or event are not considered a theoretical explanation or description. For example, the assumption that people suffering from depression abuse substances because their lives lack meaning, based on one case study, is not a valid theoretical explanation. An assumption must be transferable to a bigger range of events in order to be classified as theoretical. For example, assumptions inherent in the systems theory are applicable not only to closed biological systems but to all types of systems in all fields of inquiry. Assumptions used in the general systems theory by biologist Ludwig von Bertalanffy in 1928, for instance, are also applicable in the social systems theory of sociologist Niklas Luhmann, which he postulated in 1983.

Appropriateness

Appropriateness relates to the soundness of a theory and its underlying assumptions, and the level of consistency between them. It refers to whether the philosophical assumptions of epistemology, ontology and axiology (see Chapter 2) are reflected in the conceptual framework; research purpose, goals and questions; hypotheses and the research methods selected by the researcher. In this evaluation of the criterion of a theory we may pose the question: is there is a clear and discernible link between the tradition within which a study is grounded, its philosophical assumptions, the supporting theoretical framework, the research problem and question, and the research methodology selected?

For example, imagine you decide to investigate how organisations use the principles of the green marketing theory in their advertising strategies. Your problem statement is: 'Organisations use the principles of the green marketing theory in their advertising strategies as covert practices to manipulate and exploit consumers and conceal green crimes.' However, one of your theoretical assumptions is that organisations are committed to ethical and responsible advertising practices and the principles of the green marketing theory by emphasising consumer choices and honest business practices. This means you are assuming that organisations *do not* take advantage of the attitudes of consumers towards the preservation of the environment in their advertising. However, the theoretical assumption inherent in your problem statement is that organisations use advertising as a deceptive promotional device without any attempt to analyse or modify a product and its impact on the environment. There is therefore no consistency between your problem statement and the theoretical assumption you made based on your choice of theory. Your assumption should rather have been that green marketing and advertising are used as false practices by organisations, that make no attempt to change the actual impact of a product on the environment. You thus assume that current green marketing and advertising practices deceive consumers into believing that organisations are responsible corporate citizens who care about the environment, when they actually do not. Underlying theoretical assumptions and concepts must be consistent with the research in question.

Dainton and Zelley (2019) refer to internal and external consistency as part of the appropriateness of theoretical assumptions and concepts:

- *Internal consistency* is the logical use of ideas and constructs in the development of a theory. If a theory makes a leap from one concept to another without adequately explaining a logical relationship, it has no internal consistency. For example, a theory that describes how individuals make decisions based on freedom of choice, but then describes a formula of how decisions should be made, lacks internal consistency. In this case, there is no logical movement from describing freedom of choice as a basis for decision-making and providing a formula for decision-making that contradicts the idea of freedom of choice.
- *External consistency* relates to how understandable a theory is in comparison to other theories in the same theoretical tradition. If a researcher, in proposing a theory, contests and disagrees with other theories without substantive argumentation, the theory has no external consistency. For example, a researcher disagrees that intrapersonal communication (communication with oneself) is a valid level of communication because she proposes that an individual has no inner sense of self. She theorises that a sense of self

is only constructed through communication with others or interpersonal communication and describes theories on intrapersonal processes as based on 'airy-fairy science'. However, there are several theories from different research traditions that propose the concept of an inner sense of self. If the researcher does not provide an extensive explanation of why she disagrees with the concept of an inner sense of self, the theory has no external consistency.

Heuristic value

The heuristic value of theory means that a particular theory stimulates further investigation and allows the discovery of new ideas related to that theory. The word 'heuristic' stems from the Greek word '*heurisko*', which means 'I find'. The word 'heuristic' therefore refers to a researcher finding a new idea based on an existing theory and applying it in a different research study. If a theory inspires thought and aids in the discovery of new ideas or generates new research questions and problems, it has heuristic value.

Validity

The validity of a theory relates to its 'truth value' in describing an experience (Littlejohn et al, 2017:16). The truth value, or validity, refers to how truthful a theory is in describing an experience or phenomenon. The validity of a theory is measured in terms of three kinds of validity, namely value, correspondence (or fit) and generalisability (Littlejohn et al, 2017:16):
- We attempt to determine how *valuable*, important or worthy a theory is in its application in a specific context.
- We also try to determine whether there is a fit, or *correspondence*, between the explanations of the concepts and relationships of a theory and whether the concepts and relationships can be observed.
- The *generalisability* of a theory is similar to the concept of theoretical scope that was mentioned before, but mostly refers to a quantitative study grounded in the positivist tradition, where the aim is to generalise the findings on which a theory is based to a larger population. In the interpretivist tradition, the aim is to provide an in-depth understanding of a research study where a relatively smaller sample size is used. The theory can therefore only be generalised to a particular context.

Parsimony

Parsimony refers to how simply and concisely a theory explains complex aspects of a phenomenon. It is also sometimes referred to as the law of parsimony or the principle of simplicity (Feldman, 2016; Gibbs, 1996). The idea is that the simpler the explanation, the better the theory, if it does not oversimplify and overlook important concepts of the theory.

How parsimonious a study is may also be described in terms of its acuity. Explaining a complicated issue in a theory with acuity, or insight, may lead to the proverbial 'wow factor' or 'aha moment' (a moment of clarity and insight) for others who read the explanation of a theory (Dainton & Zelley, 2019:11).

In explaining the need for parsimony or simplicity in describing a theory, theorists and scientists often refer to Occam's razor (or Ockham's razor). This principle was first used by a 14th-century theorist, William of Ockham (Ockham was the village in which William lived). Since then, scientists have adopted or reinvented Occam's razor, but the basic principle remains the same: when you have two competing theories that make the same predictions, the simpler one is the better. The metaphor of the razor explains that theorists should 'shave away' the complexity of a theory to present it in its simplest form.

Openness

This aspect refers to the degree to which a theory is open to other possible explanations, interpretations and improvement. Thus, theories that are open can be tested and applied in different contexts. In this way, the theory can be reinterpreted and improved. We have to be aware that theories consist of constructs and concepts (as described earlier in this chapter) and are thus subject to change, reinterpretation and reapplication (which relates to their degree of openness). The systems theory is an example of an open theory because its principles have been and can be applied to different fields of study.

Theories versus models

A model is a basic and simplified illustration of a process that can be used to help understand the nature of theories, constructs and concepts in a specific context. Models assist us to identify and illustrate the most important concepts of a theory and the dynamics of the relationship between concepts. Models allow the researcher to visually depict something that is otherwise difficult to explain. Models serve as 'intermediaries between theories and the real world' by aiming to deconstruct and represent the component parts, processes and relationships between the parts of a given phenomenon (Fried, 2020).

Because of their nature, models illustrate the 'what' and the 'how' of complex concepts, but are limited in explaining the 'why' of the concepts of a theory. They are therefore mostly used to illustrate how the concepts of a theory are related, and they cannot be used in isolation to explain a theory. Models are thus more concrete 'instantiations' of theories and focus on a specific aspect of a theory (Fried, 2020).

Characteristics of theories

In the same way we describe humans in terms of characteristics such as their height, body type, weight, race, language preference, and so on, theories can be categorised in terms of various aspects or characteristics. Although researchers use several categories of characteristics to classify theories, we will focus only on the most important and widely used ones. Remember the Russian dolls we mentioned earlier? In the same way that you find increasingly smaller dolls inside the bigger dolls, in categorising the characteristics of theory we can move from broad overarching aspects to finer and more specific aspects of theory. The characteristics included in the discussion below include the direction of theorising, levels of analysis and the paradigm or tradition.

Direction of theorising

There are essentially two directions of theorising, namely inductive and deductive theorising. The aspects of inductive and deductive reasoning or argumentation are discussed in various chapters of this book (see also Chapters 6 and 10). The point of discussing them here is not to be repetitive, but to establish a link between the various discussions on deductive and inductive reasoning and their use in theory.

Deductive theorising

Deductive theorising involves reasoning from general assumptions to more specific assumptions. It is sometimes referred to as top-down theorising. Deductive theorising could also be likened to an inverted pyramid, where the researcher moves from exploring broad and general aspects of a theory to applying them to a specific topic under investigation or observation. Deductive theorising allows the *testing* of an existing theory through conducting a research study. In deductive research, a relevant theoretical framework is identified before a specific study is conducted. Deductive theorising (or reasoning) can be illustrated as shown in Figure 3.2.

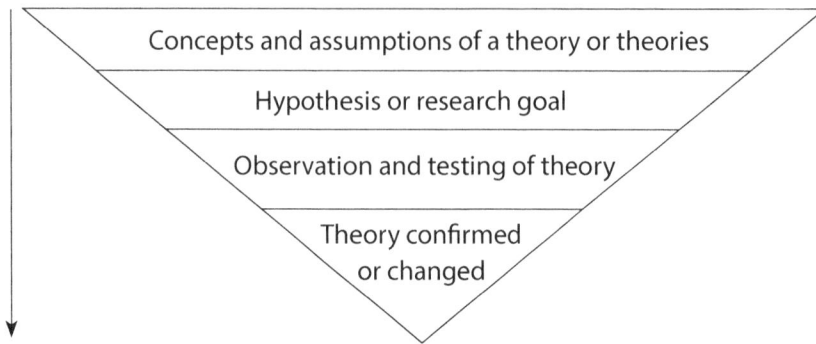

Figure 3.2 Deductive theorising or top-down approach

Inductive theorising

In inductive theorising, we infer theoretical concepts from the data collected and analysed in a specific study. We move from the specific to the general and apply our findings to more abstract and broad theoretical constructs. Inductive theorising is often referred to as a bottom-up approach. Hence, inductive theorising allows the *building* of an existing or new theory. For example, in grounded theory, researchers first conduct their research and then develop the theory based on the data they collect. The theory emerges from the study and, in this way, the research findings inform the theory. The process of inductive theorising (or reasoning) may be illustrated as shown in Figure 3.3.

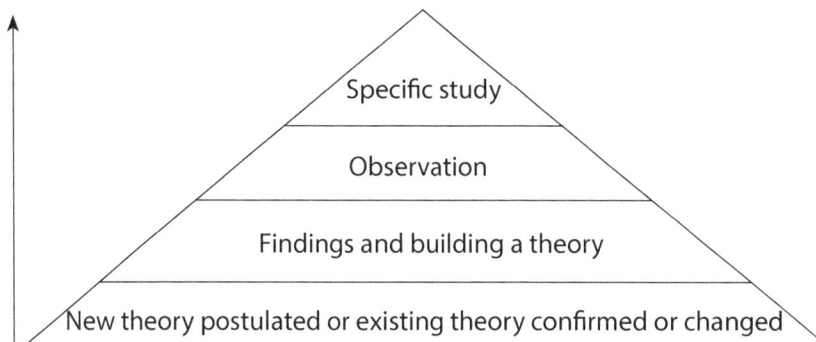

Figure 3.3 Inductive theorising or bottom-up approach

Levels of analysis

Theories may be categorised in terms of the level at which they are analysed. This relates to the scope of a theory, the units of analysis used in a research study and the period of time in which a study is conducted. It includes macrotheory, mesotheory and microtheory (Babbie, 2021; Serpa & Ferreira, 2019):

- When a researcher takes a broad approach in a research study and tries to get an overview of large collectives (such as societies) or global issues (such as the plight of the poor) he or she is engaging in *macrotheory*. Macrotheory usually focuses on processes that develop over decades or a century. Charles Darwin's theory of evolution through natural selection is an example of a macrotheory, since it involves the theory of the evolution of animals and humanity at large and was developed over a long period of time.
- A *mesotheory* is midway between micro- and macrotheory and is used when smaller categories of society are investigated over the medium term, such as several years, a decade or longer. An example of mesotheory is studying an organisation, gender or youth culture in a particular community and how, for example, perceptions or customs may have changed over the medium term.
- A *microtheory* involves the study of occurrences at an individual or small-group level over a short period of time. For example, investigating an aspect of social life, such as how an individual employee may increase productivity and investigating group dynamics are forms of microtheory. Most undergraduate research studies fall into the microtheory category because they are limited in terms of the time and the budget available for conducting the research.

Another important level of theory is *metatheory* (see Chapter 2). Generally, metatheory involves an analytical probing of the theoretical and conceptual frames, or lenses, that guide the research process. It also involves an exploration of the theory that was generated by a research study in a particular field of inquiry or discipline. Metatheory may be defined as the theory of theory—the study of those underlying assumptions which shape particular theoretical perspectives. Methatheorising involves the examination of existing theories using existing theoretical concepts (Frauley, 2017).

The paradigm or tradition

Every discipline has several ranges, genres, traditions and classes of theories. In the social sciences, Babbie (2021) describes early positivism, the conflict paradigm, symbolic interactionism, ethnomethodology, structural functionalism and feminist paradigms. Moreover, some authors categorise theory according to traditions and topics, and others in terms of different contexts and perspectives, such as the systems perspective.

Hundreds of theories have been developed, which makes any clear and inclusive discussion of different categories of theories in the scope of this chapter virtually impossible. An example of the diversity and magnitude of the theories in one discipline is the following: in 2009 Littlejohn and Foss compiled *Encyclopedia of Communication Theory*, two volumes in which they describe more than 300 theories. Clearly, since this textbook you are reading is an introduction to research for scholars from a diversity of disciplines, schools and faculties, favouring one category over another is not wise. We hence focus on the main traditions and how we use theoretical and conceptual frameworks in our own research studies in this chapter.

We use the term 'tradition', which groups theories according to shared philosophical assumptions and research approaches. However, some theories and research studies include more than one tradition and use both quantitative and qualitative methodologies — a mixed-methods approach. You should refer to the discussions in Chapter 2 for a more detailed explanation of the traditions. What follows is a very brief description of the characteristics of theories in three dominant traditions.

Positivist theory

In the positivist tradition, theory is developed from rational and objective reasoning and can only be justified by direct observation. French philosopher Auguste Comte (1798–1857) suggests that theory and observations have a circular dependence on each other. This means that observation in a research study lends itself to theory building, but also that theory stimulates the observation of phenomena. Theory thus depends on observation and vice versa, forming a circle of dependence like a snake that swallows its own tail or a cat that chases its own tail. Comte rejects religion, metaphysics and superstition as the foundation of knowledge and stresses that only scientific knowledge can reveal the truth about a phenomenon.

Positivism assumes that we can know an objective reality with a high degree of certainty and precision. A scientific theory in the positivist tradition is considered as valid if predictions are consistent with the information we can gather through our senses. You should also refer to the discussion on the relationship between theory and hypotheses in Chapter 6 for additional information on theory in the positivist tradition.

Interpretivist theorising

Interpretivist theorists, also sometimes referred to as anti-positivists, claim that focusing on the objective measurement and quantification of observable phenomena conceals the rich and 'deep' knowledge that can be mined from interpreting the personal yet unobservable subjective experiences and accounts of people. In interpretivism, studying behaviour or an aspect of a phenomenon is based on an understanding of the meaning and purpose that individuals attach to their personal actions and experiences.

Theories play a crucial role in interpretive research and can be used as a tool by researchers to sensitise others to the unobservable, subjective difficulties and experiences of individuals. Thus, theories in interpretivism are used to describe a phenomenon in an in-depth, rich, robust, 'thick', empathetic and subjective manner. Interpretivist theory leads to the understanding of phenomena. It does not predict outcomes and is not based on generalisations.

Critical theorising

The critical tradition includes, for example, critical and feminist theory, and aims to describe theories that are emancipatory, educative, transformative and participatory. Critical theories question power positions and dominant, discriminatory practices and ideologies in institutions and society at large. This tradition uses theory as a potential tool for socio-political activism by encouraging the individual to question his or her circumstances and to participate in changing those circumstances.

The systems approach: a group of theories

The following discussion is included as an example of how a theory includes several assumptions, constructs and relationships. The description is very basic and does not represent the total complexity and comprehensiveness of systems theory. We do not expect you to use or describe the systems approach based on the following brief and incomplete explanation. It is merely an illustrative example.

The systems approach is applied in the research studies of many disciplines in different traditions. The result of the multidisciplinary use of the systems approach is that there are many discipline-specific terms used to describe similar concepts, with small changes added as more evidence is gathered by scientists in that discipline and theories are tested and built upon. Consequently, only the very basic relationships, assumptions and concepts are described in this section to illustrate some of the components of theory that we discussed in this chapter.

Defining systems theory and relationships in systems

A system may be defined as a set of elements that are dependent on one another and work together in a stable way as a total and whole unit or entity. This definition focuses on the internal and external relationships and interdependence among the components of a system.

Concepts used in systems theory

According to the systems theory, economic, biological, psychological and sociocultural systems encompass certain common and universal characteristics, concepts and relationships. These systems are described as relatively *open* or *closed*, depending on the extent of a continuous flow of matter or energy between the system and the environment in which it operates. For example, a modern organisation may be viewed as an open system consisting of basic elements or parts and processes. A closed system is not influenced by the environment in which it functions, whereas an open system interacts with its environment. Systems thus vary in terms of their openness and interaction with the environment in which they function.

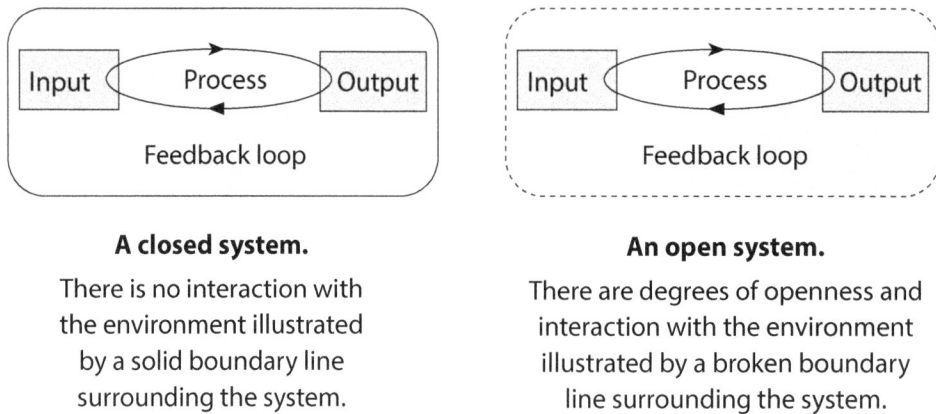

A closed system.

There is no interaction with the environment illustrated by a solid boundary line surrounding the system.

An open system.

There are degrees of openness and interaction with the environment illustrated by a broken boundary line surrounding the system.

Figure 3.4 Closed and open systems

Systems are also described in terms of, among other things, input, output, process, feedback loops, boundaries and the environment.

- *Input* in organisational systems, for example, is matter and energy in the form of raw materials for production, and information in the form of data about the environment, knowledge of sales and marketing techniques, and so on. Organisational systems have input subsystems (the concept of a subsystem is discussed below) to cope with input processes, such as public relations departments to communicate with employees, supply departments for production materials, marketing departments for analysing market data, and so on.
- Through work *processes*, inputs are transformed into outputs by means of transformation subsystems. For example, products are created and produced and services are organised.
- *Outputs* in an organisation, for example, include products or services crucial to its survival. They also include waste from the production processes. In

organisations, outputs are managed by subsystems such as sales and the control of pollution.

- Systems have *boundaries* to control output and input processes. Boundaries define the system's identity and may be concrete or intangible. A concrete boundary may be a physical border, such as the organisation's buildings. Intangible boundaries may include the cultural or psychological aspects of an organisation, such as norms that regulate employees' behaviour.

- Many systems are goal-oriented and regulate their behaviour through *feedback loops*. A *feedback loop* also refers to how systems use part of the output of a situation for new input. A system uses feedback loops to control its activities and maintain a steady state. In certain instances, balance or equilibrium is the goal of a system. Balance, referred to in the systems approach as homeostasis or equilibrium, is a form of self-maintenance and self-regulation, which implies that a system has mechanisms to detect and resist change.

- In general systems theory, the *environment* of a system includes the bigger systems of which it is part. This is called the suprasystem. For example, the suprasystems of an organisation include the community, the economic system and the wider society of which it is a part. Systems also have subsystems, such as the different departments of an organisation. Suprasystems, systems and subsystems form the hierarchy of a system. Subsystems are thus embedded in increasingly larger suprasystems. This hierarchy is like the Russian dolls we mentioned earlier in the chapter.

Some assumptions of the systems theory

One of the most important qualities of systems theory is interdependence, which means every part of a system is dependent on and constrained by the parts of a larger system, forming increasing levels of complexity (Littlejohn et al, 2017). Because of this interdependence, one of the assumptions of systems theory is that if there is a change in the bigger suprasystem, all the subsystems will be affected. This also means that if something changes in one of the subsystems of a system, the whole system or suprasystem will be affected. For example, through the lens of systems theory the coronavirus (Covid-19) pandemic has had a ripple effect on all the world systems with no parts left unscathed, illustrating the interdependence of systems.

As you can see, a theory consists of various assumptions, concepts and relationships which you have to consider if you want to apply it to your study. In the next section, we discuss how you can develop your own theoretical framework.

Theoretical frameworks

A theoretical framework is a specific collection of thoughts and theories that relate to the phenomenon that we choose to investigate. A researcher develops a theoretical framework based on the identification of one or more theories and several studies (Passey, 2020). It is the conceptual starting point and the frame or blueprint of our research study. Consider how a framed picture or photograph provides a snapshot of a specific moment in our lives. In the same way, a theoretical framework is a framed snapshot of a particular topic that we select and describe in terms of specific and related theories. By using a theoretical framework, we select and elevate specific theories and their concepts and assumptions from hundreds of theories and bring them into focus because they are relevant to our topic.

The quality of a research study is affected by its theoretical framework as an essential component since it shapes the study, determines its scope and provides an underlying structure. Theoretical frameworks allow the identification of concepts and constructs that may have been overlooked or may initially seem unrelated. They facilitate sense-making by highlighting concepts and constructs and informs researchers to avoid the risk of a limiting and narrow focus.

Functions of a theoretical framework

It is critical to develop a thorough and integrated theoretical framework within which to investigate and scrutinise a specific research topic, problem and question. If we do not do this, our research may have flaws and conflicting assumptions, which will distort or skew our findings. A theoretical framework serves several functions, such as the following:

- We use a theoretical framework to delineate or outline the theoretical scope of our studies; in other words, what is and what is not relevant to our study.
- It provides guiding principles and a specific perspective through which we examine a topic.
- It points to the concepts on which we need to focus.
- It assists us to identify the relevant key variables or aspects to include in our investigation of a topic.
- It guides how we collect, analyse and interpret the data of the study.
- It provides a way by which to identify important new issues and concepts to include in the study.
- It points to the most critical research questions that need to be answered in order to improve an understanding of a particular phenomenon.

Strategies for developing a theoretical framework

Developing and compiling your theoretical framework can be a demanding and time-consuming process. You have to concentrate your efforts on being as systematic as possible. What follows are steps and strategies you can follow to develop your theoretical framework:

1.   Write down or type a provisional title and problem statement for a topic you are interested in. In the next chapter, we explain that the research problem anchors your study. It forms the basis on which you construct your theoretical framework. Consider the consistency of the terms you use to describe the title and problem statement. Remember that there should be an obvious link between them. The words and concepts you use should be similar. Also note that these are initial statements; they will need to be refined and even changed once you have done a comprehensive search for previous studies and theories relevant to your research topic.

2.   Identify and underline or circle the most important words and concepts that you used in these statements. For example, if your title is 'An exploration of online users' experiences of cyberbullying on social networking platforms', you could highlight and underline the following words: 'experiences', 'cyberbullying' and 'social networking platforms'. Your problem statement could be: 'There are increasing occurrences of cyberbullying on social networking platforms. However, why people use this form of bullying, and how online users experience it, is not known or well researched.'

3.   Use the underlined terms to create a mind map. Remember that a good mind map is based on free association, so try to think as far out of the box as possible. This step is important in order to determine what you know about your topic and what areas you have no knowledge of. A mind map for the concept 'cyberbullying' could look like Figure 3.5.

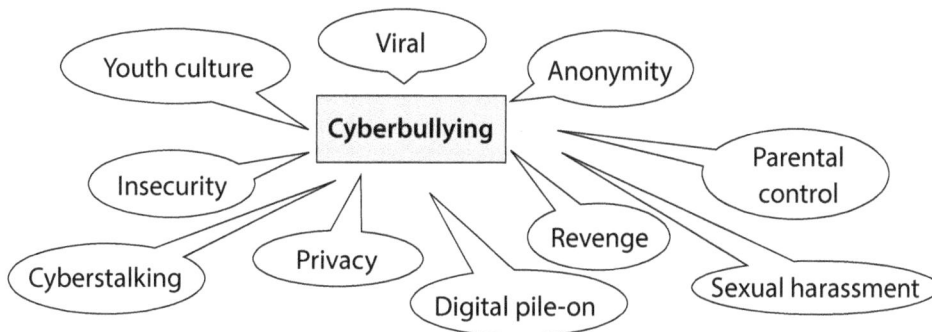

Figure 3.5 An example of a mind map

4.   The words you wrote down when you elaborated your mind map may or may not relate to or fall into the scope of your study. They are points of

departure for you to start searching for studies and theories that relate to your research problem. Use the mind map terms and do an Internet search (by using Google Scholar) to find previous studies conducted on these topics. Although Wikipedia is not a valid or reliable academic source, the case studies described and the references provided at the end of the entry may assist you in finding relevant studies and, thus, related theories. You should also use these terms in an online library search of your college or university, which will direct you to related studies in journals and books.

5. Once you have found similar studies to the one you want to research, explore the theories that researchers used in their studies. Identify which concepts and theories relate to your study.

6. You may find that after exploring all the sources, you want to refine or change your title and problem statement. This is part of the process and should not discourage you. You will note that drafting and redrafting a title and problem statement are essential parts of finding a fit between your area of interest and related theories.

7. In your search for relevant theories, it is also important to try and identify who the main researchers and theorists of a particular discipline are. For example, when you come across the theory of the social construction of reality, it is necessary to refer to the seminal authors or postulators of the theory, Peter Berger and Thomas Luckmann (1966). This will provide you with the historical context of the theory. You may also notice that theorists from one discipline often use theories from other disciplines. This practice is encouraged because there is an increasing trend in modern research to be multidisciplinary in nature.

8. An important step in the process is to consider what criticisms have been launched against a theory or what specific limitations it has. This may influence your choice between two related theories and which one you eventually use in your theoretical framework. You can refer to the criteria that we discussed earlier in this chapter regarding evaluating a theory.

9. After identifying relevant theories, you may have to embed your framework into a broader context, such as identifying your study's theories as belonging to the post-structural paradigm or cybernetic tradition. In previous research studies, researchers may specify what the overarching framework of their studies is. It is important to note that in some disciplines this step is not needed and is thus excluded. Consult with your supervisor or advisor to determine if this step should be included or not.

10. Repeat the process you followed in steps 2 and 3 in order to construct your conceptual framework. The difference between a mind map and a conceptual framework is that with the conceptual framework, you make more informed decisions on which concepts relate directly to your chosen topic.

11. The next step involves writing your framework. Use the present tense and write in clear and simple language. Long-winded sentences often indicate that a researcher is not absolutely clear on the theory he or she is describing. You should make your theoretical assumptions as explicit as possible and describe the concepts as precisely as possible. This step is more difficult than it appears. Academic writing is a skill that you develop, and you have to be prepared to rewrite your theoretical framework several times. Based on experience, we suggest that you remove yourself from your writing from time to time. This will allow you to gain a fresh perspective when you start writing again. We are not suggesting you take breaks lasting days or weeks; however, writing is a creative process and sometimes it happens in leaps and bounds. You should thus plan in advance for dry periods, and not cram in your work to meet looming deadlines.

12. Remember to use an accepted academic referencing method consistently when you source and describe your theories. Try to use the most recent sources, unless you are describing the original theory that was published long ago. For example, the construction of reality theory by Berger and Luckmann was first published in a book in 1966. These sources are sometimes called seminal sources.

One final note: although you may have started out with one or a few relevant theories, you may end up with too many alternatives. Having to deal with loads of information is cumbersome; we suggest that you list the theoretical assumptions and concepts in order of their direct relevance to your study. Resist trying to include everything. You can always do a second and third study based on the information you have gathered.

Summary

Theory matters in research because theory is indispensable in the research process. It integrates the various steps in the research process.

It is important to be able to define and understand the components of theory because they allow you to understand the 'language' of theory. For example, we use terms such as 'concepts' and 'assumptions' in describing a theory. By exploring theories, we come to realise that concepts can be described in terms of different levels of abstractness and complexity.

Understanding the nature of theories and the various types of theories assists you to determine what the processes of different types of research involve. This is also the reason why we need to know how theories function and how to evaluate their worth in the research process. Similarly, using inductive or deductive theorising steers us towards the research approach we need to use.

Realising that there are several levels of theory helps us to embed the theories we use in our studies into bigger theoretical traditions.

Developing a theoretical framework for our studies is a crucial step because it frames all the subsequent steps in the research process.

Review the chapter

Answer the questions and complete the tasks to assess whether you understand the content of this chapter:

1. How would you define 'theory' in your own words?
2. What are the three types of theories?
3. What is the nature of theories?
4. What are the basic components of a theory?
5. What are the functions of a theory?
6. What are the criteria for evaluating a theory?
7. What is the difference between a theory and a model?
8. How would you illustrate and explain deductive and inductive theorising?
9. How would you define a theoretical framework in your own words?
10. What are the functions of a theoretical framework?
11. What steps would you follow to develop a theoretical framework for your research study?

From topic to research question

Rose-Marié Bezuidenhout and Corné Davis

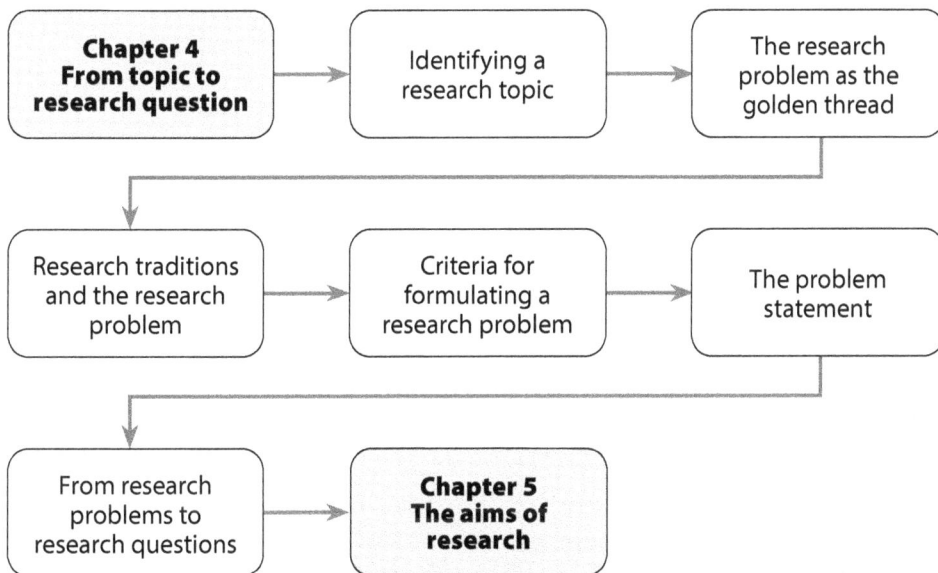

```
┌─────────────────┐      ┌─────────────────┐      ┌─────────────────┐
│   Chapter 4     │      │  Identifying a  │      │  The research   │
│  From topic to  │ ───→ │ research topic  │ ───→ │ problem as the  │
│research question│      │                 │      │  golden thread  │
└─────────────────┘      └─────────────────┘      └─────────────────┘
                                                           │
       ┌───────────────────────────────────────────────────┘
       ↓
┌─────────────────┐      ┌─────────────────┐      ┌─────────────────┐
│Research traditions│    │   Criteria for  │      │   The problem   │
│ and the research │ ───→ │  formulating a  │ ───→ │    statement    │
│     problem     │      │research problem │      │                 │
└─────────────────┘      └─────────────────┘      └─────────────────┘
                                                           │
       ┌───────────────────────────────────────────────────┘
       ↓
┌─────────────────┐      ┌─────────────────┐
│  From research  │      │   Chapter 5     │
│  problems to    │ ───→ │  The aims of    │
│research questions│     │    research     │
└─────────────────┘      └─────────────────┘
```

Overview

Identifying an area of interest or concern that will translate into a researchable topic is the first step in your research quest. Most of us identify and deal with issues and problems daily, but we do not always conduct formal research on them. However, even these aspects of our everyday experiences, and seemingly unimportant situations that we take for granted, could embody the next pursuit to understanding or explaining a certain aspect in the vast field of human existence.

In this chapter, we consider various sources which may inspire interesting research ideas, topics, problems and questions. We also take a closer look at how your direct experience or observations can be translated into research topics, problems and questions. The aim of this chapter is to help you to identify broad research topics and problems. We also explain how you can translate them into research questions in order to position them within your areas of interest. The examples used in this chapter are included only to guide your own curiosity towards the process of choosing a topic and to help you to formulate your own research problem and question. Keep in mind that one of the greatest challenges in research is to translate an area of interest into a researchable problem and to articulate that problem as a research question.

Objectives of this chapter

By the end of this chapter, you should be able to demonstrate your understanding of the following:
- identifying a research topic;
- different sources of research topics;
- the research problem as the proverbial golden thread running through the research process;
- the relationship between research traditions and the research problems they tend to address;
- the transition from research idea to problem;
- the formulation of a research problem;
- the transition from a research problem to research questions; and
- how to formulate research questions.

Identifying a research topic

The vast number of choices available to you in identifying and selecting a research topic makes it impossible for us to give you absolute guidelines; instead, we describe broad potential areas of interest that may encourage you to conduct research. It is helpful to imagine that you are at the centre of concentric circles,

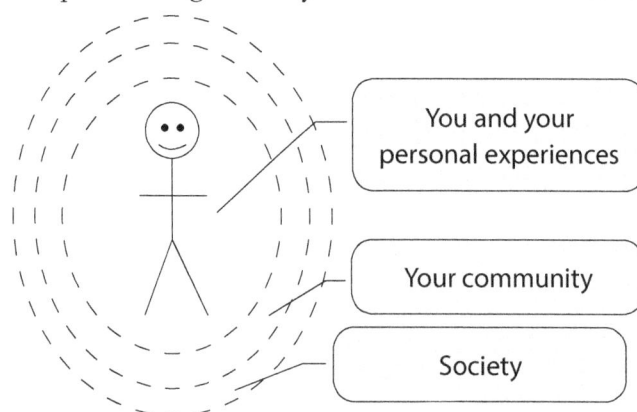

Figure 4.1 There are a wide range of sources you could use to identify a research topic

with each level, dimension or field representing different sources you could use to identify a research topic. The different levels represent your personal involvement, from direct experience and observation to more distant and global areas of concern.

In the sections that follow, we look at several different sources of research topics that you may relate to easily, ranging from everyday experiences to specific interests that may trigger your curiosity.

Direct experience and observation

Most people would relate to topics and problems revolving around personal issues, such as career opportunities, personal well-being and happiness, social belonging and any other issues that directly affect them. Direct experience and the observation of your immediate environment and the situation in which you find yourself could be meaningful sources from which to identify a relevant research topic. These are only a few examples of how your immediate environment and careful observation may generate research topics:

- If you experience or observe relationship problems, you may be interested in the role of communication in improving the quality of intimate relationships.
- You may be inquisitive about how your inner self-talk influences your confidence and success in life.
- You may observe that some people seem to have more self-discipline than others, which could awaken your interest.

In addition to the different worldviews, paradigms or traditions and theoretical perspectives to which you have been introduced in previous chapters, there are different ways, or modes, of observation. These modes range from a very broad to a very narrow focus. What you see is determined by the way you are looking at a phenomenon. For example, if you look at something through a microscope, you notice things that are not visible to the naked eye.

You may also consider that you do not always look at things in the same way on different days. For example, if you are late for a meeting, the congested traffic may upset you, while on other days you may not notice it at all and enjoy listening to the radio. In other words, the way you look at things — your mode of observation — may determine whether you consider an issue as a potential topic to research.

Social contexts

Society is constituted by social systems (families, organisations, schools, universities, and so on) created through communication or interaction (Kühl, 2020; Luhmann, 2002). These social systems create many different contexts from within which we could source research topics. For example, the context of your college or university, which is a social system, may be described as an educational system within South Africa. If you therefore decide to research a topic within your tertiary institution, it is likely that you will describe the context as an educational system. The context will change, however, if you are interested in your fellow students' tendency to use a certain brand of mobile phone. The context will then be described slightly differently because you are including a consumer product, which will shift the focus to a socio-economic context. Can you see that contexts are dynamic and that they change whenever you change the focus of your inquiry? You can test this for yourself by entering a keyword into a search engine. You will find that the same keyword occurs in many different fields, and that it is used in many different social and professional contexts.

Tradition and culture

Most of what we know about the natural and social world is based on what our parents, teachers and other significant people in our lives have told us, what we are exposed to by the media and our personal experiences. We rarely question our beliefs. We assume that certain things are true or false based on what we were taught. However, our knowledge may be based on partial information and incorrect or false evidence. There is therefore a real need to explore and even rediscover both the scope and depth of our knowledge gained through tradition and custom. For example, because of our upbringing and social background, which form our culture and traditions, we have adopted certain stereotypical views of the world and developed specific ideas about certain phenomena. These stereotypical views are sometimes so deeply rooted in our thinking that it is difficult to find their original sources and research them adequately. Researchers must reflect on these stereotypical notions and learn to practise open-minded thinking so that they can explore new and interesting thoughts and ideas.

Theories and previous research

We can also use existing theories and previous research to assist us in defining researchable topics. Theory formulation follows a systematic process of finding evidence, based on a selective and meaningful process of observation. Theories are not all-inclusive or complete in explaining all aspects of a phenomenon, and they are continually scrutinised, debated, refuted, debunked and refined. For example, if a theory states that increased exposure to online gaming will produce antisocial behaviour in gamers, the theory needs to be reformulated if you find in your research study that there is no evidence to support this view. The question of social isolation caused by online gaming is deeply debated and widely researched and, consequently, theories on interactive games and the social aspects of online social interactions are constantly being refined.

At this stage it should be clear that both existing theories and previous research studies are valuable sources of research topics. Additionally, when you look at existing research you may come across research topics that you would never have considered. It is thus crucial that, once you have identified a broad area of interest, you start searching for theories, literature and previous studies. This will allow you to focus on a more specific aspect of the topic. Studies also often include a section where the researcher makes suggestions for further research.

The media

The media provides interesting topics for research. The different forms of media have a powerful influence on our knowledge base. Social media networks are a case in point. Consider, for example, the confusing Facebook posts and fake news distributed in 2019 about the origin of the Covid-19/Novel Coronavirus. This reflects the increasing difficulty in determining the credibility of sources on social media platforms such as Twitter and Facebook. Comments about this incident also relate to issues such as citizen journalism, media ethics and the credibility of sources in the media. These aspects of the media are important topics to research.

In media advertising, norms of defining and portraying concepts such as beauty, sexuality, femininity and masculinity may have a far-reaching influence on the physical and psychological wellness of audiences. Images of women and men in advertising are digitally enhanced in order to remove all imperfections, creating unrealistic and unattainable standards of beauty. The media's portrayal of only certain body shapes and types as beautiful or desirable also contributes to creating an unhealthy and unrealistic notion of what beauty entails. This has been shown to have a real impact on both men and women's views of themselves, for example creating feelings of inadequacy. These issues point to researchable topics such as the second-wave feminist notion of the beauty myth, the objectification of women and men in the media and the possible exploitation of children in reality programmes.

The research problem as the golden thread

Identifying the research problem and providing a description that reflects its exact nature are the most important steps in any research project. Leedy and Ormrod (2019:30) refer to the research problem as 'the heart of the research process' since the main aim of research study is to find a solution to a problem.

Anyone knows that you need time and patience to tease apart a tangled rope or thread. The same process of teasing apart a thread can be applied to a research problem. We need to tease the problem apart in order to unearth and describe the various layers of a researchable aspect of a phenomenon. Once we have disentangled it, it becomes the proverbial golden thread that should flow right through our research proposal and report. Exploring or investigating a problem could also be likened to unpacking a suitcase or peeling an onion. Researchers need to unpack, unearth or uncover various layers or dimensions of a problem in their exploration of a certain phenomenon in different contexts. It is very important to consider that all the steps in the subsequent research process (discussed in the rest of this book) serve to solve a research problem and answer a research question, hence the importance of formulating a clear research problem.

The matching of succeeding steps to a research problem and congruent design decisions in research are referred to as the internal coherence and transparency of a study (Coombs, 2017). Conceptual coherence, progression and rigour mean that the researcher establishes the alignment of a selected research paradigm with the stated research problem, theoretical aims and methodological design decisions of the study (Coombs, 2017).

Research traditions and the research problem

It is apparent that no two people experience the same situation in the same way. Considering the different types and levels of theories that were discussed in the previous chapter, it is evident that the same phenomenon may be addressed from different vantage points. This is also true for researchers who use different research traditions or specific ways of looking at phenomena in the social and natural world. The research tradition that researchers follow determines what research topics they consider worth studying. Similarly, the research problems that they identify are influenced by the research tradition they follow. Since embedding a research idea, problem and question in an appropriate foundation is essential, these aspects should always be traced back to a research tradition and should be matched to that tradition during every step of the research process.

Identifying problems in the positivistic tradition

The main aim of a *positivistic* study is to predict, control and manipulate phenomena in the natural and social environments. Causal (cause-and-effect) relationships between dependent and independent variables form the basis of research problems and questions in this tradition. If, for example, a positivistic researcher is concerned about what influence the increased portrayal of crime on television will have on the behaviour of children, she or he would most likely expect a causal relationship between an increase in television viewing and behavioural problems such as criminal behaviour. The research problem could then be: 'The increased viewing of television programmes that depict criminal behaviour results in an increase in antisocial behaviour in children.' The researcher would want to establish a positive correlation between increased viewing of criminal activities on television and antisocial behaviour in a particular sample of children. See Chapter 6 for more information on dependent and independent variables and hypothesis formulation.

Identifying problems in the interpretivist tradition

The main aim of a researcher in the *interpretivist* tradition is to gain a deeper and more empathic understanding of aspects of social life and human behaviour. In contrast to the positivistic tradition, interpretivist researchers want to gain an in-depth understanding of a phenomenon and how people make sense of and give meaning to their daily 'lived' experiences. They do not aim to predict and control outcomes.

If we take the same example of antisocial behaviour and television viewing, the focus from an interpretative perspective would be to understand *why* children are drawn to programmes on television that involve crime or violent behaviour. The research problem could be: 'There is a lack of understanding of why children are fascinated by crime and violence on television.'

Identifying problems in the critical realist tradition

In Chapter 2 we explained that critical realists propose that research should liberate people from oppression by empowering them through knowledge. Critical researchers question the status quo, traditions and practices and, in so doing, create awareness of oppressive societal practices and ideologies that may marginalise or disregard certain sections of society. Critical researchers believe that certain dominant and potentially harmful ideological positions (or dominant ideas) are maintained through structures and rules, which, in turn, govern or guide people's behaviour. Therefore, by scrutinising the status quo, people may be empowered to think differently about their world.

Feminist research serves as an example of how a research problem can be formulated in the critical tradition. A typical research problem in the critical feminist tradition could be: 'Mothers with small children are perceived as ineffective employees and are, as a result, not promoted to executive positions in organisations.' It may be argued that mothers with small children are seldom promoted to executive positions because child-rearing is perceived to interfere with the demands of executive positions.

Criteria for formulating a research problem

A research problem should adhere to several criteria in order to allow the researcher to make a sound contribution in explaining, exploring or describing aspects of the social and natural world. Some of the criteria include the following:

- *Answerability*: the problem must be researchable and answerable through the observation of a phenomenon
- *Feasibility*: the research study resulting from the identified problem should be manageable in terms of time, sample size, methodology and cost.
- *Scope*: the scope and focus of the problem should not be too broad or narrow.
- *Theoretical value*: the problem should imply a study of theoretical importance and should contribute to the advancement of knowledge.
- *Relevance*: the problem should be relevant and should aim to explore, explain or question certain phenomena. The study should make a noteworthy contribution and not be trivial or insignificant.
- *Specificity:* the problem must be stated explicitly and clarify the specific context within which the study will be conducted.

The first criterion is about distinguishing between questions that can and cannot be answered. For example, if you see yourself as a feminist, you may want to argue that women are better parents. This may be your point of view. However, it is very unlikely that you could do any research to arrive at such a conclusion because, firstly, women cannot be classified as a homogeneous group (where all women are exactly the same) and, secondly, you will find it very difficult to justify the relevance of such a project.

If you are interested in how people eat Smarties (do they pair different colours, eat certain colours before others, pour them out of the box or eat them from the box?), you have to consider the 'so what' aspect of the research. *So, what* if you know how people eat Smarties? The results would not necessarily add any value to our knowledge base. The study would therefore not have theoretical value and it would not be relevant. However, if you use the results to determine people's subconscious criteria for making choices and to categorise people into different classes of decision-makers, it would be a different story.

Incidentally, how do *you* eat Smarties? Doing research out of curiosity is referred to as blue-sky, or blue-skies, research and has been a pioneering force in, for example, genetics and stem cell research. It is a contested form of basic research (also known as pure research, as discussed in Chapter 1) in which researchers question the notion that all research should be agenda-driven or goal-directed. It is argued that this type of research could radically change our thinking about aspects of reality.

When formulating a research problem, consider the above-mentioned criteria as guidelines in focusing the study. It should be apparent by now that the final analysis of the worthiness of a research study lies in how you formulate and justify your problem.

The problem statement

Once you have identified your research problem, you need to describe it in clear and understandable language. According to Leedy and Ormrod (2019), the problem statement should be stated as a grammatically complete sentence, implying and representing the purpose of the study.

An example of a problem statement could be: 'The portrayal of the female body on Instagram is idealised, unrealistic and unhealthy and a failure to achieve this ideal may lead to the poor body image of teenage females.' The resultant research purpose for a quantitative study could be: 'To determine if there is a negative correlation between the body image of teenage female learners between the ages of 13 and 18 years who attend Weston's School for Girls and the use of Instagram.' Conversely, the research purpose for a qualitative study could be: 'To gain an in-depth understanding of the reasons why teenage girls who use Instagram are likely to develop a poor body image.'

Once you have stated your problem, you have to determine if it meets the criteria stated earlier in this chapter. In other words, is it researchable, feasible, focused and relevant, and does it contribute to an understanding of a specific phenomenon?

Identifying and stating sub-problems

Sub-problems or secondary problems are, according to Leedy and Ormrod (2019), comprehensive researchable units which add to the main problem, can be linked to the interpretation of data and are small in number. If, for example, the purpose of the above-mentioned study was to gain a deeper understanding of the influence of Instagram on the body image of teenage girls, previous research findings may indicate that body image is closely related to self-esteem and the identity construction of teenage girls. The following two sub-problems could then be identified:

1. 'Teenage girls are likely to develop low self-esteem if they continuously reference Instagram images, which portray idealised and unrealistic images of female bodies.'
2. 'The identity construction of teenage girls who continuously view images on Instagram portraying idealised and unrealistic body images is likely to be influenced by the superficial value of the beauty ideal promoted as opposed to the value of positive role models which they could base their identity construction on, such as educated and successful businesswomen.'

Both these sub-problems relate to the main research problem and could enhance an understanding of the significance and relevance of the study.

From research problems to research questions

Research questions are means by which we narrow down a broad topic to a focused area that a study could address. Knowing the difference between questions that can and cannot be answered through research is a very important part of the formulation of the research question.

A research problem (such as the problem statements we discussed above) should be articulated as a research question that does not speculate about the outcome of your research study. Hence, a research question should not imply a desired outcome or assume that a condition or situation exists before the research study has been conducted. For example, if your problem statement is: 'Corporations in South Africa discriminate against obese employees', the following would not be an appropriate research question: 'Why do more people not care about the discrimination against obese employees in corporations?' Your question is speculative and based on **guesswork** because it assumes that only certain people are concerned about discrimination against employees. It does not reflect the open-mindedness and impartiality necessary in order to conduct worthy research.

Research questions should be directly related to the research problem statement and should address issues arising from the research problem statement. On page 75 we used the following example of a research problem: 'Mothers with small children are perceived as ineffective employees and are, as a result, not promoted to executive positions in organisations.' We could derive several research questions from that problem statement, each with a different focus:

- How are mothers with small children perceived as employees in organisations?
- How are mothers with small children perceived in executive positions in organisations?
- How many employees who are mothers with small children are promoted to executive positions in organisations in the financial sector in South Africa?

Research questions could indicate what data needs to be collected and how the data could be interpreted (Leedy & Ormrod, 2019). If we use the example in the previous paragraph, we could interview the CEOs of organisations or use a survey to determine how the employees of an organisation perceive female executives with small children. An interview and a survey are both data collection methods (see Chapters 12 and 13). If we use interviews, it is most likely that we will gain an in-depth understanding of how CEOs perceive executive employees who are also mothers with small children. The data that we will interpret will be the interview responses of the CEOs. We may use descriptive or inferential statistics to interpret the data we collected from a survey (see Chapter 15). Note how this example illustrates the research problem as the golden thread that runs right through the research.

The following section presents categories of typical research questions:

- *Exploratory questions* attempt to answer the question 'How?'; for example: 'How are female executives in South Africa perceived?'
- *Descriptive questions* attempt to answer the question 'How many?' or to determine whether a relationship exists between variables; for example: 'Is there a negative correlation between a negative body image and the consumption of fashion magazines?' or 'How many females are appointed as executive directors of South African companies?'
- *Causal questions* attempt to answer the questions 'Why? and 'What?' or to determine the causes of a phenomenon; for example: 'Does playing video games cause increased aggressiveness in gamers?' or 'What are the main causes of schoolground bullying?'
- *Evaluative questions* attempt to indicate the outcome or success of an endeavour; for example: 'Has the use of Facebook improved the effectiveness of crisis communication?'
- *Predictive questions* address the effect of one aspect of a situation on another aspect; for example: 'What effect do strikes have on investor confidence?'
- *Historical questions* investigate how the history of a situation influenced the current situation; for example: 'What caused the pre-eminence of male dominance in dating behaviour?'
- *Meta-analytical questions* attempt to determine the current state of or debates regarding a topic; for example: 'How is consciousness viewed in research on the systems perspective?'
- *Conceptual questions* attempt to determine the meaning of constructs; for example: 'What is metro-sexuality?'
- *Theoretical questions* attempt to identify appropriate theories, models, frameworks and explanations; for example: 'What is the predominant theoretical standpoint regarding reputation management and stakeholder theory?'
- *Philosophical/normative questions* address issues of an ideal state of being; for example: 'What would be an ideal relationship?'

The above-mentioned categories are useful not only in formulating a research question but also serve to indicate what type of research is required and what the appropriate methodology for a study could be. For example, predictive questions generally point to a quantitative research design embedded in the positivistic tradition, whereas non-empirical questions point to a qualitative approach explored from within an interpretivist tradition. However, not all research questions can be definitively categorised. As was indicated in Chapter 2, critical realism conjoins the positivist and interpretivist traditions, and thus it gives rise to questions that defy clear categorisation.

Summary

There are many different sources for research topics, depending on how we look at different phenomena. We may consider how different traditions and cultures consider the same topic in very different ways. We may also use existing theories and previous research to inform and guide our research topic. An important source from which one can identify research topics is the media, which plays a significant role in shaping our perception of what is important and significant.

We should also consider how we use different research traditions to identify different kinds of research problems and to ask different kinds of research questions. It is therefore imperative that you focus on the research tradition from within which your research problem emerges, so that you can ensure that your topic and questions correspond with the other choices you make during the research process.

We suggest that you follow the research problem formulation criteria we provided in this chapter. The research problem statement describes your research problem in clear and understandable language. Sub-problems can be described as other problems that are related to the research problem. Research problems lead to research questions. These questions should correspond with the aims of your research (see the following chapter).

Review the chapter

Answer the questions and complete the tasks to assess whether you understand the content of this chapter:

1. What sources can be used to identify research topics and problems?
2. How are each of the three dominant research traditions orientated towards the formulation of research problems?
3. How would you assess whether a research problem you find in existing research meets the problem formulation criteria identified in this chapter?
4. How would you formulate a problem statement for your research topic?
5. How would you formulate a research question related to your research problem?

CHAPTER 5

The aims of research

Corné Davis

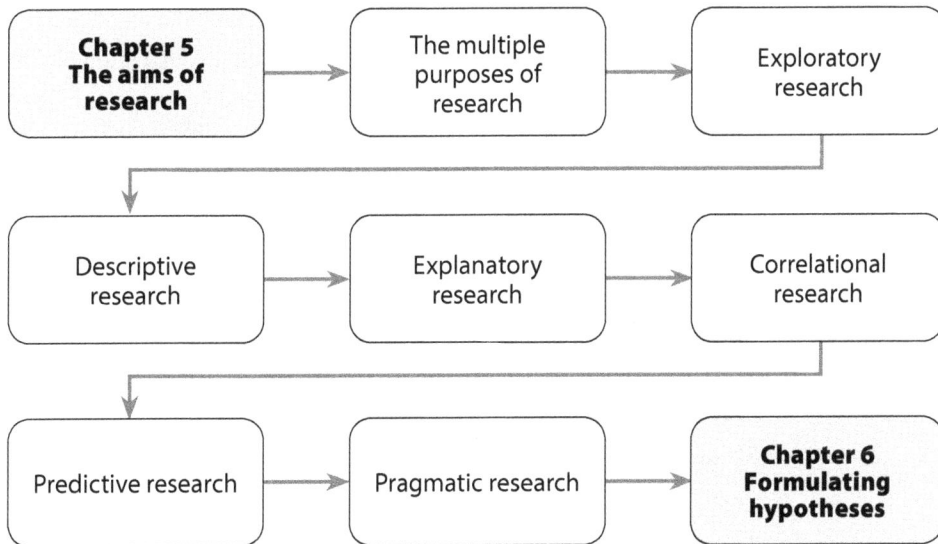

Overview

One of the many challenges we face when we engage in research is keeping in mind what we aim to achieve with our research. In this chapter, we take a closer look at the aims of research by giving you a more detailed description of different types of research so that you can see how their aims and objectives may differ. First, we distinguish three main categories of research, which are pure (basic), strategic and applied research. Next, we distinguish the types of research in terms of their narrower aims, namely exploratory, descriptive, explanatory, correlational, predictive and pragmatic.

You may, for example, start your process of inquiry with an exploratory aim and progress towards a descriptive aim. Research is a dynamic process that changes with every choice you make. This chapter focuses on explaining how to understand and articulate your choices by keeping the purpose of your research in mind. We will also show you the difference between research aims and research objectives, which can be confusing without clarification.

Bear in mind, at all times, that the choice and articulation of your research purpose are linked to your choice of paradigm or tradition (see Chapter 2). Remember the inverted triangle we discussed in Chapter 1? Study the descriptions of different types of research and their general aims or purposes carefully, so that the choices you make during the various steps of your research do not contradict each other in any way—your choices should always be consistent.

Objectives of this chapter

By the end of this chapter, you should be able to demonstrate your understanding of the following:
- the difference between research aims or goals and research objectives;
- pure, strategic, applied and action research;
- the aims of exploratory research;
- the aims of descriptive research;
- the aims of explanatory research;
- the aims of correlational research;
- the aims of predictive research; and
- the aims of pragmatic research.

The multiple purposes of research

In Chapter 1, we identified the many purposes of research to show you how research matters to us all. The most important lesson in this chapter is that the aims of research inform its processes and outcomes. Therefore, you have to be clear about what you want to achieve and what objectives you will set to do so. Your aims may change along the way and you may have to revisit the aims you identified in the earlier steps in the research process. It may be helpful to distinguish between research aims and research objectives at this point. In simple terms, research aims state what you are doing. It will start with something like 'The aim of this study is to ...'. It is important to be clear upfront about the main aim or purpose of your study. Usually, you have one main aim or purpose that you will need to break down into two or three smaller aims that fit into the main one. For example:

Main aim: The aim of this study is to identify key drivers of gender inequality among the employees of a selected group of private sector organisations in Johannesburg.

Sub-aims:
- to conceptualise gender inequality from current employees' perspective;
- to identify drivers of inequality among the selected group of participants; and

- to facilitate conversations about gender inequality among private sector organisations in Johannesburg.

The difference between research aims and objectives is that the aims focus on what you are studying, while the objectives focus on how you are going to achieve those aims. Based on the example above, the objectives of the study may include the following:

- Conducting a survey among a representative sample of employees in the population to determine how they conceptualise inequality in the workplace.
- Conducting focus groups to probe how employees perceive the drivers of gender inequality.
- Conducting a thematic analysis of participating organisations' public communication to assess gender representation.

Some scholars may include details about data analysis in the objectives, but we want you to focus on the difference between the aims and objectives only at this point. You must pay attention to how aims are derived from the different kinds of research discussed in the following section and then think about how you will identify different research objectives for different aims. You may have to return

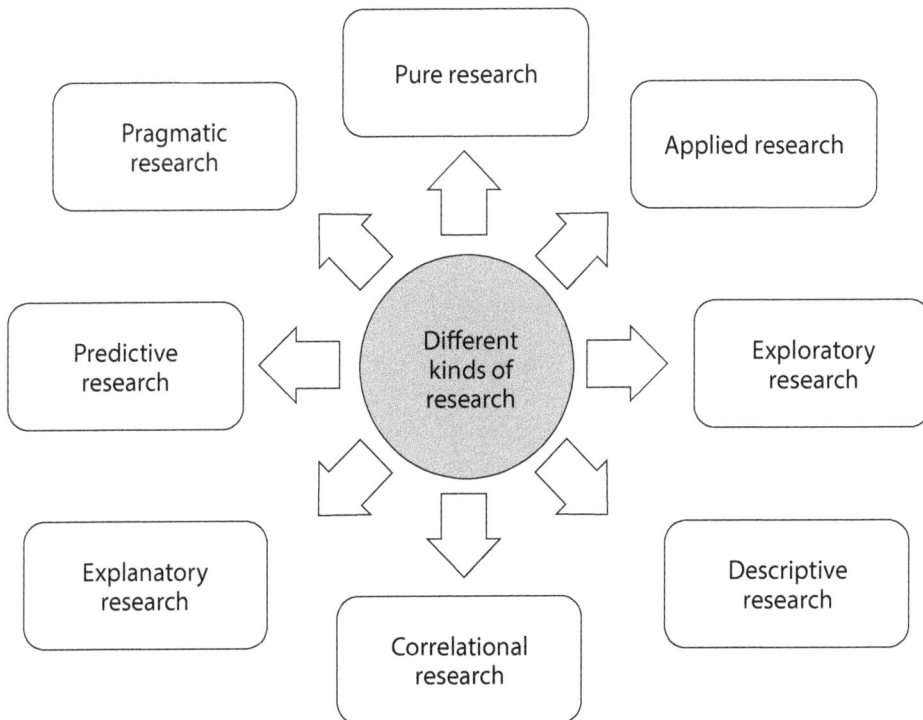

Figure 5.1 Different types of research have different aims

to this exercise after you have worked through the other chapters of this book. As Hall (2018) shows, research has traditionally been grouped into three broad categories, namely basic/pure research, strategic research and applied research. The different goals or aims of research fit into these categories to some extent, as you will derive from the discussion below.

Pure (or basic) research

Pure or basic research is done to produce knowledge for understanding things (Blaikie & Priest, 2019). It is usually concerned with testing theories to better understand our knowledge about the world. The knowledge produced through pure research is sought in order to add to the existing body of knowledge in the field concerned. We know that things change all the time so the way we look at them also needs to change. This means that we need new ways of doing research; that is, to do research about research methods. This is what pure research is. It aims to find or develop new methods, techniques, instruments, measuring devices, software programs, terminologies and so forth. Think about the Square Kilometre Array project, which is currently the biggest scientific project in the world. The project entails developing gigantic telescopes which can see further into the universe than humankind has ever been able to see before. Who knows what pure research we may see?

Besides doing the research about research methods, we also put criteria in place to make sure that all the information we collect in whatever format is legitimate. In the social sciences this is often a major challenge, especially when we select qualitative methods. Human beings are so complex and diverse that we have to do extensive research on how research on human behaviour is conducted. Examples of pure research are developing new sampling techniques, developing new methods to test people's responses to situations, developing new instruments to test children's attention span in class or developing new concepts to assess people's observations. You can see from these examples that pure or basic research has practical and useful applications even though, as Hall (2020) points out, it is 'an incidental consequence of basic research rather than its goal'.

Pure research is often used to formulate new theories and it is unlikely that you will conduct pure research during the early stages of your academic career. Hall (2020) also adds that basic research is typically conducted in universities or research centres and is usually funded by governments or other institutions. Hall (2020) adds the category of strategic research, saying that it is similar to basic research because it is conducted by research centres created by governments or non-governmental organisations. He says strategic research has a narrower focus but a broader scope. For example, if you look at the National Strategic Plan for South Africa, launched by President Ramaphosa in March 2020, the research on gender-based violence (GBV) can be categorised as strategic because it is narrowly focused on finding solutions to the many different kinds of GBV and also adds to the existing research on GBV as well as informs policies on GBV. Strategic research will probably use more mixed research methods, as Hall (2020) points out.

At this point, you will probably be more interested in applied and action research.

Applied research

Applied research usually focuses on addressing specific issues or problems that require practical solutions. Action research is a form of applied research. Broadly, speaking we can say that applied research is undertaken to:
- investigate whether solutions to social problems can be found;
- describe and assess social needs;
- assess and evaluate existing policies and practices;
- recommend and implement change; and
- identify new areas of research.

You can see that the categories of research overlap because just as GBV requires strategic research, as shown above, it also requires applied research because it is a persistent societal problem. Action research, as a form of applied research, seeks to bring about societal change. Changing societal perceptions often requires participatory action research, as Hall (2020) shows, in order to overcome injustices and suffering, for example. Hammond and Wellington (2021) add that action research addresses these kinds of social problems through an 'iterative cycle of action and reflection'. They say that action research appeals to practitioners across many different fields ranging from community development to implementing climate change, for example. As a form of applied research, action research is popular because it typically focuses on solutions and improvements and makes a difference for the better. You may find it interesting to read up on some of the challenges for researchers new to action research.

We now look at how research within these different categories can be further distinguished from each other in terms of their particular research aims.

Exploratory research

Research that has the overall purpose of exploration usually refers to the study of an unknown area. As our social, economic and technological systems evolve, new areas of research emerge. Think about how things have changed during your lifetime. When your parents were your age, for example, social media such as Facebook or Twitter — and the complications that come with them — did not exist. Social media are therefore an example of a topic that gives rise to many exploratory research projects. Exploratory research can be based on one or more of the following research purposes:

- to obtain insights into emerging problems or issues;
- to formulate problems;
- to formulate hypotheses;
- to develop and clarify new key concepts;
- to identify key stakeholders;
- to illuminate social needs; or
- to identify potential consequences of research problems.

In exploratory studies, data replication (reliability) and accuracy (validity) are usually not scientific criteria because the research design has to be flexible to enable an understanding of an unknown area of research. Exploratory studies typically include qualitative methods such as personal and focus group interviews, but also quantitative methods such as surveys or case studies.

Descriptive research

The purpose of descriptive research is to describe as accurately as possible the characteristics of phenomena, relations between variables or relationships between phenomena. There are many different ways of describing phenomena and objects, and therefore descriptive research can be the purpose of both qualitative and quantitative studies. Descriptive studies aim to:

- describe a situation, problem or phenomenon under investigation;
- provide information about certain phenomena, such as individuals' experiences in a specific context;
- answer how, what, when or where questions;
- enable visual representations of data, such as infographics and graphs; and
- provide information for further research.

In diverse sociocultural contexts, such as South Africa, a descriptive study can aim to compare attitudes towards issues of great significance, such as load shedding, corruption and vaccines for Covid-19. Think of the need to describe the impact of the pandemic on people's personal lives and on the economy in South Africa. These descriptions are often given in narrative form (by telling a story). People understand and remember stories more easily than they remember information presented as facts. Storytelling has become a powerful method of presentation in the field of branding. Hence, descriptive research focused on narratives has also gained popularity. You may also find it interesting to read up on narratology.

Descriptions can also be grouped according to classification systems or typologies which can be used to compare different responses. Note that descriptive studies can also be based on statistical data displayed in formats such as infographics and graphs, as mentioned earlier, that represent data instantly and comprehensively as indicated in figure 5.1 below. You can see how it represents information about how many companies involved in the study, percentage of men and women, how many employees were involved and how the companies were ranked.

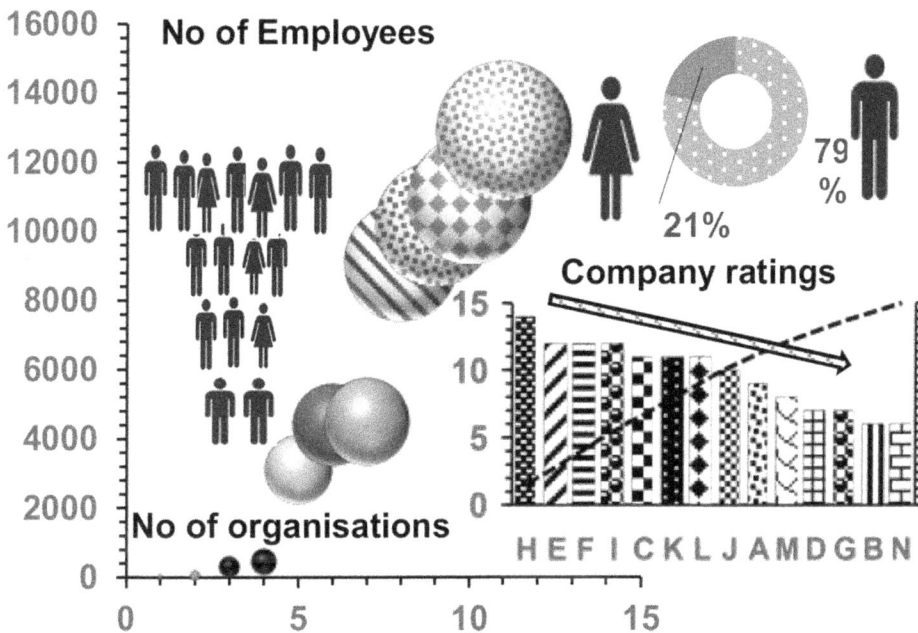

Figure 5.2: Example of Descriptive research

Explanatory research

As researchers, we have to find explanations for why certain things happen if we want to find solutions to remedy such situations. While correlational studies usually aim to identify relationships between variables, explanatory studies typically investigate the varying degrees to which these relations exist. In other words, if a correlational study established that a relationship between phenomena exists, explanatory research may attempt to clarify how and why this relationship exists. For example, you may aim to establish why peer pressure among adolescents in a particular school has a higher-than-average impact on their pass rates. You may find out that the divorce rate is very high among parents in that school and you may want to explain how this influences peer pressure.

The overall purposes of explanatory research are:
- to clarify *how* and *why* there is a relationship between different phenomena; in other words, whether you can find reasons why certain things happen; and
- to 'indicate the *direction* of a cause-and-effect relationship between an independent variable (X) and a dependent variable (Y)' (Du Plooy, 2006:50).

We said earlier that research aims are not exclusive. Therefore, explanatory studies can coincide with research that aims to predict or evaluate. This may seem confusing, but it simply means that:
- you have to keep focusing on what you aim to achieve with your research; and
- you have to articulate clearly what the overall purpose of your study is when you formulate your research design, with the understanding that you are involved in a dynamic and ever-evolving process.

Every decision you make during the research process creates further questions, just as every solution may identify further problems. The two research methods typically used in explanatory research are experimental (and quasi-experimental) designs and correlational studies, which are *quantitative* methods (see Chapter 12).

Correlational research

The primary aim of correlational research is to find out whether there is a relationship between different things as contained in the words 'co' and 'relation'. Similarly, if you look at the word 'interdependence', you will see that it is a compound word that consists of the prefix 'inter-', which means 'between', and the adjective 'dependent'. Thus, correlational studies look at:
- the relationship *between* certain variables or how one variable (usually called the dependent variable) is affected by another variable (usually called the independent variable); and
- the kinds of relationships between variables that can be identified using analytical tools such as factor analysis or Atlas Ti, among many others.

These correlations are typically referred to as positive or negative correlations (see Chapter 6). For example, you may want to establish whether there is a relationship between students' academic performance and their relationships with their parents. Thus, you want to determine whether there is a *positive correlation* between academic performance and the quality of the relationship between students and their parents. This implies that the better the quality of the relationship between the student and their parents, the higher the student's academic scores will be.

Many research questions require correlational research. You probably hear and read about the findings of many correlational studies without realising it. In fact, there are so many of them that you may find it difficult to decide what to believe, since the findings of some studies may contradict each other. For example, one study may show a positive correlation between depression and peer pressure, while another may show a positive correlation between peer pressure and high levels of motivation.

Predictive research

We know that all kinds of research are important, but predictive research is probably at the top of the list in terms of utility value. Think about how different things could have been if the Covid-19 pandemic was predicted earlier than it was. On the other hand, many things are predicted but are simply not paid attention to immediately. Think of the global gender gap report and the consequences of gender inequality that have remained an unresolved global sustainability challenge for decades. In essence, the primary aims of predictive research are to:

- prevent undesired outcomes;
- promote desired outcomes;
- anticipate probable outcomes; and
- to direct further research.

Research that aims to predict is particularly challenging when it involves human perceptions, attitudes and behaviour. Think about your own behaviour and experiences. How many times have you been in situations that you could not have predicted? We see those kinds of situations every day when we watch the news, for example. People who have lost their pensions through poor investment decisions never predicted that it could happen. The parents who lost children in the school shootings in the US, for example, never predicted that a school could become a tragic crime scene.

It will always be difficult, if not impossible, to predict human behaviour accurately. However, many studies aim to predict certain human behaviour; in fact, we rely on predictive research every day. If you think of the amount of money spent on advertising, you will realise that market research, for instance, is an attempt to predict how consumers will behave. Research into people's buying behaviour may show their preference for specific brands. Certain human behaviour can therefore be predicted to a certain extent. If a popular motor vehicle brand, such as Mercedes, launches a campaign whereby all students who pass with distinction can purchase a certain model at a discount of 25%, we can predict that there will be a noticeable increase in average marks in the student population affected by the campaign. We therefore have to agree that certain human behaviour can be predicted, even if we disagree on why individuals behave in predictable ways.

Pragmatic research

If we look at the description of the above kinds of research, we can identify the action words 'explore', 'describe', 'compare', 'explain' and 'predict'. We can link these purposes to the traditions or paradigms (see Chapter 2) and their related theoretical perspectives (see Chapter 3). These paradigms determine, to a large degree, the purposes and methods of certain kinds of research. The way you think and the assumptions you make about knowledge and reality lead you to question what is true and how to find, or create, knowledge that is credible. All these kinds of research ultimately aim to contribute to solutions of some kind, as they lead to further research or become integrated within other research.

Pragmatic research can be described as research that aims to find solutions to specific problems using both qualitative and quantitative research methods. We have transcended the time in research methodology history where researchers argue about the validity and utility of qualitative research. We acknowledge both positivist and interpretivist paradigms in this textbook, as you would have seen in Chapter 2. However, we specifically include pragmatic aims to show you that there are many more nuanced positions within these two broad frameworks. In fact, it is generally known that qualitative and quantitative methods most often complement each other when the research purpose is to solve a problem. Considering that so much emphasis is placed on global sustainability and solving the world's problems, it makes sense that pragmatic research is becoming more prominent. We encourage students at every stage of their learning journey to be solution driven since it makes sense to put your knowledge to use.

What distinguishes pragmatic research from other types of research is its worldview. It does not simply employ both qualitative and quantitative methods, but selects specific methods in a complementary way to find answers to questions and solutions to problems. It departs from the assumption that objective reality cannot be represented accurately. In other words, empirical observation alone cannot represent objective truth, since observation always takes place from a particular point of view, and people view and experience things differently. Pragmatic research therefore includes both qualitative and quantitative research. From the reflexive perspective of pragmatic research, any inquiry begs the following questions:
• What is the inquiry for?
• Who is it for?
• How do the researcher's values influence the research?

If you think about the topic of researchers' values, you touch on the notion that we are all people and that the roles we fulfil, such as researchers, do not necessarily change who we are. If you are passionate about a topic and wish to participate in solving a problem, such as students' safety on campus, arguing about the superiority of a specific method will probably not occur to you. If you are intent on bringing about change or improving a situation, you will be more interested in the best outcome for everyone and be more open to trying different methods to achieve it. It is only through looking at the world from many different perspectives that we can see the bigger picture.

Summary

Different kinds of research enable us to accomplish different aims. Research aims are, in turn, linked to different worldviews, paradigms or traditions, and theoretical perspectives. As you make different choices during different stages of the research process, you may find that your overall purpose or aims change as you learn more about your topic. It is therefore necessary to revisit your aims during all the different stages in your research process so that you can synchronise the many decisions you make. You should also ensure that at all times the purpose or aims of your research correspond with the worldviews, paradigms, theoretical perspectives and methodology you choose and apply throughout your research project.

Table 5.1 The different types of research and their corresponding aims

Type of research	Aims
Exploratory research	<ul><li>To obtain new insights</li><li>To identify key concepts</li><li>To identify key stakeholders</li><li>To prioritise social needs</li><li>To identify consequences of research problems</li><li>To develop hypotheses</li><li>To confirm assumptions</li><li>To become familiar with unknown situations, conditions, policies and behaviours</li></ul>
Descriptive research	<ul><li>To describe a situation, problem or phenomenon systematically</li><li>To provide information about things, such as living conditions of a community</li><li>To draw comparisons</li></ul>

→

Type of research	Aims
Explanatory research	• To clarify how and why there is a relationship between different phenomena • To indicate the direction of cause-and-effect relationships between variables
Correlational research	• To establish whether a relationship, association or interdependence between two or more aspects of a situation exists
Predictive research	• To prevent undesired outcomes • To promote desired outcomes • To anticipate probable outcomes
Pragmatic research	• To employ mixed methods and different modes of observation to obtain solutions for specific problems

Review the chapter

Answer the questions and complete the tasks to assess whether you understand the content of this chapter:

1. What is the difference between pure and applied research?
2. What is the difference between research aims and research objectives?
3. Identify topics in your field which are most suitable for action research.
4. Compare correlative and explanatory research.
5. Explain why you would do pragmatic research.
6. Identify some of the methods you would use doing pragmatic research.
7. How does a research topic relate to the research purpose?
8. Identify a research topic and compare how different research aims lead to different research questions.

CHAPTER 6

Formulating hypotheses

Nola Payne

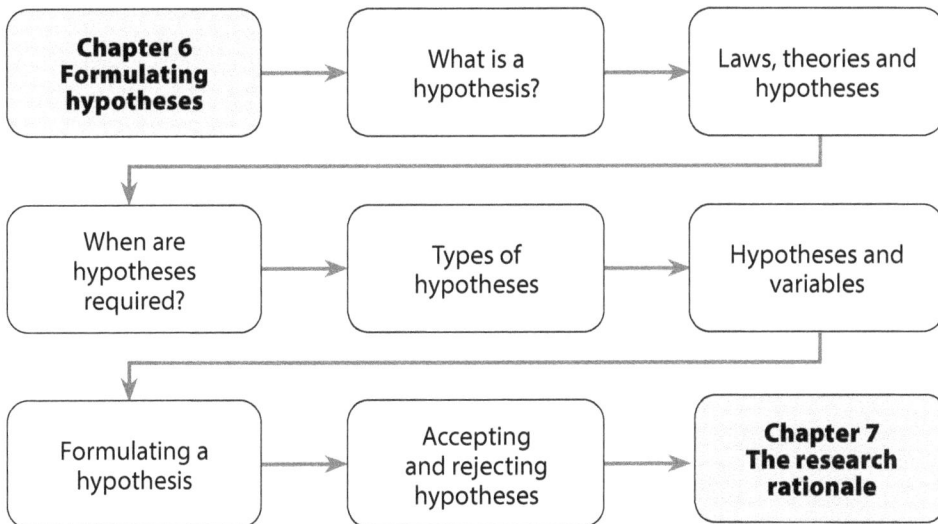

Overview

In Chapter 5 you learnt about the aims or purposes of research. You will recall that one aim of research is to explain the relationship between variables, also referred to as explanatory research. In order to explain the relationship between variables, we first need to test whether a relationship actually exists. This is where hypotheses and hypothesis testing come into the picture.

A hypothesis is a tentative or conditional statement or explanation about a phenomenon or about the relationship between certain variables. An important thing to know about hypotheses is that they can be tested. We tend to use hypotheses only in quantitative studies, and then also only in those that are explanatory in nature, as was already mentioned. We hardly ever use hypotheses in qualitative studies because the aim of qualitative research is not to predict causal relationships.

Another matter that you need to keep in mind is that your hypotheses should always be logically linked to your research question. Thus, testing your hypotheses must assist you in answering your research question. Moreover, your hypotheses need to be falsifiable. What this means is that you should be able to find empirical evidence to show that they are correct or incorrect. Keep in mind, though, that we do not say that we have 'proved' a hypothesis. 'Prove' is a strong word that implies absolute certainty, something that most scientists are cautious about and would not like to claim. Instead, we talk about 'providing evidence'. This means that we have substantial support for our claims, but we do not view it as the absolute truth. Another important thing to remember in terms of research is that when we test hypotheses, we work deductively, so we make deductions based on the evidence we find.

Objectives of this chapter

At the end of this chapter, you should be able to demonstrate your understanding of the following:
- what a hypothesis is;
- how a hypothesis differs from a law and a theory;
- different types of hypotheses;
- the difference between independent and dependent variables;
- falsification and how it affects the validity of a hypothesis; and
- applying a given framework to formulate a hypothesis.

What is a hypothesis?

A hypothesis is a tentative statement about a relationship between variables, a statement that you aim to accept or reject at the end of your research. Put differently, it is a statement that a researcher creates in order to assist him or her to predict a certain outcome. It is therefore an educated guess about a predicted outcome. If you think back to what you have learned in Chapter 2, why did we say the positivists want to use research to be able to predict things? The main reason why we want to predict something is that accurate predictions can actually give us a form of control over the outcome. For example, if we can predict what makes people sick, we can control the outcome (people not getting sick) by getting them to avoid certain behaviours (eg not overeating, avoiding smoking and excessive drinking, etc) or encouraging others, such as exercising or getting vaccinated.

A hypothesis is always testable and can be shown to be correct or incorrect. We will therefore make certain predictions about what makes people sick, and then we will test these predictions against reality to see if this is indeed the case. Hypotheses are therefore used to test theories. Through the process of hypothesis testing, the researcher is able to determine whether his or her speculation or prediction was correct or incorrect. Based on the outcome of the test, the researcher will then be in a position to predict certain outcomes. As was mentioned, you will remember that this is one of the main aims of positivistic research (see Chapter 2). Testing theories or hypotheses against reality is also a form of deductive reasoning, which you will learn about more in this book as well.

Theories, laws, and hypotheses

Laypeople often use the terms 'theory', 'law' and 'hypothesis' interchangeably, as though they are synonymous. This is not the case, and it is important that you, as a researcher, can make the distinction and know the major differences between them. Remember that being precise is essential in research to ensure that we share meaning when we use certain concepts. In order to understand the differences, keep the above definition of a hypothesis in mind as you read the following sections.

Theories

Theories are based on the careful examination of data that serve as evidence for a particular explanation of a phenomenon. The key feature of a theory is therefore that it is based on evidence and not on speculation or opinion. There are many types of theories. One way of classifying theories is as deductive or inductive (also see Chapters 3 and 10).

Some researchers prefer to address theory at the beginning of the research process. They will typically formulate a theory and then hypotheses that they want to test based on the theory. They will then test the hypotheses against reality and, based on the results, will accept, reject or modify their original theory. In this approach to theory testing, a set of theoretical assumptions and concepts drive the collection, analysis and interpretation of data (Bryman, 2016). This method of theory testing is known as *deductive theorising*. In a deductive approach, the researcher attempts to explain a causal relationship. The researcher consequently develops hypotheses to test whether certain causal relationships exist.

- Certain *controls* are put in place to allow the testing of hypotheses. By putting in place controls (see experimental designs on page 184 in Chapter 12), the researcher can be relatively certain that it is indeed the independent variable that is causing the effect on the dependent variable, and that nothing else is causing the effect.
- Because we want to test certain concepts, these concepts also need to be *operationalised. Operationalisation* refers to 'the process of turning abstract concepts into measurable observations' (Bhandari, 2020). For example, height is easy to measure, but how religious somebody is, is not. We therefore have to operationalise religiosity by breaking it up into things that we can measure (quantify) such as how often a person prays, goes to religious gatherings, reads religious texts, etc.

- A final characteristic of the deductive approach is *generalisation*. In order to generalise your findings, your sample size must be large and random enough to be representative of your population (Saunders, Lewis & Thornhill, 2019) (see Chapter 11).

Other researchers are of the opinion that theory should be an outcome of the research process. These researchers typically use more open-ended strategies, where they begin with observations and data collection. They then look for patterns and regularly occurring events or themes. Theoretical ideas subsequently emerge out of the data, and these ideas are used to build a new theory based on the data (Bryman, 2012). In this case, the theory follows the data (rather than vice versa as in the case of a deductive approach). This method of theory building is known as *inductive theorising*:

- Research with an inductive approach is usually very concerned with the *context* in which the research takes place.
- The aim here is not to generalise the results to a broader population, and thus smaller sample sizes are seen as more appropriate.

In general, theories are more robust than hypotheses. Most established theories, such as Festinger's cognitive dissonance theory and Maslow's hierarchy of needs theory, have stood the test of time. The theories that you will find in most textbooks and academic journals are therefore well supported by evidence and serve as substantiated explanations of conclusions reached during research.

It should be clear to you that certain theories developed and are still being developed out of the validation of certain hypotheses. In other words, researchers look for supporting evidence to determine the correctness or incorrectness of hypotheses through, for example, experimental designs (see Chapter 12). The validation of hypotheses verifies the theories. Yet we use our existing knowledge to formulate hypotheses of what we assume will happen. A hypothesis is therefore nothing more than an educated guess.

For example, Darwin's theory of evolution has been supported by substantial evidence that life on earth evolved from single-cell life forms into complex and multicellular organisms. Using this evidence, it can be hypothesised that organisms must constantly adapt and evolve to survive in an ever-changing environment. We can therefore speculate and form hypotheses about what will happen to living organisms over time, based on the theory of evolution.

Laws

Establishing a law is incredibly difficult and it is limited to the natural sciences. A theory becomes a law when the same things happen the same way every time they are observed under the same conditions, without any variation. A law is therefore based on a phenomenon of nature that has been proven to occur without variance under certain circumstances.

Although laws describe things, they do not explain them. Newton's law of gravity is an example of a natural or scientific law. We can use this law to predict that whenever we throw an object, such as a ball, into the air, it will always come down because of gravity. However, Newton's law cannot explain what gravity is. The causes of gravity are, at this stage, still only theories. Thus, a law is based on facts, which are indisputable observations, while theories are based on evidence, which is still disputable.

When are hypotheses required?

If you want to know whether your research requires a hypothesis—or even several hypotheses—you can ask yourself the following questions:
- Does the research approach require quantitative or mixed methods?
- Are you using an experimental design to answer your research question?
- Is the purpose of your research to predict an outcome or to find a correlation between two or more variables?
- Is the purpose or aim of your study explanatory in nature?

If your answer to these questions is 'yes', then you most likely need a hypothesis. If not, then you most likely only need a research question and maybe sub-questions. It is important to know that not all quantitative research needs hypotheses and that hypotheses are hardly ever used in qualitative research.

Remember that a research problem is solved by answering the research questions. In some instances, you will need hypotheses to help you answer the research questions to solve the research problem. Your hypotheses must therefore be aligned to your research questions. Your hypotheses will then provide you with direction and will help to keep the focus of your research on the actual purpose of your study.

Generating hypotheses in order to test theories against reality (whether what is predicted in the theory actually occurs in the 'real' world) is very often not a once-off event. In an attempt to find support for a particular hypothesis, more questions are likely to surface, questions which often cause us to review, revise and refine our initial hypothesis. We can therefore say that, in some instances, hypotheses form an integral part of scientific methodologies and the generation of knowledge.

Types of hypotheses

The main objective for the researcher in developing a hypothesis is to test it and, ultimately, to accept or reject it when examining the results of the research. There are mainly two forms or types of hypotheses: null hypotheses and alternative hypotheses.

A *null hypothesis* makes a prediction that no relationship exists between the variables that are being tested (Adams & Lawrence, 2018). For example, if you would like to know if reading more often improves a person's ability to spell correctly, then your null hypothesis would state that there is no relationship (or correlation) between reading and a person's ability to spell correctly. A null hypothesis can also state that there is no difference between two or more groups. For example, your null hypothesis can also be that there is no significant difference between the spelling ability of students who read a lot and those who read very little. In this sense, any difference will be due to chance and nothing else.

The *alternative hypothesis* is where the researcher predicts an expected outcome. This prediction is often based on prior literature and studies on the chosen topic. Using the same example, in your alternative hypothesis you would predict that students who read more are also able to spell better. Note that alternative hypotheses are often directional, similar to correlations. Thus, you predict that if reading increases, the ability to spell correctly will also increase. This is known as a positive correlation because if the one variable increases, so does the other. A negative correlation occurs when one variable decreases as the other one increases, for example: 'The more television a student watches, the lower his or her grades will be.' However, hypotheses do not always have to be directional. Sometimes they merely state that 'there is a difference' (Creswell & Creswell, 2018).

Table 6.1 The difference between the alternative hypothesis and a null hypothesis

Alternative Hypothesis (H1)	Null Hypothesis (H0)
Predicting the expected outcome	Predicts **NO** relationship between variables
Predicts a relationship between the dependent and independent variable	Predicts **NO difference** between groups
eg There is a positive correlation between attending lectures and academic performance	eg There is no correlation between attending lectures and academic performance

Hypotheses and variables

As was mentioned before, hypotheses tend to predict a relationship between variables. If you look at the stem of the word 'variable', you will see that it refers to something that varies or differs. Gender, for example, is a variable, since it varies between males and females. Most of our behaviours are also variables.

In the previous example, the amount of time spent reading is a variable. Variables are therefore quantities that change values, states or actions. In other words, they do not remain the same and can vary in form, status and/or value.

Think of a variable as a light with a dimmer switch fitted to it. The light can be in different (or variable) states. It can be on (to varying degrees, depending on how far the dimmer switch is turned) or off. We can change the state of the light switch, and when we do this, it has an effect. If I switch the light off, the room becomes dark because there is no electric current travelling to the light bulb. If I turn the dimmer switch on, then the light becomes increasingly brighter because the electric current is increased.

There are several kinds of variables. However, in terms of hypothesis testing, the two most important variables are dependent and independent variables. Determining which variable is the dependent and which is the independent variable is sometimes challenging:

- *Independent variables* are variables that are likely to cause an effect. The independent variable is changed or manipulated by the researcher to test the effect this change or manipulation will have on the dependent variable and the outcome.
- *Dependent variables* are the variables affected by the independent variable. Thus, the dependent variable will change as a result of the independent variable being manipulated by the researcher. It is therefore dependent on the independent variable.

Table 6.2 The difference between independent and dependent variables

Independent Variable	Dependent Variable
Cause	Effect
Before	After
Input	Output
Manipulated	Measured
What you do	What you get

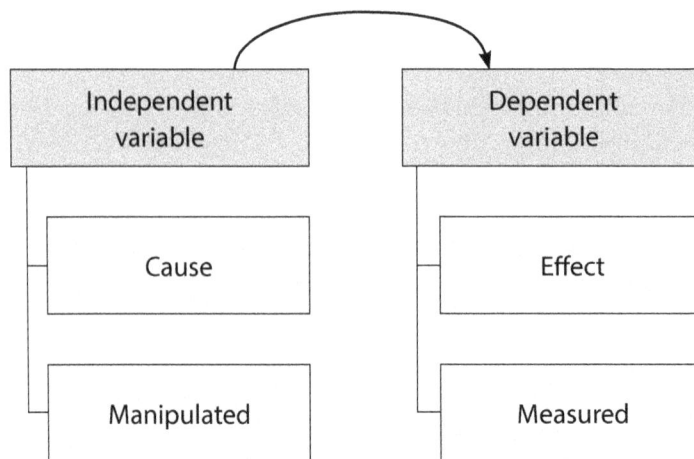

Figure 6.1 Independent versus dependent variable

In the example of the relationship between reading and spelling, spelling ability is the dependent variable. It depends on how much a student reads (the independent variable). However, whether or not a student reads will not be affected by how well she or he spells. When we test hypotheses, the outcome usually depends on how much the researcher manipulates the independent variable.

Hypothesis formulation tends to follow this simple format:

'If {this happens}, then {that will happen} because {this happened}.'

You should formulate your hypothesis in such a way that it describes what will happen to the dependent variable if you make changes to the independent variable. The basic format is:

'If {cause: independent variable}, then {effect: dependent variable} because {reason}.'

For example: 'If {the light switch's status is off}, then {it will be dark} because {there is no current going through the light bulb}.'

Another way of putting this is as follows:

'If {these changes are made to the independent variable}, then {we will observe a change in a dependent variable} because {this made me come to that conclusion}.'

For example: 'If a student reads more, her or his ability to spell correctly will increase because she or he will be exposed to the correct spelling of words more often.'

There are other variables that also need to be considered, but they do not play a role in the formulation of hypotheses. *Intervening* or *mediating variables*, for example, are variables that influence the effect of the independent variable on the dependent variable. For example, whether someone is dyslexic can also influence his or her ability to spell. Thus, the student's dyslexia will interfere with the outcome.

Sometimes we need to control for certain intervening variables, such as age, level of intelligence, level of education, and so on. These are known as *control variables*. It is important to be aware of them, since they influence the dependent variable. We control these variables in order to attempt to balance the effect they have, so that we can ignore the effect and focus the research on the relationship between the independent and the dependent variables. You can control a variable by keeping it constant. For example, you can make sure that all the respondents in your study have similar IQs. You can then determine how much or how little each of them reads without having to be concerned about what the influence of their IQ will be on their ability to spell correctly. Selecting your sample randomly can also cancel out some of the effects of the intervening variables.

Formulating a hypothesis

There is no set process for formulating a hypothesis. Instead, we provide you with a guideline that you can follow in order to ensure that your hypothesis:
* is related to your research question;
* assists you in solving your research problem; and
* helps you to achieve the aim of your research.

Follow these guidelines when you formulate your hypothesis:
1. Based on the theory, model, conceptual framework or literature you have studied, identify the theory or idea you would like to test.
2. Make sure that you know what the major intent or purpose of your study is and what you would like to achieve.
3. Identify the dependent and independent variables.

4. Find the right connecting word that will link the dependent variable to the independent variable. For example, use phrases such as 'the relationship between . . .'; 'a positive correlation between . . .'; or 'a comparison of . . .'. You can also use the 'if . . . then' format described on page 100.

5. Write your hypothesis. State the independent variable first, followed by the dependent variable. For example: 'A positive correlation exists between how much a student reads {independent variable} and his or her ability to spell accurately {dependent variable}.'

6. In order to refine your hypothesis statement, you need to ensure it is robust and testable. Consider the following criteria or questions when you refine your hypothesis:
    *   Is your hypothesis based on your research problem?
    *   Is your hypothesis logically linked to your research question?
    *   Can your hypothesis be tested?
    *   Does your hypothesis include independent and dependent variables?
    *   Can your hypothesis be falsified?

Falsification refers to the idea that your hypothesis must be inherently disprovable. Say, for instance, you make the following statement: 'If you hold a bee in your hand, it will sting you.' This may happen hundreds of times every time you repeat the experiment. However, if it happens only once that a bee does not sting someone who holds it in his or her hand, your statement is falsified. The statement cannot be proven to be unequivocally true if there was even one incident where the outcome was not in line with what was predicted. Thus, when you are testing hypotheses you are not actually setting out to 'prove' them to be true. Instead, you are looking for the single incident that will falsify your hypothesis. If you are unable to find such an incident, the only thing you can prove is that you cannot disprove your hypothesis. However, the more supporting evidence we find for our hypotheses, the higher the probability that they are correct, which, in turn, enables us to make certain predictions and formulate theories.

Accepting and rejecting hypotheses

We use hypotheses to help us answer research questions, test and verify theories, and solve research problems. Researchers consequently attempt to establish whether their hypotheses are correct or incorrect and whether they can be accepted or whether they need to be rejected. Most researchers hope to find some form of confirmation for their hypotheses. However, they often find that, after completing some research, they need to adjust or refine their original hypotheses.

As we mentioned in the discussion on falsification, most hypotheses can never be proven to be irrefutably true. This is because it is impossible to determine how many times you need to test something in order to be absolutely certain that the answer will always be the same. There is always the possibility that the millionth or billionth time something is tested, it will be falsified. How would you know when to stop testing if the very next test may produce the one and only false result? The answer is that you cannot know. Every time you retest a hypothesis and you are unable to falsify it, you are collecting further evidence to support your hypothesis. Once you have substantial supporting evidence, your hypothesis is likely to be highly probable and you can consequently consider it to be a theory.

Finally, if you cannot find any supporting evidence for your hypothesis, you reject the alternative hypothesis (the one predicting the relationship) and accept the null hypothesis (the one that states that there is no relationship between the variables). If you cannot find a relationship, it does not mean you have wasted your time and that your research was done in vain. Finding that there is no relationship between variables is still a research finding, and also contributes to the body of knowledge. It may also help you to refine your thinking or to adjust your hypotheses.

Summary

We use hypotheses to help us test theories. Hypotheses are tentative statements which assist us to establish whether certain relationships exist between dependent and independent variables. The more support we find for our hypotheses, the more evidence we have that our prediction is probably correct. Once we can make relatively accurate predictions, it enables us to control certain variables in real situations in order to get a desired result. For example, if we know that reading improves spelling ability, we can encourage students to read more in an attempt to improve their spelling ability. Hypotheses are therefore valuable tools, mostly used in quantitative research, that we can use to test, find support for, and modify theories.

Review the chapter

Answer the questions and complete the tasks to assess whether you understand the content of this chapter:

1. Explain in your own words what a hypothesis is.
2. Which variable does the researcher manipulate in an experiment?
3. A researcher conducts an experiment to see if increasing water intake lessens the visible effects of acne, a common skin condition. What is the dependent variable in this experiment?
4. Formulate a hypothesis based on the following information:
    (a) Independent variable: hours of sunlight per day
    (b) Dependent variable: number of eggs laid by chickens
5. Express the following research question as a hypothesis:
    'How does behaviour affecting health differ between people who exercises regularly and those who do not exercise at all?'
6. You want to know whether listening to music whilst studying affects academic performance. Write a hypothesis that will help you to test your idea.
7. Explain the differences between a theory, a law and a hypothesis. Provide an example of each to illustrate the difference.
8. Based on the information presented in this chapter, create a diagram which indicates where hypotheses fit into the research process

CHAPTER 7

The research rationale

Corné Davis

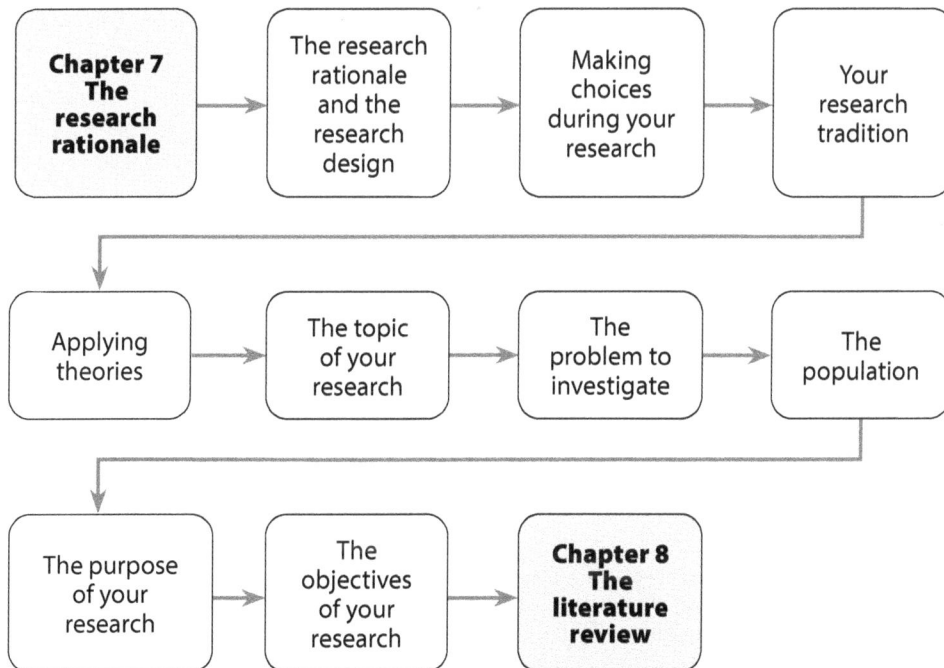

Overview

From what you have learned so far, you would have gathered that doing research can be complicated and challenging. There are many things to consider, many decisions to make and many uncertainties. The primary purpose of this chapter is to recap what you have learnt so far, so that you can start thinking about your own research and how you will apply your new knowledge to it. We avoid using very specific examples in this chapter so that you can focus on what you want to do without distraction.

You already know about the many steps involved. You probably have some idea of the research tradition that appeals to you, that sounds right to you. From your disciplinary perspective, you also probably have some theories in mind for your research and what the purpose of your research can be. Perhaps you have written down some of the problems, questions or hypotheses you have in mind or have decided exactly what the scope of your research may be. You will most certainly have a very specific time frame for the completion of the research, so you should be aware of the limitations that you need to start considering at this stage. What we are saying is that by now you should be aware that in research you are constantly making decisions. In this chapter we cover the rationale behind these decisions. A rationale is the justification for every decision you make during the research process, and keeps you focused on how you are going to execute your decisions.

In this chapter we look at how you can start thinking in terms of your own research design and research proposal at an early stage so that you can keep track of the reasons for all the decisions you make during your research. Keep in mind that what seems obvious to you may not seem obvious to your examiners, so your research rationale is meant to keep you on track and help your examiners to understand your research question.

Objectives of this chapter

By the end of this chapter, you should be able to demonstrate your understanding of the following:
* aspects to consider in justifying your research;
* why it is important to justify your choices during each step of the research process; and
* the research rationale and the research design.

The research rationale and the research design

The rationale for your research fits into your research design. The rationale is a justification; it details why you are doing your research and why it is worth spending time investigating and finding solutions for the problem you have identified. When you write your research essay or mini dissertation, your literature review will inform and support your research rationale, as we will discuss in Chapter 8.

Think of a research design as a house plan. You cannot get approval from the city planning department without a house plan. Similarly, you cannot get approval from your department and faculty's research and ethics committee without a proper research proposal and research design. The research design is a complete plan for your entire research project. It is an outline of what you will do, from formulating the question(s) or hypothesis to collecting the information and completing the final analysis. Even though you are not yet ready to draw up such an extensive plan for your research, it helps to know where you are heading.

Making choices during your research

At this point, you need to think more carefully about what you are going to research, why you will be doing this research and what contribution you want to make to the existing knowledge of your topic, if any, besides passing your research module, of course.

The overarching questions you should be asking are:

- Why am I doing this?
- What do I want to achieve with this research?
- What do I know at this stage?
- Who or what will guide my decisions?
- How did previous scholars approach this research topic?

It is easy to get lost along the way during a research process; you can avoid this by having a clear understanding of your objectives or purpose. As you will see in Chapter 8, there are volumes of literature out there. If you are not really interested in your research topic and finding out what it is actually all about, it is unlikely that you will distinguish the best literature to read, unless your supervisor prescribes some. However, in our experience, students like coming up with novel topics such as sneaker culture, for example, which is most definitely not our area of expertise. We learn many things from our students' choice of research topics.

Without deciding for yourself why you want to do your research and how it will fit into the existing body of knowledge, you will find it difficult to choose which literature to read. This is why the planning of your research has to start here. We give you a few guidelines to help you.

It is not unusual for decisions to change continuously during your research journey. You may think you understand what a certain theory is all about, but when you delve deeper, you may discover that it is not suitable for the kinds of questions you want to ask. This is why research often takes longer than anticipated and time is usually a challenge. As I remarked earlier, you may not have the luxury of a few years to complete your study, so in the rest of this chapter we discuss some questions and guidelines you may find useful, namely:

1. What research tradition best fits the purpose of your study?
2. Which theories do you subscribe to?
3. What is the topic of your research?
4. What is the problem you want to investigate?
5. What questions do you want to ask relating to the problem you want to investigate?
6. Who or what is the population in your research?
7. What is the aim of your research?
8. What are the objectives of your research?

Your research tradition

In Chapter 2 you read about some of the most common research traditions. You may be under the impression that research is about being objective, but that is only the case to some degree. Your worldview and opinions necessarily influence the way you look at phenomena. For example, you may look at a piece of art and find it breathtakingly beautiful and the person next to you may think it is awful. Similarly, you have been informed by your upbringing, including value systems, vocabularies and experiences that all shape the way you think. When you engage in something as important as research the role you play in the findings has to be considered. In other words, you need to observe yourself in the process of observing. You must understand your own point of observation; in other words, 'where you are coming from' in layman's terms. Let's see if the following questions give you more direction:

- What do I believe about knowledge?
- How have I come to know the things I know?
- How are my experiences related to what I know?
- What values do I associate with my knowledge and experience?
- How do I feel about the topic I want to research?
- How does my personal experience relating to this topic influence the questions I am asking?
- What values do I associate with the topic I want to research?

These are difficult, but important, questions, since their answers will determine how you ask the many other questions that follow. If you believe, for example, that knowledge already exists and that you can identify 'facts' that exist in an external and objective reality, you will probably try to find more objective information as evidence to prove those 'facts'. If, on the other hand, you believe that knowledge is created or constructed and that what people consider facts are dependent on their interpretations of information, you may see the information or evidence you collect as your own creation, in other words, as more subjective. A key insight you will gain from this line of thinking is that there is not one right answer to everything, as we have been taught in mathematics, for example. This may sound simple, but as you know world wars have been fought and millions have lost their lives throughout history because of the insistence on single narratives. When you discover what your worldview is, you can assess it, appreciate it, reassess it, build on it, and so forth. Embrace the notion of observing yourself and of recognising that whatever you are observing could also have been something else—the notion of contingency that is referred to by Luhmann (1996). Along with these ideas comes the appreciation of multiple realities and worldviews that are imperative in social research in particular.

Applying theories

While you are planning your research, you will have to decide on the kind of theory you want to apply, as we briefly discussed in Chapter 3. We said that there are thousands of theories, which makes choosing a theoretical perspective for your research a difficult task. It means you have a lot to read and learn about the theories that may interest you. Choosing theories again involves asking several questions, and the following may help:

- Which theoretical perspective interests me, and why?
- What are the key assumptions in the theory that interest me?
- What issues can be addressed by applying the theory that interests me?
- How does the theory of my choice relate to the research I want to do?

The topic of your research

Your choice of qualification — for example, corporate communication, information technology (IT), marketing, commerce, among many others — should position you within a certain field of interest. In previous chapters you learnt how to identify topics and formulate questions and hypotheses. You may have already decided on the topic for your research and should be able to formulate it clearly in your research proposal. You can ask yourself the following questions to ensure that you are clear about the topic of your research:

- In which field is my topic positioned?
- In which other fields is this topic being researched?
- Why is this topic relevant?
- What kind of research has been done relating to this topic?
- What else do I need to find out about this topic that I do not already know?
- Who are the key sources of information in this field?

Asking yourself these questions should enable you to identify and describe the problems you want to address in your research.

The problem to be investigated

You will find as you progress through the various steps and processes during your research that you continuously become more specific about what you are trying to achieve. One of the most important reasons for very clearly articulating the problem you want to investigate is that you need a justification, or a good reason, for wanting to investigate a particular topic. If you are interested in studying feedback processes between individuals in a business environment, for example, you must have some idea of what problems may exist. You may have read something or seen something in the media that formed your perception of a problem that may exist. For example, an Internet search may have shown that

South Africa has an Internet penetration of 40%. This kind of information may be relevant to researchers in many different fields for many different reasons. If your area of interest is IT, for example, you may identify a problem that relates to the possibility of reaching all segments of the population.

As you have seen over the past year, things can change unexpectedly and rapidly. Look at how your needs as students have changed during the Covid-19 pandemic and how suddenly most things started taking place online. In other words, your research is bound to focus on people or things happening that affect people or our planet on a continuous basis. Nothing is static and therefore we constantly need new information and thus new research.

You would have gathered that research is a complex and time-consuming process and that you will be investing a considerable amount of time in your research. The problem you choose should therefore be something that interests you and that you can work with, considering your level of expertise. To narrow your focus, you may ask yourself the following questions:

- What are the problems related to the topic of my research?
- Why does a particular problem exist?
- Who is affected by this problem?
- Where does this problem exist?
- What kinds of solutions to this problem am I considering at this stage?

These questions may appear straightforward, but you may find them difficult to answer. Choosing and formulating a research problem can be compared to choosing a puzzle to build. The way you formulate your problem can help you to determine whether you are building a 50-piece puzzle or a 5 000-piece puzzle. It may help to think about questions relating to your problem carefully so that you get an idea of the size of the puzzle you are choosing to build.

Asking questions about your research problem

Since the formulation of your research problem is one of the most critical steps of the research process, you need to ensure that you understand it thoroughly by asking some questions. You may not be able to answer all these questions at this stage, but it may help you to see what kind of information you will be searching for when you do your literature review. It is just like building a puzzle: you do not know where all the pieces fit when you begin building the puzzle, but it helps to get an idea of how many pieces you can identify. Draw up a list of questions about your research problem so that you can identify the size of the research puzzle you want to build. Think of as many questions as you can at this stage. You can always eliminate questions you consider irrelevant at a later stage.

The population

A population refers to the all the possible people, things or places where you can find the information you need. It does not refer to people only. For example, if you want to know what people's responses were on Twitter on the day that the first Covid-19 lockdown was announced, your population will be the Twitter content posted by stakeholders that you specify on that given date. The content will be downloaded and will be your population and from there you will draw a sample if there is too much data to analyse. Sometimes it is possible to analyse the entire population. If you need to gather your information from people, you will need to group them. For example, you may want to find out from primary school teachers in rural areas with poor Internet connections how they coped with lessons during the Covid-19 lockdowns. The population will be too big for you to interview so you will need a sample. If you choose to do a survey, you may be able to reach the entire population, but they may not all respond. There are several things to consider when you decide about your population and sample, as we discuss in Chapter 11. While you consider the multiple questions you are dealing with at this point, your selection of a population should inform your choices at all times.

The purpose of your research

Once you have identified the problem you wish to investigate and formulated questions relating to the problem, you can determine what the purpose or aim of your particular research may be, considering the broader aims or purposes we identified and described in Chapter 5. You can ask yourself the following questions to help you to determine the purpose of your study:

- Do I want to explore new phenomena to gain a better understanding of an existing problem?
- Do I want to test the feasibility of a more extensive study?
- Do I want to determine the best methods that can be used in a future study?
- Do I want to give an accurate description of a certain population at a particular point in time?
- Do I want to draw a comparison between different people, problems, programmes or phenomena?
- Do I want to identify relationships that may exist between people, problems, programmes or phenomena?
- Do I want to look for explanations for the nature of certain relationships?
- Do I want to make predictions relating to people, problems, programmes or phenomena?
- Do I want to solve a particular practical problem by doing my research?

Answering these kinds of questions will enable you to determine the purpose of your research, so that you can formulate your objectives more clearly. The purpose of your research should also assist you in justifying the importance of your study.

The objectives of your research

You have been asking yourself many questions and you have now reached the point where you have to turn some of these questions into objectives. Objectives are the goals you want to achieve through your research.

You will need to identify the main objective as well as sub-objectives. Your main objective is an overall statement of the motivation or impetus for your study. The sub-objectives are formulated using action words, such as 'to explore', 'to determine', 'to describe', 'to compare', 'to establish', and so forth.

You may experience some frustration while you are trying to formulate your objectives, but do not feel discouraged. It is not an easy task and it requires a lot of thinking and planning. Remember that research is a *process* of asking questions and finding answers and that you have to ask good questions to guide you in your search for worthy answers. Turning your questions into objectives will give you an indication of whether your questions can be answered and whether you have the resources, such as time, funds, access to information, and so forth, that may be required to conduct your study.

Summary

The overall aim of this chapter is to demonstrate the complexity of research by illuminating the multiple questions you should consider after studying the first six chapters of this book. The second aim is to help you understand that research is a continuous process of asking questions and that some of the answers you find may change your initial questions and lead to further questions. Research is therefore a dynamic process, meaning that it changes all the time. What is important to understand, though, is that you must always be able to justify the choices you make along the way; you must convince your reader not only that your study is worth doing, but that you have considered every step and action in the process carefully and that you can justify all your decisions.

Review the chapter

Answer the following questions to assess whether you understand the content of this chapter:

1. How would you describe your worldview?
2. Which theoretical framework appeals to you most, and why?
3. What type of research topic seems feasible to you at this stage?
4. What do you want to achieve with your research?
5. Why should you be able to explain why the research you plan to do is necessary and important?
6. Why should you be able to justify your choices in every step of the research process?
7. Why should you be able to convince your reader of the importance or significance of your study?

CHAPTER 8

The literature review

Ghita-Michelli Howard

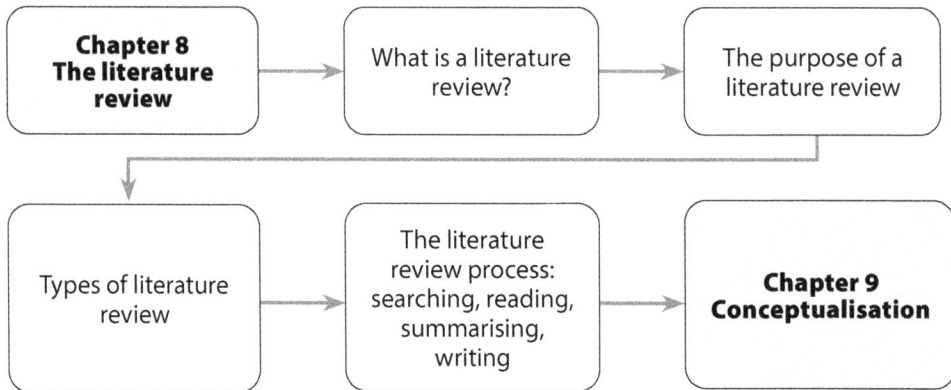

```
Chapter 8
The literature
review
```
→
```
What is a literature
review?
```
→
```
The purpose of a
literature review
```

↓

```
Types of literature
review
```
→
```
The literature
review process:
searching, reading,
summarising,
writing
```
→
```
Chapter 9
Conceptualisation
```

Overview

The literature review can be an exciting part of your research journey. It is a very important step in the research process because it frames your study in a theoretical as well as a real-life context. You also get to know much more about the topic you are interested in. In this chapter we discuss the purpose of a literature review and the role it plays in the research process. We also explain different types of literature review, or different ways you can approach your literature review, depending on the purpose and nature of your research problem. Finally, we explain the steps in the literature review process and give you guidelines on how to write a literature review.

Objectives of this chapter

By the end of this chapter, you should be able to demonstrate your understanding of the following:
- what a literature review is;
- the purpose of conducting a literature review;
- different types of literature review; and
- the process of writing a literature review.

What is a literature review?

A literature review involves searching for, reading, evaluating and summarising as much as possible of the available literature that relates both directly and indirectly to your research topic. In this sense, the word 'literature' is used broadly to refer to all kinds of published information, including textbooks, journal articles and material available online. To produce a good literature review, you need to show that you have read widely and researched the topic as much as possible. The literature review process involves:

1. identifying sources that may be relevant;
2. assessing these sources for their reliability and validity as they relate to your research;
3. analysing the relevant sources of information; and
4. writing a review of these sources to summarise the main findings of your research on the literature.

When conducting a review of the literature, you should be able to apply your knowledge and skills in two areas, namely:

*   *information seeking*, which concerns searching for and identifying only relevant sources that are applicable to your research; and
*   *critical assessment*, which involves scanning, analysing, summarising and integrating your sources to identify reliable, valid and credible material.

The purpose of a literature review

You might be wondering what the point of a literature review is, and you might think it is a waste of time. The purpose of a literature review is to put the research study at hand into perspective, to determine what previous scholars have written on the topic as well as to identify the main models and theories that are relevant to your research study.

While the main aim of the literature review is to unpack information concerning your research topic, the purpose is also to discover any relevant material that could enhance your research. A literature review is therefore also useful to determine what has not yet been written about the topic you are researching.

A literature review not only allows you to refine your research but also serves as a benchmark against which you can compare and contrast your results. In other words, reviewing the literature on your research topic will help you to determine the most important issues to focus on. It will help to guide your research in the right direction.

Furthermore, your review will determine whether or not your research problem is too large to handle or too narrow to make a worthwhile contribution to the field, or perhaps to establish if it has already been researched many times by other scholars. Further reasons for reviewing the literature available on your topic include:

- defining key terms and concepts related to your research topic;
- determining any relationships between topics and variables that are important to your research purpose and problem;
- narrowing down and defining your specific area of study (in other words, your research topic);
- establishing a theoretical framework on which to base your research;
- identifying any relevant theories, models, case studies and journal articles that may support your research or the arguments you want to put forward;
- generating new ideas for topics or issues that you could research that you may not have thought of; and
- determining if there are any information gaps your research will possibly fill.

Types of literature review

There are a few traditional types of literature review that we need to examine, each with their own purpose and material. Broadly, your literature review can focus on one or more of the following:

- *Historical reviews* trace the chronological order of the literature, looking at stages or phases of development from the past to the present and vice versa. For example, if your research involves the role of mass communication in a technologically advanced world, you could conduct a historical review of mass communication theories and how they have evolved over time.
- *Thematic reviews* focus on different schools of thought and group the literature into differing views, perspectives or themes. For example, if you are doing research on the effects of smoking on the risk of developing cancer, a thematic review would include a variety of sources that present opposing views on the issue.
- *Theoretical reviews* consider theoretical developments relating to the research problem, often linking each theory to empirical evidence. For example, a search for theories about social responsibility can take the form of a theoretical review which shows how different disciplines approach this concept.
- *Empirical reviews* generally focus on the various methodologies used and summarise any empirical evidence for the phenomenon that you are interested in. For example, you could conduct an empirical review of various methodologies that have been used to conduct research on the relationship between child-headed households and literacy levels.

The literature review process

To create a good literature review you will need to work methodically and diligently through a process that entails searching for, analysing, integrating and comparing relevant sources, and then compiling a review, or report, of your work. In the following sections we discuss each step in the literature review process.

Searching for literature

Your literature review will begin with a search for any published material that could supplement your research topic or research problem. This is a time-consuming process as it involves a dedicated, organised search for relevant sources and literature. These can take the form of either primary or secondary sources:

- *Primary sources* could include interviews, eye-witness accounts and any research that you need to conduct for the purposes of answering your research question and solving your research problem.
- *Secondary sources* could include published journals, books, databases, online sources, and more.

Regardless of the sources you use, your search for information must be well planned and executed logically.

Reading the literature with a purpose

Once you have collected a large amount of material, you will need to begin to sort through it all. This entails scanning, reading and evaluating the sources with a specific purpose. When sorting through your literature, you need to scan for information that you think is relevant to your research and leave everything else out. You can do this by looking at the table of contents, the abstract, the summary and all the headings, and then deciding if the source is appropriate. Once you have decided that a source is suitable, you can then read it in detail to find information that supports your arguments.

Bear in mind that sources that reject or contradict your research problem should not be abandoned; rather, these sources should help to further refine your search and point out the possible gaps or flaws in your research. In this way you are also ensuring that you remain an unbiased researcher, which is a vital element of any research proposal. Your sources may also suggest possible research methodologies you may not have considered, and will help to refine your research problem and question.

In evaluating your material you should generally establish whether or not your sources meet the following criteria:

- *Who?* This criterion concerns who wrote the literature and whether they are a reliable and credible source. It is important to verify the author of your source, as not all information you come across will be valid — especially when it comes from online sources. For example, a source authored by an established academic who has years of experience and a high level of education is much more credible than a potentially unqualified source you found on a site such as Wikipedia.
- *What?* This question involves looking at exactly what the subject of the source is and how relevant the subject is to your research. You also need to check whether the information is accurate and complete, and whether it will actually contribute to your research. For example, literature on the effects on sales of using images instead of text in advertising will not be of any use if your research concerns the levels of illiteracy in rural areas and the resulting effect in terms of poverty.
- *Where?* The location where the research was conducted and where the article was published could play an important role in terms of your research. For example, if you are performing research on the effects of media violence on teenagers, research carried out in the United States could produce very different results to that of the same study conducted in South Africa.
- *When?* This question relates to when the source was created or published. The question that you need to ask yourself is whether there is any information that is more up to date than the source you have. While it is not always feasible to find a considerable amount of current material that relates to your research, it is advisable to search for a few sources that are as current as possible. For example, when conducting research on the effects of online learning tools in enhancing the school curriculum, it is wise to search for current sources to support your research, rather than material from the 1990s, which will probably be both outdated and impractical and therefore irrelevant to your research.

Summarising the literature

Now that you have worked your way through a considerable amount of literature, you should have a reasonable number of sources that need to be analysed and summarised before you begin writing your literature review.

First, identify any similarities and differences between your sources and group this information together to form topics, themes or arguments that are both logical and coherent. You will then be able to work out whether there is any information outstanding and whether any issues remain unaddressed and any questions remain unanswered. If this is the case, you may need to conduct some of your own primary research to provide the missing information. Alternatively, this missing information could guide your research in the right direction.

Writing the review

Now that you have done all the groundwork of gathering and sorting through your sources, it is time to write your literature review. This is a lengthy process. Do not expect to get a final product in your first few attempts; instead, you will need to complete several drafts before you are satisfied with the final review.

It is important that your literature review follows a clear and logical line of reasoning and explanation. To this end, we suggest that you do the following:

1. Begin with an appropriate *introduction,* which clearly outlines exactly what your literature review entails and how it connects to your own research.
2. Follow the introduction with various paragraphs that expand on the sources you evaluated, integrating them by showing their similarities and differences, and also their relation to your research. Remember that you should not only describe the literature you analysed, but also conduct a *critical review* of these sources. When doing this, you should point out any strengths, weaknesses and differences you came across, and the potential reasons behind them. You could also point out any missing information your research intends to explore.
3. Your literature review should end with a strong *conclusion,* summarising all the main points of the literature review and placing the review in the context of your own research. The reader is thereby provided with a clear background of not only the literature that relates to your research but also to your research issue as a whole.

Summary

The aim of this chapter is to give you a brief insight into what a literature review involves and why it is important to conduct a literature review when doing research. You should now also understand the various types of literature review that can be conducted.

You should now be able to appreciate the very real necessity for a literature review—not only in terms of searching for and describing the sources you come across, but also in terms of those sources that are in contrast to your research. It is also important to search for current sources and to determine if there is insufficient information relating to your research topic and whether or not you intend to carry out your own research to fill in the gaps.

Finally, you have seen that writing a literature review is no simple task. It involves a number of detailed steps, all with the ultimate goal of placing your research problem into context and outlining, or framing, the literature in terms of the research you plan to do. Also keep in mind the importance of referencing all the sources you have included in your literature review, both within the text and in your reference list (see Chapter 22 for a discussion on referencing).

Review the chapter

Answer the questions and complete the tasks to assess whether you understand the content of this chapter:

1. What is a literature review?
2. What are the purpose and benefits of conducting a literature review?
3. What are the different types of literature review?
4. Name the steps to follow when conducting a literature review.
5. Discuss the components that make up a literature review.

CHAPTER 9

Conceptualisation

Corné Davis

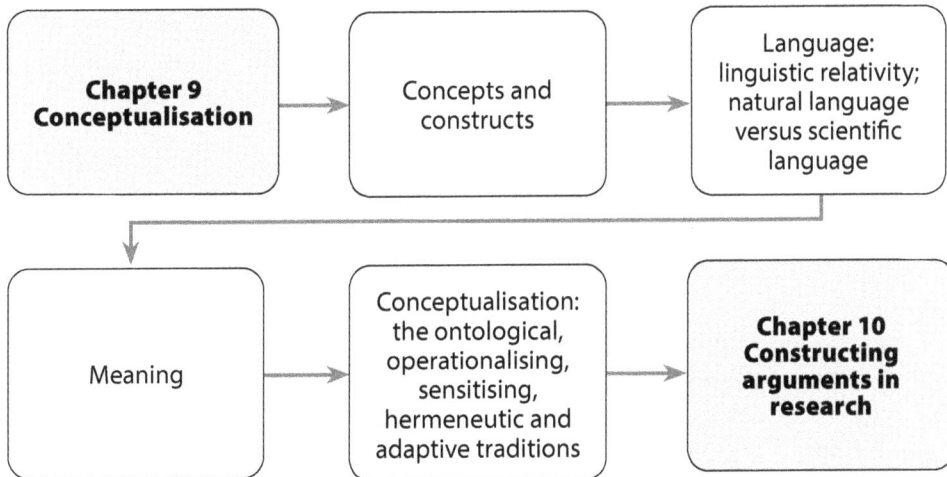

Overview

Conceptualisation refers to the refinement and specification of abstract concepts to create specific meanings for the purposes of a specific research project. It is one of the most fundamental processes in research—you must *develop* the specific meanings you are referring to when you use the key words you identify for the purposes of your study. It becomes your explanation of how you will use, observe or measure these meanings in your study.

Both meaning and communication are created through language, and we highlight some considerations about language specifically so that you keep them in mind when you choose words. It is a common misconception that we understand or mean similar things when we speak the same language. Here, we will show you that this is not necessarily the case.

At the end of this chapter, we briefly introduce five traditions of conceptualisation identified by Blaikie (2009). Each tradition views the identification and definition of concepts in a different way, which, again, highlights the complexity of the research process and the different ways in which all its aspects can be approached.

Objectives of this chapter

At the end of this chapter, you should be able to demonstrate your understanding of the following:

- the difference between concepts and constructs;
- the relationship between concepts and constructs;
- the challenges language poses in sharing meaning;
- how meaning is created;
- the choices that create communication within its scientific context;
- conceptualisation as a process; and
- conceptualisation as an important component of the overall research process.

Concepts and constructs

We introduced the terms 'concept' and 'construct' in Chapter 1. We said that concepts, generally, refer to abstract, non-tangible ideas. A concept is a *word* that can have many different *meanings* depending on where it is used or who is using it—or, rather, creating it. Concepts are also regarded as the building blocks of theories.

Let us look at communication as a concept. Your definition of communication will depend on your conception of it, in other words, the mental images you associate with it. You may define communication as people talking to each other, but what if we defined communication as the integration of *information*, *utterance* and *understanding*, driven by *expectation*? We have just used four different concepts that probably did not even feature in your existing definitions of the word 'communication'. This definition of communication is an example of a theoretical definition, in which you provide links between different concepts for the purpose of a specific study.

When we provide a theoretical definition for a concept, it becomes a construct in a particular research study. A theoretical definition also explains, to a certain extent, the *denotative* and *connotative* meanings of a construct in a logical and systematic manner. Denotative meaning refers to the most specific, direct or literal meaning of a word, while the connotative meaning refers to ideas or meanings associated with a word, in addition to its literal meaning. For example, the denotative meaning of 'equality' is 'the state of being equal', while the connotative meaning could involve associations of human rights, power relationships in society, societal change, and so forth.

By linking a concept to other concepts, you are constructing (or building) a specific meaning for what now becomes known as a construct. A construct thus consists of a combination of concepts that form a theoretical definition that is used to share meaning for the purposes of a particular study. We therefore refer to constructs in research because we are linking certain concepts (and terms) to each other in order to construct meaning. There are additional terms related to constructs, such as 'indicators', 'dimensions' and 'variables'. Figure 9.1 illustrates the relationship between the terms we are introducing.

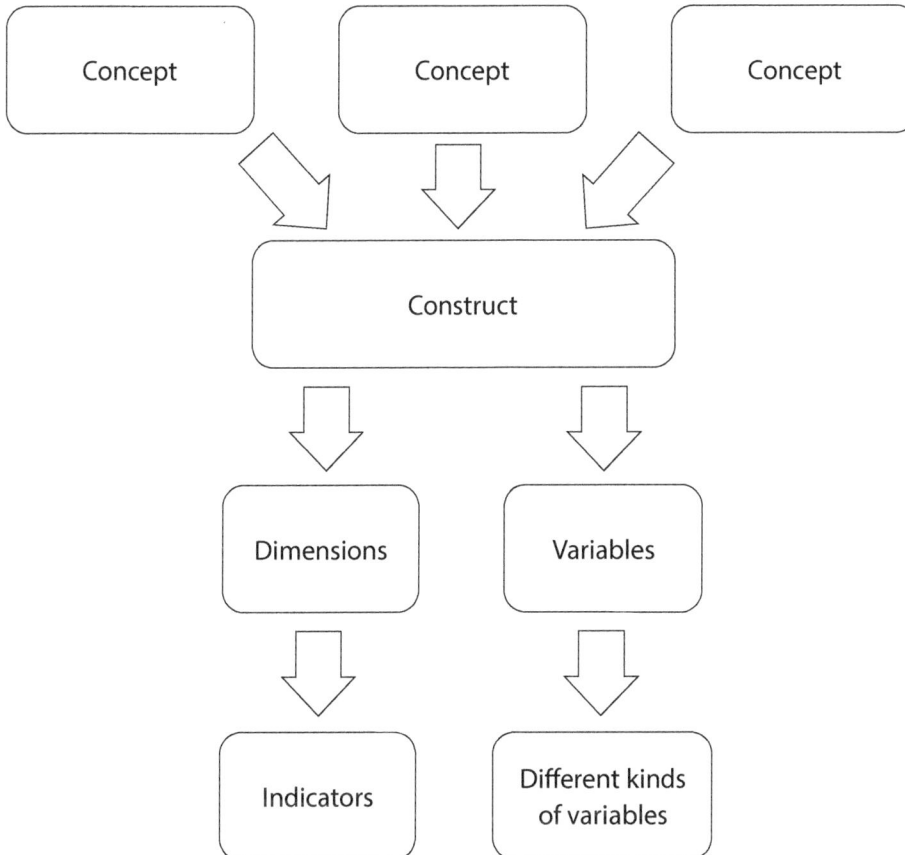

Figure 9.1 From concepts to constructs

Most constructs consist of dimensions and indicators, depending on how complex the construct is. If, for example, we want to look at social status, we can ask the question: 'What is social status?' We can then say that some of the *dimensions* of social status are a person's level of education, wealth, prestige and power. However, when a dimension is not directly observable, we make use of *indicators*. An indicator can be described as a sign of the presence or absence of the concept or construct we are studying. Thus, to determine whether or not a person has power (one of the dimensions of social status), we need to unpack power as a concept, or break it down into several indicators. Some of the indicators for the dimension of power could, for argument's sake, be whether a person:
- owns things that are valued in society;
- has the ability to govern or influence other people's behaviour;

- is most likely to win an argument;
- makes important decisions;
- stands out in the eyes of society; and
- is respected or feared by a large number of people.

In other words, if these indicators are present, we can say that it is likely that the person they are being applied to is powerful. If the other dimensions are also present (the person is wealthy, has a doctorate and is well respected in her or his field), then this person can be classified, according to the definition we used above, as someone with social status. Indicators thus indicate the presence or the absence of a construct. You will gather that the more complicated the definition of a construct becomes, the more complicated the dimensions and indicators will become.

Another question you may want to ask is how to identify the dimensions and indicators of a construct. Researchers usually describe the theoretical foundations of their research study in their literature review, and they are likely to identify the dimensions and indicators from their literature review. However, you will only use what is applicable and relevant to your own research goal. For example, if you want to investigate gender equality in the workplace, you would not consider racial equality or gender equality in religion because it falls outside the scope of your research. You would therefore have to specify that it is a study of gender equality in the workplace only.

Returning to our explanation of indicators, it is important for you to understand exactly what indicators are, since they are typically observed *indirectly*. They are often described as variables that can be used to measure whether and to what extent the constructs developed for the purposes of a specific study feature in the study. In this sense, a variable is a statistical term, meaning a quantity that can take on different possible values. Both a dimension and an indicator can be variables. When a concept has only one dimension with one indicator, the concept is practically equivalent to a variable.

Our experiences and observations are real to us, but the conceptions, concepts and constructs we derive from our experiences and observations are created in our minds for the purpose of communicating about them. Regarding constructs as real is referred to as reification. Babbie (2002:117) explains that '. . . we fall into the trap of believing that terms for constructs do have intrinsic meaning, that they name real entities in the world'. We consider what we can observe or perceive directly to be real. For example, if you learn through your HR manager that a male colleague, who has the same qualification and experience as you do, gets paid a higher salary than you do, the concept 'inequality' will probably be very real to you. However, someone who has never been on the receiving end of inequality or discrimination will not experience it as a real concept. We therefore have to be aware that everyone does not consider the same things to be real, particularly if they have not experienced it in the same way.

Therefore, based on our understanding that the 'reality' we perceive is constructed by both direct and indirect observation, we must consider that reality is to a large degree our own construction as well. Reification therefore becomes a problem in research when you want to indicate and measure concepts and constructs that are real to you but may be nothing more than words to another person. Because of this, it is imperative for you to gain some insight into the obstacles that language and meaning can present in research matters in particular. We therefore discuss a few matters relating to language to broaden your understanding of some of the many facets that play a role in how we create meaning for ourselves.

Language

It often happens that people who seem to understand the content of a text find it very difficult to explain it to others or write it down in their own words when they are asked to do so. If English, for example, is not your first language, as is the case for the majority of South Africans, it becomes challenging to deal with concepts, constructs and all the other complicated terminology used in English in various disciplines, and in research specifically. We therefore consider it relevant to explain *why* it is difficult to understand the language of research. Luhmann (1981:125) captures it well:

> The medium that extends our understanding of communications beyond basic perception is language. It uses symbolic generalizations to replace, to represent or to put together perceptions and to solve the resulting problems of mutual comprehension. In other words, language specializes in creating the impression of mutual understanding as the basis for further communication, however fragile the grounds for that impression may be.

Luhmann is saying that because we speak the same language, we think that we mean the same things. This is not necessarily the case. Language is a *medium*; in other words, it is a way of putting our thoughts into words that we can all understand in some way, even though our understanding is never exactly the same.

The next sections focus on two specific reasons — linguistic relativity and the difference between natural language and scientific language — why people find it difficult to express their thoughts in language and why you should understand this difficulty in matters of research in particular.

Linguistic relativity

Linguistic relativity is a principle that states that the grammatical structure of a language shapes the ways in which speakers conceptualise their worlds. This principle was developed many years ago and we will not discuss it in depth in this book. The reason we include it here is to help you understand that meaning cannot be translated exactly between languages. Think about the Afrikaans word 'braaivleis', for example: you can translate it as meat on the barbeque, but if you are a South African, you know that it means much more than just that — there are cultural connotations to it too.

Remember that science is created globally and that you find scholars who speak many different languages. Dictionaries provide us with translations, but in terms of linguistic relativity the meanings we create through a specific language cannot be translated directly to another. Rather, it is the structure of a language itself that steers us to observe things in particular ways in different contexts. Culture and experience are embedded in language. For example, if you read the work of Luhmann—who wrote all his books and articles in German—you will find that German words such as 'verstehen' often appear in these texts. This indicates that the English translation, 'understanding', does not fully translate the meaning of the German term. Take this into account when you make decisions about the language you use in your research.

Natural and scientific language

You may have observed that different fields of study use different terminology and that you continuously learn new terms, almost like when you had to learn times tables in primary school. As mentioned before, concepts are similar to building blocks that you use to build or create constructs. We also explained that different experiences described through different languages create meanings that are relative to those particular languages. In the same way, scientists observe things differently for different purposes. They create concepts and constructs for the specific purpose of describing what they are observing.

Concepts developed from natural scientific studies are often developed into constructs used in social scientific studies. Let us use an example to demonstrate this point. The term 'equilibrium' was developed in studies of thermodynamics (the study of heat and energy in natural systems) many years ago. It referred to a state of 'system death', in other words, a situation where a system reached a state of maximum entropy (Bailey, 1997:74). However, you will find that the concept 'equilibrium' is also used to refer to *balance* between, for example, an organisation and its environment. Another example of this is the term 'entropy', which was also coined in the field of thermodynamics to refer to chaos or uncertainty, or something that cannot be determined specifically at a given moment. The term 'entropy' has been adapted in social sciences to become 'social entropy', which refers to uncertainty that arises from social situations, or the tendency of systems such as organisations to become chaotic when structures are not in place.

You need to know how concepts are developed and how they become constructs in different fields of study. Both natural and social sciences create their own jargon. This means that the same words may mean very different things in different subject areas.

Meaning

A common mistake that people make is to equate language to meaning, while meaning is actually in the minds of people and not in the language. If a person speaks a language you don't know, what they are saying has no meaning for you. The study of meaning is called semantics. It constitutes a broad field that includes linguistics, communication theory, anthropology, neurobiology, philosophy and several others. All of these fields articulate 'meaning' differently. As a matter of interest, how would you describe 'meaning' based on your existing knowledge? You will probably agree that this is not an easy question since it is difficult to find another word for 'meaning'. We can possibly use the terms 'significance', 'representation' or 'interpretation', but you will have to agree that 'meaning' can only refer to meaning—in other words, meaning is *self-referential*: it always refers to itself.

We use language and other symbols to represent what we mean, and we assume that it represents the same things for different people, but it cannot and does not. Meaning has its own fingerprint, so to speak. If you look at a person's fingerprint, you will see that it is unique to that person, even in the case of identical twins. In a similar way, nobody ascribes exactly the same meaning to a message. In research we need to understand this so that we can create meanings that are similar enough for us to accomplish our purposes. We use the term 'interpretation' to refer to our experience of meaning. To show you how meaning(s) may differ, let us take a look at a theory of meaning developed by a well-known social psychologist, Charles E Osgood, in the 1960s. This may be an old source, but it is still applicable and relevant today.

Osgood's theory deals with the way in which we learn meaning and how meaning relates to our thoughts and behaviour. As we have shown, meaning is created in our minds; therefore, it proceeds from denotative meaning (which is learnt to some degree) to connotative meaning (which is based on our experience of objects and concepts). Osgood developed an instrument called the semantic differential scale (also see Chapter 12) to give some indication of how meaning differs. The scale uses opposite adjectives to show people's different associations with words. We will use the concept 'examination' to demonstrate how meaning differs from person to person. Osgood's theory postulates that meaning can be measured in terms of three main attitudes, namely evaluation, potency and activity. If you look at Figure 9.2 (below) and you connect the points on the semantic differential for each person, you will see that it forms a different pattern for each person. This shows that even though Wendy and Nontsasa are referring to the same concept, namely 'examination', the attitudes they have towards it are very different. A more abstract concept may need more binary codes (opposites) to distinguish between different attitudes and, hence, different meanings associated with the same concept.

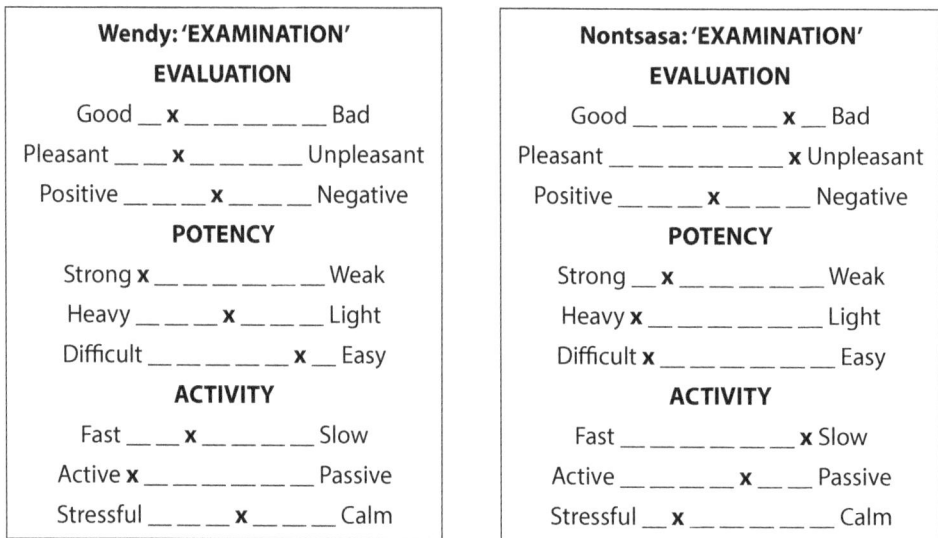

Wendy: 'EXAMINATION'	Nontsasa: 'EXAMINATION'
EVALUATION	**EVALUATION**
Good __ x __ __ __ __ __ Bad	Good __ __ __ __ __ x __ Bad
Pleasant __ __ x __ __ __ __ Unpleasant	Pleasant __ __ __ __ __ __ x Unpleasant
Positive __ __ __ x __ __ __ Negative	Positive __ __ __ x __ __ __ Negative
POTENCY	**POTENCY**
Strong x __ __ __ __ __ __ Weak	Strong __ x __ __ __ __ __ Weak
Heavy __ __ __ x __ __ __ Light	Heavy x __ __ __ __ __ __ Light
Difficult __ __ __ __ __ x __ Easy	Difficult x __ __ __ __ __ __ Easy
ACTIVITY	**ACTIVITY**
Fast __ __ x __ __ __ __ Slow	Fast __ __ __ __ __ __ x Slow
Active x __ __ __ __ __ __ Passive	Active __ __ __ __ __ x __ __ Passive
Stressful __ __ __ x __ __ __ Calm	Stressful __ x __ __ __ __ __ Calm

Figure 9.2 Illustration of the semantic differential (developed from Osgood, 1964)

The semantic differential demonstrates how the same concept can have different meanings for different people. When you select and use concepts in your research, you have to consider all the possible meanings that can be associated with that particular concept in order for you to describe the particular meaning you want to refer to in your study. In other words, you have to *deconstruct* the concepts you are using. Think of deconstruction as an activity similar to unpacking a cardboard box that contains many smaller boxes. When you deconstruct (or unpack) a concept, you identify several meanings that can be associated with it, so that you can indicate which meanings you want to include and exclude when you use a concept.

In the next section we take a closer look at formulating concepts, so that you can gain a better understanding of the process of conceptualisation.

Conceptualisation

There are different views about the sources of concepts. In Chapters 2 and 3 you were introduced to different paradigms, or traditions, and theoretical frameworks that identified different sources of concepts and their definitions. Because concepts have so many different sources and can be used in so many different ways, there can be no single view of the role of concepts in research. Thus, the researcher plays a deciding role in the identification and definition of the most appropriate concepts in a research project.

There are several things you can use to assist you in conceptualisation. You could, for example, turn to theory or literature for definitions of the key concepts that form part of your research, or you could develop your own definitions through your interactions with participants or engagements with certain phenomena.

Blaikie (2009) identifies and discusses five traditions that each view the identification and definition of concepts differently. These are the ontological, operationalising, sensitising, hermeneutic and adaptive traditions, which we describe in brief. You should note that Blaikie is a seminal source and that nobody else has described conceptualisation quite like this since, hence its inclusion in the current version of *Research Matters*.

As you know, concepts can be found everywhere in research. These traditions show how different kinds of concepts can be identified and developed to guide you through the process of conceptualisation in your own research. These traditions can also be linked to the kinds of arguments that are created in research studies. Your choice of either an inductive or deductive research strategy, for example, will determine whether you work with broader or more specific concepts. This choice will also determine, to some extent, how you develop these concepts, as you will learn in Chapter 10.

The ontological tradition

The ontological tradition emphasises concepts that identify the basic features of the social world. These concepts aim to explore how people experience realities. Such concepts are identified and developed into constructs that specify the concepts' meanings in specific research studies. If we look at the concept 'institution', for example, it can be further defined in terms of whether it refers to relational, regulative or cultural institutions (Blaikie, 2009:114). You may, for example, describe marriage as a relational institution, government as a regulative institution and a museum as a cultural institution.

When concepts such as these are used in a research study, the researcher sets out the relationships between them. In other words, if you were the researcher, you would explain how these concepts are different and how they relate to each other, and what is relevant or not relevant for the purposes of your study. In your particular study you may want to indicate which concept is present, absent or dominant, whichever the case may be. Broadly speaking, concepts relating to culture, power, rules and resources, to name a few, can be positioned within the ontological tradition.

The operationalising tradition

We said earlier that when we want to measure concepts, we turn them into variables. In the operationalising tradition, the emphasis is placed on transforming theoretical concepts into empirical (measurable) concepts. In other words, we take abstract concepts and turn them into things that we can *observe directly* and, consequently, measure.

The difficulty in transforming concepts into operational definitions with variables that can be measured is that certain concepts are incredibly abstract. This means that if you want to operationalise a concept, you have to identify the indicators and variables that you will use to measure it. It also means that you will limit its meaning in terms of what you are aiming to measure. You have to turn concepts into variables by defining them with the purpose of developing ways of measuring them.

We referred to theoretical definitions earlier, saying that we use these definitions to position concepts within a particular theoretical framework for the purpose of linking them to other concepts in order to create understanding among researchers who work with similar concepts. Within the operationalising tradition, however, theoretical language is transformed into empirical concepts. Blaikie (2009:116) explains that 'this is done by specifying procedures by which the "eoretical" concept will be measured'. In other words, if you work with the concept 'equality', for example, you may identify equal remuneration, equal working conditions and equal career opportunities as variables of equality that can be measured.

These variables are then used to create an operational definition. The operational definition sets specific limits on the meaning of a concept, which means that you will focus on only a limited aspect of the phenomenon under investigation. Another research study may develop an entirely different operational definition for the concept of 'equality'. The aim of your study is probably the most important consideration when you decide on the theoretical and operational definitions for the purposes of your specific research study. Because the purpose of operationalisation is to measure, it is mostly used in quantitative studies.

The sensitising tradition

You will find that researchers frequently disagree about whether concepts can be operationalised or not, in other words, whether — or to what extent — concepts can be measured. In the sensitising tradition it is argued that concepts need to be sensitising rather than definitive or absolute. Sensitising concepts provide clues and suggestions about the meanings we can explore and the common features we may be able to identify when we observe certain phenomena.

A researcher may start with a loosely defined concept and may then develop more specific definitions during the course of the research. Let us say, for example, you are studying the role of friendships in the development of self-esteem among primary school children in a rural area in South Africa. You may start with a broad definition of 'friendship' and develop more specific definitions as you progress with the study. Your engagement with children will sensitise you to the meanings they associate with 'friendship'. As a researcher, you will make decisions about the meanings of the concept as the study develops.

The hermeneutic tradition

The hermeneutic tradition looks for concepts in the everyday language of the people under investigation and not in the language of the discipline (Blaikie, 2009:119). In other words, rather than turning to academic and scientific literature to conceptualise 'friendship', you would spend some time with primary school children in rural areas to learn how they view and experience friendship. Based on the insight you gain through spending time with these children, you may develop an altogether new concept, or you may adapt existing definitions or meanings associated with 'friendship' to align with your new insight into the concept.

As Blaikie (2009:120) puts it, the aim is 'to generate concepts that fit the problem at hand and work to provide useful descriptions and understanding'. Within the hermeneutic tradition, concepts are developed by mediating between the particular language used by the participants, or people under observation, and some version of the theoretical language of the subject of the research study. This process of mediation is similar to interpreting a text.

Developing concepts from within the hermeneutic tradition requires the researcher to become immersed in the world of the participants. Researchers who adopt the operational tradition work according to a top-down approach by applying their own judgement of the relevance of concepts; researchers adopting the hermeneutic tradition work from a bottom-up approach by becoming learners rather than experts (Blaikie, 2009:16).

Concepts developed in the hermeneutic tradition are also not static; they keep evolving as new information emerges.

The adaptive alternative

You will recall from previous discussions that paradigms, or traditions, and theoretical orientations influence how researchers approach phenomena. The adaptive alternative to the definition of concepts means, in essence, that we have to build bridges between phenomena which can be observed and those that we cannot observe but that we aim to explain in terms of how we perceive and define them. The adaptive alternative was developed and published by Layder in 1998 for the purpose of building bridges between empirical and theoretical data without giving preference to one over the other. With this purpose in mind, he identified four types of concept. Figure 9.3 illustrates the adaptive alternative as well as the broad orientations of the different traditions.

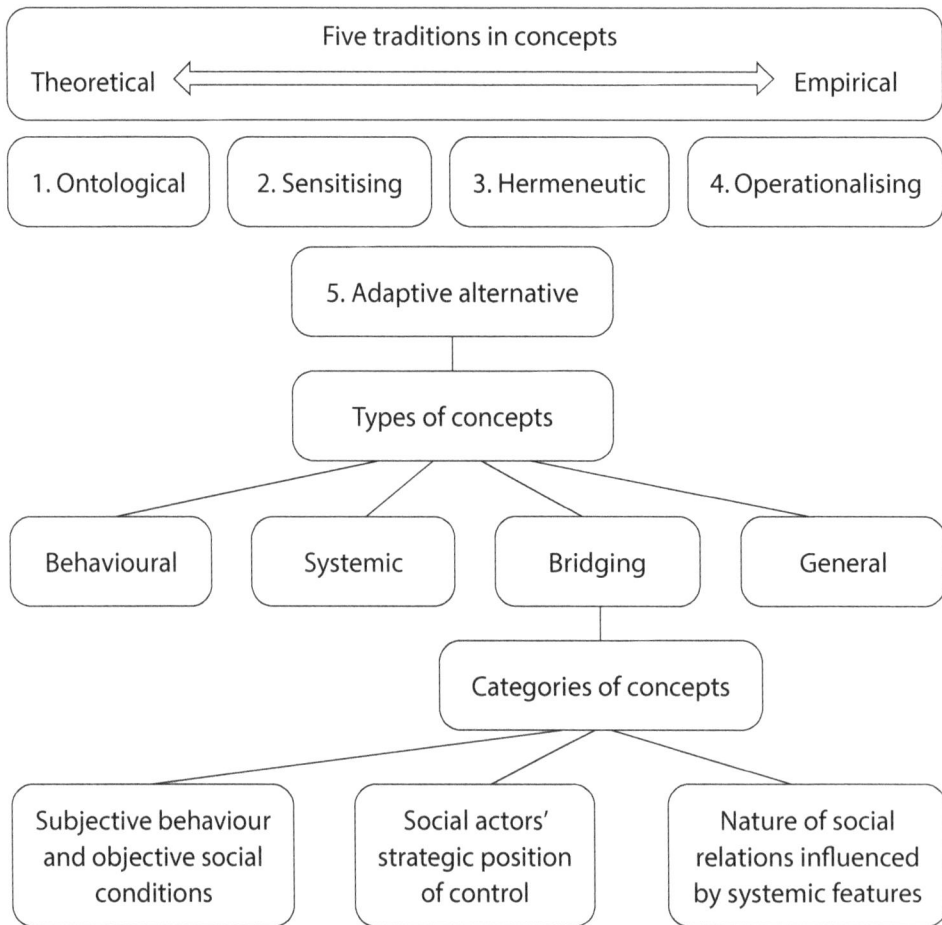

Figure 9.3 The adaptive alternative in relation to other traditions in the use of concepts (developed from Blaikie, 2009)

Behavioural concepts focus on individuals and how they describe the world from their perspectives. Behavioural concepts directly describe certain aspects of the behaviour of the people participating in the research. These can be described either from the researcher's perspective or from the participants' perspectives, but they must be understandable to the people who are being studied (Blaikie, 2009:121).

Systemic concepts are structural concepts. Think of a physical building — it has a particular structure, such as walls, windows, corridors and doors. Without us realising it, these structures guide us in terms of our behaviour. In other words, you will automatically walk in the direction of the door if you want to exit or enter a room. You will not climb through the window, for example. Thus, the structure of the building influences your behaviour, or where you will go and what you will do. Similarly, we are born into social systems, so to speak, and these systems (such as culture, religion, politics and language) actually govern our behaviour without us always being consciously aware of it. Thus, things such as institutions (schools, churches, and so on), cultures and even language constitute the social environment in which we live and they provide us as researchers with systemic concepts that are closely linked to behavioural concepts.

Bridging concepts build bridges between behavioural and systemic concepts. Bridging concepts focus on three kinds of phenomena:

1. There is a link between people's experiences and behaviour (which is subjective) and the objective social conditions in which their behaviour takes place. For example, the university where students are studying creates the objective social conditions, while their personal behaviour and experiences within the university create the subjective phenomena.

2. Certain individuals occupy strategic positions of control which can affect the behaviour of others. For example, lecturers form part of the objective social conditions in a university and their judgements can influence individual students' behaviour and performance.

3. The nature of social relations is influenced by the features of the system. For example, in some educational systems there are close relationships between lecturers and students, while in others, lecturers maintain their distance, which may include concepts such as 'engagement' or 'alienation'.

General concepts are the fourth type of concept illustrated in Figure 9.3. They refer to concepts that are invented by social theorists and that are 'embedded in their theories of society and social life' (Blaikie, 2009:122). A good example is Festinger's concept of cognitive dissonance, which refers to a mental imbalance or uneasiness that people experience when their behaviour (for example, smoking) is in contrast with their beliefs (for example, that smoking is a health risk), and the justifications they then come up with to support their behaviour. These kinds of concepts can be positioned in the ontological tradition with its emphasis on theory.

General theoretical concepts are often neglected because they are considered to be too abstract to link to empirical evidence. However, general theoretical concepts can offer great insights, and researchers should continue to build bridges between those phenomena that can be experienced and observed and those that can be described in theoretical terms only at given moments in time. It forms part of the evolution of knowledge that is crucial to the development of solutions and progress in society at large.

Summary

Conceptualisation refers to the refinement and specification of abstract concepts to create specific meanings for the purposes of a particular research project. Meaning is created through the use of language. Even though we think that language and therefore meaning is shared between people, each person actually has a unique interpretation of each message they receive. Specific meanings are also developed within specific fields over time and then become part of the academic discourse and jargon of that particular field. Denotative meanings are learnt, whereas we build connotative meanings through different conceptualisation processes.

More importantly though, when you conduct research, you need to define the concepts you are working with to create constructs that contain the dimensions, indicators or variables that are relevant to your particular research project in order to share meaning with others.

The five different traditions in the use of concepts indicate how concepts can be identified along a continuum, where the emphasis moves between theoretical and empirical conceptualisation. The challenge for researchers is to build bridges between theoretical concepts that cannot be observed directly and empirical concepts that cannot be described sufficiently without thorough theoretical grounding and argumentation.

Review the chapter

Answer the questions and complete the tasks to assess whether you understand the content of this chapter:

1. What are the differences between concepts and constructs?
2. What is the relationship between concepts and constructs?
3. How would you use the same concept to create different constructs by using different dimensions and indicators?
4. How would you go about creating an operational definition through the process of identifying measurable variables? Provide an example to illustrate.
5. How, in your view, do the different conceptualisation traditions influence the construction and description of concepts?

CHAPTER 10

Constructing arguments in research

Corné Davis

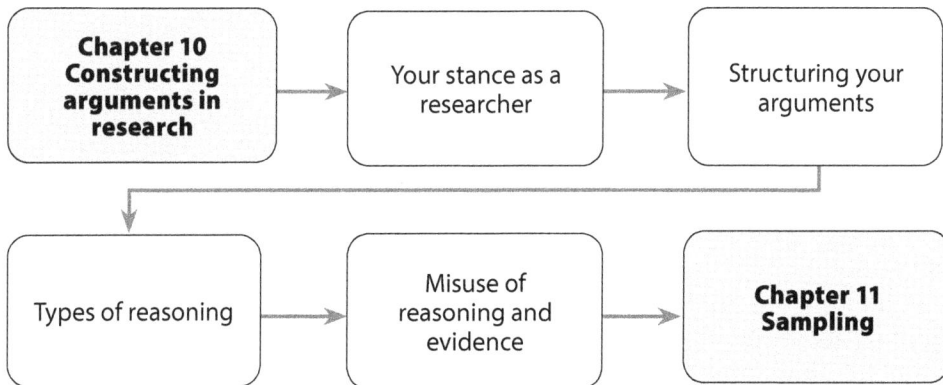

Overview

Argumentation is a crucial skill in research since you need to convince your readers and critics that you have made the most appropriate decisions in every step of the research process. Remember the concept of double contingency, which means there are always choices that could have been made differently. In this chapter, we look at the skill of argumentation and the necessity for logic in research matters.

Your research project is an accumulation of many arguments that all constitute the bigger argument in which you answer your research question and show how you (a) have met the objectives of your research, and (b) solved the research problem.

We focus on the planning, construction and assessment of arguments by identifying the key elements that should be present in sound arguments. First, we consider your stance as a researcher; in other words, where you are coming from. Then we introduce a well-known model developed by Stephen Toulmin in 1964, which is still relevant and applicable today. This model will assist you to construct logical arguments in your research. We discuss the elements in the model so that the claims you make and the evidence you choose to substantiate your claims are clear.

As you will learn in this chapter, arguments require structure in order to meet the requirements of logic. However, as you gathered in Chapter 2, 'logic' and 'truth' are not universal concepts. Therefore, your selection of claims and evidence must correspond with your philosophical orientation, research tradition, approach, theoretical orientation and methodological orientation. We also discuss the misuse of reasoning and evidence in research, so that you avoid errors that may compromise the credibility of your work.

Objectives of this chapter

By the end of this chapter, you should be able to demonstrate your understanding of the following:
- your stance as a researcher;
- structuring arguments in research;
- types of reasoning; and
- the misuse of reasoning and evidence in research.

Your stance as a researcher

We have touched on the notion that objectivity is not possible because we all see things from our own perspectives that are made up of opinions, preferences, worldviews, and so forth. Say, for example, you are opposed to abortion, your beliefs and perceptions will naturally shape the content you choose to read and the arguments you will create. Your stance as a researcher will also determine the kind of involvement you will choose to have with the participants in your research. This may involve the following considerations:
1. Will you be an insider or an outsider?
2. Will you be an expert or a beginner?
3. Will your research be about, for, or with people?

The answers to these questions will most certainly play a role in the construction of your arguments during the research process. Always keep the relationship with your participants in mind because it may also influence other parts of your research.

Insider or outsider

If you are doing research involving people, you have to choose both the kind of relationship you wish to have with the people you are researching and the kind of role they will play during the process of generating new knowledge (Blaikie, 2007:11). In other words, you will have to decide whether you will be making observations as an outsider or as an insider. If you choose to observe people as an outsider, they will not participate in your observations. If you choose to observe them as an insider, you may aim to observe phenomena through your participants' eyes. Should you choose the latter option, you need to be aware that not only could you be influenced by the people you are researching, you could also have an influence on them.

Expert or beginner

It makes a big difference whether you are doing your research as an expert or as a beginner. As an expert, you are equipped with theoretical knowledge and a clear understanding of the concepts you will be dealing with. Your knowledge of these concepts will influence the way you formulate research questions and the way you seek answers. On the other hand, you may decide to keep an open mind and to enter the social world of the participants in your study to observe how *they* conceptualise the social world that you want to study. This means that your research questions and answers will emerge from a learning process that will then influence the way you construct the arguments in your study.

About, for, or with people

The final consideration pertaining to the relationship between you and the people you are researching is whether your research is about, for, or with people:

- If your research is *about* people, it will be conducted primarily for your own purposes, such as completing a research essay or a dissertation.
- If you are doing research *for* a client, for example, you will be guided by their requirements, which will influence the arguments you develop.
- Doing research *with* people means that you are part of a research project or team, typically to solve a particular problem, to evaluate a programme such as a campaign, or to bring about change. In this case, the people you are doing your research with will probably participate in articulating the claims and arguments for the research project.

Structuring your arguments

You will be gathering many different kinds of information during your research project which all fit into different parts of your document. For example, information from the academic articles and books on the theories you are using should support the theoretical arguments you will apply to your arguments about the information on your research topic. There are specific ways to structure arguments and the Toulmin model has been used to teach this skill for many decades.

The model created in 1964 by Toulmin identifies three basic elements and three further substantiating elements that constitute a sound argument. The three basic elements are the *claim*, the *data* and the *warrant*. These basic elements can be observed in everyday conversations, and you may recognise them in some of our earlier discussions. The three substantiating elements are the *backing*, the *qualifier* and the *rebuttal* (reservation).

During the research process, you will engage with the topic of your research in more and more depth. As your knowledge increases, you may come to assume that your readers know what you know when you create your argument. However, this may not be the case. Therefore, you must apply sound reasoning skills throughout to ensure that your claims correspond with your evidence. A closer look at these elements will improve your understanding of the reasoning process.

Claims

A claim is the proposition or premise that you hope will be believed, adopted or followed by the reader or critic of your research. When you identify your research problem, you claim that a problem exists that requires research for a specific purpose. When you construct the rationale for your research, you make certain claims about the relevance of and necessity for your research. While you are writing your literature review, you are consulting primary and secondary sources whose research you may use to make new claims about the phenomenon you are investigating. Claims can therefore be described as 'facts', evidence or conclusions that can be based on your general observations, assumptions, other research and your own research. What qualifies as a fact or evidence also depends on your worldview(s) and research tradition, as you learnt in Chapter 2.

Keep in mind that your claims or the facts you present will be scrutinised by your examiners or critics. Therefore, you need to give evidence for every statement you make and apply logical reasoning, bearing in mind that 'logic' does not necessarily mean 'truth'. Let's use an example to demonstrate this point: 'All women like shopping. Mary is a woman. Therefore, Mary likes shopping.' This seems to be a logical argument. However, it is clear that the major claim in the argument, namely that all women like shopping, has no substance because this is not true of all women. When you deal with more complex phenomena and concepts, it becomes more difficult to recognise insubstantial claims. For example, people readily believe statistical information without questioning its sources or substance. You must keep in mind at all times that there is not one truth about anything and this requires you to look at claims more carefully. We can broadly distinguish between conceptual claims and practical claims as follows:

- *Conceptual claims* generally aim to provide explanations, for example: 'Credibility of participants is a key requirement for expert research reports on Covid-19 vaccinations.'
- *Practical claims* generally aim to initiate some kind of action, such as solving a problem: 'All citizens have to be vaccinated against Covid-19 to combat it.'

As we discussed in Chapters 4 and 5, a clear understanding of your research problem, its purpose and the questions you ask is crucial, as these inform the claims you will be making. To broaden your understanding, we further identify four specific types of claims, namely designative, definitive, evaluative and advocative. The type of claim you make has to be supported by the type of reasoning you choose, as we will discuss a bit later:

1. *Designative claims* assert what is, by stating facts. If you argue, for example, that all countries use vaccinations to combat disease, you are making a designative claim.
2. *Definitive claims* state how some situation, idea or fact should be classified or defined. If you argue that vaccinations should be made freely available to all citizens, for example, you are making a definitive claim, since freely available vaccinations are defined as necessary to combat a disease.
3. *Evaluative claims* stress the value or importance of some idea, situation or fact. If you claim that delaying immunisation is immoral, for example, you are evaluating the situation by a standard of value, in this case morality.
4. *Advocative claims* contend what policy should or should not be adopted or followed. If you claim that the selection of the vaccines used in this country should not be made if it is not verified that no corruption was involved in the selection process, for example, you are making an advocative claim.

Data

The evidence you collect during the various stages of the research process is referred to as data. It provides a reason for the claim you make. For example, if you claim that 'Students at College X who submit fraudulent doctors' certificates will be expelled from university', you will require data to support this claim. You may show, for example, that the university has a policy stating that the submission of fraudulent documents qualifies as an offence which may result in the dismissal of the students. Thus, any evidence that substantiates or confirms a claim may be classified as data. Bear in mind that such a classification in itself does not mean that the evidence is sound.

The data you present to substantiate the claims you make in your research must be relevant. You may have several pieces of data that support a given claim, and it will be up to you to choose the most appropriate data in every case.

The more support you can provide for a claim, the more valid that claim is likely to be.

Warrants

A warrant refers to how you reason that the evidence you are giving supports your claim. It involves some assumption that we find in proverbs, for example 'Actions speak louder than words'.

Warrants may be difficult to grasp. This may be because warrants are often not clearly stated in arguments. As knowledge develops over time, certain things are assumed. For example, you will not see the need to provide evidence that the Earth is round. Certain things become what we refer to as general knowledge.

Returning to our previous example, the claim that students who submit fraudulent documents will be expelled—a claim backed by the data of the university's related policy—rests on the warrant that students do not wish to be expelled from university. In this argument the warrant is assumed, as is often the case in arguments. It may therefore be necessary for you to state a warrant explicitly if you think your reader may not follow your reasoning. In other words, in certain instances, you will need to tell your reader what assumptions you are making.

The backing, qualifier and rebuttal

Backing refers to any other additional information which further supports a claim and a warrant, thus backing your claims. If you say, for example, that 23 students were expelled from College X in 2020 following the submission of fraudulent doctors' certificates, such information may be categorised as backing.

A *qualifier* refers to words that indicate the level of probability of a claim, such as 'It is probable that . . .' or 'It can be assumed that . . .'. You may introduce your claim with a qualifier by saying, for example: 'It is probable that students who submit fraudulent doctors' certificates will be expelled from university.'

A *rebuttal* indicates the circumstances under which the claim does not follow from the data. For example, in the claim that students who submit fraudulent documents will be expelled from university, you may use a rebuttal such as 'unless College X changes its policy'. A rebuttal is used when you want to indicate that you have considered other possible outcomes to your claim. Depending on the topic, it may add to the credibility of the argument. In other words, it helps if you show that you considered all options.

The Toulmin model

The Toulmin model has been popular among scholars for its visual representation of the structure of sound arguments, as shown in Figure 10.1 below.

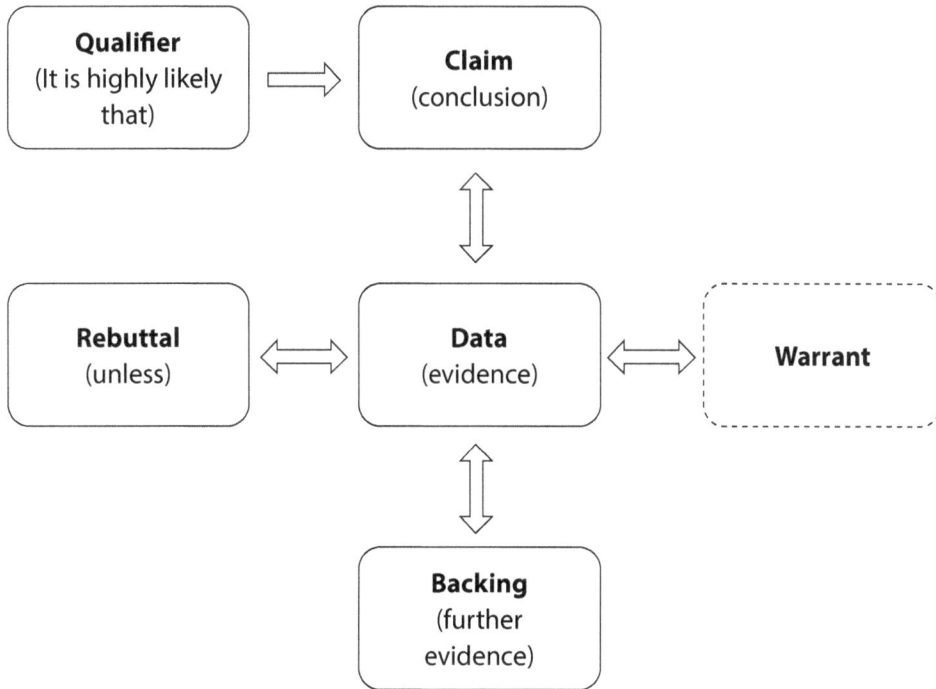

Figure 10.1 The Toulmin model (adapted from Scheidel, 1972:205)

Types of reasoning

Besides the structural elements of sound arguments we have discussed, we can identify several types of reasoning to show you how data may be arranged in a different order, depending on what you aim to achieve with a particular argument. In research, you will first consider the distinction between inductive and deductive reasoning.

During *inductive reasoning*, you gather specific data to formulate a general claim.

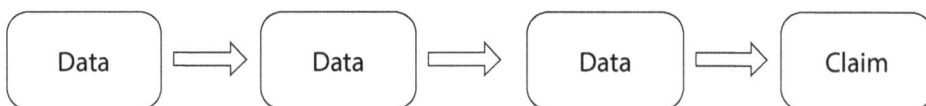

Figure 10.2 An illustration of inductive reasoning

For example:
- Data: The University of Johannesburg has expelled 23 students who had presented falsified doctors' certificates.
- Data: The University of Pretoria has expelled 16 students who had submitted falsified doctors' certificates.
- Data: The University of the Witwatersrand is investigating 50 cases of falsified doctors' certificates.
- Claim: Universities in Gauteng follow strict disciplinary procedures for falsified doctors' certificates.

Inductive reasoning is often applied to reason *from effect to cause*. Using the example above, you may use the data pertaining to students being expelled from university as the effect, while identifying the falsification of doctors' certificates as the cause of the students being expelled.

Deductive reasoning, on the other hand, argues from a general claim (major premise) to a narrower claim (minor premise) to a specific conclusion (claim).

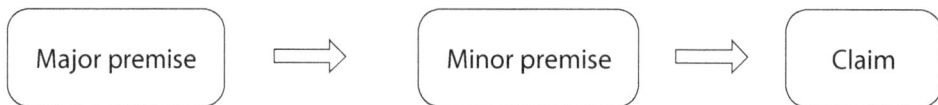

Figure 10.3 An illustration of deductive reasoning

For example:
- Claim: There is a significant occurrence of fraudulent activities among university students in Gauteng.
- Claim: The University of Pretoria is situated in Gauteng.
- Conclusion: Therefore, there should be an occurrence of fraudulent activities at the University of Pretoria.

Deductive reasoning is also used to reason *from cause to effect*. For example, you may argue that the submission of falsified doctors' certificates (cause) has resulted in a high number of students being dismissed from tertiary institutions (effect).

Other types of reasoning include reasoning from sign or symptom, reasoning from criteria to application, and reasoning from analogy or by comparison.
- An example of *reasoning from sign* would be if you argued that the submission of falsified doctors' certificates was a sign (or symptom) of the decay of social values.
- *Reasoning from criteria to application* typically aims to assign a label to phenomena or social entities. For example, if you argue that an increase in fraudulent activities, combined with a decline in pass rates and financial

constraints, is putting universities at risk of closure, you may argue that the universities in Gauteng are at risk of closure, provided that you have the data to support such a claim.

- *Reasoning from analogy or by comparison* involves identifying behaviours or characteristics in a certain setting or phenomenon to make assumptions that the same behaviours or characteristics can be anticipated in another similar setting or phenomenon. For example, you may argue, that the University of Johannesburg has the same sociographic composition as the University of the Witwatersrand, and that a similar increase in the number of fraudulent doctors' certificates submitted by students should therefore be found at both universities.

Misuse of reasoning and evidence

As we suggested earlier, the confusion that often occurs between 'logic' and 'truth' remains a challenge in research. It is therefore worth considering how reasoning and evidence can be misused.

As you may have found, statistics and testimony are often misused or misrepresented in arguments. This may be because people tend to believe statistics without question, as we said earlier, since they provide specific information that may seem to be well researched. Therefore, keep in mind that in research reports, the selection of the sample and sample size is frequently under scrutiny. You must demonstrate that:

- your statistics are drawn from a representative sample, and
- the sample was not selected in a way that might bias the results.

In a similar way, researchers provide testimony of their observations, which may also be biased. In other words, you may want to prove that your hypotheses are correct and consequently only identify data that support your stance. It is therefore important that you demonstrate your integrity as a researcher by collecting and assessing all the relevant data.

We also recommend that you familiarise yourself with common fallacies used in argumentation. Fallacies are unsound arguments that may sound believable in spite of being based on invalid reasoning. For example, you may argue that the high failure rate of secondary pupils in Gauteng was a result of teachers' strikes in a particular year, while there may have been several other causes for the failure rate in that particular year. An argument stating that because certain people or groups share some attributes, they share all other attributes, is another kind of fallacy. If you argue, for example, that fraudulent activities at the University of Pretoria have probably increased, since they have increased at the University of Johannesburg, your claim may be challenged based on differences between these universities that you have not identified or specified. You should therefore ensure that you steer away from claims that cannot be verified or supported by sound evidence.

Summary

The construction of arguments in your research project will evolve as you progress through the various stages in the research process. The claims you make throughout the research process will depend, first and foremost, on your philosophical and theoretical orientations, and other factors such as your stance as a researcher and the aims of your research. We suggest that you familiarise yourself with the general principles of argumentation and the types of reasoning introduced to you in this chapter by also consulting other sources to increase the depth of your understanding. We reiterate that sound structures of argumentation and reasoning alone do not guarantee success in research, since many other considerations present unique challenges in every research project.

Review the chapter

Answer the questions and complete the tasks to assess whether you understand the content of this chapter:

1. What is your stance as a researcher at this stage and how does it influence the claims you are making about your research topic?
2. What basic elements in the Toulmin model can you identify in everyday discourses you observe?
3. Can you draw a distinction between sound and unsound arguments that you observe in everyday discourses? Explain.
4. Construct your own argument using the elements in the Toulmin model.
5. Analyse some arguments you see on social media platforms and apply what you have learned in this chapter to critically assess them.

Sampling

Gerald Pascoe

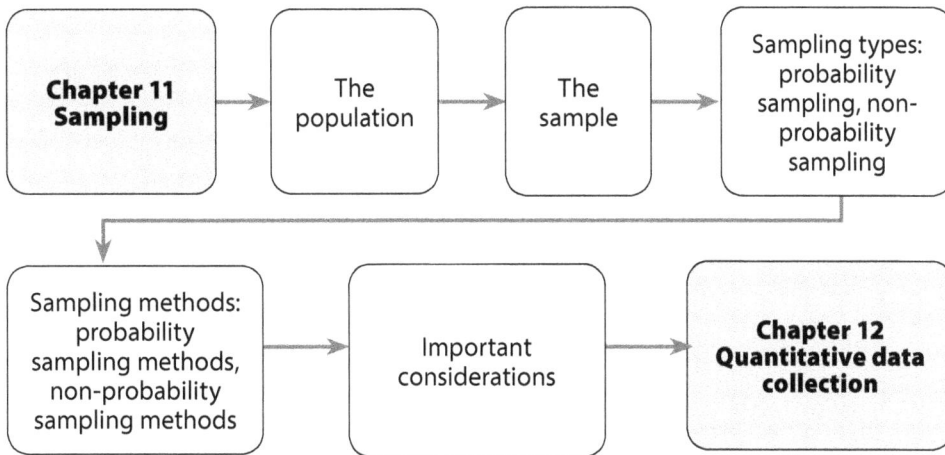

```
┌─────────────┐     ┌─────────────┐     ┌─────────────┐     ┌─────────────────┐
│  Chapter 11 │ --> │     The     │ --> │     The     │ --> │ Sampling types: │
│  Sampling   │     │  population │     │   sample    │     │   probability   │
│             │     │             │     │             │     │  sampling, non- │
│             │     │             │     │             │     │   probability   │
│             │     │             │     │             │     │    sampling     │
└─────────────┘     └─────────────┘     └─────────────┘     └─────────────────┘
```

```
┌───────────────────┐     ┌─────────────────┐     ┌───────────────────┐
│ Sampling methods: │     │                 │     │    Chapter 12     │
│    probability    │ --> │   Important     │ --> │ Quantitative data │
│ sampling methods, │     │ considerations  │     │    collection     │
│  non-probability  │     │                 │     │                   │
│ sampling methods  │     │                 │     │                   │
└───────────────────┘     └─────────────────┘     └───────────────────┘
```

Overview

Have you ever left a hotel or a restaurant and on your way out filled in the customer satisfaction survey? Congratulations, if you have—you are one of many who form part of a research sample. By filling in forms and providing places such as hotels, restaurants or shops with feedback on your experience, you are helping them gather important information about how well the business is performing.

You will recall that research is a process of gathering knowledge by looking for answers to questions. How we get the answers to the questions depends on the kinds of decisions we make during the research process. One of these decisions is deciding from whom or what we are going to get our answers. Sometimes we get our answers from people and sometimes we get them from other places, such as newspapers, books, television shows or social media platforms (we refer to these as social artefacts). There will also be times when there are so many people or social artefacts that can provide you with answers to your research question that it is impossible to include all of them in your study. The process of selecting who or what we will include in our research is called sampling, and different sampling strategies are used based on our research problem and question, and is guided by our research approach.

It is important to be mindful of the divergent principles underlying the sampling strategies used in qualitative and quantitative approaches in research studies. Kumar (2019) explains that impartiality and representation prompt the selection and size of a sample for a quantitative study. The basis of a smaller sample selection for a qualitative study is accessibility, the lived experiences of individuals and typical or 'thick' examples of phenomena from which a researcher can gain an in-depth understanding. In this chapter we explain the process and methods of sampling in greater detail.

Objectives of this chapter

By the end of this chapter, you should be able to demonstrate your understanding of the following:
- population;
- unit of analysis;
- population parameters;
- sample;
- sampling;
- the differences between probability and non-probability sampling methods;
- numerous sampling methods; and
- what to consider in the process of sampling.

The population

A population is described by Babbie (2021:199) as 'the theoretically specified aggregation of the elements of a study', thus the elements (people or artefacts) from which a sampling unit is selected. For example, if the manager of a hotel wants to know what guests think of her or his hotel, she or he should choose to ask the people who would know best—guests at the hotel. The manager can only get the information she or he requires from people who have experienced the hotel; therefore, all the guests staying or who have stayed at the hotel will become the population for her or his research.

As we can see from this example, we need to go back to the research problem and research question to determine who or what would best help us get the answers we need to identify and define the population for our research. Once we know *what* or *whom* to observe to find our answers, we can ascertain what they have in common—what characteristic they all share. This will help us when we need to define our population in our research proposal and report.

Unit of analysis and unit of observation

A unit of analysis is the 'what' or 'whom' being studied and is the smallest unit or entity under observation. It is the focus of your study. Identifying a suitable unit of analysis is crucial since it affects the research process, specifically the choice of sampling elements and methods, sample size and data collection and analysis methods. Identifying your unit of analysis seems relatively easy but it becomes difficult when it is a complex study, and it may be confused with the unit of observation. A unit of observation is the element that you observe and measure while attempting to learn more about your unit of analysis. Although they are the same for most studies, the unit of observation and unit of analysis may be different in some studies. For example, if you are interested in how couples interact, you are observing couples (your observational unit), but your unit of analysis is an interaction.

A unit of analysis may be described in terms of different levels and Babbie (2021) describes them as the individual, group, organisation, social interaction and social artefacts. Descriptions of the categories are not exhaustive, and we briefly explain some levels of units of analysis:

- *The individual* is a typical unit of analysis and can involve *individual* experiences with and feelings about, for example, Covid-19, the lockdown restrictions in South Africa or the 2021 protests and looting in Kwa-Zulu Natal and Gauteng.
- *Groups* include the collective behaviour of social groups as a single entity and your typical unit of analysis would be gangs, families, cults, and social clubs such as a book club and online or web communities.
- *Organisations* include formal organisations such as corporations and conglomerates, religious congregations, universities, colleges, campuses and schools.
- *Social interactions* include the interactions and communication patterns between individuals and not the individuals themselves and may consist of, for example, arguments, gaslighting (a colloquial term for insidious and often covert emotional abuse), messaging exchanges (on WhatsApp or Telegram) and online shaming (cancelling or callouts on Twitter or Facebook).
- *Social artefacts* are the products of creations by humans consisting of concrete objects (paintings, photographs, movies, video games, books, television programmes, documents, Twitter tweets and Facebook posts).
- *Geographical units* include geographic areas (a town, a census tract, a province or a territory).

Units of analysis and observation units are thus related but distinct concepts. An observational unit is the entity that is being observed, and the unit of analysis is the focus of a study's analysis. The units may be the same in a study, and both have an influence on design decisions and sampling strategies and the population parameters or shared characteristics of sampling units.

Population parameters

An important aspect to keep in mind is that all the people or social artefacts in the population should share at least one specific characteristic that relates to the research question. Let's look at an example to illustrate this: let's say we want to research whether more action shows are aired on Channel Z than situation comedies (sitcoms). For this example, we will use the following question: 'How many sitcoms compared to action shows are aired on Channel Z?'

1. The first step is to decide what we need in order to get the information that will answer this question. In this case, we will have to turn to Channel Z and the programmes aired on this channel. From this we can deduce that we are studying social artefacts. We can therefore say that our unit of analysis is social artefacts, or television programmes.

2. We then need to determine what characteristics these social artefacts will need to share in order to be a part of the population of our study. Again, we return to our research question. From our research question it is clear that we are focusing on one particular television channel—Channel Z. The question also specifically states that we are only concerned with two specific genres, namely sitcoms and action shows.

3. We can now define our population as any social artefact that meets the requirements of being a television programme belonging to either the sitcom or action genre that is aired on Channel Z.

Another research question we could ask is: 'What are viewers' opinions of the comedy sitcoms aired on Channel Z?'

1. Who will we approach to answer this question? In this example, the viewers of Channel Z are the population for the study because we want to know what they think of the sitcoms aired on Channel Z.

2. What characteristics do these people share? They all have access to and watch sitcoms on Channel Z.

3. We can therefore define our population as individuals (people) who watch sitcoms on Channel Z. The shared characteristic for this second question is that for each person to be a part of the sample they must be a viewer of sitcoms on Channel Z.

The shared characteristic and the number of people or social artefacts in a population are referred to as the *population parameters* of the study. The population parameters of a study therefore refer to the nature (people or social artefacts), size and unique characteristics of the population. It is this that we use to define the population of our study. If we continue with our example above of comparing sitcoms to action shows, the population parameters of the study will be:

- *the nature of the population*: social artefacts in the form of television shows;
- *the size of the population (denoted by the letter N)*: all the sitcoms and action shows aired on Channel Z on a weekly basis; and
- *the unique characteristics* of the population: the television shows have to belong to the sitcom and action show genres and must be aired on Channel Z.

Once the population parameters have been set and we have defined our population appropriately, we need to distinguish between the target population and the accessible population. The difference is that the target population is everyone or everything that falls within the population parameters, whereas the accessible population refers only to the section of the population that we can include in our study. There will be times when the population is so large and widespread that we will not be able to determine who all the members of the population are. Only those that we can reach (when questioning or observing people) or get copies of (when analysing social artefacts) will be our accessible population.

Using the example of the study of what audience members think of the sitcoms on Channel Z, the target population will be *all* the people who meet the population parameters for this research. In other words, the target population will be all viewers of comedy sitcoms on Channel Z. The problem is that there are so many viewers of Channel Z that we will not be able to contact all of them. We therefore need to ascertain which of the viewers we will be able to contact. We might choose to focus only on those people who live in the same province or city as we do, as they may be easier to contact. These people will form our accessible population. The accessible population in our example is the portion of the target population that we will be able to reach to ask questions about Channel Z.

For ease of reference, we summarise the key considerations for defining the population for your research as follows:

1. Go back to the research question and determine the nature of the population by asking whether your question will be answered best by turning to people, groups, organisations or social artefacts (the units of analysis).
2. Once you know the nature of the population, determine and describe the common characteristic(s) of your units of analysis.
3. You now have your population parameters and can define the population based on this information.
4. Now you can begin to distinguish between your target and accessible populations.

The sample

Up to this point, we have worked through a number of research choices. We have reviewed our question and problem and identified our population parameters. We can now also distinguish between our target population and our accessible population. Our next step is to select a *sample* from our accessible population using a list of the people we would like to contact or a list of the objects that we will be analysing. A sample is a subset of your population which you select to be the respondents or the artefacts in your study The individual people or objects that form the basis for your sample selection are referred to as your sampling *element* or sampling unit.

You will find that, often, the accessible population includes too many elements to reach or analyse — many more than our time and resources will allow for to finish our research. So we have to reduce the number of our accessible population to a more manageable number. We can work out how many people or social artefacts we need to include in our sample in a quantitative study by using a sample size calculator (such calculators can be found online). Ordinarily, the number of elements that need to be included in a sample for a quantitative study is vastly greater than the number of elements that need to be included in the sample of a qualitative study. Thus, the purpose of your study and your research approach will play a role in determining your sample size (sample size is denoted by the lowercase letter 'n').

When choosing our sample for a quantitative study, it is unfortunately not as easy as just picking and choosing whom or what we want to include in our sample. We need to narrow down our accessible population by carefully drawing a sample. As a subset of a population, the sample should be *representative* of the population. Think about when a doctor takes a blood sample for testing. That one sample of blood will provide the doctor with enough information about what is happening in the rest of the body to draw certain conclusions (also called generalisations) about your general health. It is not necessary to test all your blood to come to certain conclusions about your health. If a problem is identified in the sample, then there is more than likely a problem in the body (Bradley, 2013).

A representative sample, usually required for a quantitative study, shares the characteristics of the larger population (like the sample of blood). Their responses to your research should therefore be very closely related to what the response would have been if the entire population were included. For example, let's say we want to investigate people's opinions of online shopping. The population for this research would be all the people who had shopped from an online site such as Takealot.com. If Takealot.com has to date had 1 000 customers, an ideal sample of 278 shoppers will be a representative sample with a 95% confidence level (associated with a confidence interval (CI) in statistics, which is an estimate computed from the observed data) with a 5% margin of error. The margin of error is a statistical expression of the random sampling error in the results of, for example, a survey. The larger the margin of error, the less confidence there should be that the results gained from a sample represent the entire population.

If the sample is selected acceptably and is representative of the population, we will be able to generalise the findings from our research to the rest of the population. We will then be able to predict the possible opinions of all the other people in the population who were not included in the research.

The extent to which we can generalise the findings to the rest of the population can be measured using a calculation to determine the *sampling error as discussed above*.

A related term is *selection bias* or the *selection effect* when proper randomisation is lacking, and the selection of the sample obtained is not representative of the population. It mostly relates to the distortion of a statistical analysis because of the method of collecting samples. It is thus crucial to be as systematic as possible during the selection of a sample.

In order to draw a representative sample for a quantitative study, you need a list of all the people or objects in that particular population. We call this list our *sampling frame*, which we use only if the elements of the study population are individually known (Kumar, 2019), and may include a telephone directory, a list of customers, tax records, driver's licence records or a mailing list. The key in deciding on a sampling frame is that the people or items on the list must match the characteristics of our population. We would not use a telephone directory, for example, if our population only included guests of a specific hotel. The telephone directory would include people who had not stayed at the hotel and would therefore not be appropriate for the research. A guest list of the hotel would be more relevant — this way, we could ensure that all the people who form part of the sample have stayed at the hotel.

The sample size for a qualitative study is not based on representation and a predetermined size is often not necessary since the researcher may reach a point of data saturation during the data collection phase. The data saturation point is discussed in more detail later and in Chapter 13.

So how do we go about drawing a sample? Once the population has been identified, we will need to determine what sampling method — a probability or a non-probability sampling method — will be most suited to our research. Several choices are available to identify the most appropriate sampling method to use. Remember these key points when choosing a sampling method:

- A sample is a subset of the accessible population.
- The sampling frame is a list of the elements included in the population.
- The final sample must have the same relevant characteristics as the population in order to be considered representative of the population.

Sampling types

Keep in mind that the selection of sampling types and methods for studies using qualitative and quantitative research approaches is guided by different philosophies and underlying principles. In a qualitative study, the researcher's judgement of the participants' experiences and knowledge of a phenomenon drives the sample selection. This subjective judgement is not acceptable in the selection of a sample for a quantitative study and the researcher takes extensive steps to remove all forms of bias during sample selection. The two broad categories of sampling types used by researchers are discussed below.

Probability sampling

Probability sampling includes methods where each unit (whether an individual or social artefact) in the population has an equal and independent opportunity to be a part of the sample. If there are 150 000 people in our population, we need to make sure that every one of them has the same chance of being included in the sample.

This method is preferred, and therefore often used in quantitative studies, because it removes human bias from the sampling process by using methods that are random and systematic (following strict step-by-step procedures). Human bias is said to occur when researchers select a sample that does not reflect the population accurately. This can happen when we choose to draw a sample that favours some population parameters or characteristics over others. If our population includes both males and females, but we want to focus more on women's opinions of a particular topic, then we may choose to bias the sample by including more women in the sample than men. However, if we want the sample to be truly representative of the population, systematic random sampling will ensure that each element in the population has a fair chance of being selected as an element in the sample. How this systematic procedure unfolds is explained later in this chapter, since there are several options available to us in this regard.

Probability sampling therefore lends itself to those research situations where we want to draw a sample that:
- fits with the parameters (shared characteristics) of the research;
- is drawn randomly from the population;
- requires little influence from the researcher; and
- leads to generalisable findings.

Non-probability sampling

Non-probability sampling is used when it is nearly impossible to determine who the entire population is or when it is difficult to gain access to the entire population. As explained previously, you might not always have access to a sampling frame that includes the entire population. For example, if we wanted to question recovering alcoholics on the effectiveness of a 12-step recovery programme, the population will be hard to determine — the nature of the topic makes it a sensitive subject and getting a comprehensive list of alcoholics in a particular area will be nearly impossible. Instead, we will carefully select our sample from an accessible population and through those who can recommend other possible participants. The sample will still meet the population parameters for the study; however, the sample will be selected using the researcher's judgement and the participants will therefore not be randomly selected from a list. Any inclusion in the sample will be based on coincidence or our ability to contact participants and not necessarily on a random or systematic selection.

The sample is, therefore, different to one selected by means of probability sampling, in that the elements in the population will not all have an equal opportunity to form part of the sample. However, the representativeness of the sample is not considered important in non-probability sampling when compared to probability sampling, especially in the case of qualitative research. Rather, the focus is more on how many people we need to interview or how many artefacts we need to analyse to allow us to gain an in-depth understanding of the research problem that we are exploring. If, for example, you interview students studying at a particular university or college about their perceptions of the value of higher education, you will find that, at some point, your participants are no longer providing you with new information and that everything that is being said has already been said. This is referred to as *data saturation*. Thus, in qualitative research the emphasis is not so much on ensuring that the sample size is big enough to be representative of the entire population, but instead on including enough participants in the sample so that the data saturation point is reached.

Also keep in mind that the findings from non-probability sampling are often not used to generalise results to the larger population. Moreover, the findings of a non-probability sample are not considered reliable in the same way that the results from a probability sample would be. This is because there is a greater likelihood of researcher bias influencing the findings. Since generalisation is not an aim of most qualitative research studies, non-probability sampling methods are most often used in qualitative studies. Non-probability sampling can be used when we want to draw a sample:

- that is in line with the parameters (shared characteristics) of the research;
- where not all individuals or social artefacts in the population are easy to access or are known; and/or
- where drawing a representative sample to generalise results to a broader population is not the goal of the study.

Sampling methods

Once the choice has been made as to whether a probability or non-probability sample is more appropriate for your research, you can decide on which sampling method to use. The following sections summarise several sampling methods.

Probability sampling methods

The following are explanations of different probability sampling methods. They can be used when the findings of a study need to be generalisable to the larger population.

Simple random sampling

A simple random sample is the most basic type of sampling method. It can be used when each element of the population has the same and equal chance of being selected to be a part of the sample. The sample is drawn following a precise procedure to reduce the influence of bias. A popular example of a simple random sample is drawing names written on slips of paper from a hat or a fishbowl, assuming that the population of your study is small enough to fit into the hat or bowl. If you then need 50 people to form your sample, you could randomly draw one name at a time out of the hat until you have your sample of 50 people. By doing this, you are ensuring that everyone that forms part of your population has had a fair chance of being included in the sample.

The drawing of names or numbers from a hat or fishbowl or other random selection methods can be done using two methods: sampling with or without replacement. Sampling without replacement entails that names are drawn, but the slips of paper with the names or numbers of the elements are not placed back into the bowl. When you select the first name or number from 100 names of your study population, the probability of the selection of the first name is 1/100. With the selection of the second name, the probability of the selection of the second name is 1/99. However, by doing this the randomisation of the sample selection is affected and the probability of sampling may be reduced to, for example, 1/71 after the drawing of more names. Sampling with replacement occurs when a selected element is replaced and thus placed back into the population (for example, a hat or fishbowl). If the same element is selected again, it is disregarded; however, the chance of the reselection of an element is slim when the population is large. What is important, though, is that the equal chance of selection of elements remains intact.

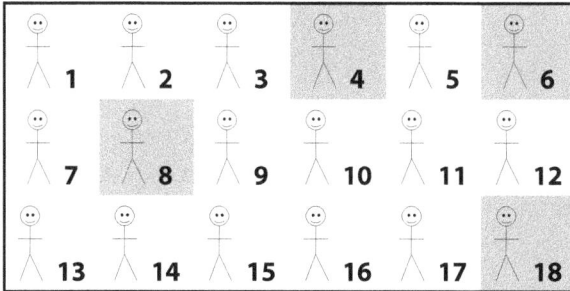

Figure 11.1 Simple random sampling

For larger populations that require a larger sample, numbers can be allocated to each member of the population. This can often be done using computer software, which would randomly select the sample for you. This method of sampling removes the chances of researcher bias, as you will not be able to choose a sample that includes only those elements that would provide answers favouring the research question.

Systematic sampling

In the systematic sampling method, each element in the population needs to be numbered on the sampling frame list. Each element of the sample will be randomly chosen from this list using a *sampling interval*. A sampling interval is the distance between each element selected for the sample. For example, if we need a sample size of 25 from a list of 100 names, the process would be the following:

1. We can work out our sampling interval by dividing the number of elements included in the population by the number of elements to be included in the sample: 100/25 = 5. Our sampling interval is 5.
2. Next, we need to determine at which number on the list to start. You can write down the numbers 1 to 10, each on a separate piece of paper, and then randomly select a number. Let's say you select the number 3. You then start at the element numbered 3; the element listed third on the list will be the first element in our sample.
3. You then need to count the same number as your sample interval down the list to get the next element in your sample. If you start at 3, and count down 5, the next element in your sample will be the element listed as 8, then 13, then 18, then 23 and so on until you have your sample of 25 elements.

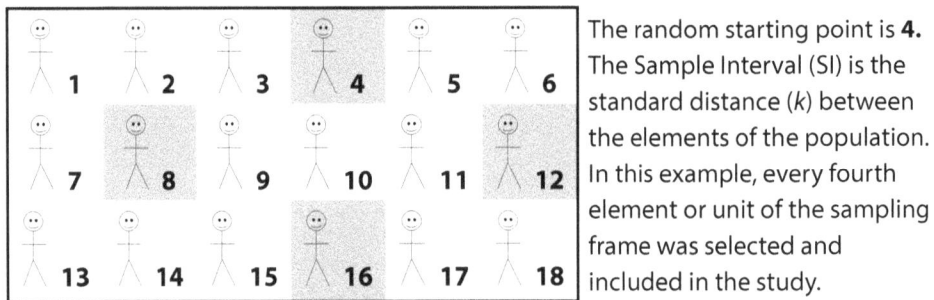

The random starting point is **4.** The Sample Interval (SI) is the standard distance (*k*) between the elements of the population. In this example, every fourth element or unit of the sampling frame was selected and included in the study.

Figure 11.2 Systematic sampling

Stratified sampling

With stratified sampling, the first step is to split the population into sub-units or strata. Strata (the singular form is stratum) are groups of elements that share the same characteristics within the same population. These strata will be decided based on characteristics included in the population parameters. Samples are drawn from each stratum using either simple random sampling or systematic sampling (Babbie, 2021). The two types of stratified sampling are: *proportionate* stratified sampling and *disproportionate* stratified sampling.

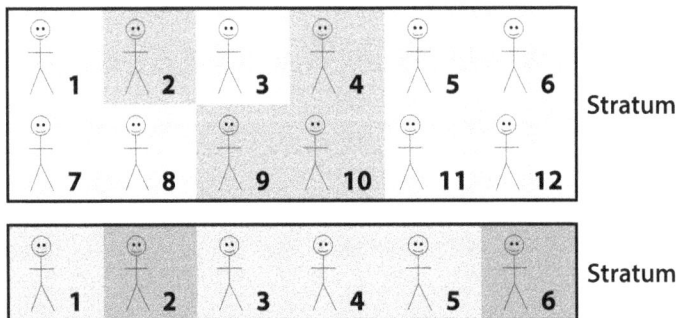

Figure 11.3 Proportionate stratified random sampling

This method can be used to ensure that the final sample is representative of the population in those situations where the population has multiple characteristics that are proportionately uneven. For example, if we want to determine the popularity of a new nightclub, our population will include all the people who have been to the club. The population, however, is split unevenly, with 60% of the nightclub-goers being women and 40% being men. We therefore have at least two strata in this population: one stratum is all the women and the second all the men from our population. The proportion will be 6 : 4 — for every six women in the population there are four men, if we use proportionate stratified sampling. It is possible that men's and women's experiences of the club will differ and thus we will want to make sure that both strata are represented proportionately. Our sample will therefore need to have the same ratio as the population in order to be considered representative. As the two strata are based on gender, we will draw a larger sample from the female stratum than from the male stratum. The final sample will match the population ratio and will have six women for every four men. In disproportionate stratified sampling, the researcher does not select elements based on the size of the strata in the population.

Cluster sampling

Cluster sampling involves the division of the sampling population into groups or clusters based on specific population characteristics. Clustering can be based on geographical proximity or other common characteristics. Cluster sampling may be done on different levels, referred to as single, double, or multi-stage cluster sampling.

Multi-stage cluster sampling is used when the population for a study is widespread (for example, across a country) or where reaching each element of the sample is difficult (Kumar, 2019). If you want to look at, for example, waiter satisfaction with wages in a national restaurant chain, you will be working with clusters, each separate restaurant in the chain representing a cluster. Here we would start by drawing a sample from a broad category, thereby creating a cluster of smaller categories. Another sample will then be drawn from each of these smaller categories to get to our final sample.

For example, an analysis of waiter satisfaction with wages in a chain such as Purple Plum would be a very time-consuming and costly exercise if we tried to draw a sample from a list of all the waiters working across the country. However, using multi-stage cluster sampling, we could do the following:

1. We first create broad categories using each of the nine provinces of the country.
2. We then draw a sample of restaurants from each province.
3. Finally, we draw a random sample of waiters from each cluster (selected restaurant).

This gradual narrowing of the population from one cluster to the next allows us to obtain a more manageable sample size.

Cluster 1

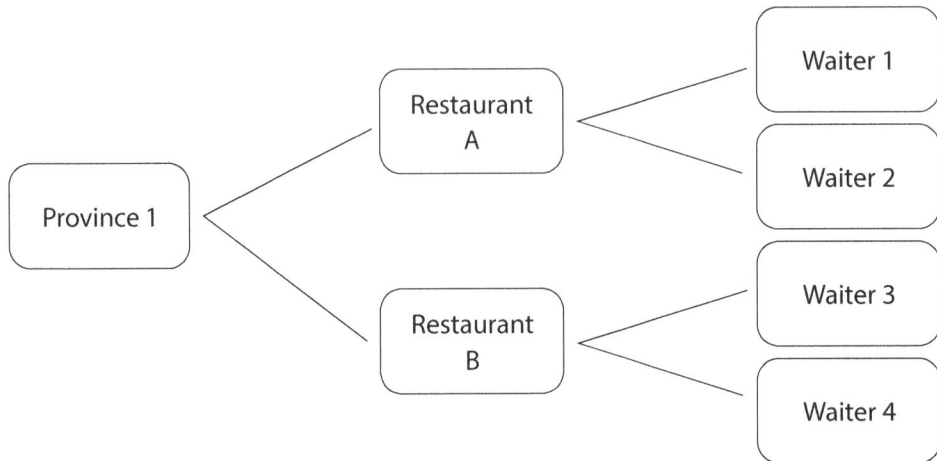

Cluster 2

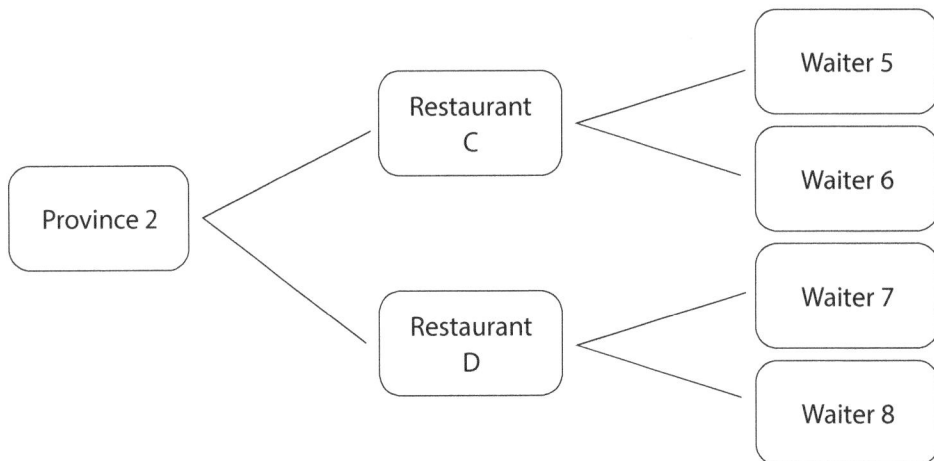

Figure 11.4 Multi-stage cluster sampling

The size of the sample drawn from each cluster can be decided in one of two ways:

1. We can draw a sample from each cluster that is proportionately the same as the cluster. Thus, if Restaurant A is larger than Restaurant B, the sample drawn from Restaurant A will be proportionally larger than that of Restaurant B. We refer to this as *probability proportionate to size sampling*.

2. The other option is *disproportionate sampling and weighting*. Here we may choose to have a larger sample size from one cluster than from another in order to include a sufficient number of elements. If Restaurant C (a Purple Plum in a small rural town) is much smaller than Restaurant D

(a Purple Plum in a big city), a proportionate sample might result in only one or two waiters from Restaurant C being included in the sample. This will not help us get the answers we need because the experience of waiters working in rural areas could be very different from those of waiters working in the city. We would thus draw a sample from Restaurant C that is proportionately larger than what it is supposed to be, so that we can ensure the views of waiters from rural areas are also incorporated. In this way, the waiters from Restaurant C can be included in the research and provide a sample that is likely to add more value to the research.

Non-probability sampling methods

The following are explanations of different non-probability sampling methods. These methods can be used when the findings of a study do not need to be generalised to the larger population, specifically in exploratory and qualitative studies.

Accidental sampling

This method of sampling does not use a sampling frame; instead, the sample consists of elements that were included purely because they happen to be in the right place at the right time. Stopping people in a shopping mall is an example of accidental sampling. Here, the people are included in the sample purely because we were able to see them walking past and they were willing to answer our questions.

This non-probability sampling method is risky, as the results obtained from the participants cannot be generalised to the rest of the population. The reason for this is that some important elements of the population may be left out, and the location could be biased towards one segment of the population. Depending on the time of day and the day of the month, the sample will include only certain segments of the population. For example, if you go to the mall in the morning on a weekday, you are like to find mostly pensioners, students and other individuals who are not full-time workers. This method is usually used only when a researcher wants to pre-test questionnaires or during the conduction of a pilot study on which a more comprehensive study will be based.

Convenience sampling

Convenience sampling is also most often used to pre-test questionnaires. The reason for this is that a sample gathered using convenience sampling can be heavily biased towards the social or professional context of the researcher. As the name suggests, our sample consists purely of elements that we know or that we can get quick and easy access to. Where convenience sampling differs from accidental sampling is that the people most likely to be convenient are those that we already know or have some form of contact with. If we are doing research on the teaching styles of lecturers, for example, a convenience sample would be made up of the lecturers that we see daily at university or college—they are convenient because we know them and see them every day.

Quota sampling

Quota sampling is similar to purposive sampling in that we purposefully choose our sample. Where quota sampling differs from purposive sampling is how the sample is drawn to match the ratio of different characteristics stipulated in the population parameters—we make a list of the characteristics of the target population and then allocate proportions to these characteristics.

Quota sampling assists in making sure that the characteristics stipulated in the population parameters are represented proportionately in the final sample. Let's say that we are analysing films within two specific genres, namely comedies and action films: if the number of action films in the population is larger than that of the comedy films, we would want this to be reflected in our final sample. When choosing our sample, the ratio of action films to comedy films will be the same as the ratio in the population. Let's say action films outnumber comedy films by two to one. We will then purposefully select one comedy film for every two action films included in the sample.

Snowball sampling

Also referred to as chain-referral sampling, a snowball sampling method is a recruitment technique often used in qualitative research. As with the previous non-probability sampling methods, the results obtained from such a sample cannot be generalised to the larger population. If you roll a snowball in snow, it collects more snow and gets bigger and bigger as the snow accumulates. Snowball sampling, then, makes use of referrals to increase the sample size. Participants in the study provide suggestions of others who also fit the population parameters of the study, and who could and want to participate in the research.

We would contact a few people who match the population parameters of our study. After approaching these people to form part of our sample, we would ask them to suggest names of others who may be interested in participating in the research. We would continue to do this until we have reached the number required for our sample.

This method is often used when members of the population are difficult to locate because they are not listed in databases or records. For example, if you wanted to gain an in-depth understanding of the lived experiences of gangsters, you could contact one gangster known to you and ask him to put you in contact with another gangster. You would continue to do so until you have a big enough sample.

Volunteer sampling

Volunteer sampling or voluntary response sampling, as the name suggests, is a sample put together from people who volunteer to participate in the research. Participants self-select to become part of a study when asked, or they may respond to an advertisement, notice or a public online survey. This method of sampling is not very reliable and tends to provide a lot of erroneous research results. One reason for this is that people who volunteer to participate in research will inherently be more likely to respond for personal gain. Note that some research authors classify volunteer sampling as a form of purposive sampling.

- An example of volunteer sampling is placing a questionnaire in a magazine or newspaper and then requesting that people fill it in and submit it. There is usually an incentive associated with this kind of research, such as being entered into a competition to win a prize. The volunteers are therefore motivated to participate in the research only because of the possibility of gaining something through their participation.
- In other instances, people volunteer because they are unhappy about something and want to voice their unhappiness. For example, convenience stores, fast food franchises, hotels and restaurants often use short questionnaires to determine customer satisfaction regarding their food or services. The only problem is that people tend to fill these in only when they are displeased with something, and hardly ever when they are satisfied with the food or service.
- In some instances, volunteers tend to provide what they believe is the desired answer instead of what they truly think. Another problem with this method is that the people who volunteer might not meet all the population parameters of the study.

Purposive sampling

Purposive or judgemental sampling (also referred to as purposeful sampling) means we purposefully choose the elements we wish to include in our sample, based on a set list of characteristics. We would look at our population and our research question and determine what characteristics from the population are important for the research. We would then carefully select a sample from the population that have these characteristics, and we would disregard those that do not.

Using our previous film genre example, our population would include all films from the comedy and action genres. In order to narrow our focus, we would select only films that fall within these genres and that were produced in South Africa. We would then select those films that we need to make up our sample, and disregard all films not from South Africa, even though they are classified as comedies and action films. The advantage of this method of sampling is that we can ensure that each element of our sample will assist with our research because each element fits with the population parameters of the study. If an element does not fit, we can disregard it.

There are several types or forms of purposive sampling explained in the table below:

Table 11.1 Types of purposive sampling

Purposive sampling	
Type	**Description**
Maximum variation/ heterogeneous	The selection of cases with maximum variation for the purpose of analysing unique or diverse variations that have emerged, and to identify important common patterns that cut across variations. It involves selecting participants across a broad range of cases that relate to the topic being researched.
Homogeneous	The selection of homogeneous cases to reduce variation, simplify analysis, and facilitate group interviewing. The focus is on participants sharing similar traits or specific characteristics relating to the topic being researched.
Typical case	The selection of participants based on the likelihood that they may exhibit typical or standard behaviour patterns. For example, selecting participants with the same socioeconomic status or similar educational backgrounds.
Extreme/deviant case	The selection of extreme or divergent cases to explore unusual indications of phenomena of interest. Participants are known to exhibit atypical or unusual characteristics related to a topic being researched.
Critical case	The selection of important or critical cases in the initial stages of research to establish if a more in-depth exploration is needed.

→

Purposive sampling	
Type	**Description**
Total population	The selection of an entire population when the whole population meets the criteria for inclusion in the sample, specifically when the population is very small.
Theoretical	The sampling of new research sites, cases, incidents, time periods or data sources to compare with those that have already been studied. It is used to gain a deeper understanding of the constructs of a particular topic, typically in systematic reviews and the theory construction stage of a grounded theory approach.
Expert	The selection of known and established experts in a particular field related to the topic being explored. The method is used when, for example, a population is inaccessible due to the topic being too sensitive or dangerous to interview people, for example, child rape victims or victims in a conflict-affected area. Experts in, for example, in human trafficking in conflict-affected areas could be interviewed to explore the prevalence of the phenomenon. Some research authors such as Kumar (2019) do not view expert sampling as a form of purposive sampling because sample selection is not based on the judgement of the researcher but on the known expertise of the participants.

Important considerations

From the very outset of the sampling process, there are several considerations that need to be taken into account. These considerations may be helpful in setting the boundaries for the kinds of sampling alternatives available to us.

- *Budget.* Every research project will have a budget. It is important to consider cost versus value, in that the sampling method chosen will need to be cost effective while still providing valuable data. A large sample might provide us with a lot of valuable data, but it may cost too much to get a team large enough to collect and analyse the data. The alternative is to carefully choose a sampling method which will provide us with the same kind of data from a smaller number of elements.
- *Time.* Researchers typically work within time constraints. We must keep in mind that we need time to source our sample, contact them, collect the data from them and then still analyse and write up our findings. We therefore

need to make sure that our sample size and sampling method are not too time-consuming.

- *Resources.* The resources we have at our disposal will also affect our research. If we have a team of researchers, we will be able to take on a larger sample than if we have to manage the collection and analysis on our own. Access to statistical programmes, pre-established questionnaires, computer equipment and recording equipment will all play a part in the kind of sampling decisions we will have to make.
- *Purpose.* Some research is not designed to be generalisable to the larger population. Exploratory research for the purposes of designing questionnaires or measurement instruments, for example, does not need to be generalised beyond the sample.
- *Error allowance.* When error control is not a main concern — as in the case of pilot studies, for example — larger or more generalisable results are not required. In such cases, sampling methods can be chosen according to the specific requirements.

Summary

Each decision we make during the sampling process leads to a range of other decisions, until we have finalised the sample for our research. The best approach is to be systematic, following steps — almost like following a recipe. Our research question and the goals of our research will guide these decisions. We must be aware that each decision we make will have an impact on the representativeness of our sample and the generalisability of our research findings. It is therefore important to know from the outset what we want to gain from the research and to work towards this goal.

Review the chapter

Answer the questions and complete the tasks to assess whether you understand the content of this chapter:

1. When doing probability sampling, an important consideration is how representative the sample is. What is meant by the representativeness of the sample?
2. What is the difference between a research population and a sample? Explain how these two terms are related.
3. A researcher needs to decide whether she or he is going to use a probability or non-probability sampling method. What criteria would the researcher use to make this decision?

→

4. Social media is increasingly becoming more influential in the lives of people across the world. University students are using social media for numerous reasons, from starting and maintaining personal relationships to product sourcing and brand feedback. You want to confirm how much time university students are spending on each of these activities through social media.

    (a) Develop a research question that would be appropriate for the above scenario.

    (b) Define the population for this study by identifying the population parameters.

    (c) Choose a sampling method that best fits the research question and explain why you have chosen this method.

CHAPTER 12

Quantitative data collection

Franzél du Plooy-Cilliers and Johannes Cronje

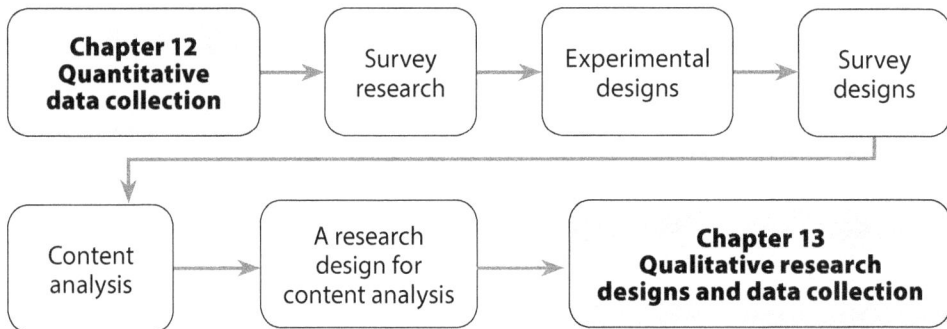

Overview

Data collection is one of the most important aspects of any research study. Researchers need to take great care when they collect data because incorrect data collection will lead to invalid results and findings. However, before you can start collecting your data, you need to consider a very important factor, namely time.

In designing your research, you have to consider three aspects regarding time:

1. Consider the placement of your study in time—is it a current study, a retrospective/historical study or a future study?
2. Consider the time span—is it a longitudinal study over a number of months or years, or a cross-sectional study that takes a snapshot of a single moment in time?
3. Thirdly, you have to consider the time that it will take to do the actual research, including collecting and analysing the data.

The researcher also has to decide *where* the research will take place. If you study the phenomenon where it occurs, it is called a field study. Experimental research is usually conducted under controlled conditions, such as in a laboratory, while literature analyses and historical studies are often called desk studies.

Finally, the researcher must consider the *tools and methods* that will be used to collect and analyse the data. (You will learn more about how to analyse quantitative data in Chapter 15.) The way in which data is collected for quantitative research differs significantly from the way in which data is collected in qualitative research. In this chapter we briefly deal with some of the most common quantitative data collection techniques, namely surveys, experiments, and content analysis. However, keep in mind that there are many more quantitative data collection techniques available that you can investigate and use for quantitative data collection.

In general, quantitative data collection methods tend to rely on random sampling (see Chapter 11), since one of the aims of quantitative research is to generalise results to a broader population. In instances where it is not possible for a quantitative researcher to draw a random sample for a quantitative study, he or she will at least attempt to control for the influence of the dependent variable through the use of statistical tests that can indicate significance (see Chapter 15).

Furthermore, quantitative data collection methods are often used to test hypotheses derived from theories (see Chapter 6). The purpose of quantitative research, then, is frequently to find causal (cause and effect) relationships or correlations that can be generalised, and the data collection methods that these researchers use are therefore designed with this aim in mind.

Objectives of this chapter

By the end of this chapter, you should be able to demonstrate your understanding of the following:
- the purpose of surveys;
- compiling a questionnaire for a survey;
- the advantages and disadvantages of surveys;
- different types of surveys;
- the four levels of measurement;
- the development of measurement scales;
- the advantages and disadvantages of using measurement scales;
- experiments as a mode of scientific observation;
- the different components of experimental designs;
- the factors that can be a threat to the internal and external validity of experimental designs;
- the advantages and disadvantages of experimental research; and
- the uses and characteristics of content analysis.

Survey research

The word 'survey' means to inspect something carefully. In the research context, surveys refer to a data collection tool that consists of a series of questions designed to gather information about a relatively large group of people. It is a very popular research tool and is often used to gather demographic information (age, gender, race, income, and so on) as well as data about people's attitudes, opinions, impressions, levels of satisfaction and more. This research tool is often used to provide a quantitative or numeric description of the trends, attitudes or opinions of a population by asking questions of a sample of respondents and then generalising the results to the population from which the sample of respondents were selected.

Survey designs

Various types of survey designs are available, each providing a unique research focus. A *cross-sectional survey design* is used to create an overall picture of a phenomenon by collecting information from lots of people at a single point in time. Thus, you collect data from your respondents only once. There are no repeats. For example, you hand out a questionnaire to a large group of students in class and collect it after the students (referred to as 'respondents') have completed it, right there and then. This will be the first and last time you collect data from these respondents.

A *before-and-after survey design* is also known as a pre-test/post-test design (often used in pre-test/post-test experimental designs). It can measure changes in a situation, problem, attitude, and so forth. It is the most appropriate design to use when measuring the impact or effectiveness of an intervention. In this design there are usually two data collection points using the same population to measure any change between the two points in time. The change is measured by comparing the differences in a situation before and after an intervention (Kumar, 2019). For example, you would ask students to write a maths test and capture their results. You would then expose them to a maths programme for a few weeks and make them write another maths test. You would then compare the two sets of results to see if there was an improvement in their performance.

A *longitudinal survey design* is used to determine the long-term effects of an intervention. Longitudinal studies are useful when you need to collect factual information on a continual basis. You may, for example, want to determine trends in the demand for a specific skill in the job market. For such a study, several data collection opportunities over a period of time are required (Maree, 2019). This method makes provision for changes that can occur over time. There are three major types of longitudinal surveys:

1. *Trend studies* are sometimes also referred to as retrospective studies. These types of studies usually look back in time to determine what kind of changes have taken place. For example, if you look at fashion magazines over a long period of time, you will see that the body types and sizes of female models used in these magazines have changed rather dramatically.

2. *Cohort studies* are used when a different sample from the same population is studied at different points in time. Thus, every time the survey is repeated a new sample is drawn, but from the same population. An example of a cohort study would be the Millennium cohort study, where almost 20 000 children who were born in the years 2000 and 2001 are being tracked over time to determine, for example, the influence of parenting styles, income, parents' level of education, school choice, and so forth on the academic performance and ultimate success of these children. The last time information was collected on them was in 2018. One of the findings from this study, for example, is that parents' level of education and qualifications remain one of the most powerful predictors of a child's success in life.

3. In *panel studies*, the same sample (or the same respondents) from a population, now called a panel, is used every time the survey is repeated. For example, you may select a group of first-year students and measure whether there is a decline in the panel's physical and mental health as they progress through their studies from first to third year.

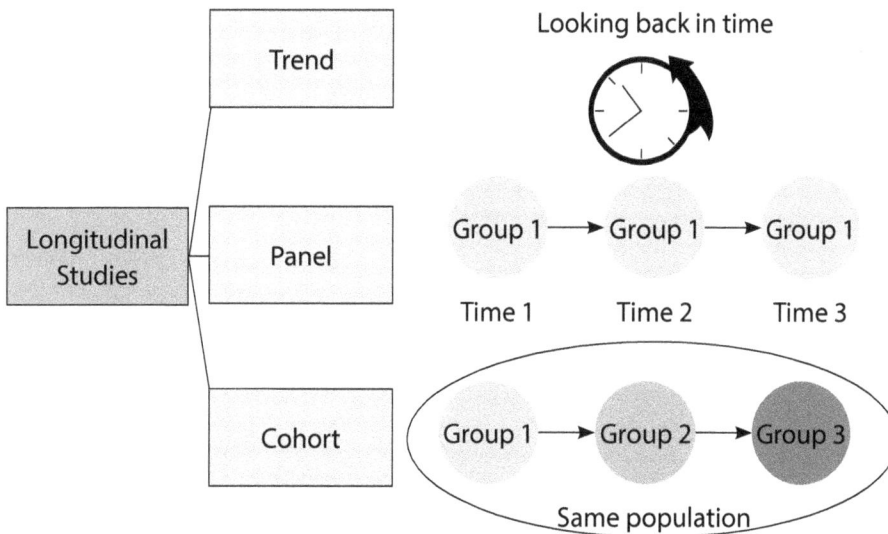

Figure 12.1 Types of longitudinal studies

When you include a discussion of a survey in your research proposal or report as part of your data collection method, ensure that you can answer the following:
1. Are the purpose and reasons for selecting a survey clearly stated?
2. Is the design of the survey clearly stated (cross-sectional vs longitudinal)?
3. Are the advantages and disadvantages of using surveys clearly stated?
4. Is the population described in terms of size and demographics?
5. Are the sampling size and method described and justified?

6.   Is it clear whether the survey will consist of questions, scales, or a combination of both?
7.   What procedures will be used to pilot or test the survey?
8.   How will the scale, if included, be tested for reliability?

Types of surveys

Surveys take on different forms. In this section we briefly look at different types of surveys.

Mail survey

In a mail survey you send questionnaires to individuals in the sample, which they fill in at their leisure and return by a given date. You can send these via mail or email. When you use email, you can either attach the questionnaire or you can send your potential respondent a hyperlink that will take him or her to a secure website to complete the questionnaire. Since people complete it on their own without any help from the researcher, it is called a self-administered survey. This type of survey is relatively inexpensive and you need few human resources to conduct it. It is particularly useful when you investigate sensitive topics, such as people's drug use. A major disadvantage is that you cannot clarify what you meant by a certain question if the respondent does not understand the question. Most people do not like to fill in questionnaires, so you are also likely to get a low response rate. In addition, it takes a long time to collect the data. Illiteracy and semi-literacy are also potential problems and even language usage can be a problem. If the language is too complicated, the respondents may misunderstand the question and respond inaptly. Access to data and technology could also be a stumbling block in electronic surveys.

Telephone survey

A telephone survey is similar to a mail survey, except that you call the respondents and interview them over the phone. The advantages of using a telephone are that it is relatively inexpensive, the data collection time is short and you tend to get a better response rate than with mail/email surveys. You also have the opportunity to clarify questions for your respondents if they do not understand. In addition, your respondents do not have to be literate. A major challenge in using this method is getting access to an appropriate sample. Moreover, because of telemarketers, most people are very suspicious of telephone surveys and are likely to be reluctant to participate, so your response rate may be low as a result.

Personal interviews

Survey interviews must not be confused with in-depth interviews used in qualitative studies. Qualitative in-depth interviews are usually unstructured or semi-structured, and the researcher has the opportunity to ask additional probing questions if a response is unclear or incomplete. On the other hand, survey interviews are structured, face-to-face interviews in a certain setting, where a set of standardised, closed-ended questions is asked and the responses are recorded. These interviews can also take place via electronic means, such as *Skype™, Zoom™, Microsoft Teams™*, etc. In most instances, researchers use laptops or tablets to capture the data, as opposed to completing a pen-and-paper questionnaire for each respondent. This method saves time when it comes to data processing.

The major advantages of using survey interviews are that questions can be clarified, response rates are high and respondents do not have to be literate. The researcher also has an opportunity to build rapport with the respondents and thereby ensure their co-operation. However, collecting quantitative data by means of a personal interview is extremely time-consuming and expensive — in the case of a large sample, it is actually impractical. Another major problem is that interviews lack anonymity. Thus, if the topic is sensitive, people tend to be less honest, and their dishonesty can affect the validity of your findings.

Group administration

A group administration survey involves a group of people who make up your sample all filling in the questionnaire at the same time during one session. Again, the response rate in these types of settings is high, the data collection time is short and the questions can be clarified. It can, however, become expensive in terms of printing costs.

Surveys using questionnaires

Questionnaires often use closed-ended questions, checklists and rating scales. These devices are very useful because they simplify and quantify responses, and people are usually more willing to tick boxes than they are to write or type out long answers. Keep the following in mind when you construct a questionnaire:
*   Always include an introduction in which you explain who is doing the survey and why you are doing the survey. When possible, provide the respondents with a good reason why it will be worth their while to fill in the questionnaire.
*   Assure respondents of confidentiality or anonymity, whichever is applicable.
*   Indicate the estimated time it will take to complete the survey and be honest about this.

- Provide clear and simple instructions. Try not to include too many instructions either, otherwise your respondents will get confused.
- Make sure that you use clear, simple and respectful language and keep in mind the problems that can be caused by the wording of questions (see Table 12.2).
- Use a logical sequence and group questions on similar topics together.
- Do not include too many questions. People are more willing to complete a short questionnaire than a long one. Thus, fewer questions will ensure a higher response rate. Also, only ask questions related to your research question(s) (or hypothesis).
- Consider asking for demographic characteristics at the end. If we start with them, people often lose interest and, if demographic characteristics are not essential to the survey, it will not be problematic if your respondents do not complete them.
- Always thank your respondents for completing your questionnaire.
- Always try to pre-test your questionnaire to see whether it is understandable and clear.

Types of questions

Different types of questions are used in questionnaires. Table 12.1 summarises the different types of questions and gives an example of each.

Table 12.1 The types of questions that appear in questionnaires

Type of question	Example
Direct questions demand a response in a frank and often confrontational manner.	Do you plagiarise?
Indirect questions are asked when we want to be more polite and less confrontational.	Do you ever consider plagiarising?
General questions are applicable to a whole situation.	How do you feel about plagiarism?
Specific questions are similar to direct questions and focus on a particular aspect of a whole situation.	Do you think plagiarism is unethical?

→

Type of question	Example
Closed-ended questions contain a fixed number of answers, from which the respondent must select one.	Have you ever plagiarised? ☐ Yes ☐ No ☐ Maybe ☐ Not sure
Open-ended questions invite respondents to answer in their own words, in any way they wish. The question can elicit underlying ideas, feelings, etc that the researcher might not have considered.	What do you think motivates students to plagiarise?
In *paired-comparison questions*, the respondent must choose between two options.	Which one of the following should be used to address plagiarism? (a) Expulsion (b) A disciplinary hearing
Contingency questions instruct the respondent to answer another set of questions, but only if the respondent gave a particular response to a previous answer.	Do you think plagiarism is unethical? If not, please answer questions 11–14. If you think it is unethical, please answer the questions in the next section.
Ranking questions ask the respondent to rank several options.	Please rank the following options from the most severe to the least severe form of plagiarism: (a) Taking another person's work and presenting it as your own work. (b) Not including in-text references but providing a reference list at the end. (c) Not using quotation marks to indicate that you are using someone else's direct words.

→

Type of question	Example
Inventory questions ask respondents to list options that apply to them personally. Inventory questions are not mutually exclusive. Thus, more than one option can be chosen, and a category called 'other' is usually included if the respondent wants to add to the list.	Which of the following forms of punishment do you think should be used when a student plagiarises? ☐ Expulsion ☐ A disciplinary hearing ☐ Giving 0% for the assignment ☐ Giving the student a written warning ☐ Other_____
Matrix questions are scaled questions. The respondents are asked to select the option that best reflects their attitude, opinion, etc. The same scale is repeated for each question (eg Likert or semantic differential scale).	Plagiarism is unethical. ☐ Strongly agree ☐ Agree ☐ Disagree ☐ Strongly disagree
In *multiple-choice questions*, certain units are grouped together. They are usually mutually exclusive (only one answer is applicable to the respondent). The respondent then chooses the category applicable to him or her.	For how long do you think a student guilty of plagiarism should be suspended? ☐ One week ☐ One month ☐ One semester ☐ One year

Problems associated with the wording of questions

Constructing a questionnaire is not as easy as it seems. You need to be aware of some of the common mistakes researchers make in the wording of questions, as listed in Table 12.2

Table 12.2 Problems associated with the wording of questions

Type of problematic question	Description	Example
Double-barrelled questions	When you have two or more questions in one, it confuses the reader because the different questions may have different answers.	Do you think single mothers face more financial and social problems? (Your respondent may think they face more financial problems but not more social problems, or vice versa.)
Questionable assumptions or presumptive questions	This type of question is objectionable because it makes assumptions about the respondents or participants.	Have you stopped using drugs? (You are assuming the respondent has used or is using drugs.)
Questions making use of loaded language	Your questions should be stated in an unbiased way; a position for or against the issue must never form part of the question.	Do you believe re-implementing the death penalty will help to save the lives of innocent people, since it will make criminals think twice before they kill? (It is obvious that you are in favour of the death penalty.)
Leading questions	In a leading question, you 'lead' your respondent through subtle pressure and manipulation to give a desired response.	Do you agree with the majority of South Africans who believe that politicians are corrupt? (You are leading the respondent to agree by using 'majority'.)

→

Type of problematic question	Description	Example
Negative items	Negative statements or questions must be avoided because people often misinterpret them and then respond based on their misinterpretation.	Should children not be allowed to watch movies with age restrictions? (If the respondent answers 'Yes' to this question, it could mean 'Yes, they should not be allowed' or 'Yes, they should be allowed'.)
Incomplete questions	This type of question forces the respondent to express an opinion based on incomplete information.	Should the government spend more money on education? (The information is incomplete: education as opposed to what?)
Vague questions	If a question is too vague and broad, the answers will not yield very useful information because it is not clear what is expected of the respondent.	What do you think of poverty? (The question is not providing the respondent with any direction: poverty in terms of what or in what context?)
Lengthy questions	Lengthy questions tend to confuse people and obscure what we actually want respondents to think about and respond to.	Do you think single mothers, given the fact that they are responsible for all household chores, child-rearing and building a career, experience more stress than mothers with a committed partner who shares in these responsibilities?

→

Type of problematic question	Description	Example
Ambiguous language	Ambiguous language is open to interpretation and can have multiple meanings.	Under which circumstances will you deviate from socially acceptable behaviour? (What is meant by 'socially acceptable'?)
Abbreviations and acronyms	Unless explanations are given for abbreviations or acronyms, you cannot expect respondents to understand them and interpret them correctly.	Do you think the goals that are set out in the NDP are realistic and being sufficiently addressed in South Africa? (Your respondent may not know that NDP stands for the National Development Plan.)
Complex questions	Avoid using jargon or language that your respondents may not understand.	Do you experience cognitive dissonance when you eat chocolate while you are on diet? (If your respondents do not know what cognitive dissonance is, they will not be able to answer your question.)

Using the table above, state what is wrong with the wording of the following questions?

1. Should people be allowed to not wear masks at the office?

2. Do you think it is important to pay tax since it assists in looking after the poor?

3. Have you stopped beating your wife?

4. Does smoking cause health problems?

5. Why do you think so few people see solipsism as a plausible explanation for human existence?

➜

6.   Do you think women who have children have a responsibility to quit their jobs in order to stay at home with their children, since the absence of a mother at home can cause children to become maladjusted adults who have difficulty forming meaningful relationships with other people?

7.   Do you agree with most people who believe the death penalty will lead to a decrease in the crime rate?

8.   Do you think it will one day be possible to download your memories on a computer?

9.   What do you think about religion?

10. Do you think transcendental meditation can be considered a form of intrapersonal communication?

The use of scales in a questionnaire

Measurement scales, such as the Likert scale and the semantic differential scale, often form part of questionnaires, but they are also used on their own. It is important to understand the general properties of scales and the types of scales which may be applied under various circumstances.

The measurement scale or level of measurement you decide to use has certain implications for the analysis of data. Keep in mind that certain quantitative analysis techniques require minimum levels of measurement. The *ratio scale* is the highest level of measurement, while the *nominal scale* is the lowest (we explain these concepts in more detail below). You can often measure the same variable with different scales, so make sure you use the correct scale for the purposes of your study. For example, you can either determine respondents' age through a nominal scale (for example, younger than 20, 21–40, 41–60, older than 60) or you can determine it through a ratio scale, where you ask respondents for their exact age. Also, some variables, such as age or income, are easily measured through a single question, while other variables, such as prejudice, cannot be measured by making use of a single indicator (see Chapter 9). Thus, we cannot determine how prejudiced someone is through asking a single question.

In a measurement scale, numbers should be assigned according to rules, which should correspond to the properties of what is being measured. Rules may be very simple or more complex. Consider, for example, when you need to catch a flight to another city. Each flight is given a number to help passengers understand which route it is travelling on. Here the only property is identity, and any other numerical comparison would be meaningless. The number essentially acts as a name for the flight. This is a nominal scale. At the other extreme is the ratio scale, which has very specific properties.

Scale properties put significant restrictions on the interpretation and use of the resulting measurements. The following sections discuss the properties of scales and different types of scales.

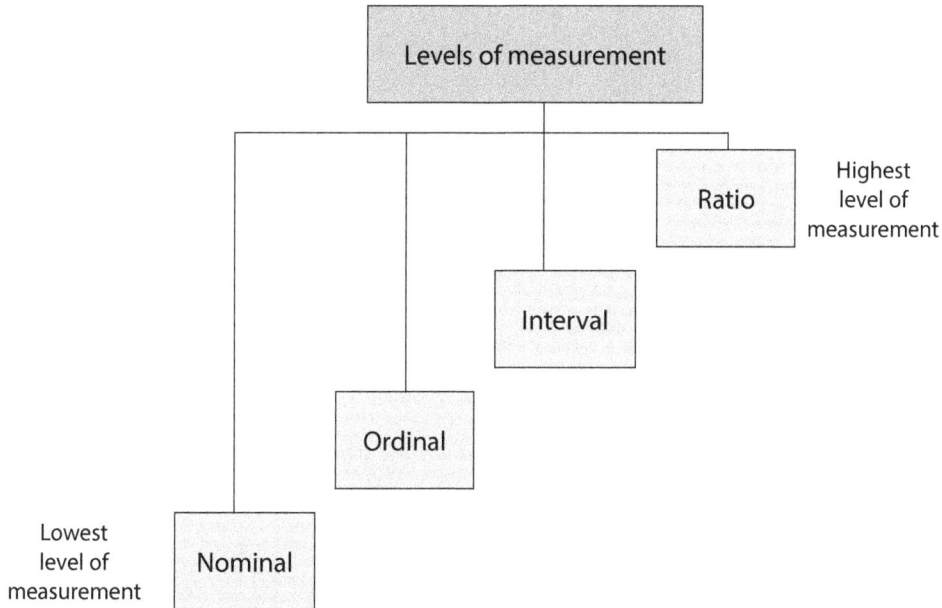

Figure 12.2 Types of scales, from lowest to highest level of measurement

Nominal scales

Sometimes we use numbers to name or label variables, as in the flight number example previously mentioned. If, for example, you want to distinguish between smokers and non-smokers, you can label smokers (1) and non-smokers (2). You could also label non-smokers (1) and smokers (2), or even (a) and (b). Thus, on a nominal level of measurement the number is merely a numeral, meaning that it is only used as a symbol and it has no mathematical significance in this context. We therefore cannot use these numbers in any calculations. When we use numbers to label categories or variables on a nominal level of measurement, we need to keep the following criteria in mind:

- The categories used must be *exhaustive*. What this means is that all the elements of your population or sample must fall into one of the categories and that none of the elements must be excluded. If you have two categories, namely smokers and non-smokers, all the people in your population will fall in either one or the other category because people either smoke or they do not.
- Categories must be *mutually exclusive*. What this means is that if an element of your population or sample belongs to one category, it must not be able to

belong to any other category. Thus, you either smoke or you do not. Even if you are just a so-called 'social smoker', you still smoke and will therefore fall in the 'smokers' category.

* When we label variables or categories on a nominal level of measurement, we use a different number for each variable or category, but the number we assign to each category is of *no mathematical significance*. There is therefore no order or space implied by the number.

Examples of nominally scaled variables include geographic location, gender, income and age. The only arithmetic operation that can be performed in such a scale is a count of each category. In other words, we can only count the number of respondents from Gauteng, or the number of taxis on a given route on a certain day, for example, and express it as a percentage.

Ordinal scale

An ordinal scale is created through ranking objects or arranging them in order with regard to a common variable. The only question that the use of this scale answers is whether each object has more or less of a particular variable than some other object. The scale does not indicate how much of a difference exists between the objects being observed.

A good example of this scale in application would be the results of a race in which the runners' times were not recorded—you would be able to discern first place from second and third; however, you would not be able to tell the degree to which the runner in first place beat those in second and third place. Similarly, brands of chocolate could be ranked from most preferred to least preferred. This scale would express which brand rated most highly, but not the differing degrees of preference which exist between the various brands. However, even though it is not possible to determine the difference between the ranked variables, the rule of correspondence applies, meaning that the element that was rated first is better than the second, which is better than the third, and so on.

Interval scales

The interval scale is very similar to the ordinal scale, but the intervals between the numerals are of equal distance, and the numbers can therefore be used in mathematical or statistical calculations. In an interval scale the numbers used to rank the elements are equal increments of the attribute being measured. This means that differences can be compared. For example, the difference between 1 and 2 is the same as the difference between 2 and 3, but is only half the difference between 2 and 4 (Kumar, 2019).

When using this scale, it is important to remember that the number zero is actually a value. The scale therefore does not include what is known as an 'absolute zero'. The measurement of temperature is a good example. When a thermometer reads 0 °C, it does not mean that there is no temperature, just that it is really cold.

Ratio scales

A ratio scale is an interval scale which has been taken one step further, in that this scale includes an absolute or true zero. In a ratio scale, zero means that the element or variable is absent. Let's say you want to measure how many friends you have that believe in aliens or extra-terrestrials. If you have none, then we use zero to show that the element (friends who believe in aliens) is absent.

With a ratio scale it is possible to say how many times larger or smaller one object is in relation to another, in terms of variables such as weight, age and money. Thus, you can measure how much older one person is than another.

Table 12.3 Different levels of measurement

Nominal	Ordinal	Interval	Ratio
Categorises, labels, names, or classifies	Ranking order	Ranking order	Ranking order
Identifies types, not rank (eg smokers vs non-smokers)	From best to worst (eg best brand to worst brand)	Distance between intervals is equal and measurable	Distance between intervals is equal and measurable
Cannot be quantified	From first to last (eg winner, runner-up, etc)	Zero (0) is a value (eg 0 °C)	Has an absolute zero (zero means the variable or phenomenon is absent)
Cannot be used for statistical calculations other than percentage	Distance between intervals is not equal and not measurable	Can include values below zero (eg −10 °C)	Ratio variables never fall below zero
Categories are exhaustive and mutually exclusive	Cannot be used in statistical calculations	Can be used in statistical calculations	Can be used in statistical calculations

Figure 12.3 Types of scales, from lowest to highest level of measurement

---

Using the table above, state on what level of measurement the following examples are:

1. TV news items containing political topics and TV news items that do not contain political topics.

2. Children ranked on aggressiveness while watching television.

3. Preference of political parties in order of preference.

4. Ranking speeches made by three politicians.

5. You give your respondents photographs of 10 people and ask them to arrange them in terms of physical attractiveness from top to bottom, top being most attractive and bottom being least attractive.

6. The duration of advertisements in YouTube videos in seconds.

7. Readers of newspapers compared to non-readers of newspapers.

8. Top five online games.

9. Nudity in magazine advertisements.

10. A quantitative content analysis of a chairperson's interaction during an important trade-union meeting. The purpose is to determine how often the chairperson uses a certain phrase.

The Likert scale

The Likert scale, named after Renis Likert (1903–1981), is one of the most widely used approaches to scaling responses in survey research. This type of scale requires respondents to indicate their degree of agreement or disagreement with a variety of statements related to an attitude or object. Likert scales are also known as summated scales, as the responses to individual items are added to create a total score for the respondent that usually indicates how positive or negative the respondent feels towards a particular issue. The scale is most often composed of two parts, namely the item (which is likely to be a statement) and the evaluation (whether the respondent agrees or disagrees with the statement, and to what extent). The evaluation part usually consists of a five- or seven-point scale. For example, if you wanted to measure respondents' attitudes towards smoking in public, one of the items could be:

(Item) *Smoking in public puts the health of non-smokers at risk* (negative item)
(Evaluation: a five-point scale)

1	2	3	4	5
Strongly Agree	Agree	Undecided	Disagree	Strongly Disagree

An important assumption when using this scale is that each item measures some aspect of a single common construct, such as 'attitudes towards smoking in public'. Moreover, it is important to remember to reverse the scoring for positive and negative items. If you look at the item in the example, you will see that it is a negative item. If you then include a positive item about smoking in public, you need to reverse the scoring. For example:

(Item) *Smoking in public places such as clubs contributes to the ambiance of such places* (positive item)

5	4	3	2	1
Strongly Agree	Agree	Undecided	Disagree	Strongly Disagree

The semantic differential scale

The semantic differential scale is also a five- or seven-point rating scale. It uses adjectives that are polar opposites, such as 'hot' and 'cold'. In a similar way to the Likert scale, the scoring of the evaluation changes depending on where the adjective is placed on the scale. Look at the example in Figure 12.4.

The visual design of Company X's website is:

Amateurish	□1 □2 □3 □4 □5 □6 □7	Professional
Ineffective	□1 □2 □3 □4 □5 □6 □7	Effective
Interesting	□7 □6 □5 □4 □3 □2 □1	Dull
Cluttered	□1 □2 □3 □4 □5 □6 □7	Simple
Balanced	□7 □6 □5 □4 □3 □2 □1	Unbalanced
Clear	□7 □6 □5 □4 □3 □2 □1	Confusing

Figure 12.4 An example of a semantic differential scale

The semantic differential scale measures the meaning and connotations we ascribe to verbal and non-verbal symbols. The scoring is also reversed for positive and negative items, as indicated in Figure 12.4.

Advantages and disadvantages

One of the major advantages of using a survey is that you can collect a lot of data from an individual respondent at any time. Surveys are also versatile and can be conducted in almost any setting. A survey that involves a self-administered questionnaire also has some additional advantages:

- It is relatively inexpensive.
- It is less time-consuming than most other data collection methods.
- The questionnaire can be filled in anonymously, which tends to encourage candid responses to sensitive issues.
- A large amount of data can be collected, and the data can be standardised.

However, in order to conduct successful surveys, the researcher needs to have an extensive understanding of the nature of the errors that may occur during the process of collecting and interpreting surveys. Another disadvantage of surveys is that they tend to be artificial and, potentially, superficial.

Experimental designs

The basic intent of an experiment is to test the effect of an *intervention* on an *outcome*. In the process, the researcher also tries to control other factors which might influence the result. In experimental research (also known as true experiments or randomised experiments), researchers *randomly* assign individuals to experimental and control groups, as one form of control. The experimental group is subjected to an intervention, and the control group is not. The researcher then looks for differences between the two groups. It is assumed that any differences observed in the two groups after the experiment will be the result of the intervention — also known as the *treatment effect*. Since the two groups were randomly assigned, it is assumed that had any member of the control group been selected for the intervention, that member would also have shown the intervention effect that was displayed by the experimental group.

For example, if you want to test whether involving students in more class activities (intervention) improves their overall academic results (outcome), you can randomly assign students to a control group and an experimental group. The experimental group will then be exposed to the intervention (class activities), while the control group will not be exposed to the intervention. At the end of the experiment you will be able to compare the overall academic results of the control group (who did not do the activities in class) to that of the experimental group (who did the activities). You can, for example, do a t-test to determine whether the academic results of the experimental group were significantly higher than the results of the control group, and if you then find a significant difference, you can attribute it to the intervention. You may ask the question, *What about intervening variables such as students' IQs or the amount of time they spend studying?* You would be right to ask the question; however, because students were *randomly* assigned to both the experimental and control groups, these kinds of variables are likely to balance out, so we can be relatively confident that any change is due to the intervention.

Experiments, then, usually involve manipulating a certain condition or set of conditions. This condition or set of conditions is referred to as the *independent variable*. Once the experiment has been conducted, the researcher measures the effect that the change to the independent variable (for example, class activities) has had on certain outcomes, called the *dependent variables* (for example, academic results). It is assumed that the manipulation of the independent variable caused the change in the dependent variable (also see Chapter 6 for an explanation of independent and dependent variables). There are several different experimental designs. They differ in terms of how they are administered. We discuss only a few of them in the sections that follow. You can read up on experimental designs if you would like to know more about the different types.

Elements of experimental designs

The most conventional type of experiment involves three major pairs of components, namely:
1. the independent and dependent variables;
2. pre-testing and post-testing; and
3. the experimental and control groups.

The visual representation of research designs also follows certain conventions. Each symbol represents an aspect of the experimental process.

A classical experiment would be represented as follows:

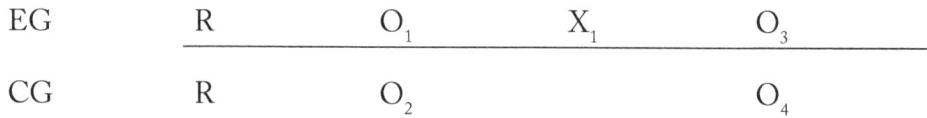

EG	R	O_1	X_1	O_3
CG	R	O_2		O_4

Table 12.4 The meanings of symbols used in experimental designs

Symbol	Meaning
EG	Experimental group
CG	Control group
R	Respondents or test units were *randomly* assigned to either the EG or the CG.
O_1, O_2, O_3, O_4	Observations 1, 2, 3 and 4
X_1	Intervention 1 (independent variable)
Everything left of X	Pre-test
Everything right of X	Post-test

We can explain the various elements as follows:
- The *experimental group* (EG) indicates the respondents or test units that will be exposed to the intervention or independent variable (class activities). Multiple EGs may exist in one experiment and should be indicated as per the same method outlines for Os (observations) and Xs (interventions/ independent variables).
- The *control group* (CG) indicates a control group of respondents or test units that will not be exposed to the intervention or independent variable (X). Multiple CGs may also exist and should be indicated as per the same method outlines for Os (observations) and Xs (interventions/independent variables).
- *Random assignment* (R) indicates that all respondents or test units were randomly assigned to either the experimental group (EG) or the control group (CG). Randomisation is useful because it contributes to experimental validity thanks to increased control over extraneous or intervening variables, as was explained earlier.
- The *independent variable* (X_1) indicates the intervention that the researcher introduced (eg class activities). Essentially, experiments examine the effect

of an independent variable (eg class activities) on a dependent one (academic performance). The independent variable takes the form of an intervention, which is either present (EG) or absent (CG). In such an experiment the researcher then compares what happens if the intervention is present to what happens when it is not present.

- *Pre-testing and post-testing*: Respondents, or test units, are measured in terms of a dependent variable in the pre-test (observation 1, or O_1), exposed to an intervention representing an independent variable (X_1), and then measured again in terms of the effect the independent variable had on the dependent variable in a post-testing (observation 3, or O_3). Any difference between the first (O_1) and last (O_3) measurements on the dependent variable is then attributed to the independent variable (X_1). In the example provided earlier, X_1 would thus have been exposure to class activities.

Also note the following:

- Xs and Os in a given row are applied to the same specific persons, group or test unit.
- Xs and Os in the same column, or placed vertically relative to each other, take place at the same time.
- The left-to-right dimension indicates a time sequence in terms of the procedures in the experiment. Thus, the pre-test takes place first, then there is an intervention, and then the post-test is conducted.

EG	R	O_1 Pre-test	X_1 Intervention	O_3 Post-test
CG	R	O_2		O_4

- Everything above the solid line is associated with the EG and everything below the solid line is associated with the CG. If the horizontal line separating the parallel rows is a dashed line, and the symbol R is not included, it indicates that the respondents were not allocated randomly.

Quasi-experimental and true experimental designs

Experimental designs are often used to test causal or correlational hypotheses. For example, we want to know if an intervention, such as more activities in class, causes better academic results. Determining the cause of something is often difficult, so several researchers opt for correlational studies instead. In these types of studies you can indicate, for example, if an increase in class activities correlates with better academic results.

Broadly speaking there are two types of experimental designs, namely quasi-experimental and true experimental designs.

Quasi-experimental designs

The word *quasi* comes from Latin and means 'as if', or pseudo, which means 'false'. Quasi therefore refers to something that is almost the same as something else but missing some of its features. In the case of experiments, quasi-experimental designs are similar to true experimental designs, but they lack certain important qualities. They are experiments where the respondents are not randomly assigned to the experimental and control groups. Instead, the similarity of the two groups is based on other variables which can be predetermined. These designs are also referred to as correlational research designs. Three popular quasi-experimental designs are propensity score matching (PSM), regression discontinuity (RD) and difference in differences (DID):

1. *Propensity score matching* would match two groups for characteristics that are arguably the same. For instance, the researcher may use an income bracket, the size of a business or level of education as a variable. The researcher would then select from that target population a group of people who meet certain criteria and compare the two populations. For instance, one could compare middle-class schoolchildren who grew up with dogs in the house to those who grew up without dogs and see if there is a difference in their propensity for hay fever.

2. *Regression discontinuity* involves comparing the instances above or below a certain threshold. Typical of this type of research would be comparisons of the university pass rate of people who graduated with very high marks at school and the pass rate of those who graduated with lower marks.

3. *Difference in differences* is probably the most commonly used quasi-experimental design and is often used in cases where randomisation is either not feasible or unethical. In this design, it is not the difference between the pre-test and the post-test of two groups that is being compared, but the size of the difference between the two groups. This is done through a four-step process. The first step is to determine the score of both groups before the intervention. This is called the *baseline*. Then the score of both groups after the intervention is determined. This is called the *end-line*. The next step is to determine the difference between the end-line and baseline scores of both groups. The difference between the two is then compared and the result will be the difference in difference. For example, researchers could compare the long-term health effects of people who were inoculated against the coronavirus against people who opted not to get inoculated against the virus.

The biggest advantage of correlational designs is that they are relatively easy to conduct. The disadvantage is that, although they describe the correlation, they are usually silent on the cause of the correlation. Unlike true experimental designs, where the cause can actually be demonstrated, quasi-experimental designs can only indicate the possibility of cause. The cause is often likely to be looked for in non-experimental research.

True experimental designs

You can have more confidence in the results obtained from a true experimental design than in those obtained from a quasi-experimental design. The reason for this is the degree of control that is incorporated in its implementation. In true experimental designs the variables are carefully isolated from others, so that you can be sure that it is indeed the independent variable that you are testing which is causing the effect, and nothing else. These designs therefore have very high internal validity. Table 12.5 summarises the different factors that can have an influence on internal validity.

Table 12.5 Factors that influence internal validity

Threat to internal validity	Example
History: Specific events can take place between the pre-test and the post-test that could influence the results.	In a pre-test the members of an experimental group are given a test on their perceptions of the crime rate in South Africa. They are then exposed to news programmes for a week and tested again in a post-test to see if the news content changed their perceptions of the crime rate in South Africa. However, between the pre-test and post-test, some members of the experimental group are involved in an armed robbery, which is likely to now interfere with their perceptions of the crime rate in South Africa.
Maturation: Changes take place in individuals over time.	You want to test whether a subliminal advertisement will encourage respondents to buy a particular soft drink. However, after watching a two-hour movie, most of the respondents will be thirsty and will buy something to drink because of their thirst and not necessarily because of the subliminal advertising.

→

Threat to internal validity	Example
Testing: Sometimes the pre-test can have an effect on the post-test.	You want to see if a short learning programme on mathematics will improve the maths scores of respondents. You give them the test, expose them to the programme, and give them the same test again. The fact that they have already done the test could now influence their results and cause them to do better in the test, regardless of the intervention.
Instrumentation: This refers to a situation when the measurement instrument is not actually measuring the construct it is supposed to be measuring.	A common critique against IQ tests is that they do not actually measure all the dimensions that make up a person's level of intelligence.
Statistical regression: When you choose a group based on extreme results, regression to the mean (average) is very common.	If you include all the students who failed the first test in your experimental group, and you expose them to an intervention to see if it will improve their test results, your results could be problematic. There is a chance that the students who failed the test will work much harder for the second test and are likely to do better even without an intervention.
Selection bias: The members of the control group and experimental group must be compatible.	If you want to do an experiment on how a particular intervention can change perceptions of gender inequality, you cannot include only males in your experimental group and only females in your control group — the two groups would be incompatible. Both groups need to include both genders.
Selection maturation interaction: Similar to selection bias, this is where your experimental and control groups are incompatible because of maturation.	You cannot use first-year students in your experimental group and third-year students in your control group in a study on self-esteem. First-year and third-year students are not compatible in terms of their level of maturity and self-esteem, which generally improves from first to third year.

→

Threat to internal validity	Example
Experimental mortality: This is when you lose some of your respondents between the pre- and post-test. The groups are thus no longer the same as the original groups. You could lose some of the unique characteristics of the respondents who dropped out.	You want to test if a new nasal spray alleviates the symptoms of sinusitis. If some control group members who have severe sinusitis drop out of the experiment, it will skew your results. It will likely look like the nasal spray is working better than what is actually the case.

The *pre-test/post-test control group design* is one of the most common experimental designs used by researchers. The design looks like this:

$$EG \qquad R \qquad O_1 \qquad X_1 \qquad O_3$$

$$CG \qquad R \qquad O_2 \qquad \qquad O_4$$

What this means is that two groups were selected randomly (R) and were tested at the same time before and after the experimental group was exposed to the intervention (X). One of the major problems with this design is that the pre-test can have an influence on the final outcome. One way in which the researcher can control for the influence of the pre-test is by using the *Solomon four group design*, which looks like this:

$$EG_1 \qquad R \qquad O_1 \qquad X_1 \qquad O_3$$

$$CG_1 \qquad R \qquad O_2 \qquad \qquad O_4$$

$$EG_2 \qquad R \qquad \qquad X_1 \qquad O_5$$

$$CG_2 \qquad R \qquad \qquad \qquad O_6$$

The Solomon four group design is a 2×2 factorial design that is used to measure the effect of the pre-test on the outcome. This design involves the random assignment of respondents to four groups. The first experimental and control groups (EG_1 and CG_1) take the pre-test, while the second experimental and control groups (EG_2 and CG_2) do not. However, all four groups take the post-test. The groups who were exposed to the pre-test are then compared to the groups who were not, to determine if the pre-test had an effect on the outcome. In this design, the following observations are compared, via a t-test:

- O_1 with O_3
- O_3 with O_4
- O_5 with O_6
- O_3 with O_5

A t-test is used to determine whether there is a significant difference between the outcomes of the experimental and control groups, but also whether there is a significant difference between the outcomes of the groups who have and have not been exposed to the pre-test. If the difference in outcome between the experimental groups (who were exposed to the intervention) and the control groups (who were not) is significant, the assumption that the intervention (X_1) caused the effect is reinforced. This method also allows you to investigate the interactive effects of the pre-testing on your results. However, you will work with the post-test results; the pre-test results are used only for control.

One can also test the simultaneous effect of more than one independent variable upon a dependent variable. You could, for example, test the effects of noise and temperature on people's productivity. These are called factorial designs. Similarly, you can test multiple levels of the same independent variable(s) in one experiment, for example the influence of high and low levels of noise on productivity. Finally, there are instances when researchers can do experiments outside of controlled settings, often in the course of normal events. These experiments are known as natural experiments. Our example of children who grew up with or without dogs is an example of a natural experiment.

Advantages and disadvantages

The advantages of experimental designs are that the experimenter can attempt to eliminate, or control for, all unwanted, extraneous variables. Since the experimental design involves the manipulation of the independent variable and the observation of its effect upon the dependent variable, it is possible to determine causal relationships. Since experiments are conducted in strictly controlled environments, they can be repeated again and again, and the results can be compared. This increases the reliability of the research, which results in greater confidence in the results.

A major disadvantage of experimental research is that it is not always possible to eliminate extraneous variables. Sometimes, even the fact that an experiment is being conducted can lead to a distortion of the results. (Read more about the Hawthorne studies, for example.) Moreover, not all experiments can be directly related back to the real world; experimental research's greatest weakness therefore lies in its artificiality. People do not live in laboratories under controlled circumstances, so what happens in the lab is not always the way things work in reality. It may also be unethical to assign people to groups on a random basis. In education, for instance, if we were to compare two teaching methodologies and it can be shown that one method is much better than the other, then those learners who were subjected to the weaker method have been disadvantaged in relation to their peers.

Content analysis

Content analysis is a data collection technique as well as a data analysis technique. It helps us to understand information as symbolic phenomena. It is used to investigate symbolic content such as words that appear in, for example, newspaper articles, comments on a blog, political speeches, and so on. Content analysis, then, is a quantitative technique in which the researcher attempts to describe the denotative meaning of content in an objective way. There are two levels of meaning, namely denotative and connotative meaning (see Chapter 9). The denotative meaning of a word refers to the literal meaning you will find in the dictionary when you look up that word. This meaning is free from any form of interpretation. The connotative meaning of a word refers to the connotation we ascribe to a particular word, based on the feeling or idea the word evokes in us, which is often based on our experiences. For example, the denotative meaning of the word 'Rottweiler' is 'a medium- to large-sized breed of domestic dog'. However, depending on your experiences with Rottweilers, for you the connotative meaning of 'Rottweiler' could be 'a vicious, scary dog' or 'a confident, fearless, courageous dog', among many others. As was already mentioned, in content analysis we only work with the denotative meaning of words to make valid and reliable assumptions of data within context. When conducting a quantitative content analysis, you can only work with what is reported and you are not allowed to make any assumptions about the author's intended meaning. Because this is a retrospective data collection and analysis technique, a major advantage is that the researcher can make certain observations about a communicator, such as a politician, without influencing the communicator. Yet, because of the symbolic nature of words, we have to be context specific in our analysis, since the meaning of words changes depending on the context. We can also only make context-specific assumptions when we do a content analysis.

In most data collection methods that involve collecting data from humans, data collection is deliberate, and the respondents are aware of the fact that the researcher is collecting data from them. When people are aware of the fact that information is being collected from them, they often give distorted responses, or what they believe are desired responses. In content analysis, however, the researcher has no control over the situation in which a response is given, and the sender of the message is also unaware that the message will be analysed.

Moreover, the researcher does not run the risk of collecting information that then becomes invalid because the data was not correctly gathered. With content analysis, data does not have to be gathered in a structured way. A major advantage of content analysis is that it allows you to collect and analyse large amounts of data because you can use more than one researcher to analyse the data, as long as you can establish high inter-coder reliability. Inter-coder reliability is the extent to which two or more independent coders evaluate a message and come to the same conclusion. Inter-coder reliability is imperative in quantitative content analysis because we are supposed to work with only the exact denotative meanings of words. Neuendorf (2002:141) states that '[g]iven that a goal of content analysis is to identify and record relatively objective (or at least inter-subjective) characteristics of messages, reliability is paramount. Without the establishment of reliability, content analysis measures are useless'. Inter-coder reliability not only makes coding more efficient but it also helps to dismiss sceptical reviewers and critics. It is also for this reason that you must report inter-coder reliability carefully, clearly and in a detailed manner in your research report.

Quantification of the data

Since content analysis is considered a quantitative technique, you must be able to express the results numerically. Quantification is a prerequisite for those who see content analysis as a scientific method. Some researchers feel that there is no purpose in content analysis unless the results are measurable; in other words, unless it can be quantified. Proponents of quantitative research are also of the opinion that quantitative methods describe the quality of communication better. Thus, researchers who employ quantitative research use frequency to determine, for example, how often certain concepts and themes are used. These researchers further believe that if we use statistical methods, it helps us to make more precise interpretations; therefore, the quality of our interpretations increases. However, to restrict content analysis to quantitative methods can lead to certain problems. For this reason, textual analysis (a qualitative version of content analysis) is used to analyse the connotative meaning of communication, since the denotative meaning of messages does not always provide insight into the intentions of communicators.

A research design for content analysis

Similar to other research, content analysis follows a particular design. However, in this case the design needs to be appropriate for the context of the data; it must therefore be sensitive to the context. This design is also used to answer a research question and to test hypotheses related to the research question. The researcher also needs to select an appropriate sample (for example, a selection of political speeches made by Julius Malema). Once the data has been collected, the researcher codes the data according to objective rules. The researcher will then get numerical values for the codes and categories that were identified. Categories are the meaningful groups into which we allocate our units of analysis. They form the conceptual framework of the study and give an indication of the important variables that are connected to the research question. Formulating and defining categories are some of the central problems of a content analysis design, yet they are the most important part of content analysis. The categories must be a reflection of the goal of your research, which means that you must specify all the variables with which you are working. You must also specify why certain data falls into a certain category. Thus, operational definitions of your categories are crucial to the success of your content analysis. Moreover, knowledge of the data is important to form valid and reliable categories. In this regard a thorough literature study becomes invaluable. You should select the number of categories based on the context and necessities of the research. Ideally, you should not have too many or too few categories: too many categories may obscure results and too few categories could lead to unreliable and, possibly, invalid conclusions. The final results will then be interpreted in line with and referring back to specific theories and literature.

Criteria for evaluating categories

All the categories must reflect the goal of your research and must assist you in answering the research question and testing your hypotheses. All categories must fulfil the following criteria:

- *Mutually exclusive:* Each unit of analysis should fit into only one category. If your data falls into more than one category, you need to restructure or redefine your categories. It is for this reason that your operational definitions must be clear and specific. Have a look at Figure 12.5 to get an idea of what we mean by categories being mutually exclusive.
- *Exhaustive:* All your data should fit into a category. You can include a 'diverse' category to cover all possibilities. For example, if you take a pack of cards, and you sort the cards according to their suits, there should be no cards left when you are done. Thus, the categories are exhaustive because each card fits into a category (see Figure 12.6).
- *Equivalent:* Each category must carry equal weight; thus, no category is more important than another. In the case of playing cards, all the suits are equally important.

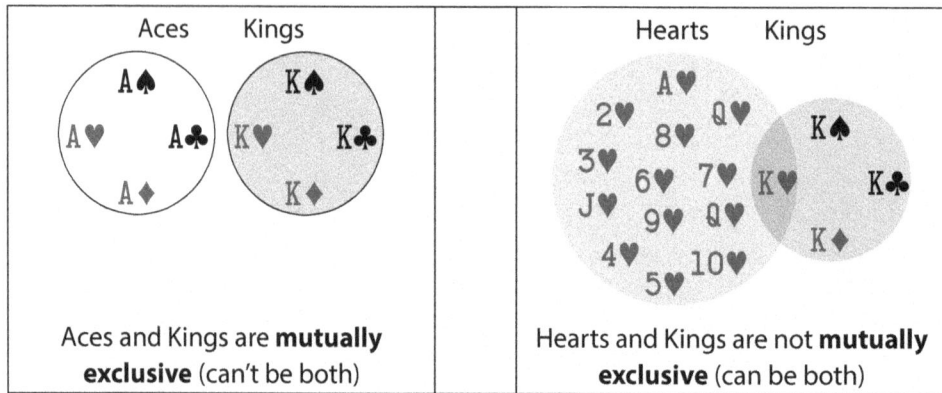

Figure 12.5 Mutually exclusive versus not mutually exclusive categories

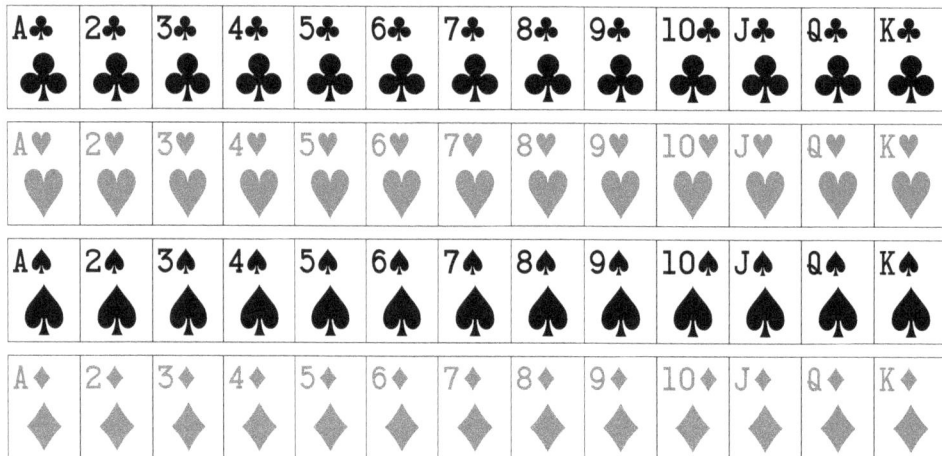

Figure 12.6 An example of exhaustive categories

Steps in content analysis

If you want to do a content analysis of the political speeches of Julius Malema, for example, you will first need to get hold of his speeches. If these speeches are only available in audio format, you will need to transcribe the speeches. When you transcribe something, you put it into written or typed words. Once you have transcribed a sample of Julius Malema's speeches that you would like to analyse, you can follow these steps:

1. Read through the text several times and make brief notes in the margin when you come across interesting or relevant information.
2. Go through the notes made in the margins and list the different types of themes that emerge — what are the things that reoccur in his speeches or to which he refers in all his speeches?

3. Read through the list and categorise each item in a way that describes what it is about. These are your operational definitions.

4. Use your operational definitions to code your data and place the information in a particular category. If you are using additional coders, you will need to train your coders and do an inter-coder reliability test to ensure that the coding is reliable.

5. Once you have all your categories, identify whether the categories can be linked in any way or grouped together. Determine whether each major category consists of other minor categories. Also remember to check whether your categories are mutually exclusive.

6. If you are working with more than one transcript (in this case speeches), repeat the first few steps again for each transcript.

7. When you have done the above with all the transcripts, collect all the categories. Examine each category in detail and consider its relevance. Thus, ask yourself if it will help you to answer your research question or to test your hypotheses.

8. Check to make sure that you have captured all the relevant data from the transcripts and coded it to fit into one of your categories.

9. Depending on what you wish to achieve through your content analysis, you can now apply an appropriate statistical test to analyse your data.

The process of content analysis is lengthy and may require the researcher to go over and over the data to ensure that he or she has been thorough. Today, content analysis is used more as a method of analysis than a data collection method. It has come to encompass all sorts of approaches to studying content — even the responses to open-ended questions in questionnaires. However, all these approaches are reliant on a coding scheme based on a set of coding categories that the coder applies with the goal of quantifying the frequency of occurrences of coding categories. Moreover, the validity of your findings is likely to increase if you combine quantitative content analysis with qualitative textual analysis.

Summary

In this chapter you were introduced to three of the most prominent quantitative data collection methods, namely surveys, experimental designs, and content analysis.

One of the key considerations for the use of surveys is time. Surveys that are conducted over a period of time are referred to as longitudinal surveys, whereas surveys that collect data only at one point in time are referred to as cross-sectional studies. There are several kinds of surveys, such as mail surveys, telephone surveys, personal structured interviews and group administered surveys. The precise formulation of questions in surveys is imperative and, therefore, researchers should familiarise themselves with the different types of questions that can be used and also the many problems that can arise when wording questions. Measurement scales are frequently incorporated into questionnaires, but they can also be used in quantitative studies as a stand-alone methodology. Researchers should develop a clear understanding of the general properties of scales and the types of scales which may be applied for different purposes.

Experimental designs are used to test the effect of an intervention on an outcome by, essentially, comparing a group that is exposed to an intervention to a group that is not.

Content analysis as a quantitative data collection technique is used to describe the denotative meaning of content in an objective way. A major advantage of quantitative content analysis is that it enables the researcher to collect and analyse a large amount of data, as more than one coder can be used. In fact, it is desirable to use more than one coder in a content analysis because it increases the validity of a study.

Review the chapter

Answer the questions and complete the tasks to assess whether you understand the content of this chapter:

1. What are some of the advantages and disadvantages of using surveys?
2. Identify the different kinds of surveys and explain the application of each kind.
3. What is the difference between an interval scale and a ratio scale?
4. What is the difference between quasi-experimental and true experimental designs?
5. What is an alternative name for 'the independent variable'?
6. What are the threats to internal validity in an experimental design? Provide an example of each to illustrate your answer.
7. What criteria will you use to evaluate the categories of a content analysis?

CHAPTER 13

Qualitative research designs and data collection

Rose-Marié Bezuidenhout and Annemi Strydom

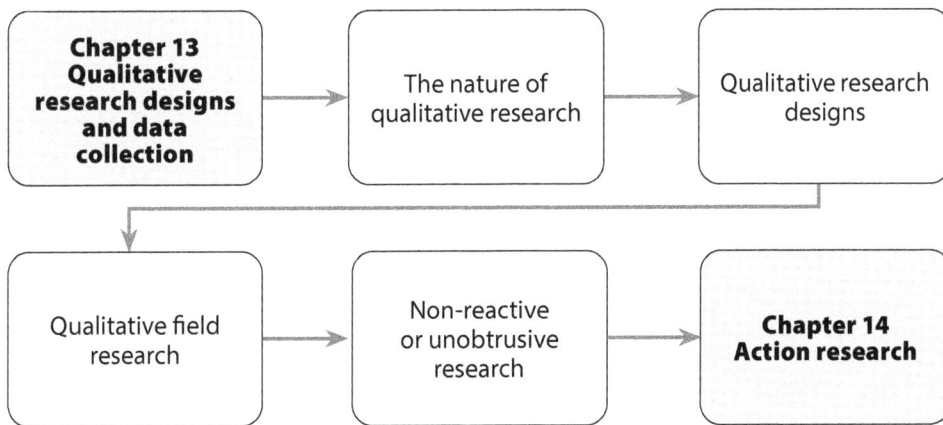

Overview

Qualitative researchers explore the underlying qualities of subjective experiences and the meanings associated with phenomena. As qualitative researchers, we assume that it is difficult — if not impossible — to measure and quantify these subjective experiences and meanings. Therefore, quantifiable measurements are not appropriate for researching the lived experiences and experiential meanings of individuals, small groups and communities. The qualitative research process includes a research design, data collection, analysis and interpretation methods, and culminates in the representation and presentation of findings in the form of a capstone report, publication or thesis. The components of a research design are discussed in various other chapters in more detail (for example, sampling methods in Chapter 11). In this chapter we focus on some design perspectives, including phenomenology, ethnography and others, and the choice of data collection methods used within these design perspectives. By using qualitative data collection methods, the researcher finds deepness in rich data gathered from complex and multi-faceted phenomena in specific social contexts. The aim of this chapter is thus to describe the nature of qualitative research and guide you in selecting a design perspective or approach and data collection methods when you conduct a research study. It is impossible to discuss the full spectrum of qualitative designs and data collection methods in one chapter. We provide a summary of the major research design perspectives and then explore some data collection methods used within these designs. We use two overarching approaches or categories to group the data collection methods, namely field research and non-reactive or unobtrusive research.

Objectives of this chapter

By the end of this chapter, you should be able to demonstrate your understanding of the following:
- the nature of qualitative research;
- qualitative design perspectives;
- phenomenology;
- narratology;
- ethnographic research;
- grounded theory research;
- case study research;
- field research;
- participant-observation in field research;
- data collection: focus groups;
- data collection: in-depth interviews;
- non-reactive or unobtrusive research;
- comparative and historical research;
- qualitative content analysis; and
- comparative and historical research.

The nature of qualitative research

Qualitative researchers often refer to a 'whole-world experience' because they are interested in the depth of human experience, including all the subjective peculiarities that are characteristic of individual experiences and meanings associated with a phenomenon. For example, knowing how many people viewed a particular movie is not the goal of a qualitative study; instead, we want to explore how a participant experiences, perceives, and attaches meaning to the content of the movie. We are thus interested in people's 'voices' and how they make sense of and give meaning to their life worlds and constructed realities. As qualitative researchers we need to keep in mind that when selecting a research design and methodology, our ultimate aims are to explore and understand and not to measure, quantify, predict and generalise, as quantitative researchers do. Yin (2016:9) explains five distinctive features of qualitative research as:

- the study of the meaning of participants' authentic experiences under 'real world' conditions as opposed to the restrictive and controlled environment of a laboratory or the intrusiveness of artificial research protocols;
- representing the perceptions and values of the participants and not the predefined notions and values of the researcher;
- containing the social, institutional, cultural and environmental conditions within which participants' lives are rooted;
- explaining social behaviour through the application of current and emerging theoretical constructs; and
- collecting, integrating and presenting multiple sources of information and thus triangulating data collection methods such as interviews, field observations and social artefacts to 'create converging lines of inquiry' in exploring complex social experiences and contexts (Yin, 2016:11).

Qualitative researchers systematically analyse everyday actions to provide a better or deeper understanding not only of others but also of the researcher him- or herself (Tracy, 2020). Three fundamental concepts of qualitative research are identified by Tracy (2020) as self-reflexivity, context, and thick description, explained below.

Self-reflexivity refers to how researchers need to consider and acknowledge that their frames of reference and experiences may influence their interactions with participants. Their interpretation of these interactions and contexts, and the resultant data gathered and interpreted, may be subjective and biased. Qualitative researchers must thus be aware of their ontological and epistemological positions within the research framework and design. For example, as researcher, you need to self-examine your possible prejudice towards participants and their sometimes thoughtless and spontaneous remarks and reactions during an interview. The interview in this example is the *context* within which the interactions take place, but context also relates to other circumstances within which data is collected. The qualitative researcher should actively and purposefully take note of both significant and seemingly insignificant cues during the process to make sense of the contextual environment while being immersed in the interview process. 'Immersiveness' and active involvement are unavoidable and even desirable during a qualitative research process. It allows the researcher to provide *thick descriptions* or detailed accounts of the process, participants' contributions, the context and the researcher's self-reflection. The researcher does not try to control the environment or context, does not infer any causation or generalise findings, as would be the case in a quantitative study. Rather, researchers interpret participants' subjective meanings, perceptions, views and opinions by providing thick descriptions of individual and peculiar lived experiences within socio-historical contexts (Leavy, 2017).

We explain various qualitative design *perspectives* that emphasise these distinctive features in the following section of the chapter.

Qualitative research designs

A research design is the complete plan that you choose for the integration of the different components or elements of a research study. It is a map used to address the research problem and answer the research question flowing from the problem and it guides the collection, analysis and interpretation of data.

Since research is a continuous and cumulative process, the decisions and choices you made in the previous steps of the process determine what your choices of design and data collection methods could be. For example, it is crucial that your data collection method allows you to achieve the desired outcomes of your study, as anticipated in the research problem, goal and question that you have formulated. Equally, your choice of data collection, analysis and interpretation methods determines what findings you will eventually report on and present. This alignment is referred to as *design and methodological coherence*.

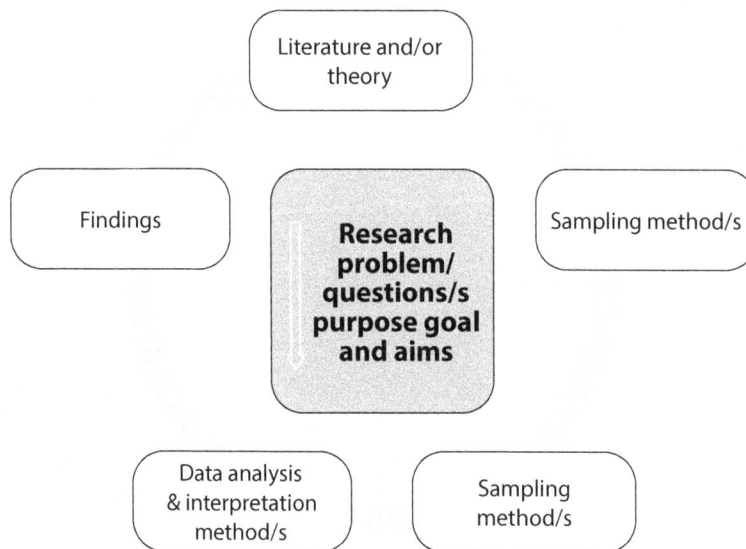

Figure 13.1 Elements of a research design based on the pivotal research problem and nested in a paradigm, reflecting design and methodological coherence

Design and methodological coherence occur when the researcher demonstrates the alignment of, for example, research problems and questions and data collection and analysis methods within a specific paradigm. The concepts of design and methodological coherence thus relate to the congruent and consistent arrangement of the research purpose, goals, question and methods within a specified perspective embedded in a paradigm or tradition (Pouchera, Tamminen, Caron & Sweet, 2020). Maintaining research design and methodological coherence in any study is essential and is comparable to the golden thread that needs to run through a study, as mentioned in Chapter 4. Coherence confirms the soundness and overall trustworthiness of a research study (see Chapter 17).

The qualitative researcher mostly works within an interpretivist or constructivist paradigm or tradition. The interpretivist or constructivist worldviews include a range of perspectives, also referred to as approaches and theoretical schools of thought. The most widely applied perspectives in qualitative research are summarised matched with different data collection methods in Table 13.1. These perspectives are then briefly explained in the sections that follow.

Table 13.1 Qualitative design perspectives

Qualitative design perspectives	Description	Data collection methods
Phenomenology	Explores everyday phenomena and participants' conscious awareness of their life worlds in the 'real world'. It aims to understand people's perceptions and perspectives of a particular situation.	Field research: interviews, focus groups, field notes and participant observation.
Narratology	Chronicles stories and sequences events. Narrative designs can be either biographical or autobiographical.	Field research: interviews, focus groups, field notes and unobtrusive research.
Ethnography	Explores social phenomena in their 'natural' and cultural environments or contexts for a lengthy period, often several months or several years.	Field research: interviews, focus groups, field notes, participant observation and unobtrusive research.

→

Qualitative design perspectives	Description	Data collection methods
Grounded theory	Creates theory from the dynamic interplay between data collection and analysis.	Field research: interviews, focus groups, field notes and participant observation.
Case study research	Studies a particular individual, programme or event in-depth for a defined period. Examines bounded exemplars and systems. Also referred to as idiographic research (Leedy & Ormrod, 2015). May include a single or multiple cases.	Field research: Interviews, focus groups, field notes, participant observation, and unobtrusive research.

Phenomenology

Phenomenology involves the study of individuals' immediate experiences of, as the term suggests, 'phenomena' and specifically the conscious perceptions and sensations of their life worlds. The School of Phenomenology was established in the early 20th century by Edmund Husserl, a German philosopher. The current application of phenomenology as a research goal emerged from Husserl's phenomenology to explore 'the meaning, composition, and core of the lived experience of specific phenomena' in their totality as opposed to their component parts (Edmonds & Kennedy, 2017:168). Participants share their conscious experience of phenomena and the researcher interprets these concrete and authentic experiences to grasp human experience in the 'real world'. Phenomenology seeks to understand the participant's preconceptions, while the researcher 'brackets out' their own.

Different phenomenological perspectives are summarised briefly in Table 13.2 below. The descriptions are inadequate for a comprehensive understanding of the complexities of all the notions underpinning phenomenology. The summary mainly serves the purpose of illustrating how qualitative research has been imbued with the qualities of phenomenology and its branches.

Table 13.2 Phenomenological perspectives

Phenomenological perspectives		
Perspectives	**Proponents**	**Goals**
Transcendental phenomenology	Edmund Husserl (1859–1938)	It seeks to understand the conscious awareness of the participant's experiences of phenomena without the predefined notions and ideas of the researcher.
Existential phenomenology (ontological phenomenology)	Martin Heidegger (1889–1976) Maurice Merleau-Ponty (1908–1961).	The focus is on the existential or lived experience and not only on the conscious awareness of phenomena. Through a systematic analysis, the research goal is to explore the meaning of lived experience itself.
Hermeneutic phenomenology	Hans Georg Gadamer (1900–2002)	The researcher seeks to interpret descriptions of lived experiences and co-construct meaning.

Narratology

The focus in narratology is on ethical, moral and cultural ambiguities. For example, in feminism the lives from the narrator's perspectives and experiences are emphasised. A subtle understanding of their life situation is obtained through an analysis of their 'stories'. A narrative analysis includes scripts and frames which uncover the complexities and contradictions in specific contexts such as organisations (Gray, 2014). Edmonds and Kennedy (2017) explain that a narrative design explores a single participant or a small sample of participants by gathering data through stories, retelling the stories (restorying) and reviewing the story with participants to confirm the meaning and interpretation of narratives.

Ethnography

Ethnography, or ethnographic research, is a field research approach which involves the description of a particular culture that a researcher is interested in exploring. It allows the researcher to gain a better understanding — directly from the people involved — of the way of life of a particular cultural group or subculture. It thus involves studying a topic from a participant's frame of reference. The decision to conduct ethnographic research should be contemplated very carefully, since it is expensive and time-consuming, and gaining prolonged access to a research site may be difficult.

There are several types of ethnographic research, including among others, anthropological ethnography, audience ethnography, street ethnography, autoethnography, virtual ethnography and institutional ethnography.

Anthropological ethnography entails the researcher spending lengthy periods of time, sometimes years, immersed in foreign or unknown cultures and subcultures. The researcher obtains an insider's view of the cultural customs, rituals and interactions of group members. Field notes, journals and interviews, among others, are used to record and report on the researcher's observations and participation in the cultural groups.

Audience ethnography is used when researchers want to explore how audiences make sense of and derive pleasure from their interaction with their favourite television and/or radio programmes and within the context of everyday life. The researcher spends relatively short periods of time in the company of media users. For example, you spend a few weeks in the company of a family to study their television viewing or streaming behaviour.

Street ethnography is focused on a particular setting with people who, by choice or due to circumstances, spend most of their time on the streets of large cities or live on the fringes of these cities. For example, the homeless, street gangs, prostitutes and runaway or abandoned children fall into street cultures. These people may have developed a culture alien to that of the mainstream culture. Street ethnography is also conducted in bars, shopping centres, clubs or hostels. Street ethnography is often problematic since involvement with certain street populations may present a physical danger to the researcher. It is also often difficult to gain entry and earn the trust of street group members. People are often suspicious if you tell them that you are a researcher. Some researchers conceal their identities and become members of the groups. By doing this, the researcher learns details about rituals and other practices that are kept secret from outsiders. An advantage is that the researcher can penetrate the social context of participants, which provides a great deal of insight. However, the researcher's own biases and values can be a limitation.

Autoethnography is an ethnographical and autobiographical study about the cultural connection between an individual researcher and others in a specific social context. It focuses on the relationship between self (the researcher as participant) and others. The primary data consist of the autobiographic observations of the researcher about her or himself in a particular social setting. 'Autoethnographic stories are artistic and analytic demonstrations of how we come to know, name, and interpret personal and cultural experience' (Adams, Jones & Ellis, 2015:2). An example of an autoethnographic study is a researcher examining and describing her or his own experiences as a political refugee in a foreign country.

Virtual ethnography is conducted when a researcher uses ethnographic techniques to gain an understanding of people's behaviour in cyberspace (Babbie, 2021). Essentially, the researcher observes and participates in, for example, a blog discussion on a particular topic and hence gains a deep understanding of the cybergroup's interactions. For example, the massively multiplayer online role-playing game (MMORPG) *World of Warcraft* has a feature called a 'whisper' (also called a 'tell'), which only gamers can use to communicate with each other during game playing (ZAM, 2013). A researcher may subscribe to and start playing the game — and hence participate in the interactions or whispers — and observe the content of the statements made in the whispers. In doing so the researcher gains a deeper understanding of the virtual gaming culture. The researcher thus becomes immersed in the virtual cyberculture and can report on the gamers and their typical activities.

Institutional ethnography was developed in the late 1970s from a critical feminist perspective by Dorothy Smith. It was extended to be applied as a frame of inquiry to understand how the workplace is shaping the subjective experiences of people. It focuses mostly on the subjective experiences of oppressed people in institutions. The researcher is particularly interested in 'the personal experiences of individuals but proceeds to uncover the power relations that structure and govern those experiences' (Babbie, 2021:307). Thus, instead of observing the official processes of an institution, the researcher attempts to understand how individuals experience institutions by attempting to understand hidden and possibly oppressive activities. In this way, individual microlevel personal experiences relate to the macrolevel of organisations (Babbie, 2021:307).

Grounded theory

Grounded theory was developed by Glaser and Strauss (1967) as an alternative to positivism. Contrary to other methods where the researcher draws on theory from existing studies through a literature review, in the grounded theory approach, theory is *grounded* in the data that the researcher is collecting. Researchers use a grounded theory approach when theories on a certain topic are scarce and in need of development — thus, when there is a need to create new thoughts and patterns of argumentation on that topic.

You will recall from our discussions on inductive and deductive reasoning (see Chapters 3, 6 and 10) that, when following a deductive approach, the researcher argues from the general to the specific, and when following an inductive approach, from the specific to the general. In grounded theory the researcher uses an inductive process and develops theory from specific data collected in the social setting being explored. Glaser and Strauss (1967) suggest that researchers keep an open mind when pursuing grounded theory as an approach by steering clear of other existing theoretical frameworks.

The theory thus emerges from the data. As such, this type of research is seen as an ongoing process. The more data the researcher collects, the firmer the theory that emerges. Here the researcher is not trying to test a theory; instead, the theory is developed by looking at real-life occurrences. Consequently, the theory and methodologies are shaped as the researcher progresses.

Grounded theory is mostly used to study human behaviour by way of comparative analysis. By comparing groups of people and observing their behaviour and reactions we generate a new theory. The more groups are analysed, the firmer the theory that can be described. A researcher using grounded theory usually collects data through semi-structured interviews, field studies, participant observation and social interaction.

Case study research

A case study is a thick and detailed description of a social phenomenon that exists within a real-world context. The case study recounts a real-life situation by rigorously describing the scenario in which the phenomenon occurs. It is an attempt to understand a phenomenon within specific circumstances. The case study method allows a deep exploration within a natural context and hence provides a full and thorough understanding of the particular and lived experience of a participant.

These characteristics of the case study method facilitate the goal of a qualitative study, namely to focus on the particular and subjective experiential reality of participants. The aim of a case study is to represent the case authentically and, in this process, to discover symbolic realities that amplify 'a contemporary phenomenon (the "case") in depth and within its real-world context, especially when the boundaries between phenomenon and context may not be clearly evident' (Yin, 2018:45).

Researchers developing the case use data collection methods such as interviews and direct observation. The most widely used case study methods are the following:

- An *illustrative*, or *typical*, case study is an attempt to understand what happened in a specific case. It entails a descriptive account of the main characteristics of a typical case example to clarify an idea or reinforce an argument.

- An *exploratory* case study involves a rigorous description of the case within its broader context to understand the nature of the case.
- An *explanatory* case study is an attempt to explain the circumstances and nuances of a specific phenomenon.

In the following section we discuss some of the aspects that researchers need to consider when they decide on conducting field research.

Qualitative field research

Field research has become an increasingly important method. It is suitable when we want to make observations of phenomena in their natural environments. Although field research can also be used to collect quantitative data, it is more qualitative in nature (Babbie, 2021:290). When conducting field research, we assume that the behaviour of the individuals we observe has a purpose and is an expression of deeper feelings and beliefs. We also assume that people can structure, experience and describe their own worlds. In field research we prefer to use the term 'participant' instead of 'respondent' when we refer to the individuals we observe.

In this book we use the term 'field research' in the broadest sense, meaning that a researcher is conducting research in the field or setting of human experience by observing and participating in specific events or circumstances. Typical field research is conducted in various social settings, subcultures and aspects of social life (Neuman, 2014:433). Field research settings are selected according to the researcher's interest and goals and may vary from observing childbirth to deathbed experiences, and all human activity in between these extremes. For example, field researchers watch or observe participants in specific settings or events such as night clubs, music festivals, college campuses, political rallies, and so on. The researcher is often immersed in a particular social setting and, in a way, becomes the research instrument used to obtain information that otherwise would not be readily available.

Field research methods

Field research has a long history. It was first used in anthropology, the study of all aspects of humanity including human cultures and development. It originated from anthropologists in the 19th century exploring documents reporting on foreign cultures and progressed to the development of the technique of participant observation between 1940 and 1960. The University of Chicago's Department of Sociology — known as the Chicago School of Sociology or,

simply, the Chicago School — first developed the technique of participant observation to include three main principles, namely (Neuman, 2014:434–435):
1.   studying people in their natural environment (*in situ*);
2.   repeated interaction with people over time; and
3.   developing theoretical concepts based on an in-depth understanding of the perspectives of people's environment.

By observing people in their natural environment the naturalist approach was developed (Babbie, 2021:300). Today, researchers use the same principles of observation and interaction to construct an understanding of people's perspectives and experiences in their natural environment. We discuss focus groups and in-depth interviews as data collection methods used in field research.

The range of participation in field research

Field research can be classified in terms of the degree to which the researcher participates in the activities of, for example, a group being observed. Babbie (2021:295) argues that some field research involves observation only and no participation at all. Conversely, some field research studies include full participation and observation. Consequently, you find observation only at the one end of the participant observation continuum and full participation at the other end.

Where there is no participation involved, the researcher is merely an onlooker of an activity in a particular setting. If the research is conducted in a public space such as a shopping mall, the researcher may observe the behaviour of a certain group and not get involved in the activity whatsoever. Observing the behaviour of teenagers at a skating rink in a shopping mall from a distance is an example of onlooker observation in field research. The researcher may observe the behaviour over a period of time, for example several weekends, and make field notes about the behaviour of the teenagers. Typical behaviour patterns observed may include the way they dress, greet each other, flirt and interact, whether they form cliques, and so on. However, by merely being an onlooker the researcher will not get a full understanding of the group's activities. To really gain an in-depth understanding of a phenomenon it is often necessary to either participate in the activity or to interview participants.

Field research also varies according to the degree to which the researcher's observation and participation are concealed or hidden from participants. Observation is *covert* when a researcher conceals her or his identity as a researcher, and *overt* when open about observing participants and if they know they are being studied.

The range of participation and degree of concealment can be classified in terms of three broad categories, namely onlooker, partial participation and full participation. Table 13.3 summarises the levels of involvement and the limitations of the three types of researcher involvement.

With full or complete participation, researchers get involved in the daily activities and experiences of a certain group, community or organisation. When you participate, you see, hear and experience events as the participants do. You thus become part of the inner circle of the group. There are several benefits to this level of involvement:

*   Active involvement within a group allows the researcher to experience the same reality as that of the group being studied, which leads to a greater understanding of the phenomena at hand.
*   Actual happenings are understood within the context in which they occur, as opposed to being observed by an onlooker.
*   The more taboo or forbidden behaviours, which group members are more likely to try and conceal, can be observed and reported on.
*   Thanks to active involvement you may also find discrepancies between what the participants say they do and what they actually do.
*   Being involved in the daily lives of participants allows you to observe and report on their actual everyday behaviour. This allows you to reflect on the findings more accurately.

Conducting field research

It is important to plan your research according to the guidelines of the research process and to choose a research setting that is both accessible and applicable to your study. Ensure that the phenomenon that you are exploring occurs with sufficient frequency in the setting you plan to use.

Consider the difficulty involved in gaining research entry into the field. Research entry depends on how public the venue is and on the willingness of the participants to be observed. Public places, such as shopping malls, are easy to gain access to, since people have nothing to conceal. In closed social settings, such as secret societies, entry is restricted because people normally have good reason to keep their identities and activities hidden. In such instances researchers need to get permission from the appropriate members of the group to gain access. If the research is conducted within a closed group or community, researchers need to be open about their research purpose and make it clear to the participants that they are part of a research project.

Table 13.3 Types of researcher involvement

Onlooker	Level of researcher involvement	The researcher has no actual contact with participants and/or the field that is being studied. When you opt for the role of onlooker, you observe a social process without becoming involved in it at all. The status of the researcher remains a secret. Observation is covert and concealed.
	Limitations	You are unable to build meaningful relationships with the community. This means you cannot ask questions when new information is identified. You do not have opportunities for immersing yourself in the community and building relationships with the people, which will also hamper your chances of gaining deeper insights into their feelings and the reasoning behind their actions. Ethical issues of deceit also need to be considered.
Partial participation	Level of researcher involvement	Your participation as a researcher is known and, hence, overt. You do not get too involved — a balance is maintained between being both an insider as well as an outsider when dealing with the group. You are involved, but not immersed in participants' daily lives.
	Limitations	Partial participation allows you a very good opportunity to be involved in the community and experience what they are experiencing, but it also allows you to remain at a distance, making detachment and some degree of objectivity more possible. However, because you only participate partially, you may not be able to immerse yourself sufficiently in all the aspects of the culture, which could undermine the depth of your understanding of a particular culture or subculture.
Full participation	Level of researcher involvement	You are completely or fully integrated within the community that you are studying. Your participation could either be known (overt) or concealed (covert). You become an active member of the group and you fully embrace all the dealings and customs that are part of the daily existence of the group. You experience everything that they do and you participate in all their rituals.
	Limitations	As you become very involved in the population that you are studying, you may lose the objectivity that you are supposed to uphold for the sake of the validity of the findings. This means that, as a researcher, you must be very mindful of not losing perspective.

As the researcher will be actively involved in all the dealings and processes within the group, the participants need to be assured that their identities will be protected — confidentiality therefore needs to be ensured at all times. If the participants feel uncomfortable or unsure about whether their identities and subsequent behaviour will be kept confidential, the information obtained by the researcher may not be a true reflection of the actual situation. The level of trust that the researcher as participant observer can establish within the group being studied will have an influence on the quality as well as the value of the information being collected. If the participants do not trust the researcher enough to be sure that the information they provide will be kept confidential, they are unlikely to volunteer intimate and detailed information — information that may be valuable to the study.

When engaging in participant observation the researcher is also able to form friendships with the participants. Although these friendships may yield valuable information regarding the inner workings of the phenomenon being studied, they may also lead to subjective and biased opinions. It is thus very important that the researcher be aware of any subjective opinions or biases and take care not to allow any preconceived notions or viewpoints to influence the way the research is conducted or the conclusions that are ultimately drawn from participation in the group's activities.

The following steps are important to keep in mind in conducting field research:

1. *Get to know the people that you are studying.* You need to establish a rapport with the community that you are studying. Rapport means establishing a close, harmonious and sympathetic relationship with the participants. Visit the area in advance if possible. You will be able to gain more valuable and appropriate data if you have a good relationship with the people that you are studying. If you are accepted in the community, people will trust you and they will share information with you more readily.

2. *Immerse yourself.* You need to conform to the society that you are studying. As the saying goes: 'When in Rome, do as the Romans do.' You need to establish some sort of connection with the society in which you wish to be immersed. This will give you the opportunity to experience the day-to-day dealings of the community. It is important that, without being patronising, you use the same levels of language and participate in the same way that the people in the community do, as they need to accept you as one of them.

3. *Make detailed notes.* You need to make detailed recordings of the thoughts and feelings of the community that you are studying. Record and reflect on not only your emotions but also your personal opinions, ideas and notions of the community. Take your own experiences and background into account and be aware of any bias that you may have. Guard against these possible preconceived feelings and perceptions when you collect the data. Detailed field notes and transcripts of discussions will make it

easier for you to make sense of your experiences. Careful report writing and note taking will aid in the process of data collection and will allow you to identify possible recurring themes and patterns that develop within the group being studied. As you are part of the community and may forge friendships with the persons being studied, you run the risk of becoming emotionally involved with the group. For example, a researcher studying street children may easily get emotionally involved in the situation. It is thus important that field researchers keep careful notes of the emotions and feelings they experience. This will allow you to establish whether the observations you made during the research process were affected by the emotions that you experienced. This, in turn, will enable you to have a more objective viewpoint at a later stage, when the data are interpreted and presented.

4. *Consolidate the data*. Search for common trends that surface during the research process. Categorise the information you have obtained according to themes, starting from broad, general observations and moving on to more specific and narrow aspects thereof. Use the information you have recorded and construct a coherent account of the data. Guard against being subjective — focus on participant responses and not your personal feelings and opinions.

Focus groups

A focus group is basically a group interview used to determine the attitudes, behaviour, preferences and dislikes of participants who are interviewed simultaneously by a facilitator. It is often used to determine participants' experiences regarding products and services, advertisements and television programmes, for example.

Focus groups consist of the meeting of a small group of people (usually between six and twelve people) and a facilitator, who is often also the researcher. Several participants are gathered for the explicit purpose of expressing their views and opinions regarding predetermined, open-ended questions related to a specific phenomenon. Broad questions and themes are identified in advance and are then used to facilitate a discussion among the participants. The discussion is conducted in a natural and unstructured way and the participants are free to express their views and opinions about the topic at hand. There is thus a free exchange of ideas between the selected participants.

The advantages of focus groups

The advantages of using focus groups are numerous and can be summarised as follows:

- Debates generated during discussions can provide you with a deeper understanding of the different opinions and viewpoints of the participants.
- Participants can learn from each other and, in turn, may assist in resolving certain issues experienced in the group.
- It is a very useful data collection method in action research, where a primary objective of the researcher may include the resolution of a problem or a situation that a group of participants or the community is facing. For example, a focus group consisting of women from an impoverished rural community discussing their experiences with water shortages may generate solutions to the problem.
- It allows you to collect evidence about the feelings and opinions that are shared and experienced by people who are in similar situations.
- It is very cost-effective, since it allows you to get the opinions of several participants simultaneously. Thus, you collect your data at a faster pace than you would with other methods of qualitative data collection.
- It provides you with an opportunity to explore and verify certain perspectives and experiences that come to light during the meetings.
- It is a very helpful methodology when the topic has never been studied before or when you are unfamiliar with the field of study.
- It provides concentrated insight into the participants' views on a topic. The participants can debate the statements made and opinions expressed by others, which will allow you to get different viewpoints from several perspectives.
- You could ask the participants detailed questions that relate to the specific aspects you are investigating. It therefore allows you to obtain rich and detailed information, as the participants can be asked to elaborate on those parts of the discussion that interest you as the researcher.
- The participants can build on and contribute to each other's contributions, which may lead to debates and discussions that would not otherwise have occurred.
- A focus group allows you to clarify contradictory responses by participants.
- You can use a focus group after the completion of your research project as a technique to test your understanding, insights and observations of a phenomenon.
- A focus group can help the researcher direct the construction (the format and content) of interview questions. For example, it can help you determine the questions for follow-up in-depth interviews you may wish to conduct with individual participants afterwards.

- It can be used to supplement the pre-testing of a quantitative measuring instrument. For example, if a researcher is using surveys as part of a mixed-methods approach, a focus group may assist in compiling a questionnaire or in testing the questions on a specific population. It can also help to determine the independent variable and the manipulation thereof.

Planning a focus group meeting

Before a researcher starts conducting focus group meetings, she or he should do the following:

- Determine whether there are sufficient funds and time available to make the meetings worthwhile.
- Decide how many focus group meetings need to be conducted. Usually three to four sessions are adequate. Keep in mind that the more homogenous the group, the fewer sessions are needed. You must have only as many focus group meetings as is necessary to answer your research question and solve your research problem adequately.
- Determine the composition of the focus group and ensure that all subgroups are included.
- Determine the level of involvement of the facilitator. If the aim of the focus group is to learn something new, little involvement is needed. However, when specific matters have to be discussed the facilitator needs to be more involved and will typically guide the discussions.
- There are several similarities between focus groups and less structured interviews and, for this very reason, you need to identify specific discussion topics. You should also formulate predetermined, open-ended questions to guide the discussion.
- Consider political and ethical issues.

There are certain key considerations that you need to keep in mind when you plan a focus group discussion, namely the size of the group, the composition of the group and ethical issues. Focus groups are small and normally consist of six to twelve participants. A group of this size allows for a varied number of opinions and viewpoints, while still being small enough for you to guide and control.

Think about the composition of the group. You need to consider carefully whom you want to include when you are planning your focus group meeting. You should refrain from inviting your friends and family members to participate in your focus group discussion, as their presence may have a negative influence on confidentiality and the quality of the feedback that you receive.

Choose the participants according to their shared experiences. The group should consist of individuals who share similar experiences, but do not know each other in a social context. Participants are thus selected purely based on their individual experiences. You should be mindful of very outspoken, possibly opinionated participants who dominate the discussion — the dominant views and opinions that are expressed by these persons may intimidate the more reserved participants, which can lead to these participants not airing their views.

Make sure that your focus group adheres to ethical principles. The participants must know that you will treat the information that they volunteer in an ethical and professional manner. You should inform participants that the information they share with you will not be used irresponsibly or in a fashion that can cause them any form of harm, whether physical or emotional, in the future. If the participants feel that they can trust you, they will provide you with more honest feedback, which will add value to your study. Participants should complete a consent form to allow you to use the information they provide. See Chapter 18 for more information on ethics in research.

Conducting a focus group meeting

The facilitator starts the meeting by asking general questions about the participants and their backgrounds to make them feel at ease and more relaxed in the group setting. The initial questions that you ask will allow the group members to build a rapport with you as facilitator and enable the individual group members to familiarise themselves with one another and with what experiences they are sharing.

Introduce the themes that you need information on by asking some basic open-ended questions about the topic that you are investigating. Your questions should be divided into broad categories that relate to the topic. This ensures that you ask questions and obtain information that is relevant and valuable to the phenomenon that you are investigating.

The participants should feel comfortable and be assured that the focus group is a safe and secure environment in which they can express their feelings and opinions without fear of being victimised, judged or ridiculed. The facilitator of the focus group should thus ensure that the participants are comfortable and that they feel that their views and opinions are valued and important.

You may obtain valuable information and insights from the various group members, and it is therefore very important that you keep a detailed report of the focus group meeting. It is helpful to record the meetings and to transcribe the discussions according to their relevance and value after the focus group meeting.

You need to monitor the contributions made by the different group members carefully to ensure that the different participants have fair and equal opportunities to air their views. Domineering group members need to be controlled and participants who are hesitant to speak should be encouraged to share their opinions. Confident, extroverted persons, as well as persons with a higher level of expertise or education, will tend to speak more than other participants, which may lead to you as the facilitator developing biased opinions towards certain members of the group. It is thus important that you take several factors, such as level of education, financial status, and so forth, into consideration when selecting group participants. If the topic under discussion is a sensitive issue, some participants may be hesitant to express their feelings and opinions, especially in the presence of their peers and other individuals that are known to them.

If you use open-ended questions, the participants may be more willing to express their views and opinions. You can follow up on the narrative presented by the participants with cues and invitations to discuss their stories in more detail. Prompt the participants to explain more and to give more details, without expressing any form of judgement or opinion which may lead to participants feeling uncomfortable or victimised. You could repeat specific words and phrases used by the participants in order to prompt further discussions. This will indicate that the opinions and viewpoints expressed are respected and understood by you. This strategy encourages further discussions and explanations on a linguistic level with which the participants are comfortable, for them to fully participate in the discussion.

The following aspects are key considerations during the process of conducting focus group meetings:

- *The involvement of the researcher.* You need to remember that the participants in the focus group are human beings with feelings and emotions, and they need to be respected at all times. They cannot be treated as numbers or mere objects as a means to an end, and during the discussions you must be sensitive to any cues regarding discomfort. Do not force the participants to answer questions that they are not comfortable with. No unethical techniques should be employed to evoke responses from them.
- *Build rapport.* It is very important that the group members feel comfortable with you, their fellow group members and the setting in which the meeting is taking place. If the group members do not feel at ease, they will most likely not volunteer information easily. This, in turn, will have a negative impact on your study, especially in terms of trustworthiness (see Chapter 17).
- *The bias of the researcher.* You need to remain impartial throughout the focus group meeting. Do not try to force the opinions of the participants into the outcome that you want. As a researcher, you must be neutral. You cannot approve or disapprove of the opinions, decisions or actions of the participants. You must be understanding of their actions, thoughts and opinions and refrain from any response that may communicate that you either condone or judge the information that they are making available to you. A possible pitfall of focus groups is that the way in which you, as

the researcher, experience and read the group, may lead to unfounded and inaccurate assumptions and conclusions.

In-depth interviews

An in-depth interview is a qualitative data collection method which allows you to pose questions to participants with the aim of learning more about their views, opinions and beliefs about a specific phenomenon. Interviews are a form of conversation, with the primary aim of obtaining information based on open-ended questions.

Interviews are valuable sources of information and, if conducted correctly, they allow you to interpret and understand the meaning of participants' answers to specific questions. In-depth interviews also allow you to ask a participant to clarify a point she or he is making and provide a more detailed explanation of, for example, her or his view of a specific question that you have asked. As a researcher, you can ask more in-depth questions about the aspects that interest you, which allows for more flexibility in the research process. Since you can observe the non-verbal reactions of participants while they are answering your questions, it is an additional source of data that you can use in your analysis and interpretation. We can distinguish between three different types of interviews:

1. During *informal, conversational interviews*, you do not ask specific predetermined questions; rather, you allow the interview to progress as it goes along. This type of interview allows you to be as open and adaptable as possible to the responses of the interviewee.

2. When you apply the *general interview approach*, the interview follows a conversational approach. Although certain themes are covered by predetermined questions, a great degree of freedom is given to the interviewee. This is a very adaptable approach and allows the researcher to adjust the focus of the interview when necessary.

3. *Standardised, open-ended interviews* focus on asking the same set of open-ended questions of all the participants. The information obtained can be analysed more easily and this format also allows you to compare notes on the views and opinions of the participants in a more organised manner.

Key considerations

A researcher should consider various aspects to gain the optimal advantages of conducting in-depth interviews. Qualitative research interviews are very time consuming and resource intensive. You and the participants need to travel to a predetermined location and you must have the necessary equipment to record what the participants say. It can be a long process, especially when detailed responses are needed. Remember to take these aspects into consideration when you plan the interviews. Consider the questions that you will ask:

- The questions should move from a broad to a narrow focus. First ask general, broad questions regarding the topic. The participant will give an answer which may contain cues indicating that there is more information to be obtained. Your more focused follow-up questions should stem from these cues and should be designed to get as much detail as possible from the participants.

- Ideally, you should not rely purely on pre-planned questions, but should allow the interview to progress and flow in a natural, conversational manner.

- You need to formulate clear and simple questions and ensure that the participants know exactly what you are expecting from them with the question that you are asking. Do not think one thing and ask another. Remember that the participants cannot see what you mean or what you are expecting from them, so make sure that the questions are structured in a way that will allow the participants to communicate clear and precise answers.

- You need to guard against asking leading questions. Instead of asking a leading question such as, 'Did the experience make you happy?', rather ask, 'How did the experience make you feel?' This will allow the participants to express how they felt, and not communicate what they think that you want to hear.

- Do not ask double-barrelled questions. Your questions should only address one aspect at a time. If you try to obtain a number of answers from a single question, the participant may become confused and the response may answer only certain parts of the question. For example, if you are inquiring regarding the availability of office equipment, a question such as, 'When did you receive a new laptop and printer?' may confuse the participant, as the question refers to separate pieces of equipment that may not necessarily have been replaced at the same time.

- Ask truly open-ended questions. Do not ask questions that lead the participant into answering in a certain way. Open-ended questions allow the participant to give varied opinions and responses that are not influenced by predetermined cues provided by you.

The information used in your study should be based on what the participants meant, and not what you feel or think they meant. To this end, effective listening is the most important aspect of interviewing. To obtain the information that you truly want, you need to listen carefully to what the participants are saying:

- Do not ascribe your own meanings and perspectives to their responses.
- Listen for hidden and underlying subtext.

- Ensure that the context within which participants are answering the question is the same as the context within which you understand and interpret the answer.
- Never assume that you know exactly what participants mean; prompt them to clarify what they mean with a specific answer.

Take the participants' feelings into consideration when you need to ask personal details about aspects of their lives and experiences. They are assisting you with your research by allowing you to interview them and you need to respect any boundaries that they put in place. If a participant is unwilling or hesitant to proceed with a certain topic, do not force a response.

It is important that you ask the participants questions about their experiences. They need to express their views regarding the experiences that they have had, as these experiences are directly related to the feelings that they had. These feelings and emotions should be interpreted in terms of the context and perspectives of the experiences in which they were felt by the participants.

Allow the participants to explain and elaborate on their answers. By allowing the participants to elaborate, you will obtain a deeper understanding of the context within which they are providing information. Ensure that you understand the context within which the responses are phrased. The answers that you obtain from the open-ended questions will be influenced by the backgrounds, circumstances and experiences of the participants. You need to take these factors into consideration and view the responses within these contexts. You also need to remember that participants' experiences *differ* from each other, and that these differences will be a major contributor to the opinions of the participants.

In the process of trying to obtain detailed information from the participants, refrain from asking questions that may probe into areas that are very sensitive for the participant, if this is not the objective of your research. If the topic of your research is a sensitive topic, you need to approach this sensitively. If the participant does not want to talk about a specific aspect, or seems hesitant, rather ask non-invasive questions that will make the participant feel at ease. The participant can then provide you with details she or he feels comfortable with. Always respect people's boundaries. If you see that the participant does not want to answer a question or elaborate on a statement, do not force him or her to do so.

The participants must be allowed enough space and freedom to give their full views and opinions, but you need to ensure that you give them adequate guidance and do not allow them to stray from the topic, as this may lead to a lot of information that is not relevant to the topic you are researching.

Non-reactive or unobtrusive research

In field research the danger always exists that researchers may inadvertently affect the outcome of the study merely because of their presence in the social setting. Participants may react differently in a social setting when they are aware of being observed, and the researcher may be perceived as obtrusive.

In non-reactive research, also referred to as unobtrusive research (in this chapter we use the terms interchangeably), the researcher is not directly involved with the research participants and hence has no effect on the findings of the study. In conducting unobtrusive research the researcher is 'studying social behaviour without affecting it' (Babbie, 2021:326). The three major methods of the unobtrusive research approach include qualitative content analysis, the analysis of existing statistics and historical analysis (Babbie, 2021:326). We discuss only content analysis and historical research.

Quantitative content analysis, which was discussed in Chapter 12, is also an unobtrusive research approach. Content analysis can be used as both a quantitative and qualitative data collection and analysis method. In the following sections we discuss qualitative content analysis as a qualitative data collection method.

Qualitative content analysis

Qualitative content analysis has been defined as the process to 'systematically transform a large amount of text into a highly organised and concise summary of key results' (Erlingsson & Brysiewicz, 2017:94). Qualitative content analysis hence involves the systematic analysis of social artefacts to provide an in-depth understanding of, for example, media texts and their specific contexts. In contrast to quantitative content analysis, it does not involve the counting of words and codes; rather, the researcher identifies subjective themes and patterns which may emerge from a particular text. In doing a qualitative content analysis, the researcher is working in an interpretive paradigm with the goal of providing a thick description of the social reality mirrored in the texts.

Qualitative content analysis is mostly an inductive approach which researchers can use to develop theories or test existing theories. This method is most effective when looking at narratives (or stories) in texts such as journals, diaries, books, brochures, written documents, transcripts, news reports and visual media. The focus here is on textual content such as stories, written and spoken words as well as visualised narratives. Transcription of interviews with open-ended questions and focus groups can also be analysed insightfully by way of this inductive method.

We discuss the coding and interpretation of qualitative content analysis or textual analysis in Chapter 16.

Historical research

Historical research is based on the analysis and description of events that occurred in the past. When conducting historical research, you are looking for patterns that occurred in the past. The analysis of decisions made in the past, as well as the consequences that these actions had, help to show us where we came from and where we are heading as a society. It also assists us to make decisions based on the outcomes of historical situations. For the purpose of this type of research, a descriptive approach to past events as well as their meanings and influences is followed.

You would conduct historical research when you want to:
- identify patterns in the past behaviour of people;
- identify the relationship that the past has with the present, and thus also with the future;
- record and evaluate the accomplishments as well as failures of individuals or organisations, or even countries;
- gain a better understanding of the culture within which we are functioning by looking at its past development; and/or
- present past events more accurately or provide a new interpretation of past events.

In essence, there are four main types of historical evidence that a researcher who is in the process of conducting this form of research can consult:
1. *Primary sources* consist of original artefacts from the past that have survived. These items have direct relevance to the event being investigated. In some cases, primary sources such as the original written text, are used by the researcher.
2. *Secondary sources* are accounts that are created after the event has taken place. These accounts are created from original primary sources.
3. *Records* are materials such as diaries, memos, yearbooks, reports, diplomas, and so on that a researcher can use to make more sense of a historical event.
4. *Oral history* is a very useful type of information and is obtained by interviewing people who have had either direct or indirect experience or have knowledge about the topic being studied.

An advantage of historical research is that the documents used as data already exist and cannot be tampered with or altered. This type of research also has some disadvantages, for example that the data available to you may be incomplete or inaccurate. The resources may also be hard to find, and the search for these documents may be very time-consuming. The information you find may also be conflicting and difficult to verify.

Summary

Qualitative research allows an in-depth, or deep, understanding of the subjective experiences of the participants of a study. Qualitative researchers are interested in describing these experiences in a substantial and comprehensive manner, without the need to measure and quantify data. This allows the researcher to provide a rich and thick description of the phenomena being observed.

We summarised several qualitative design perspectives and two major approaches to qualitative data collection. Field research plays an important role in qualitative data collection. The data collection methods available to the field researcher include case studies, focus groups and in-depth interviews, among others. The non-reactive or unobtrusive research approach includes qualitative content analysis (or textual analysis) and comparative and historical studies.

Review the chapter

Answer the questions and complete the tasks to assess whether you understand the content of this chapter:

1. Discuss the distinctive features of qualitative research.
2. Define phenomenology.
3. What is narratology?
4. What is ethnographic research?
5. Name and explain six types of ethnographic research.
6. What is grounded theory?
7. Define the case study method.
8. Name and explain three goals of the case study method.
9. What is the difference between overt and covert participant observation?
10. Explain three different ranges of participant observation.
11. What does a focus group entail?
12. How would you conduct a focus group meeting?
13. What are the advantages of using focus groups?
14. Discuss some key considerations when conducting a focus group meeting.
15. What is an in-depth interview?
16. Name and explain three types of in-depth interviews.
17. What aspects should you consider when conducting interviews?
18. Define non-reactive or unobtrusive research.
19. What is qualitative content analysis?
20. Define historical research.
21. Name and explain the different sources a researcher can use in historical research.

CHAPTER 14

Action research

Lorette Jacobs

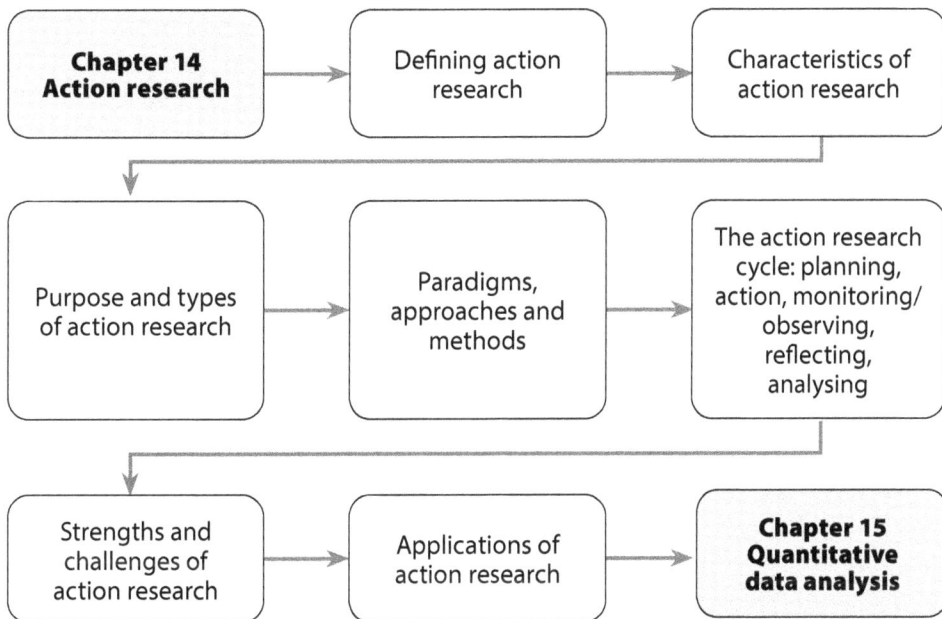

```
┌──────────────────┐      ┌──────────────────┐      ┌──────────────────┐
│   Chapter 14     │ ───► │  Defining action │ ───► │ Characteristics of│
│  Action research │      │     research     │      │  action research │
└──────────────────┘      └──────────────────┘      └──────────────────┘

┌──────────────────┐      ┌──────────────────┐      ┌──────────────────┐
│                  │      │                  │      │ The action research│
│ Purpose and types│ ───► │    Paradigms,    │ ───► │ cycle: planning, │
│ of action research│      │  approaches and  │      │ action, monitoring/│
│                  │      │     methods      │      │    observing,    │
│                  │      │                  │      │    reflecting,   │
│                  │      │                  │      │     analysing    │
└──────────────────┘      └──────────────────┘      └──────────────────┘

┌──────────────────┐      ┌──────────────────┐      ┌──────────────────┐
│  Strengths and   │      │                  │      │   Chapter 15     │
│  challenges of   │ ───► │ Applications of  │ ───► │  Quantitative    │
│ action research  │      │ action research  │      │  data analysis   │
└──────────────────┘      └──────────────────┘      └──────────────────┘
```

Overview

Have you ever encountered a problem and attempted to find a solution for it? If so, then you have already, to a certain degree, engaged in informal action research. Think for a moment about the words 'action' and 'research'. Chapter 1 introduced the meaning of research and explained that it involves an *activity* or a *process* where the aim is to search for answers to questions and solutions to problems. When you encountered the problem, you may have engaged in some activity to investigate the causes or consequences of it. Based on the outcome of your investigation, you may have decided to make some changes, and therefore to take *action* to solve the problem.

Similarly, we use action research as a research design, through the application of mixed methods, to investigate and take action towards improving personal and social situations. Action research then, is the process of planning, acting, observing and reflecting systematically and rigorously (Cohen, Manion &

Morrison, 2018) in an attempt to answer a research question or solve a research problem.

The aim of this chapter is to assist you in using action research by providing introductory information on the meaning, characteristics, and purpose of action research. We also explain the process you need to follow to conduct action research. We provide the objectives of the chapter below, but you may also want to include some of your own to ensure that you gain a thorough understanding of the scope of action research.

Objectives of this chapter

By the end of this chapter you should be able to demonstrate your understanding of the following:
- what action research is;
- what the purpose and characteristics of action research are;
- the process to follow when conducting action research; and
- the disciplines in which action research can be applied.

Defining action research

Action research is mostly associated with the work of Kurt Lewin, who viewed it as a cyclical, dynamic and collaborative process in which people address social issues affecting their lives (Adelman, 1993:8). Action research requires a personal attempt, through a process of inquiry, to improve or reform social and professional practices (Cohen et al, 2018). Action research, which often forms part of pragmatism, is therefore a systematic process in which a problem is studied scientifically, and where the results are used to take a particular action to help solve the problem. Once the action is implemented the researcher is required to reflect on the action that was taken. If certain shortcomings are identified, the intervention needs to be improved further based on these insights, or a different intervention needs to be applied. In the process, practices, such as teaching practices, are continuously improved. For this reason action research is seen as a powerful tool to bring about change and Lewin, in fact, wanted to use it originally to help minority groups to overcome the forces of exploitation and colonisation that had been prominent in modern history. Through using action research, then, we aim to answer questions such as, 'What am I currently doing?', 'What do I need to change to improve?' and 'How do I improve it?' (McNiff, 2017).

From the above statements we can conclude that action research primarily concerns investigating problems or concerns and finding practical solutions for them, hence the connection to pragmatism. For example, teachers often conduct action rescarch to determine if their teaching practices are achieving the desired outcome of assisting learners to learn new skills. By conducting action research, they improve both their understanding of the outcomes of their teaching and their own teaching practices. If you analyse the definitions, you will note that action research requires action within society and that the researchers also reflect on their own practices. In this way, the researchers are expanding on their understanding of a particular practice (eg using engaging activities in class) and also improve on or change it. These two sets of actions that occur during action research — 'out there' and 'in here'— are intertwined and of equal importance (McNiff, 2017).

Characteristics of action research

The definitions we discussed earlier may have already provided you with some clues about the characteristics of action research. Action research is about taking action to address a problem or challenge based on research and, in turn, researching the action being taken to determine the effectiveness of an intervention and to make changes based on insights gained through the research (Ary, Jacobs, Sorensen & Walker, 2017). It therefore consists of a cyclical continuation of the research process based on reflection (McCaig & Dalhberg, 2010:97). It is also based on the premise that conditions or context may vary and that solutions that have worked in other context may not work as well in a different context and researchers must therefore always consider local conditions. Action research is meant to be practical and accessible, aimed at changing practices to solve or improve identified problems. Action research is therefore problem- and solution-driven.

Another characteristic of action research is that it should include participation from participants. Participation requires a partnership between the researcher and research participants, who become equal partners, stakeholders, decision-makers and owners of the research process. This partnership should be active throughout the entire interactive research cycle, which involves the identification of practical challenges, the formulation of research questions, the implementation of the research approach and reporting on the findings in a manner that will inform further action (Maree, 2019).

Reflection is another key characteristic of action research. Reflection is the process that researchers apply in order to plan for future actions based on concrete experiences and observations. Reflective processes challenge the researcher to ask questions about what is happening and why, and what is to be changed to improve the situation or address an identified problem. By reflecting critically the researcher will learn more about the questions that are pursued through action research. It might lead the researcher to question original beliefs and understandings, and to use new insights to plan further actions. This brings us to the *purpose* of conducting action research.

Purpose and types of action research

Why would researchers want to engage in action research? Stringer (2013) indicates that there are a variety of reasons for using it, but arguably the most important of these is that action research provides the basis for formulating effective solutions to significant problems. It further involves addressing issues and improving conditions because the process of action research promotes professional growth, improvement and change (Craig, 2009:6). Within this context, action research may have an exploratory, descriptive or action-related purpose. It can be used to work out how things could be (exploratory), the way things are (descriptive) or what procedures can be taken to improve a problem (action-related). Maree (2019) maintains that, based on the purpose of the research, researchers may select a certain type of action research to investigate a particular phenomenon. These types are briefly described in Table 14.1.

Table 14.1 Action research types

Type	Description
Technical action research	The aim of this type of action research is to improve the effectiveness of certain practices. The success thereof depends greatly on collaboration with participants, who are often practitioners.
Practical action research	This type of action research involves studying a local problem in which the researcher is directly involved. It requires the identification and implementation of a plan of action. Reflection on the action is important to make suggestions to further improve the situation.
Participatory action research	This type of research is to be used when studying social issues that constrain individual lives. Collaboration with participants is imperative and the focus is on taking action that will lead to changes in the lives of participants.
Emancipatory action research	The aim here is to transform and bring about change within existing societal boundaries, conditions, and systems. The focus is on changing the system itself.

(Compiled from Adelman, 1993:13–14; Maree, 2019)

Irrespective of the type of action research applied, the main purpose of action research remains to improve understanding or bring about change. Action research is not to be used to draw comparisons, show statistical correlations, or demonstrate a cause-and-effect relationship. Its purpose is to understand a specific occurrence and how to improve it. It emphasises the researcher's intent to take action for the purpose of advancement. The ability to take action actively and to effect change lies in the researcher's interpretation of the problem and his or her ability to reflect on his or her own practices (McCaig & Dalhberg, 2010:97).

Paradigms, approaches and methods

Chapter 2 of this book introduced various research paradigms or traditions. As you know, the tradition from which we approach research will impact on the methodology used to conduct the research. Based on your understanding of the information included in Chapter 2, can you determine the tradition(s) that may apply to action research? Maree (2019) and Stringer (2013) explain that action researchers acknowledge that multiple realities exist, that research and intervention can coexist, and that subjectivity is central to and can be used through reflection to strengthen the action research process.

Action researchers are required to be familiar with the various research methodologies associated with the different research traditions, as well as the application of a variety of data collection methods used in the action research process. Action research often uses a mixed-methods approach, where qualitative and quantitative methodologies are combined to execute the actual research (Maree, 2019). Action research adds unique nuances to the research process, however, as it seeks to empower participants and achieve change through interventions. The use of multiple data collection methods is an attempt to achieve different kinds of views and perspectives, including strategies to improve research practices (the way in which we conduct research). Within the context of a mixed-methods approach, examples of methods that can be used during action research to obtain data include consultations, interviews, observations, journals, narratives (stories), distributing questionnaires, monitoring, textual and/or content analysis and case study analysis, among others.

The action research cycle

The action research cycle consists of a four-phased approach, namely planning, acting, observing, and reflecting (Adelman, 1993:10). This process should be repeated so that solutions are considered, analysed and reformulated until a successful outcome is achieved. More complex problems and issues, however, require a more sophisticated formulation of this process and include designing the study (plan), taking action, monitoring or observing the outcome, analysing data and reflecting to determine how actions should be revised to address the problem.

Figure 14.1 provides a diagram of this cyclical action research process. A brief description of each phase follows on page 232.

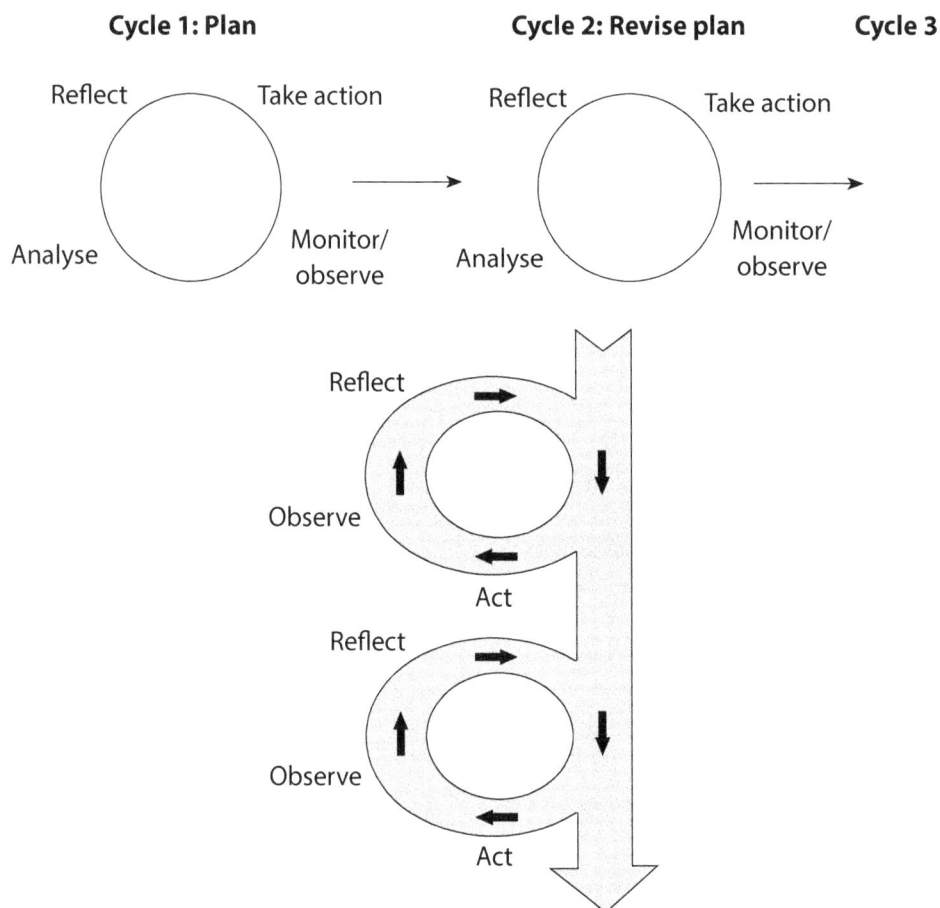

Figure 14.1 The action research cycle (adapted from Koshy, Koshy & Waterman, 2011:7)

The action research process starts with the identification of practical challenges or social issues during the *planning phase*. We need to look at the research environment and gather information to build a preliminary picture of the situation (Stringer, 2013). We can ask key questions, such as, 'What is the problem?' or 'What can be done about the problem?' Reading and assessing the current situation through the application of one or more research method may be required to obtain a thorough understanding of the problem. For example, information may be acquired through dialogue with both colleagues and potential participants, and observations to identify factors that influence the problem to be investigated. A preliminary literature review may provide further insight into and different perspectives pertaining to the problem.

Once the problem has been clearly identified, the research question related to the problem can be formulated. This research question will provide the framework from which to determine the structure or process for conducting action research (Craig, 2009:31). During this stage it is important to consider the characteristics of action research. Remember that action research is bound to a specific environment, requires some form of participation by both the researcher and participants, and focuses on a specific problem in a particular context. Thus, the participants of the study play an important role in formulating the research question and identifying the research problem.

To comply with the above-mentioned action research characteristics, the researcher, as part of the planning process, will have to decide on and select the participants. Stringer (2013) proposes that purposive or purposeful sampling be used to ensure that participants who are affected by the problem are selected to participate in the action research study. We have already dealt with sampling (see Chapter 11), so we will not go into detail on the use of purposive sampling here. However, once you have selected your sample and together you have identified and gathered sufficient data about the problem, you can engage in the following phase of action research — the identification of the action towards solving the problem.

The focus of the *action phase* is to provide structure or to identify actions which will form part of the action research process. It is important that, when you identify the action, you select an action that is manageable and relates specifically to the problem being researched. It need not be a perfect action. Remember: action research is a cyclical process, meaning that various actions may be applied, depending on the outcomes of a cycle. Also note that, within action research, the action is part of the research itself, so selecting the most appropriate action may only become clear after the implementation of various actions. Based on the selected action, participants collaborate with the researcher to mobilise resources aimed at actively dealing with the problem.

From the action phase, the natural progression is to monitor and/or observe the application of the intervention. This requires the collection of data that may be used to determine the impact of the implemented action. Such data may be collected through interviews or discussions to obtain feedback, keeping records, observing participants during the application of the action, and monitoring the implementation process of actions (Craig, 2009:138).

The *analysis* of the data obtained during the monitoring or observation phase requires that the researcher analyses the data against a set of criteria to determine whether the solution has worked to address the problem (Cohen et al, 2018). Analysing the data involves exploring the relationships between interdependent elements, the viewpoints of participants and the experiences obtained during observations. More detail on how to analyse data is provided in the following chapter.

Based on the analysis obtained, the findings should be used to spur reflection and the planning of a new action. This reflection will give birth to a new concern related to the problem or deeper insight into the cause of the problem, or it can raise an altered concern, which will restart the action research process. Findings should be presented in report format and used as a reflective tool. From these findings, deductions can be made on a future course of action which may be required to address the identified problem.

As we already explained, when we defined action research, this reflective process does not only require reflecting on what is 'out there' (research findings) but also what is 'in here' (personal reflection). The researcher should therefore embark on his or her own internal reflective process to determine what he or she has learnt through the process of implementing the action and how that will affect future plans and actions. Internal reflection will assist researchers in understanding how their own development may influence future actions (McNiff, 2017).

To illustrate the process of action research, let's use an example of a problem in a higher education classroom. Mr Makhubela is struggling to retain the attention of learners in the classroom. By comparing their first assessment marks with those of previous cohorts of learners, he is able to confirm his suspicions that the learners' lack of attention is impacting on their marks.

He conducts a brief literature review to see what others have learnt about improving the ability of learners to pay attention in class, and the relation between attention span and pass rates. Based on this background information, he decides to embark on an action research project. He follows the four steps we discussed earlier:

1. *Planning.* He interviews ten of his learners to determine what problems they are experiencing with focusing on the lessons presented in class.
2. *Action.* Based on their feedback and on the information he has obtained from secondary sources, he decides to change his teaching strategy to a learner-centred approach. Learners are grouped together and each group receives a section of a lesson to research and present. In this way, Mr Makhubela hopes that learners will engage more actively with the content.
3. *Monitoring/observing.* After applying this approach for two weeks, Mr Makhubela assesses the learners through a test. By comparing the results of this test to their previous results, as well as the results of other cohorts of learners, Mr Makhubela is able to determine whether learners are more actively engaging with the subject content. Analysis of the data will provide new insights.

4. *Reflection*. Based on the analysis of the data, Mr Makhubela also reflects on his own teaching methods and knowledge about educational practices. Such reflections may lead to further action and adaptation of educational practices.

Strengths and challenges of action research

As with any research design, action research has its strengths and challenges. One of the key strengths of action research is that researchers can use their expertise and knowledge to conduct systematic inquiries which help to improve conditions and solve problems (Craig, 2009:6). In addition, action research addresses practical problems in a positive way, with results feeding back into practice (Maree, 2019).

However, action researchers face the challenge of earning the trust of participants — a necessary step for participants to allow the researcher to gain insight into their perspectives and experiences. Because action research is often conducted within a specific social environment and related to a specific group of participants, findings from action research can often not be generalised and applied to other social environments or groups experiencing similar problems.

Applications of action research

Due to its concerns with both action and research, action research is widely used in many academic and vocational disciplines. It becomes a particularly attractive problem-solving approach because of its emphasis on collaboration between researcher and participant based on a context-specific problem (McCaig & Dalhberg, 2010:95).

The scope of action research as a method is notable: it can be used in almost any setting where there is the need for a solution to a problem involving people, tasks and procedures. The flexibility of action research makes it useful to researchers in various disciplines. It can, for example, give researchers the opportunity to conduct research that may solve many problems that are part of the complex life of an organisation. It is therefore a tool that can be used to promote career development, to enable researchers to improve career experiences and to ensure a beneficial impact on the lives of those with whom they work.

Summary

In this chapter we have provided a brief overview of action research and of what conducting action research entails. Some theoretical underpinnings of action research and examples were presented, enabling you to become more acquainted with the phases of the cyclical process of action research. However, to understand the nature of action research more fully, you will need to actively engage in an action research project of your own.

Review the chapter

Answer the questions and complete the tasks to assess whether you understand the content of this chapter:

1. What are the key components or characteristics of action research that distinguish it from other research designs?
2. What is the purpose of action research in the context of social problems?
3. Explain the types of action research that can be used to investigate social problems.
4. Explain the cyclical process applied during action research to bring about change.
5. In which context would you select action research as a research design to investigate a problem?

Quantitative data analysis

Dionne Morris and Ross Khan

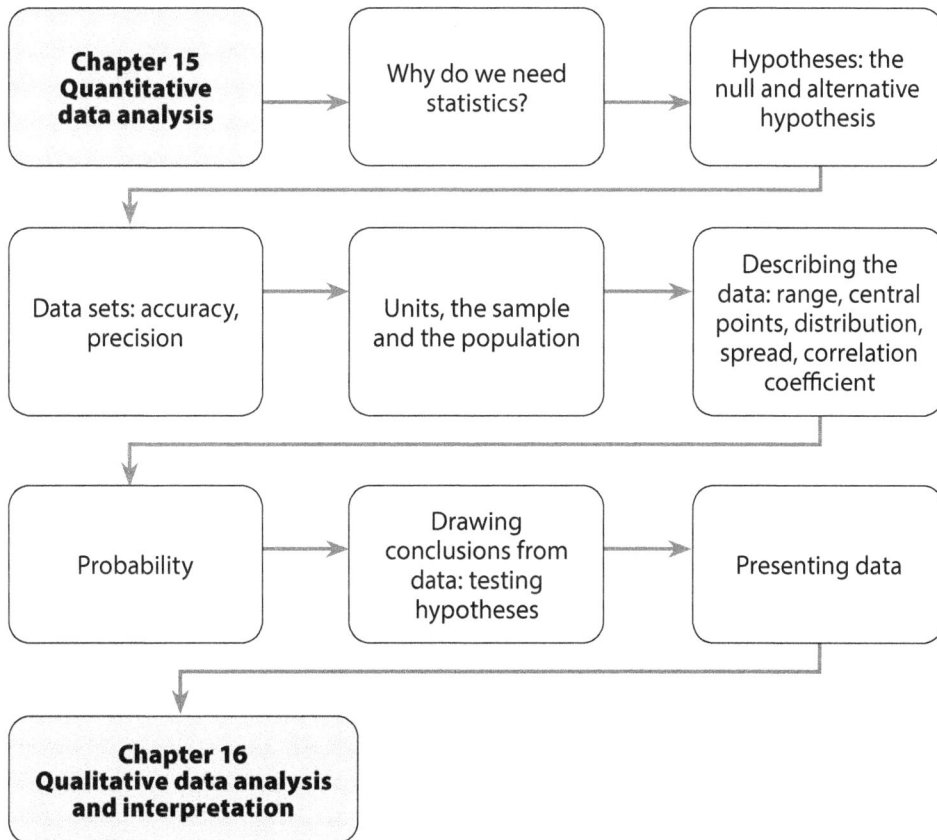

```
┌─────────────────┐     ┌─────────────────┐     ┌─────────────────┐
│   Chapter 15    │     │  Why do we need │     │  Hypotheses: the│
│   Quantitative  │ ──▶ │    statistics?  │ ──▶ │ null and        │
│  data analysis  │     │                 │     │ alternative     │
│                 │     │                 │     │ hypothesis      │
└─────────────────┘     └─────────────────┘     └─────────────────┘
         │                                                │
         ▼                                                ▼
┌─────────────────┐     ┌─────────────────┐     ┌─────────────────┐
│                 │     │                 │     │  Describing the │
│ Data sets:      │     │ Units, the      │     │  data: range,   │
│ accuracy,       │ ──▶ │ sample and the  │ ──▶ │ central points, │
│ precision       │     │ population      │     │ distribution,   │
│                 │     │                 │     │ spread,         │
│                 │     │                 │     │ correlation     │
│                 │     │                 │     │ coefficient     │
└─────────────────┘     └─────────────────┘     └─────────────────┘
         │                                                │
         ▼                                                ▼
┌─────────────────┐     ┌─────────────────┐     ┌─────────────────┐
│                 │     │  Drawing        │     │                 │
│  Probability    │ ──▶ │ conclusions     │ ──▶ │ Presenting data │
│                 │     │ from data:      │     │                 │
│                 │     │ testing         │     │                 │
│                 │     │ hypotheses      │     │                 │
└─────────────────┘     └─────────────────┘     └─────────────────┘
         │                                                │
         ▼                                                │
┌─────────────────────┐                                   │
│    Chapter 16       │ ◀─────────────────────────────────┘
│ Qualitative data    │
│ analysis and        │
│ interpretation      │
└─────────────────────┘
```

Overview

Imagine the following scenario: you are very excited because you have found a new and better way of doing something — you have found that using a red plaster cast helps broken bones heal faster. However, it sounds a little improbable. How can you convince others that your technique works better than the current accepted norm?

Statistical analysis allows you to produce such proof, when correctly applied. It produces a set of statistics that can be used to convince others and enable them to adopt your new technique.

Statistical analysis techniques may be used to prove (or disprove), among endless things, that:

- a new drug is more effective than an older formulation;
- climate change and global warming are not fiction;
- imposing and policing road speed limits result in reduced road deaths; and
- more women than men like chocolate.

The application of statistical analysis techniques may, for example, allow you to show that your technique of using a red plaster cast provides a 20% improvement in the time required to heal a broken bone. However, the results of any investigation will have to produce statistically significant results in order to encourage others to use a red plaster cast. We discuss this concept later in the chapter.

We are presented with statistics almost every day — watch the current news on Covid-19 vaccination rates or death rates. These latest numbers tell us things that affect our lives directly or indirectly, and we may be influenced to make decisions based on these statistics.

This chapter intends to provide a grounding in the methods and techniques used to generate believable and defensible statistical results.

Objectives of this chapter

By the end of this chapter you should be able to demonstrate your understanding of the following:

- what statistics are;
- why we need statistics;
- the importance of accuracy and precision in data sets;
- the range of a data set and how to determine the range;
- the central points of a data set (the mean, median and mode) and how to determine them;
- the distribution of data in a set;
- the standard deviation of data in a set and how to calculate it;
- the correlation coefficient, how to calculate it and what it means;
- what probability is;
- how to work with the probability density function and normal distribution;
- how to test a hypothesis; and
- how to present quantitative data.

Why do we need statistics?

Applying statistical analysis to a set of data removes the guesswork from the interpretation of data. Objective and defensible conclusions can then be drawn from the results of the analysis.

- *Objective* in this context means devoid of bias. If we want to convince you that red plaster casts promote faster healing of broken bones, then the reasoning must be more weighty than, say, red being someone's favourite colour.
- *Defensible* in this context means that the results show a statistically significant difference between the status quo, or an existing set of conditions (in this case, the use of white plaster casts), and our proposed alternative position (the use of red plaster casts). Something is statistically significant when you are very confident that your results are reliable and that the difference between two groups is big enough for it to be noteworthy. For example, if you find that there is a significant difference between the test scores of students who summarise work from their textbooks and students who do not, you can say with confidence that making summaries from a textbook is highly likely to improve a student's test scores.

Statistics consists of the collection and analysis of data through the use of mathematical techniques. We do this in order to ensure we make accurate and objective interpretations of the data. The analysis sets out to arrive at a set of summaries of the data and attempts to discover patterns that may exist hidden within the data. These summaries of the data create information that may then be used to inform decisions, change people's behaviour, change medical treatments, and so on. Statistics is a branch of mathematical science. It encompasses aspects of:

- *gathering* data, including formulating questionnaires (if used), encoding the data and recording data;
- *analysing* data, including finding basic characteristics of the data set, exposing patterns within the data and identifying relationships between the gathered data and external parameters;
- *interpreting* the data, including attributing patterns within the data to the external parameters;
- *formatting* and *presenting* the data, including data summaries and graphical representations; and
- *projections* derived from the data, including forecasts, predictions and systems modelling.

Governments commonly use the results of statistical analyses for making policy decisions and businesses use them to make operational and investment decisions. Ultimately, statistics may be used to influence outcomes and change societies by changing social conditions. More recently, we can see the usefulness of statistics in policy decisions around the coronavirus pandemic, with several countries using statistical data to determine the ideal time to suspend lockdowns based on the rate of infection and/or transmission versus rate of vaccination rollout (Lawton, 2020).

In general, statistical techniques are used to analyse numerical (quantitative) data and to support decision-making processes. Statistical techniques may also be used to process descriptive (qualitative) data; however, such analyses require an assignment of qualities to numeric values (Atmowardoyo, 2018). This may introduce bias in the conclusions, which is why such analyses are often avoided.

It is important to recognise from the outset that statistics may be misused or manipulated to make them appear to prove a particular position, regardless of whether that position is supported by the data. A notorious example of this is the use of statistical analysis by health and fitness experts to attempt to create proof that the use of a particular supplement will result in lower body weight within a short period of time. However, it is also important to note that using statistics may also be beneficial. We are able to make decisions about theoretical hypotheses that examine underlying behaviours through the use of statistics; for example, we may pose the question, 'Are men more likely than women to engage in extreme forms of callous behaviour that are typically associated with psychopathy?' A question like this would be difficult to address using any other analytical method.

If we ask the wrong questions or ask them in the wrong way, it is possible to derive biased answers from a statistical process. The formulation of the analysis must itself be unbiased in order to arrive at defensible conclusions — objective conclusions that are supported by the data and the analysis of the data.

Hypotheses

What is a hypothesis? Simply stated, hypotheses are statements or proposed explanations made on the basis of limited evidence as a starting point for further investigation (McKoon & Ratcliff, 1995). They can also take on the form of statements of proposed alternative 'facts' or states of affairs (see Chapter 6 for a detailed discussion of hypotheses).

Using our earlier example of the proposition of red plaster cast as a technique for healing broken bones, we can state this by defining a null hypothesis and one or more alternatives that we then test using statistical analyses.

The null hypothesis

The null hypothesis is the statement supporting the status quo. The null hypothesis is denoted by the symbol H_0. In our example, it might be:

H_0: The use of red plaster for immobilising broken bones during the healing phase has no influence on the healing time when compared to the use of white plaster.

This statement of the null hypothesis relates the two alternative states of affairs (red versus white plaster) and establishes the status quo position.

Other examples of a null hypothesis may be:

H_0: The use of drug ABC has no significant influence on the reduction of gastrointestinal inflammation.

H_0: There is no significant difference between the use of nicotine patches and the 'cold turkey' method in the long-term cessation of smoking.

The alternative hypothesis

The alternative hypothesis is a statement supporting a change in the status quo, such as supporting a new discovery or better technique — the game changer. It is the statement that indicates that the null hypothesis is wrong. The alternative hypothesis is indicated by the symbol H_a or, if we have more than one alternative hypothesis, by H_1, H_2 and so on:

H_a: The use of red plaster reduces the healing time for broken bones compared to the use of white plaster.

It is important to note that some of the words and concepts used in the above hypotheses may be considered ambiguous or vague and may require further clarification:
- Which broken bone: the femur, scapula or phalange?
- In what type of patient: child or adult?
- What kind of break: fracture or compound break?
- Under what circumstances was the bone broken? In a motor vehicle accident or as part of a surgical (orthopaedic) procedure?

For this reason, it may be possible and appropriate to construct multiple alternative hypotheses and to analyse them simultaneously or to add more specific details within your hypothesis. To be able to add sufficient detail to your hypothesis, you need to be aware of the data set you are using.

Data sets

A data set is a collection of data. It consists of separate units that make up the entire set. For example, if we wanted to improve people's future health, we could ask different individuals to provide us with information about their eating and exercise habits, the number of hours of sleep they get per night, how often they go on holiday, and so on. If we put all the information we collect from all the different individuals together, we have a data set. From the analysis of this information we would be able to make certain predictions and provide people with advice on how to improve their future health. However, in order to have confidence in our results, we need to ensure that our data or information is accurate and precise.

Something is *accurate* when it is free from error. Unfortunately, it is very easy to make mistakes and errors often have a tendency to surface, especially when it comes to measurement. Errors introduced in the process of measurement often result in a variation — this is known as measurement error.

If we were to measure heights of individuals, for example, there may be an uncertainty or inaccuracy in our measurement of between 1 and 2 mm. A height measurement would then be recorded as, for example, 1 605 mm ±2 mm. This means that the individual's true height lies between 1 603 mm and 1 607 mm, or that the individual's height is 1 605 mm within an accuracy of 2 mm. Such variation may be introduced through several different factors:

- *Observer bias*: variations in the way a human observer views a height scale (from slightly below horizontal to slightly above horizontal).
- *Environmental changes*: the goal is to measure the same individual under identical circumstances; however, this is not always the case as there would be small changes in the environment can that influence the measurement (such as time of day, temperature, lighting, etc).
- *Participant changes*: the participant can change between measurements, for example, their mood or degree of focus may be different between the testings.

Such variation must be accounted for in order to ensure that the observed values that support the alternative hypothesis are not simply due to measurement error.

Although the terms are related, *precision* should not be confused with accuracy. Precision refers to a consistent error in measurement that consistently causes measured values to be skewed either upwards or downwards. An observer's best efforts to position a height scale accurately may be thwarted if the scale is attached to the wall slightly too high or too low, resulting in consistently skewed measurements.

The combined effect of accuracy and precision factors must be taken into account when examining data sets and testing hypotheses. Statistical techniques provide the methods for dealing with issues in both accuracy and precision in data sets.

Units, the sample and the population

Units of measurement are associated with all numerical measurements. The units of the International System of Units, known as SI units, are often preferred. These include metres, kilograms, seconds, and so on. However, alternative units may also be used. For example: the number of peanuts found in packets sold by the local supermarket has an associated unit, namely packets of 50g. Values of this type are often represented as a simple approximate number (such as an average of 40 peanuts in each packet).

Either way, it is important to ensure that the units of measurement are recorded for reference, both for the researcher and for others who may wish to utilise the data later, either for their own study of a different phenomenon or for reproducing the results of your study.

If we are in the business of producing packets of peanuts for sale, we may be interested in the number of peanuts that each packet contains. We have two ways of determining this. The first is to count all the peanuts in every single packet that is produced. This would give us an exact and entirely accurate picture of the entire *population* of packets. However, counting every single peanut in every single packet can be time consuming and wasteful of resources.

Alternatively, we could count the number of peanuts in a *sample* portion of the packets produced. We can then use our findings from this sample to draw a conclusion that relates to all packets of peanuts that are being produced — this is known as inferential statistics.

Therefore, inferential statistics is an activity that uses information drawn from a sample in order to arrive at conclusions relating to a population. In order to draw accurate conclusions and to avoid arriving at generalisations about the population, we must use a sample that is sufficiently representative of the population. There are many methods that we could use for selecting our sample packets if we want to ensure that we are drawing accurate conclusions from our analysis. Sampling methodology should be a significant consideration of any study design (see Chapter 11).

Determining how to conduct a study, including determining what sample size is sufficiently representative of the population, may be considered a branch of statistics in itself and is useful in research regardless of the methodology adopted. Statistical analysis is used to determine the sample error. Sample error means that a sample does not provide a perfectly accurate representation of its population.

Describing the data

In order to begin to understand the data set we are working with, we can start by performing a descriptive analysis of the data. Descriptive statistics summarises the data and allows some basic questions to be answered, for example:

- What is the *range* of the data? This could refer to the maximum and minimum value; for example, whose bones healed the fastest and whose healed the slowest?
- What is the *central point* of the data set? This can be determined in terms of the mean (average), the median (the middle value of a list) or the mode (the value that occurs the most frequently).

Let's use the following data set to explain these concepts:

Sample	A	B	C	D	E	F	G	H	I	J	K	L	M
Value (d)	40	44	40	38	41	45	45	40	42	46	41	42	43

Here, the samples are identified using a single letter (A, B, and so on) in order to track them as we manipulate them. In this case, these labels refer to individuals and the labels are used to protect the identity of test subjects. The value is the time required to heal a broken bone. The unit used is days (denoted by the symbol 'd'). In the following sections, we answer some of the basic questions about this data set.

Range

Our question is: what is the range of the data?

- Minimum value: 38 (sample D, whose bones took 38 days to heal, the shortest period of all the test subjects)
- Maximum value: 46 (sample J, whose bones took 46 days to heal, the longest period of all the test subjects)

Central points

Our question is: what is the central point of the data? As we mentioned above, there are several ways of expressing the central point of a data set, namely the mean, median and mode. They have different uses.

Calculating the mean

The mean is the numerical average of the data. In this data set there are 13 samples (A–M). The average is simply the sum of all the data points divided by the number of data points (ie number of participants in the sample):

$$\frac{(40 + 44 + 40 + 38 + 41 + 45 + 45 + 40 + 42 + 46 + 41 + 42 + 43)}{13} = \frac{547}{13}$$

$$= 42.0769$$

Mathematically, the mean is represented as follows:

$$\bar{x} = \frac{\Sigma x}{n}$$

Where $\bar{x}$ represents the mean, Σx represents the raw values and n is the number of participants in the sample.

Certain computer programs, such as *Microsoft Excel*™, have an *AVERAGE* function to help you calculate the mean.

Determining the median

The median is the middle value of the list. To find the median, the data needs to be rearranged in sample value order:

Sample	D	A	C	H	E	K	I	L	M	B	F	G	J
Value (d)	38	40	40	40	41	41	42	42	43	44	45	45	46

These are the same samples and values, simply rearranged from numerically lowest to numerically highest, from left to right. Once this is done, we identify the middle value (the seventh value in this case). The median is sample I, with a value of 42.

If there is an even number of samples, simply find the two middle sample values — the median will be the numerical average of these two values. Certain computer programs, such as *Microsoft Excel*, can also help you to determine the median.

Determining the mode

The mode is the value that appears most often in the data set. Rearranging the data in value order assists in identifying the mode:

Sample	D	A	C	H	E	K	I	L	M	B	F	G	J
Value (d)	38	40	40	40	41	41	42	42	43	44	45	45	46

The value appearing most often in the data set is 40 (samples A, C and H).

It is possible for a data set to have multiple modal values (for instance if there were two samples with value 40 and two samples with value 45 in our example data set). You would record all modal values as the mode of your data set.

Distribution

The distribution of the data shows us the number of times a particular data value occurs. The following shows the data values of our example data set and the number of times they occur in our data set:

Value	38	39	40	41	42	43	44	45	46
Count	1	0	3	2	2	1	1	2	1

We can draw a graph of these values against their counts, as shown in Figure 15.1.

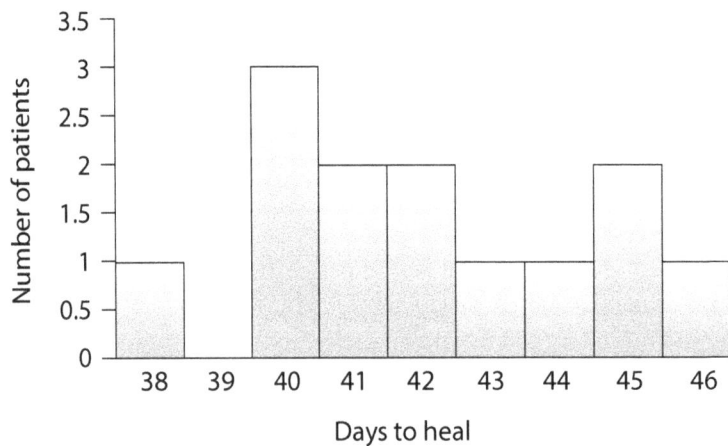

Figure 15.1 Frequency histogram of number of patients vs days to heal

This type of graph is commonly known as a frequency histogram and gives us a visual indication of the distribution of the sample values.

The spread of the data

The spread of the data may be expressed in many ways. The most useful and common way of expressing the spread of data is through the standard deviation. The *standard deviation* represents the average distance that the data values vary from the mean. The standard deviation therefore tells you how far removed a value is from the average (or mean). If the standard deviation is low, it means all the results are close to the mean. If it is high, it means the numbers are far away from the mean. For example, if the average IQ is between 85 and 114, someone with an IQ lower than 85 will be a standard deviation or more away from the mean, which means she or he is less intelligent than the average person. If someone has an IQ higher than 114, she or he will also be a standard deviation or more from the mean, which means she or he is more intelligent than the average person.

To calculate the standard deviation, we take each value and subtract the mean from each. Earlier, we found the mean value of our example data to be $\bar{x} = 42.08$.

Table 15.1 Examples of healing time values, variances and squares of variances

Sample	Value (x)	Variance from mean $(x - \bar{x})$	Square of variance from mean $(x - \bar{x})^2$
A	40	−2.0769	4.3136
B	44	1.9231	3.6982
C	40	−2.0769	4.3136
D	38	−4.0769	16.6213
E	41	−1.0769	1.1598
F	45	2.9231	8.5444
G	45	2.9231	8.5444
H	40	−2.0769	4.3136
I	42	−0.0769	0.0059
J	46	3.9231	1.1598
K	41	−1.0769	15.3905
L	42	−0.0769	0.0059
M	43	0.9231	0.8521

Next, we take the sum of the last column of numbers:

$$\Sigma(x - \bar{x})^2 = 68.9231$$

The standard deviation (s) is then:

$$s = \sqrt{\frac{\Sigma(x - \bar{x})}{n - 1}} = \sqrt{\frac{68.9231}{12}} = \sqrt{5.7436} = 2.3966$$

When treating a patient with a broken bone, these results would enable us to tell the patient fairly confidently that her or his cast would come off after around 42.08 days (or 42 days if rounded), plus or minus 2.40 days (therefore, after between 40 and 44 days).

Some computer programs may provide a *STDEV* function to help you determine the standard deviation.

The correlation coefficient

Sometimes, we want to find out whether two values are related in some way. For example, we may want to know whether there is a relationship between the maximum daytime temperature and the number of daylight hours in the day as the seasons change.

To examine such a possible relationship, we calculate the correlation coefficient (often also called Pearson's coefficient) as shown below. The correlation coefficient is represented by the symbol r.

$$r_{xy} = \frac{\Sigma(x - \bar{x})(y - \bar{y})}{\sqrt{\Sigma(x - \bar{x})^2(y - \bar{y})^2}}$$

Here, x and y stand for the two variables, temperature and number of daylight hours. The process of calculating r is quite straightforward, although it can be lengthy to do by hand if the data set is large. It is therefore recommended that you use a computer program to calculate r. However, it is always useful to know how to calculate the value without the assistance of a computer program.

The value of the correlation coefficient is always between 0 and ±1. If your answer is not between 0 and ±1, you have made a calculation error. The closer the number is to ±1, the stronger the correlation is, in either the negative or positive direction. The closer to 0 the value is, the weaker the correlation is.

- A negative number indicates a *negative correlation*. This means that if you increase the independent variable, the dependent variable decreases. For example, the more recreational drugs a student uses, the lower her or his test scores will be.

- A positive number indicates a *positive correlation*. In this case, when the independent variable increases, the dependent variable also increases. For example, the more a student studies, the higher her or his test score will be.

Table 15.2 explains how the *r* score can be interpreted.

Table 15.2 Interpretation of the correlation coefficient

Value of correlation coefficient	Interpretation	Notes
From −1.0 to −0.8	Strong negative correlation	The value of y is strongly related to the value of x. The value of y decreases as x increases (negative slope).
From −0.7 to −0.3	Weak negative correlation	The value of y may be related to the value of x. The value of y decreases as x increases (negative slope).
From −0.2 to 0.3	No correlation	No relationship between x and y.
From 0.4 to 0.7	Weak positive correlation	The value of y may be related to the value of x. The value of y increases as x increases (positive slope).
From 0.8 to 1.0	Strong positive correlation	The value of y is strongly related to the value of x. The value of y increases as x increases (positive slope).

The interpretation of the correlation coefficient (along with many other results of statistical analysis) becomes more certain as the number of elements in the data set increases. Thus, the bigger your sample size, the more confident you can be in your results. This can be attributed to the fact that the larger your sample size is, the more representative it is of the population from which it was selected.

A set of data gathered for the above example might look like the example in Table 15.3.

Table 15.3 Example values for maximum daytime temperatures

Daylight hours (x)	Maximum daytime temperature (y)
13	31.3
12.5	32.2
12	28.4
11.5	29.2
11	26.7
10.5	25.2
10	24.3
9.5	20.8
9	20.2
8.5	17.9
8	16.3

In this example data set, the number of daylight hours (x) is an independent variable: it is the quantity that is adjusted (in this case, by the changing seasons). We are interested in how the maximum daytime temperature (y) reacts to (and is, therefore, dependent upon) changes in daylight hours.

Figure 15.2 shows the maximum daytime temperature plotted against the number of daylight hours.

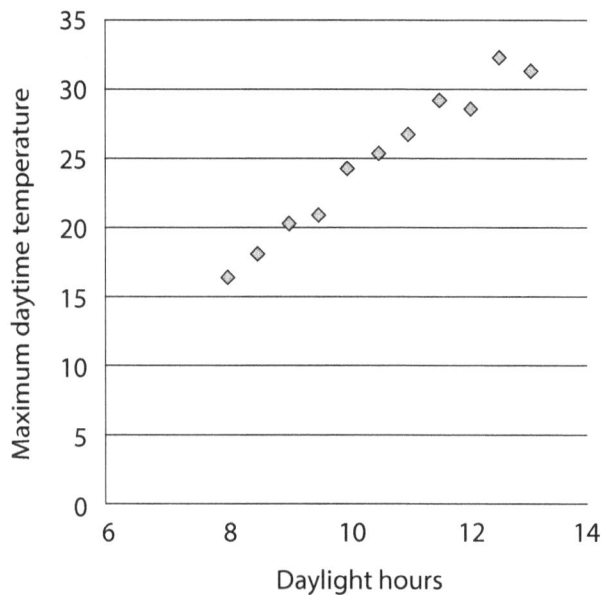

Figure 15.2 Scatter plot of maximum daytime temperature vs number of daylight hours

It looks like there is a relationship here, but how can we be sure? We can start by calculating the means of x and y:

$$\bar{x} = 10.5$$

$$\bar{y} = 24.77$$

Next, we calculate the variances of x and y, the squares of the variances and some products, as shown in Table 15.4.

Table 15.4 Intermediate values in computing the correlation coefficient

Daylight hours (x)	(x − x̄)	(x − x̄)²	Maximum daytime temperature (y)	(y − ȳ)	(y − ȳ)²	(x − x̄) × (y − ȳ)
13	2.5	6.25	31.3	6.53	42.61	16.32
12.5	2	4.0	32.2	7.43	55.16	14.85
12	1.5	2.25	28.4	3.63	13.16	5.44
11.5	1	1.0	29.2	4.43	19.60	4.43
11	0.5	0.25	26.7	1.93	3.71	0.96
10.5	0	0.0	25.2	0.43	0.18	0.00
10	−0.5	0.25	24.3	−0.47	0.22	0.24
9.5	−1	1.0	20.8	−3.97	15.78	3.97
9	−1.5	2.25	20.2	−4.57	20.91	6.86
8.5	−2	4.0	17.9	−6.87	47.23	13.75
8	−2.5	6.25	16.3	−8.47	71.79	21.18

We now take the sums of the values in the third, sixth and seventh columns in this table:

$$\Sigma(x - \bar{x})^2 = 27.5$$

$$\Sigma(y - \bar{y})^2 = 290.36$$

$$\Sigma(x - \bar{x}) \times (y - \bar{y}) = 88.0$$

We can then substitute these into the equation for the correlation coefficient:

$$r_{xy} = \frac{\Sigma(x - \bar{x})(y - \bar{y})}{\sqrt{\Sigma(x - \bar{x})^2 \Sigma(y - \bar{y})^2}} = \frac{88.0}{\sqrt{27.5 \times 290.36}} = \frac{88.0}{89.35} = 0.984$$

We now have statistical evidence of the strong relationship between the number of daylight hours in a day and the maximum daytime temperature, with a correlation coefficient of 0.984.

Some computer programs may have a *CORREL* function to enable you to calculate the correlation coefficient.

Probability

Probability is the likelihood of a particular event occurring. Mathematically, probabilities are stated to be in the range of values from 0 to 1. The higher the value, the higher the probability. For example, we may be interested in knowing what the probability is of getting heads or tails when we toss a coin. The various values we obtain when we actually toss the coin are known as outcomes. Outcomes may be the result of a single event (tossing a single coin) or the result of multiple events (tossing a pair of dice).

If we think of tossing a coin, we know intuitively that a toss will result in a head 50% of the time (probability of 0.5), and a tail 50% of the time (probability of 0.5).

Statistically, we could say:

$$P_H = \frac{1}{2} = 0.5$$

$$P_T = \frac{1}{2} = 0.5$$

This indicates that the probability of a head is 0.5 and the probability of a tail is 0.5. It is important to note that the probabilities of all the outcomes always add up to 1.

When we enumerate (count) the probabilities of obtaining the various outcomes of throwing a die, for example, we intuitively know that we will obtain a 3 one-sixth of the time. This means that:

$$P_3 = \frac{1}{3} = 1.667$$

Results from a pair of dice, however, are based on two results that occur independently of each other. The result of tossing the first die has no influence on the result of the second.

The result is a distribution of outcomes that looks like Figure 15.3.

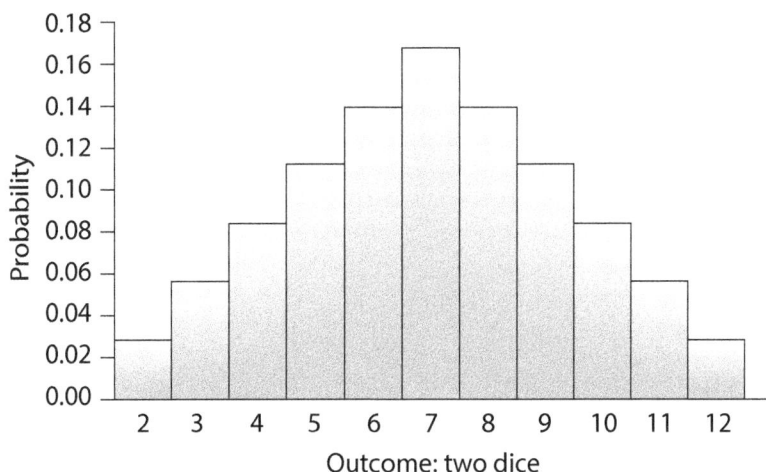

Figure 15.3 Bar graph of probabilities vs outcomes of throwing a pair of dice

If we are playing a game of chance based on the throwing of dice, it would be good to know what the chances of the various outcomes are in order to know what our chances are of winning. Given enough throws of the dice, the outcomes will closely resemble the probabilities shown in the histogram, assuming they are *fair* (not loaded).

The type of graph shown in Figure 15.3 depicts the probability of the various outcomes and is known as a *probability density function*. When we examine this graph, the probability of any of the outcomes is represented by the height of the corresponding bar in the graph. For example, the probability of obtaining a 6 is 0.14. We can also find probabilities by examining areas and portions of areas under the probability density function. If the width of each bar is 1, then the probability of obtaining a 6 is also represented by the area of the corresponding bar (height x width = 0.14 x 1 = 0.14). If we wanted to know the probability of obtaining a result of 3 or lower, the result would be the total area of the bars representing the outcomes 2 and 3 together:

$$P = P(2) + P(3) = \left(\frac{1}{36} \times 1\right) + \left(\frac{2}{36} \times 1\right) = \frac{3}{36} = 0.0833$$

If we added up all the areas of all the bars, we would obtain the value 1 (the sum of all the possible outcomes). The total area of the bars of a probability density function is always 1 if we set the width of the bars to 1.

The values of the outcomes of throwing dice are *discrete*. In many cases, however, measurements taken are more continuous in nature because their quantities are continuous (for example, length, height, weight, time). Continuous quantities that we measure are also distributed in some way. One of the most common distributions observed for real-world quantities is known as the normal distribution.

The normal distribution has a characteristic shape, commonly known as a bell curve, as illustrated in Figure 15.4. The normal distribution is very useful as it has very specific relationships to measures of central tendency and the standard deviation.

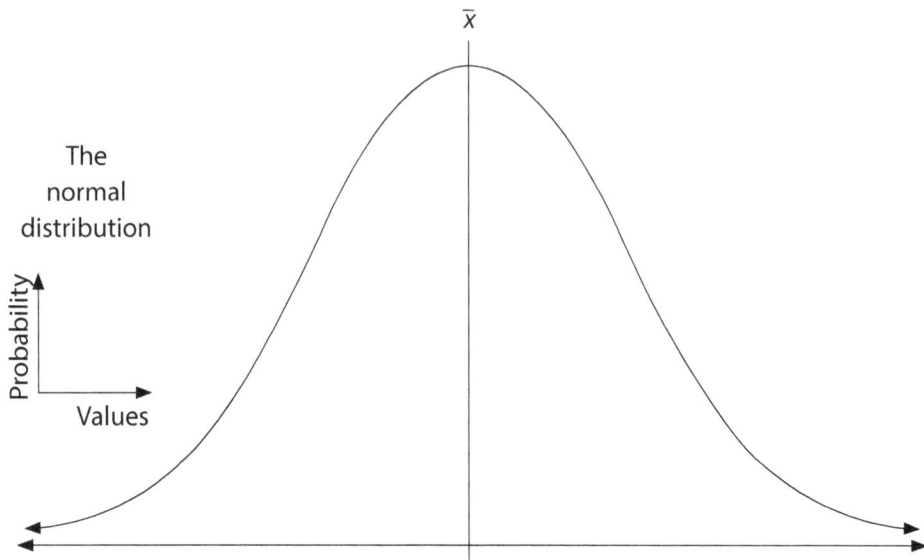

Figure 15.4 The bell curve of normal distribution

Note that the vertical line in the middle of the bell curve is the mean of an ideal theoretical data set (which we calculated earlier). Many of the analyses performed on our measured data involve comparing the data we gather to this theoretical ideal. For example, when students write a test, the ideal would be that the majority of students pass the test, with a small number getting distinctions for the test and a small number failing the test. If too many students get distinctions for the test, it means the test was too easy. Conversely, if too many students fail the test, it means the test was too difficult.

When we deal with continuous values, we use a version of the normal distribution, known as the standard normal distribution. The area under the curve of the standard normal distribution is also 1. When we determined probabilities for outcomes with discrete values, we calculated the area of the appropriate bars in the graph. When we determine probabilities for outcomes with continuous values, we are considering areas under the curve of the graph of the standard normal distribution.

Drawing conclusions from data

Once a data set has been gathered we can use it to draw conclusions or draw inferences from the data, using *inferential statistics*. For example, if we want to know what the world's population will be in 10 years' time, we would use inferential statistical techniques to arrive at an estimate. Such an estimate would be based on our knowledge of previous years' population growth, models of population growth and projections.

Gaining new knowledge requires us to draw inferences from sets of data — both old and newly gathered data, and data that is the result of our own work or that of others. Extending the data set by including another researcher's results may help to strengthen a case by increasing a sample size, if the data set is suitable for such use.

So when do we know that we have made a new discovery? When we can see, through testing our hypotheses, that the data we have gathered are statistically significant. Hypothesis testing provides a method for determining whether a result that deviates from established knowledge is the result of randomness in the gathered data or whether the data support a new understanding.

Hypothesis testing

In the vast majority of the world's legal systems, innocence is presumed and the burden of proof lies with the prosecution; in other words, they have to disprove the accused person's innocence. In hypotheses testing, the null hypothesis is presumed to be true and the 'burden of proof' lies in attempting to disprove the null hypothesis. We will follow an easy four-step process for testing hypotheses.

Step 1: Stating the hypotheses

You will recall that, earlier in this chapter, we defined two hypotheses relating to our example of treating broken bones. Let's restate these hypotheses and include some more details:

1. Null hypothesis (H_0): There is no significant difference between the use of red plaster and white plaster for immobilising humerus bones (upper arm) in humans during the healing phase and its use in reducing the healing time of bones, regardless of the circumstances under which the break occurs.

2. Alternative hypothesis (H_a): When compared to white plaster, the use of red plaster decreases the healing time for broken humerus bones in humans significantly, regardless of the circumstances under which the break occurred.

Medically, the accepted healing time for humerus fractures is six to eight weeks, or 42–56 days (Radiopaedia, nd). We shall use an average of these values (49 days) for our test.

So, stated numerically, our hypotheses are:

$$H_0 = 49$$

$$H_a < 49$$

Step 2: Setting the decision criteria

We had a sample data set and performed some basic analysis on that sample data set (see Table 15.1). When we wish to test our hypotheses, however, we need information on the population from which our sample is drawn. This information is shown in Table 15.5.

Table 15.5 Population and sample means and standard deviation

Quantity	Symbol	Value
Population mean	μ	49
Population standard deviation	σ	4.5
Sample mean	$\bar{x}$	42.0769

We start by stating that we want to be 95% confident in the decision that we make. Put another way, we want to be 95% sure that the effects of error (ie measurement error, sampling error, etc) in our sample cannot account for our finding.

Our experimental results have to 'beat the odds' in order for us to reject our null hypothesis and accept the alternative. What are those odds? In terms of probabilities, 95% of outcomes could result from error in our sample and support our null hypothesis (red plaster is no better than white). We call this possible result P_0 and assign it the value $P_0 = 0.95$

If 95% of outcomes are related to error in the sample, the remaining 5% must be related to an observed effect. If this is true, then this 5% must support our alternative hypothesis (our red plaster game changer). We call this possible result P_a and assign it the value $P_a = 0.05$

Recall that the standard normal distribution is a probability density function, which relates outcomes with probabilities. We are interested in finding an outcome value that represents the dividing line between 95% of the area under the curve and a remaining 5% of the area. We draw the standard normal distribution with these areas marked, as shown in Figure 15.5.

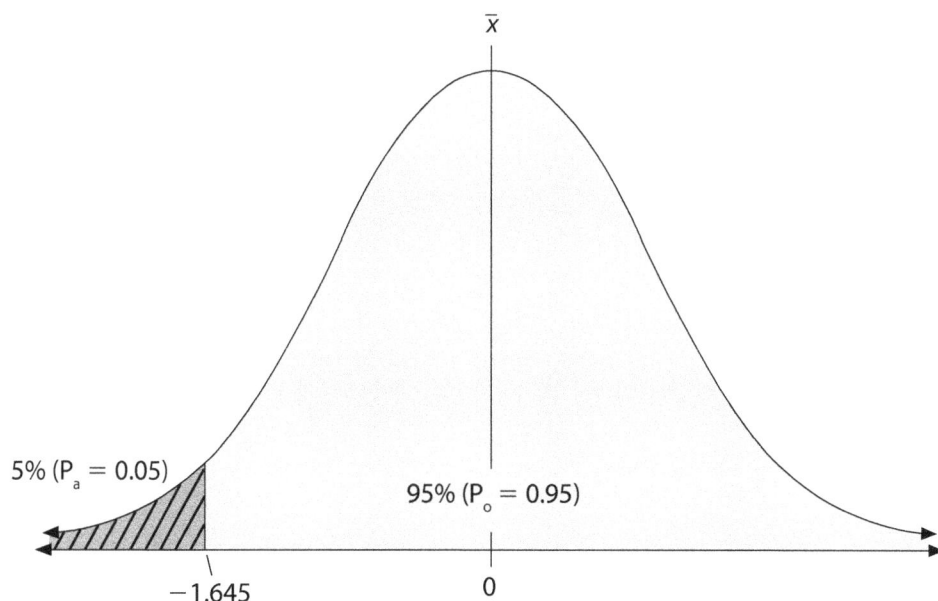

Figure 15.5 Standard normal curve with rejection region shown (striped)

Here, the shaded area to the right corresponds to the 95% of outcomes values where we will be forced to fail to reject the null hypothesis (ie accept the null hypothesis). The striped region to the left corresponds to the 5% of outcomes values that relates to low-value outcomes.

If we find that our result falls within the 5% region on the left, then our sample data allows us to *reject* the null hypothesis (ie accept the alternative). This region is called the *rejection region*.

The boundaries that we have established that separate the high-probability samples from the low-probability samples is known as the level of significance or the alpha level. For the proposed example, the alpha value (a) would be 0.05. With α = 0.05, we separate the most unlikely 5% of the sample means (the extreme values) from the most likely 95% of the sample means (the central values).

We find from our analysis of the areas that our outcome value (using our proposed alpha level of 0.05), called the z-score, is $z = -1.64$

A z-score will tell you if your score is above the mean or below the mean and by how many standard deviations. These z-scores relate confidence levels with z-scores and are commonly available in distribution tables for reference.

Table 15.6 Example z-score distribution table

(A) z	(B) Proportion in body	(C) Proportion in tail	(D) Proportion between Mean and z	(A) z	(B) Proportion in body	(C) Proportion in tail	(D) Proportion between Mean and z
1.50	.9332	.0668	.4332	2.00	.9772	.0228	.4772
1.51	.9345	.0665	.4345	2.01	.9345	.0222	.4345
1.52	.9357	.0643	.4357	2.02	.9778	.0217	.4778
1.53	.9370	.0630	.4370	2.03	.9783	.0212	.4783
1.54	.9382	.0618	.4382	2.04	.9788	.0207	.4788
1.55	.9394	.0606	.4394	2.05	.9793	.0202	.4793
1.56	.9406	.0594	.4406	2.06	.9803	.0197	.4803
1.57	.9418	.0582	.4418	2.07	.9808	.0192	.4808
1.58	.9429	.0571	.4429	2.08	.9812	.0188	.4812
1.59	.9441	.0559	.4441	2.09	.9817	.0183	.4817
1.60	.9452	.0548	.4452	2.10	.9821	.0179	.4821
1.61	.9463	.0537	.4463	2.11	.9826	.0174	.4826
1.62	.9474	.0526	.4474	2.12	.9830	.0170	.4830
1.63	.9484	.0516	.4484	2.13	.9834	.0166	.4834
1.64	.9495	.0505	.4495	2.14	.9838	.0162	.4838

Step 3: Computing the test statistic

Using the values we calculated above, we find a value called the test statistic (Z):

$$Z = \frac{\bar{x} - x_0}{\sigma} = \frac{49 - 42.0769}{4.5} = \frac{-6.9231}{4.5} = -1.5384$$

The test statistic is a normalised value which informs us of the relationship between the population and our sample. In order to interpret our result, we must compare the test statistic with normalised values which relate to our level of confidence in the result we have obtained. The standard normal distribution provides us with normalised values for direct comparison with our test statistic.

Step 4: Recording the decision

In our test above, we found:

z-score $= -1.645$
test statistic (Z) $= -1.5384$

In order for us to reject our null hypothesis, the test statistic must fall within the striped rejection region on our graph. For an alpha level of 0.05, the corresponding z-score is -1.64. Our test statistic, however, is -1.54, which falls in the shaded area on the graph, outside the rejection region.

We therefore conclude that we must fail to reject our null hypothesis, based on our analysis. Thus, based on our statistical analysis, we can conclude that the use of red plaster for immobilising humerus bones in humans during the healing phase does not reduce the healing time when compared to the use of white plaster, regardless of the circumstances under which the break occurs.

If the parameters surrounding the test had been differently selected, this result may have been different. For example, if we had selected an alpha level of 0.10 the normalised z-score would have been $z = -1.28$ and we would have accepted our alternative hypothesis. However, our choice of alpha level would then have been questionable due to being too wide a girth for error variance. By convention, commonly used alpha levels are $\alpha = 0.05$ (5%), $\alpha = 0.01$ (1%), and $\alpha = 0.001$ (0.1%).

The striped rejection region in our test tails away to the left, theoretically to infinity. This type of test is referred to as a one-tailed test and is directional. It is typically directional when we have justification for the direction. Using the proposed example of the red plaster, the direction is negative as we stated in the hypothesis that the red plaster would cause a decrease in the healing time of the bones.

Sometimes the hypothesis we are testing relates to a variation from an established baseline (either an increase or a decrease). We may want to determine whether consumer spending has changed significantly from an established baseline, for instance. To test this, we would use a two-tailed test, in which there are two rejection regions, at the left and right extremes of the standard normal graph, as shown in Figure 15.6.

In this graph, the total area under the curve is still 1, and the total area of the striped rejection regions is still 0.05 (corresponding to 5% of the total area). The same four steps are still used to construct our test. However, we would reject our null hypothesis if our obtained test statistic is less than 1.96 or greater than 1.96.

The level of significance is commonly denoted by the symbol α (alpha). Depending on the type of study being performed, various values for z are commonly used and may become familiar to you over time. Full sets of tables for z-scores are widely available and should be consulted when constructing tests.

Table 15.7 The z-scores for some commonly used levels of significance

Level of significance (α)	z-scores	
	One-tailed	Two-tailed
0.05	−1.645 or 1.645	±1.96
0.01	−2.33 or 2.33	±2.58
0.001	−3.09 or 3.09	±3.30

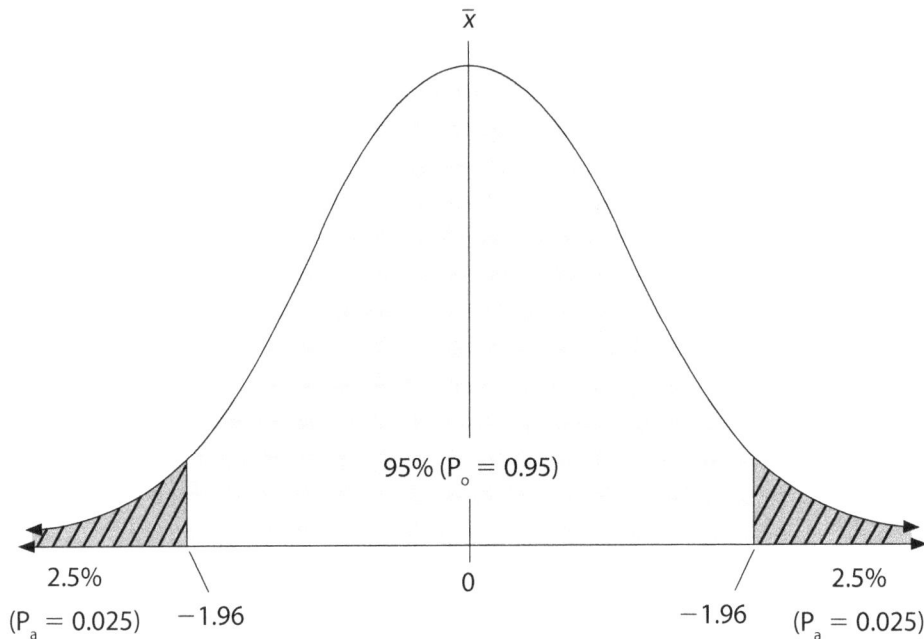

Figure 15.6 Standard normal curve with two rejection regions shown (striped)

Many other types of probability density functions exist and are used in different disciplines. Choosing the distribution to be used as a reference in testing hypotheses is an important step and may require some prior knowledge of the type of data being examined.

Presenting data

We ultimately use statistics to change perceptions or to change the way in which people do things. In order to achieve this, our data and our findings will need to be accurate and unbiased. Presenting people with raw data sets can often fail to achieve these goals due to complexity — even when we are dealing with other researchers in the same field. Data are therefore commonly presented in various ways that convey movement, changes or trends.

For example, if we wanted to demonstrate the effectiveness of the Covid-19 vaccination, we could track how many individuals have been vaccinated over a number of years and examine how the transmission rate of the virus has changed. This would be highly complex and needs to be simplified into trends or patterns that are easily accessible.

Human brains are designed to find visual patterns. Presenting quantities in a visual format can consequently convey meaning quickly and efficiently. Throughout this chapter, visual aids have been used to convey meaning by presenting numerical data in visual format (tables and graphs). Various graph types have also been presented to support the discussion.

Graphs are an effective and, generally, universally understood means of conveying trends (an upwards slope means that something is increasing, and vice versa). Various graph types may be used to show different aspects of the same data, as illustrated in Figure 15.7.

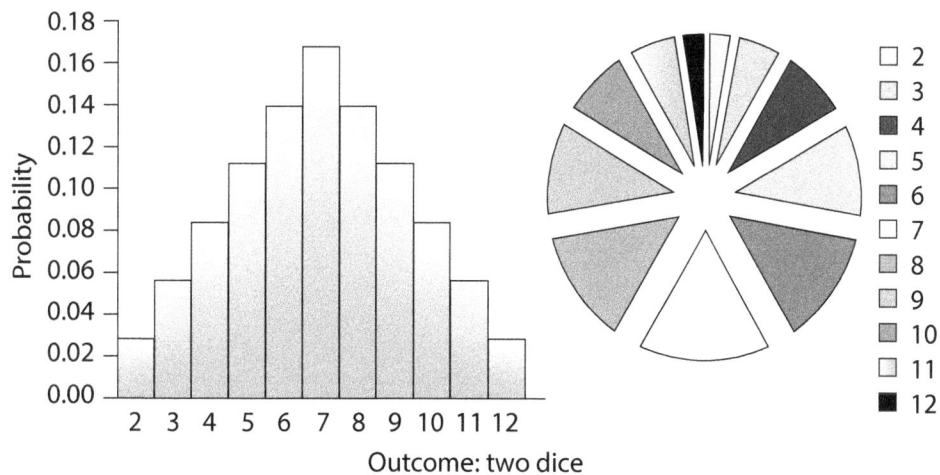

Figure 15.7 Two graphical representations of data (probabilities vs outcomes)

These two graphs show the probabilities of the various outcomes from throwing a pair of dice. In the probability histogram on the left, we can quickly see the relationship between the various outcomes and their absolute probabilities. However, we cannot easily see the proportions of the various outcomes easily, while in the pie graph on the right we can see almost immediately that almost half of the time, the outcome will be a 6, 7 or 8.

Presenting the results of a study will generally require a mixture of both text and graphics. It is generally not sufficient to present graphics and expect a reader to gain the expected understanding immediately. Explanatory text explicitly stating the intended meaning is required in order to ensure that the reader has understood the point being made.

Summary

Statistics provide us with a set of accepted methods for analysing sets of data. The two primary types of analysis allow us to characterise data and to draw conclusions from that data. Descriptive statistics allow us to develop summaries and to determine various key characteristics of the data, while inferential statistics provide us with means of drawing conclusions about populations based on a sample of data.

Probability is the study of the likelihood of observing various outcomes. Probabilities are expressed as fractions or decimal amounts, and the sum of all possible outcomes is always 1.

Inferential statistics attempt to determine whether a particular observed outcome is the result of error (supporting our understanding of existing knowledge) or whether we have discovered something new, supported by our gathered data. The accepted method for making such a discovery is to test hypotheses using the following four steps:

1. State the hypotheses.
2. Set the decision criteria.
3. Compute the test statistic.
4. Record the decision.

This established method enables us to draw defensible conclusions from a set of gathered data.

Review the chapter

Answer the questions and complete the tasks to assess whether you understand the content of this chapter:

1. Why is the use of standardised analysis techniques important when examining data sets? How do they help to remove bias and how do they ensure that conclusions are defensible?
2. What is meant by the term 'statistically significant'?
3. How can statistics be misapplied or misused and what can be the results of such abuse?
4. What is the difference between accuracy and precision when gathering data? How do they influence the data that is gathered?
5. What are the different causes of measurement error?
6. What does the correlation coefficient tell us about the relationship between two quantities?

→

7. Consider drawing a card randomly from a standard set of playing cards. State the probability of drawing:
    (a) a black card
    (b) a picture card
    (c) two pairs
    (d) a royal flush

8. How do the probabilities of the outcomes in question 7 change if jokers are present or absent from the pack?

9. What do the terms 'standard' and 'normal' refer to in the term 'standard normal distribution'?

10. How do the z-score and the test statistic relate to each other?

11. Review the graphs presented in this chapter and consider whether the choice of graph is appropriate in each case and whether it complements the discussion adequately. Would you have presented some of this data differently?

CHAPTER 16

Qualitative data analysis and interpretation

Rose-Marié Bezuidenhout and Franci Cronje

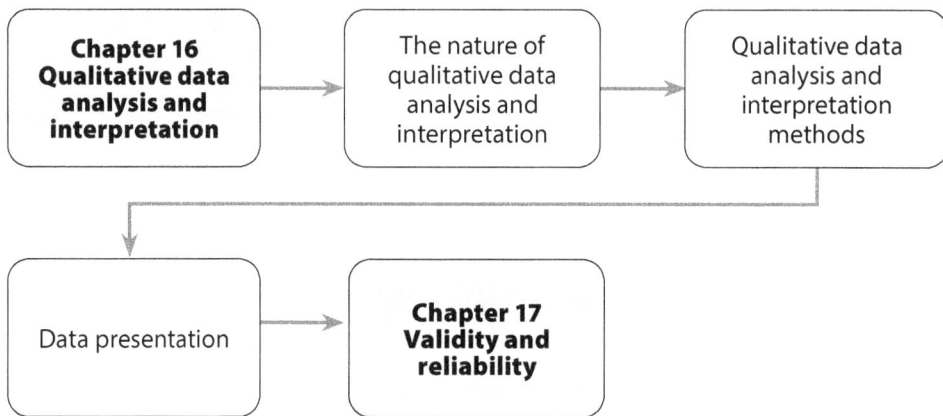

Overview

We discussed qualitative design perspectives and field research and non-reactive or unobtrusive data collection methods in Chapter 13. In this chapter we take the qualitative research process a few steps further and discuss possible ways in which you can analyse and interpret the data that you have collected. Regardless of what methods you have used in collecting qualitative data, you invariably end up with a vast amount of data that needs to be transcribed, analysed, interpreted and presented. The processes used in data analysis and interpretation are systematic and rigorous to allow a thick, rich and detailed description of meanings in presenting the capstone of your study: your findings. The aim of this chapter is to discuss some of the ways in which qualitative data is analysed, interpreted and presented. We start the discussion by briefly considering some shared characteristics of qualitative data analysis and interpretation methods.

Objectives of this chapter

By the end of this chapter, you should be able to demonstrate your understanding of the following:

- the nature of qualitative data analysis and interpretation;
- qualitative data analysis;
- conducting qualitative data analysis;
- coding and the different forms of coding;
- the steps involved in conducting qualitative content analysis;
- discourse analysis;
- conducting discourse analysis;
- conversation analysis;
- multimodal conversation analysis;
- semiotics;
- the interpretation of qualitative data; and
- the presentation of qualitative data.

The nature of qualitative data analysis and interpretation

People often mistakenly think that using a qualitative approach to research is easier than using a quantitative approach, which involves a statistical analysis of data. They typically underestimate the effort and length of time needed to perform a deep and close reading of text and to provide a detailed description of the findings. Basically, through qualitative analysis and interpretation, data is transformed into findings. This transformation is enabled by the researcher being totally immersed in the data and identifying and describing the evident and dormant patterns of meaning emerging from the data. This can be a long and arduous process, mostly due to the goals and characteristics of the qualitative research process.

In the section below we restate some typical concepts regarding qualitative research. The purpose of this summary is to provide the background against which you need to view the process of qualitative data analysis and interpretation provided in the chapter. We also suggest that you revisit the discussion on the interpretivist and critical realist approaches in Chapter 2 to refresh your memory on the goals of these approaches. Some of the distinct and unique concepts regarding qualitative data analysis and interpretation are described in the sections below.

Qualitative data is textual

Quantitative data consist of numerical information obtained from the collection of data from, for example, a standardised questionnaire, but qualitative data are more diverse and complex. Qualitative data are collected through a wide range of methods including face-to-face interviews and focus group discussions, but may also consist of social artefacts such as documents, Twitter tweets, YouTube videos, a book, a photograph, a building, a film, clothing and music, among others.

We transcribe data from all the raw information that we have collected from the written and verbal responses of participants during conversations, interviews and focus group meetings, and all the notes and journals we kept during field research projects. Transcribing data thus means that we copy and convert information into a written or visual format so that we can analyse it by using a systematic method. Thus, if you recorded an in-depth interview on a digital recorder, you would have to retype the whole interview word for word so that you can analyse it in the form of text.

Qualitative data are thus mostly transcribed into text and these textual transcripts are analysed and interpreted. Text has significance because it conveys potential meaning which the researcher interprets after doing a close and deep 'reading' of the text and following a process of analysis. Text is thus considered a meaning-creating site.

Qualitative data analysis and interpretation are iterative

In qualitative research 'iterative' and 'iteration' mean repeating the analysis and interpretation processes in a continuous cycle. The process is recursive and cyclical because the researcher is repeatedly analysing and interpreting data to isolate and refine the embedded meanings of the text under investigation. The researcher thus moves through successive cycles of analysis and interpretation, gaining new insight with each cycle. This process allows the researcher to identify emerging patterns in the text and to attain a deep and thorough understanding of the meaning of these patterns. In addition, the qualitative researcher describes the patterns of emerging meanings with increasing recombinant levels and cycles of understanding. This is made possible by fracturing the text and considering the parts in terms of the wider texts as well as the original context within which the phenomenon was studied or observed.

The initial stages of the analysis/interpretation process may also prompt the collection of additional data 'to confirm, clarify, or disconfirm' patterns identified in the data (Leedy & Ormrod, 2015:309). Leedy and Ormrod (2015:309) call this iteration between data collection, analysis and interpretation as the *constant comparison* method. For example, in inductive grounded theory the processes of data collection, analysis and interpretation are enmeshed because the focus is on the meanings which emerge from data rather than on a linear one-by-one application of methods. The methods are thus used to serve the goal of qualitative research, which is to determine how meanings are constructed in both a creative and multidimensional way.

Qualitative data analysis and interpretation are hermeneutic

The iterative cycles of analysis and interpretation resemble a hermeneutic circle or the interpretive movement between an event or phenomenon and its contextual meaning. The word 'hermeneutics' stems from the Greek term *hermeneuō*, which means 'to interpret'. In folk etymology the term is said to stem from Hermes, the god of communication and writing in Greek and Egyptian mythology. Hermeneutics includes a detailed reading or examination of text to interpret and understand the meaning embedded within text. Also known as *verstehen* (the German word for 'to understand'), interpretation is the process of giving meaning to a participant's experience by moving from the general to the specifics and from the specifics to the general (Littlejohn et al, 2017:111).

This movement between the general and specific enables you to use pure or critical hermeneutics to better understand and interpret all kinds of textual data. It allows the researcher to consider and describe a bigger and more holistic picture by looking at the interplay between specific details and the broader general context. Clarke (1994:43) explains this interplay as a 'continuous dialectical exchange to determine the sense of a text by the reiterative interplay of meanings between part and whole, and between text and context'. The researcher thus provides a deeper understanding of the specifics of a phenomenon observed by describing it in terms of its broader context.

The reiterative interplay of meanings and the iteration between analysis and interpretation of data mentioned previously present us with a challenge. Typically, analysis and interpretation are so intertwined that it is often difficult to present them separately. In this way the data that are analysed become the interpretation and, in turn, the interpretation becomes data to be further analysed, which then becomes a form of reinterpretation. There is an uninterrupted transition from the analysis to the interpretation of data. Consequently, in this chapter we discuss the analysis and interpretation of data concurrently, but also provide some guidelines for the interpretation of data.

Qualitative data analysis and interpretation are subjective

Hermeneutic analysis and interpretation are not appropriate when a researcher is looking for an unambiguous and objective outcome because it is up to the researcher to analyse and interpret the data and to make informed decisions regarding the findings of the research. In this sense, data analysis is interpretive; however, this does not imply that the qualitative research process is unscientific.

The goal of qualitative research is to gain an understanding of the subjective experiences of participants, but the processes of data analysis and interpretation are systematic and rigorous. There thus rests a great responsibility on the shoulders of the researcher to motivate the outcomes of his or her study. An interpretive approach to data analysis and interpretation rests on the foundation that there can be no absolute right or wrong answer for human behaviour. Hence, the qualitative analyst assumes that there is no absolute, factual truth independent of human interpretation. Rather, he or she regards and describes human behaviour in the context of the person who experiences a situation or phenomenon subjectively.

The notion of subjectivity also relates to the researcher as a research instrument in the data analysis and interpretation processes. Self-reflexivity (discussed in Chapter 13) and reflective practices and the acknowledgement of personal biases are essential to maintain rigour and trustworthiness throughout the qualitative research process.

Qualitative research is constructed and symbolic

When we say that qualitative data collection and interpretation are constructed and symbolic, we mean that both the researcher as research instrument and the participant interpret phenomena subjectively and express it symbolically. This refers to social constructivism and symbolic interactionism (see Chapter 2).

Symbolic interactionists view subjective experience as symbolic and constructed through social interaction. Symbolic interactionism emphasises the social dimension of symbols and views meaning as a product of social life using significant symbols (such as language) in a society.

Social constructivism (see the discussion on interpretivism in Chapter 2 for more information on the concept of social construction) is concerned with an inquiry into the construction of reality. According to constructivists, each individual constructs his or her world based on subjective experience. Symbolic constructionism considers the process by which meanings are created, negotiated, sustained and modified. The goal of constructivists is to understand the world of lived experience from the perspective of those who live in it.

By viewing reality as constructed and expressed symbolically, the qualitative researcher sets out to deconstruct text (see also Chapter 9). This is an attempt to understand how the meaning of the subjective experiences of participants is created and expressed symbolically. Deconstruction, as a method of analysing text, is the process through which the researcher fractures or takes text apart to understand how meaning is constructed. It is assumed that text contains the embedded meanings associated with the phenomena that participants experience subjectively. Deconstruction is based on the notion that language is typically imperfect and fluid in describing aspects of a phenomenon. It also assumes that the reader, rather than the author, is central in determining the meaning of a text.

Denzin and Lincoln (2018:47) refer to the qualitative researcher as a *bricoleur*, who, when applying interpretative methods, produces a *bricolage* or pieced-together representation based on an emergent construction of reality. These representations of participants' lived experiences may be likened to a patchwork quilt and the researcher to a quilt-maker. The qualitative researcher must piece together different representations of a complex situation from the data collected, and the findings that emerge from the analysis and interpretation represent the *bricolage* of the researcher. Adopting a *bricolage* approach allows researchers to revere the complexity of meaning-making processes which incorporate the intricacies and idiosyncrasies of lived experiences. The interpretive researcher (*bricoleur*) thus connects the parts (representations) to construct a whole picture (*bricolage*). In the next section we look at what is involved in the process of qualitative data analysis and interpretation.

Qualitative data analysis and interpretation methods

There are several ways of analysing and interpreting qualitative data, and these methods are increasing in number as researchers try to make sense of both our complex social and subjective world and the nature of qualitative research. Qualitative data analysis and interpretation typically involve complex and arduous processes, but it is also stimulating and rewarding since several layers of meaning embedded in the data might be discovered. The process can be likened to mining for 'gems of meaning' as the researcher sifts significance from trivia while seeking patterns of meaning.

We present several qualitative data analysis and interpretation methods in the following section to give you a sense of not only their similarities but also how difficult it is to describe and represent the dynamic nature of the processes. A preliminary review of several research sources indicates that common denominators of qualitative analysis methods are *the reduction, organisation, interpretation* and *substantiation* of data. Although this process and its methods seem straightforward, they are not linear and one-dimensional and may be experienced by the researcher as rather scrambled and ambiguous at first — which leads to the first step in analysis: the organisation of data.

Saldaña (2014:581) suggests that organising and maintaining 'an orderly repository of data' is necessary for easy access and analysis. You can use several 'cosmetic devices' such as different font styles, sizes and colours to recognise pieces of raw data and differentiate between, for example, data collected from interviews and field notes. Saldaña (2014:583–584) lists the steps after data organisation as: *jotting down* notes to capture fleeting thoughts while immersed in the data; *prioritising* chunks of relevant and significant data to 'help answer your research questions or emerge as salient pieces of evidence'; *analysing* to recognise patterns within the data and to construct meaning that 'capture their essence and essentials'; and *patterning* to discern 'similarities within and regularities among data' collected. Saldaña (2014:584–605) explains that the subsequent steps support patterning or 'pattern-making', including coding, categorising, interrelating, reasoning, memoing and making assertions. During the final stages of analysis and interpretation the researcher displays, narrates, verifies and represents the findings.

Creswell and Creswell (2018:269) describe similar steps in the analysis process as organising and preparing the raw data for analysis, reading through all the data, coding the data while concurrently developing themes and descriptions, interrelating themes and descriptions, and interpreting the meaning of the themes and descriptions. Throughout this process information should be validated for accuracy. With some variation, Creswell and Poth (2018) present the analytic process as a spiral of analysis including the following elements: managing and organising data, reading and memoing emergent ideas, describing and classifying codes into themes, developing and assessing interpretations, and representing and visualising the data. They emphasise the cyclical nature of the process and state that 'the researcher engages in the process of moving in analytic circles rather than using a fixed linear approach' and 'the researcher touches on several facets of analysis and circles around and around' (Creswell & Poth, 2018:254).

Researchers tend to describe processes for the analysis of qualitative data in detail, but often neglect or omit explaining strategies for the interpretation of data. The reason may be because the processes are so interrelated as mentioned previously in the chapter. A useful explanation is provided by Trent and Cho (2014:640), who distinguish between the often-entangled processes as analysis consisting of the 'summarising and organising' of data, and interpretation as the 'meaning-making' process. Interpretation, as an interconnected aspect of the qualitative research process, is thus 'a process of collective and individual "meaning-making"' through the selection and transformation of data, and the ascribing of meaning to data (Trent & Cho, 2014:640). Additionally, interpretations are socially constructed arguments presented as 'unique, contextualised meaning'; thus, interpretation is 'knowledge construction' (Trent & Cho, 2014:641). Through thick and rich descriptions during the meaning-making or sense-making process, researchers stamp their mark on the data 'allowing for the emergence of multiple, rich perspectives' (Trent & Cho, 2014:644). The transformation of data into contextual meanings also involves relating interpretations to existing literature and theories related to the phenomenon under investigation. As part of the interpretation process, researchers create loops and connections between their interpretations — richly presented with justified data exemplars (usually verbatim quotes from participants' responses), existing literature and their conceptual and theoretical frameworks. As researchers engage in an interpretive iteration, they may uncover similarities and differences through the comparison of their findings with existing literature and theory. Differences between findings and conceptual literature indicate the researcher's unique contribution to understanding aspects of participants' lived experiences. This interpretive iteration or looping thus embeds the findings within the contextual framework of a study with the final aim of answering the research questions.

In the following section we discuss several data analysis methods, namely qualitative content analysis, thematic analysis, discourse analysis, conversation analysis, multimodal conversation analysis and semiotic analysis. However, keep in mind that there are many more qualitative data analysis techniques available that you can investigate and use for qualitative data analysis.

Qualitative content analysis

We use the terms 'qualitative content analysis' and 'textual analysis' interchangably. Both refer to content as text and the process involved in the analysis is the same. The use of either term seems to be based on the individual researcher's discipline and preference and the origin of the method within a specific discipline. Textual analysis is thus a transdisciplinary method used in both the social sciences and humanities. Qualitative content analysis, according to Macnamara (2018), uses techniques derived from textual analysis, rhetorical analysis, discourse analysis, semiotic analysis, and interpretive analysis and, consequently, the analysis process and procedures are similar. Additionally, Drisco and Maschi (2016:83) note that thematic analysis (TA) is comparable to current forms of qualitative content analysis and may be 'an early, underdeveloped variant of contemporary qualitative content analysis'. Despite their origin, the analytic processes of qualitative content analyses and thematic analysis are very similar, with slight differences in the steps described. For example, coding is generic and can be applied to most other methods of data analysis. We discuss coding in detail in this section, but with the understanding that the same process is applicable to the other methods we discuss later in the chapter.

Qualitative content analysis is used to explore and identify overt and covert themes and patterns embedded in a particular text. It is the process of reducing data and obtaining meaningful interpretations through the identification and description of categories of themes using a systematic coding process. Schreier (2014:170) indicates that qualitative data analysis has three distinctive features: '[I]t reduces content, it is systematic, and it is flexible.' It reduces data since the researcher focuses on specific data and their meaning to answer the research question. It is systematic because it requires the researcher to first do a close reading of all the data, and then follow sequential steps to code data systematically and iteratively. The flexibility of qualitative content analysis is evident in that it 'combines varying portions of concept-driven and data-driven categories within any one coding frame' (Schreier, 2014:171). This implies that the researcher uses both a deductive and an inductive approach to data analysis.

Qualitative content analysis can be conducted inductively, deductively or abductively. When a researcher uses a *deductive approach*, he or she argues from the general to the specific. When conducting deductive qualitative content analysis (a concept-driven analysis), the researcher uses a conceptual framework derived from applicable theories (the general) to identify several specific codes within the text, which are grouped into several specific themes (the specific). Deductive codes are also called *a priori* codes and are developed before examining the data. These themes are then linked to the literature and the theoretical framework (the general) that the researcher described in his or her study and are interpreted within the context of the specific study (the specific). Note the iteration between general and specific, and analysis and interpretation. The researcher moves from the general to the specific in several cycles of analysis and interpretation. In this process the relevance and applicability of the theories are tested and, in some instances, expanded. The disadvantage of a deductive analysis is that a researcher may overlook unexpected but key aspects of the phenomenon experienced by participants 'since the main concern simply is to "prove" or "demonstrate" the theory and assert their *a priori* arguments' (Kennedy & Thornberg, 2018:51).

Reasoning from the specific to the general means that the researcher is using an *inductive approach*. When a researcher uses raw data (specific) in his or her analysis to develop themes without using a preconceived conceptual framework, it is considered as inductive (a data-driven analysis). The codes, themes and categories emerge from the data through a process of constant comparison. When conducting an inductive qualitative content analysis, for example in grounded theory, the researcher develops theory from the specific data collected from a specific social setting and develops a general theory. The theory thus emerges from the data. A critique of inductive data analysis without *a priori* codes is the 'naïve' assumption that researchers 'can collect and analyse theory-free data without any prior theoretical knowledge' (Kennedy & Thornberg, 2018:51).

The difference between deductive and inductive content analysis lies in the use of an existing theoretical framework. Contrary to grounded theory, where you create your own framework (inductive), in deductive qualitative content analysis you are led by existing theories, thus a preconceived and pre-structured theoretical framework.

A third approach to qualitative data analysis may also be appropriate in qualitative content analysis where a hybrid from of inductive and deductive analysis is used, namely, *abductive analysis*. 'Abduction is about discovering new concepts, ideas and explanations by finding surprising phenomena, data, or events that cannot be explained by pre-existing knowledge' (Kennedy & Thornberg, 2018:52). In an abductive analysis the researcher uses 'a selective and creative process' to test existing knowledge while seeking novel ways of understanding phenomena with an openness and readiness for new patterns of meaning. During an abductive analysis, the researcher adopts a questioning frame of mind and realises the need for constant reiteration between analysis and meaning-making or interpretation since 'conclusions are always fallible and provisional' (Kennedy & Thornberg, 2018:62).

Regardless of the approach, in conducting qualitative content analysis the idea is to group data together into chunks and then assign them to broader categories of related meanings. This could also be referred to as indexing textual units. In this way the researcher structures the data into codes and themes, which can then be applied to all the text. By giving the data some sense of order, the researcher can identify whether there are patterns embedded in the text. This can lead to the development of more categories and subcategories.

The process of grouping data into categories is referred to as coding. Coding is a system that makes the process of analysis manageable. It can be applied to all texts, including focus group notes, observations, interviews, written texts, visual images and any tangible interpretable artefacts. The goal of qualitative coding is not the counting of data, but what Strauss (1987:29) describes as the *fracturing* of data. Fracturing data means that the researcher breaks the text down into codes and concepts and rearranges and orders them into meaningful categories. The process of coding is critical because it will eventually enable you to contribute findings to your discipline. We discuss the process of coding in more detail later in the section.

The most prudent way to discuss the process of data analysis is to present it systematically and in the form of sequential steps. Several researchers have proposed and developed steps based on their own studies. You must also identify, adapt and describe the process you intend to follow in your analysis. The choice of which steps you need to follow will be determined by what you aim to achieve with your study. Hence, your research goal and question should be your first considerations.

In the following section we combine the steps proposed by Zhang and Wildemuth (2009: 309–311) in the process of qualitative content analysis and the six recursive phases of thematic analysis as proposed by Clarke and Braun (2014:6626–6628) and reflexive thematic analysis proposed by Braun and Clarke (2019:589–597). We have adapted the steps and phases for the purposes of this book, as follows:

1. Preparation of and familiarisation with data.
2. Defining the coding units to be analysed and generating initial codes.
3. Developing categories and a coding scheme or conceptual framework: generating initial themes.
4. Test your coding scheme on a sample text.
5. Code all text.
6. Assess your coding consistency.

7.   Draw conclusions from the coded data (interpret your data).

8.   Report your methods and findings.

Step 1: Preparation of and familiarisation with data

You need to organise and convert, or transcribe, the raw data that you have collected into written text before you can start with the analysis. This includes data derived from, for example, interviews and recordings.

Remember that not all raw data are relevant or useful. For example, when you intend to analyse existing text rather than text transcribed from an interview, your decision of what to include and what to exclude should be guided by your research goal and question. In the case of data obtained from interviews and focus groups you need to decide if you want to use summarised versions or the full range of responses, including non-verbal cues such as pauses and exclamations displayed by participants during interviews. Some data might look irrelevant at the outset but could gain significance in the second or third cycle of coding. The more complete and more organised the transcriptions, the more useful they will be during the analysis. Once again, you should be guided by what you want to know, hence your research goal and question.

By transcribing your data you also get to know your data better. During the first round of transcription, you aim to get a general feeling of information gathered during, for example, interviews. Doing a close reading of the data involves a familiarisation with and immersion in the data. Familiarisation with the data assists in identifying features that may be relevant to the research question. Every time you revisit the material it creates another opportunity for reflection. Making notes and writing down your impressions as you go through the data will improve your intimate understanding of the material. An important practice that you should adapt is memoing.

Memoing entails making reflective notes about what you glean from the data while you are reading and coding it; hence, the sense you make of the data. These notes could include remarks or questions related to the text that you are reading. You thus write memos to yourself as reminders of your thoughts and insights during the reading, coding and analysis of the text. These notes could also be used as data to be analysed. In addition, the notes could serve as evidence of the processes that you followed, and thus increase the trustworthiness of your study. Remember that data that is not transcribed or thoughts that are not recorded are as useless as trying to locate a misfiled book in a library. It might be lost forever.

In the example in Figure 16.1 a video was transcribed with time markers in place so that specific points in conversations could be traced for further transcription during the next stage

Step 2: Defining the coding units to be analysed and generating initial codes

This step refers to the basic coding unit or unit of text that you intend to analyse. A coding unit is also called a 'concept' by some researchers. This is a crucial step in the process. Here you have to indicate whether you are going to use individual words, phrases, symbols, sentences or paragraphs as your coding units. It is a way of organising your data into manageable chunks. Also consider that you are examining text for an idea or a concept which could be expressed in different ways, including a single word, a phrase, a sentence, a paragraph or an entire document. Zhang and Wildemuth (2009:309–311) state that, '[t]hus, you might assign a code to a text chunk of any size, as long as that chunk represents a single theme or issue of relevance to your research question(s)'.

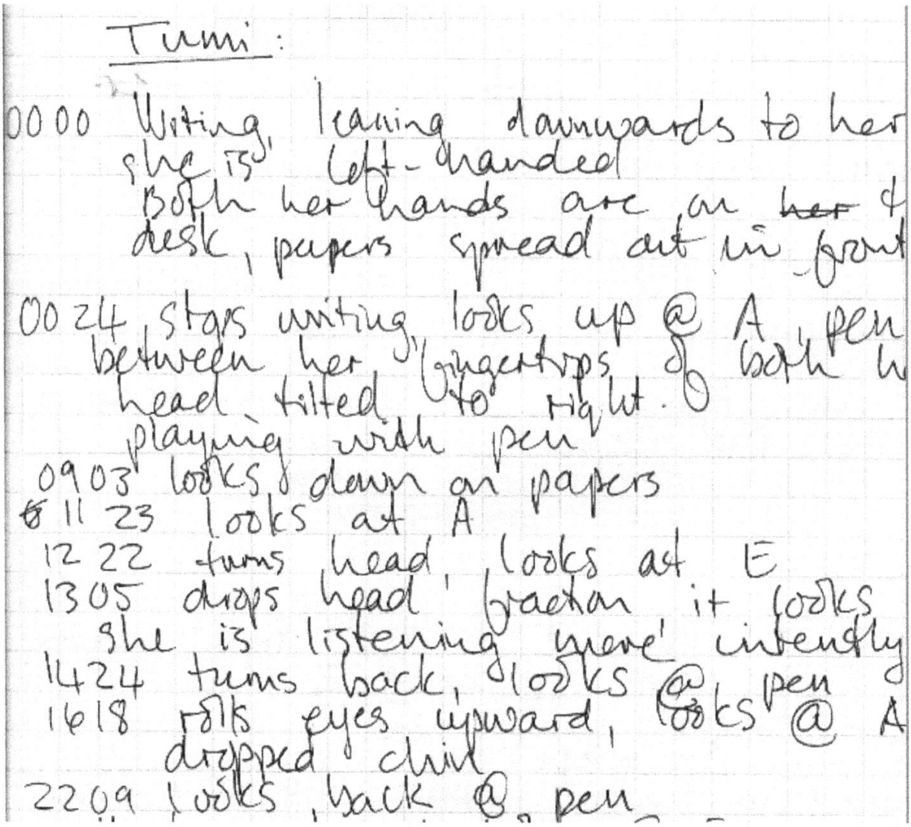
Tumi:
0000 Writing, leaning downwards to her
she is left-handed
Both her hands are on ~~her~~ &
desk, papers spread out in front
0024 stops writing, looks up @ A, pen
between her fingertips of both h
head tilted to right.
playing with pen
0903 looks down on papers
~~0~~ 11 23 looks at A
12 22 turns head, looks at E
1305 drops head, fraction it looks
she is listening more intently
1424 turns back, looks @ pen
1618 rolls eyes upward, looks @ A
dropped chin
2209 looks back @ pen

Figure 16.1 Example of a transcribed video

Clarke and Braun (2014) define a code as a concise tag/label which describes something meaningful about the data. Codes can either contain the surface and overt meaning of the data (semantic, manifest, or *in vivo* codes) or identify deeper hidden meanings of data (latent and covert codes). Latent codes are dormant and identified by the researcher based on theoretical or *a priori* concepts (concept-driven) through deductive data analysis. Semantic or manifest codes are data-driven and grounded in the data, and meanings thus emerge from the data through inductive data analysis.

In this step you examine the data (text) closely and decide how to break it down into chunks or parts. Consider that you will compare and group these chunks in terms of relations, similarities and dissimilarities. Different chunks or parts of the data will hence be marked with appropriate codes to identify them for further analysis. Use files, folders, boxes, sticky notes and labels to organise material into sections that make sense to you. Every researcher has a unique way of ordering material, and there is no standard way.

You should be led by your research question in identifying the coding units you need to use — hence the importance of formulating your research question as precisely and concretely as possible.

Step 3: Developing categories and a coding scheme or conceptual framework: generating initial themes

This step involves grouping related coding units together to form categories of codes or themes. Braun and Clarke (2019:359) define themes as 'patterns of shared meaning underpinned or united by a core concept'. Clarke and Braun (2014; 2019) explain that the process of constructing or developing categories and themes involves the identification of patterns of meaning across the data by grouping relevant codes together. You may also develop a conceptual frame or framework which could assist you in coding your data. You develop your conceptual framework or coding scheme (sometimes referred to as concept mapping) either from the raw data (inductively) or based on previously conducted studies and theories (deductively). It may also include a combination of an inductive and deductive coding scheme. In this instance, some codes are previously known and others emerge from the data.

The researcher must label or name the categories of codes or themes. Some researchers refer to labels as indicators. Naming or labelling chunks or categories of codes could be done, for example, by taking terms used by participants during interviews or observations. This is referred to as 'in vivo' labels for codes and themes. Alternatively, the researcher may construct his or her own names or labels for groups or categories of codes by using common properties of the codes or concepts based on the text that is being analysed. You may also decide to organise your codes into different dimensions and hence use a hierarchical conceptual frame (see Figure 16.2).

An important aspect of coding is that you should define every code, theme and category clearly and systematically to allow you to apply it to the text as consistently as possible. The reason for this comprehensive description is to facilitate the identification of these codes and themes in the text that you are analysing. Describing categories comprehensively also allows you to identify the differences between the categories of themes. You may also want to develop a coding book or manual to ensure the consistency of your coding. A coding manual describes category names, definitions or rules for assigning codes, and examples.

In describing your codes, themes and categories, ensure that they have the following characteristics:

- They should be *exhaustive*. There should be enough categories to accommodate all the data. More categories may emerge after several cycles of reading the text. You may also want to have a 'miscellaneous' category if some codes do not fit the existing themes. This category may be revisited at a later stage and relabelled or discarded.
- They should be *mutually exclusive*. Each theme and category should be distinct, with no overlap in meaning. Hence, there should be no uncertainty under which themes codes should be grouped. No coding unit should be placed in more than one category.
- They should be *specific*. Themes and categories should be specific. Their relevance should be obvious and discernible, even to someone not directly involved in the development of the themes.

In Figure 16.2 we provide a graphic representation of a hierarchical conceptual framework or coding scheme. In this hypothetical example the researcher identified the codes, themes and categories from concepts derived from a theoretical framework and previously conducted research studies on cyberbullying. See Chapter 3 and compare this conceptual framework with the mind map we provided there. The conceptual framework is more detailed and specific. The acronyms listed next to the themes can be used in coding a specific text. It saves the researcher the time needed to write out the label of the theme every time a section of the text is coded.

The naming and defining of categories of codes or themes form the heart of the interpretive analytic process 'where the researcher produces detailed and complex definitions of each theme, which capture its shape and texture and how it relates to other themes' (Braun & Clarke, 2014:6627).

Step 4: Testing your coding scheme on a sample text and reviewing potential themes

This step involves testing the clarity and consistency of your category definitions on a sample of your data. Coding definitions and rules need to be redefined if the level of consistency is low. During this stage, all doubts and problems related to your coding categories need to be resolved.

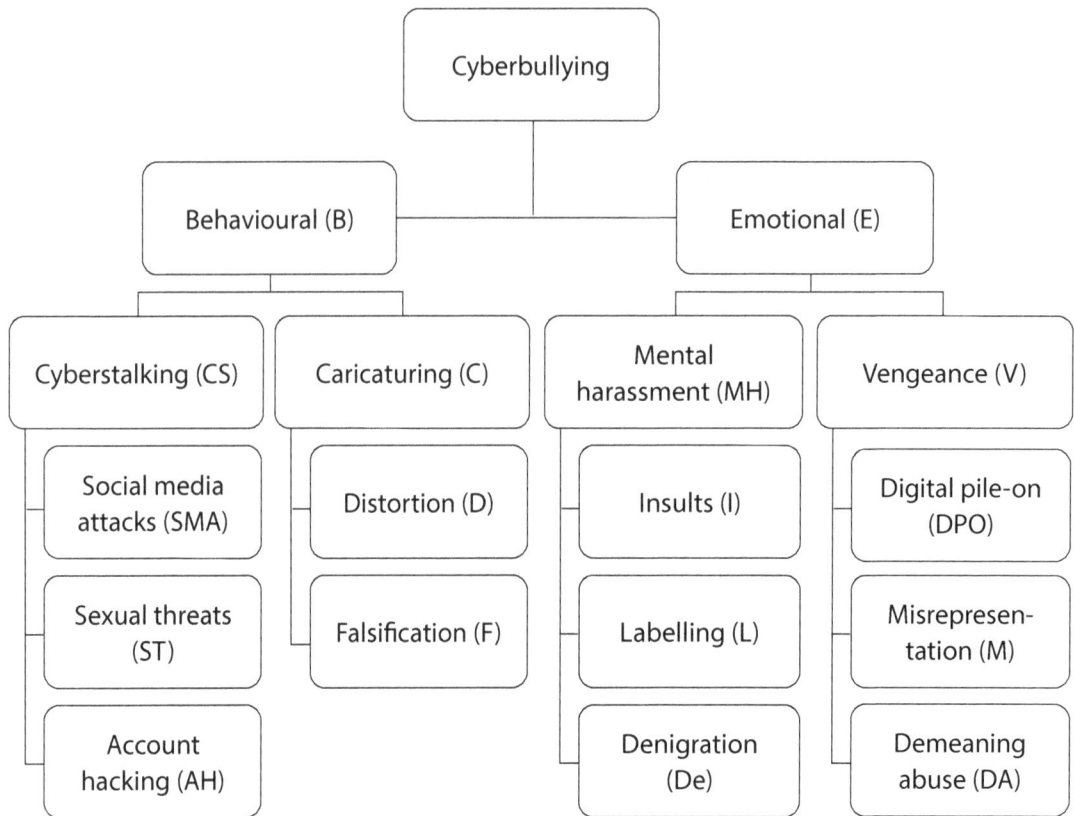

Figure 16.2 A diagrammatical representation of a hierarchical conceptual framework or coding scheme

Step 5: Coding all text

Coding data refers to the scrutiny of data and taking note of all the relevant and meaningful sections and items. You can highlight all those relevant sections with symbols, descriptive words or codes that would order the information into areas that you can refer to when you analyse your data. However, keep in mind that you could also use several forms of coding. Some forms of coding include:
- line-by-line coding;
- open or substantive coding;
- axial coding;
- selective coding; and
- thematic coding.

Line-by-line coding is a form of microanalysis and means that the researcher literally reads through parts of the text line by line while marking certain words and phrases that are relevant to the study. By doing this the researcher can develop categories within which to group the codes or concepts. Line-by-line coding can be used both inductively and deductively. It is very time consuming, but it helps to build a conceptual frame which could be applied to all the data. When no new codes or concepts are unearthed, you have reached data saturation point (see Chapter 11) and the process of coding that particular text is then completed.

In the following example the researcher took economic metaphors used to describe the value and worth of interpersonal relationships and used them as codes. The researcher read the text line by line, highlighting the relevant codes.

> People invest time in their interpersonal relationships because they believe these relationships have great value . A rewarding relationship is priceless because it supplies people with support and love. Without such relationships people feel emotionally bankrupt . Quality relationships are therefore an emotional investment and a great gift one can give oneself.

Figure 16.3 An example of linebyline coding

Open or substantive coding is similar to line-by-line coding. However, in this form of coding the researcher reads though the entire text in order to get an overall impression and understanding of the text. Concepts related to the words and phrases in the text are identified and noted either in a separate document or by making notes in the margins of the text. The researcher will then group these concepts into bigger categories of concepts. These concepts are then identified in more data and compared with any new concepts that emerge. The process thus involves breaking down, examining, conceptualising, comparing and categorising and re-categorising data.

Strauss and Corbin (1990:96) define *axial coding* as 'a set of procedures whereby data are put back together in new ways after open coding, by making connections between categories.' Hence, axial coding follows open coding and the researcher compares categories of concepts and identifies the connections and relationships across categories. The researcher may thus decide to merge categories or codes and may re-categorise others. The researcher also takes the context in which the events or incidences occurred into account in the coding.

Selective coding involves selecting the core or essential codes that closely correspond with the typical behaviour that has been observed in the field or codes that most adequately describe the central notion of the research study. In most instances it is a tentative description of the essential core codes. The core concepts are then used as a guiding principle in selecting related concepts. All subsequent data coding is based on the core codes or concepts. In a grounded study the core concepts may also be used to collect new data. This process of using core codes selectively in identifying and comparing data is also referred to as theoretical coding. The theoretical codes emerge from the process of constantly comparing the data in field notes and memos and are applicable when a researcher is building theory inductively from the analysis and interpretation of data. An example is when a researcher is exploring how femininity is constructed in text and therefore uses 'femininity' as a core code.

Thematic coding is also known as conceptual, concept or focused coding (Saldaña 2016:294). Thematic coding is hence used in a thematic analysis of a text. Thematic coding is a process of data reduction by means of identifying themes. In thematic coding you often use deductive coding by using a list of themes known or anticipated to be found in the data, usually derived from your literature review.

If you are using deductive coding, in this step the coding scheme or conceptual framework is applied to all text. You hence identify, isolate and contextualise all the bits of data that would inform your research questions based on your conceptual framework. It involves an immersive and close reading of the text whilst applying the coding scheme. It is also possible that new and unexpected codes are identified which need to be added to the coding scheme.

However, if you are using an inductive coding approach, you allow codes to emerge from scrutinising the text. The development of codes, themes and categories from raw data is an iterative process, also referred to as the *constant comparative method* (Glaser & Strauss, 1967). You should continuously and repeatedly read through the material and decide on dominant trends or patterns, inductively work with emergent categories and constantly compare them. Use your own descriptive themes and phrases and establish categories according to those sentences and phrases. Write a descriptive paragraph about each category of each of your own sections to allow you to refer to your categories at a later stage. Some themes might only emerge while working through your material for a second or third time.

Step 6: Assessing your coding consistency

Once all coding has been completed it is important to recheck the consistency with which the coding was conducted. You may want to use a second coder to confirm your coding consistency. Consistency between the coding of several coders is referred to as establishing intercoder reliability.

Step 7: Drawing conclusions from the coded data (interpreting your data)

This step involves the interpretation of the themes or categories identified. According to Zhang and Wildemuth (2009:313), '[a]t this stage, you will make inferences and present your reconstructions of meanings derived from the data.'

In this step of the process you must rely on your ability to augment the analysis with your own interpretation by drawing on existing theories and previously conducted studies, and your own sense of the meaning of the text. This process also resembles iteration. Hence, the interpretation of the analysed data is done through the consideration of theoretical constructs (general) and your own sense of the meanings imbedded in the text (specific) and the augmentation and amplification of your understanding by referring to the broader context (general) of the study.

Since this type of interpretation is context sensitive, you need to consider and describe how the meanings that you have reconstructed from the analysis of the text are linked to a broader context. The broader context includes the circumstances within which the phenomenon was observed and, possibly, cultural, social and political environments. This will depend on the research goal and question(s) of the study. Interpretation involves three steps:

1. Explaining the relationships you found.
2. Considering extraneous information.
3. Avoiding false interpretations.

Before we move on to the reporting of your methods and findings, also consider the following aspects regarding the interpretation of data:

- It is difficult and it is an art learnt through practice and experience.
- The usefulness and relevance of research findings lie in proper interpretation.
- You must look for the broader meaning of your findings.
- You must expose the relations and processes that underlie your findings.
- You can use your interpretation to link your results with the results of other studies.
- You can formulate new ideas, theories or concepts which will serve as a guide for future research.
- Ask yourself: did I really investigate the problem, and can I answer my research question?

Step 8: Reporting your methods and findings

This step requires that you report on the process that you applied in your coding, analysis and interpretation, as completely and truthfully as possible. It is important that the researcher reflexively and transparently expresses how the analysis and interpretation processes may have been influenced by his or her own assumptions, biases and theoretical awareness.

Qualitative content analysis is supported by computer programs such as Coding Analysis Toolkit (CAT) and ATLAS.ti. Although the first round of coding might be done digitally, it is not advisable to leave content and textual analysis to a non-discriminatory method. In the second and subsequent rounds, the researcher needs to assess the phrases and words to catch intonations and inferences that might lead to further thematic linkages.

Discourse analysis

Discourse analysis has a wide range of applications in different disciplines. The term 'discourse' simply means a particular way in which language, both spoken and written, is used to express certain thoughts or ideas. A general definition of discourse analysis is that it is a linguistic approach to text where the researcher tries to determine how speakers or authors choose words to construct a social object or event. Simply put, it means looking at language to determine how ideas are conveyed to construct a particular reality. Discourse analysis is thus a way to understand how language is used to construct social realties (Allen, 2017). It considers the discursive construction of actions and events and their social consequences (Willig, 2014:342). For example, it is used to make sense of the ways in which the media conveys meaning and constructs different aspects of reality, such as what it means to be beautiful or successful.

A critical approach to discourse analysis is concerned with the power relations, cultural and social backgrounds and intentions inherent in a message conveyed through language (Willig, 2014). It explores the way in which language and political and social structures and institutional practices overlap, or imbricate (how they overlap in layers). Critical discourse analysis reveals sources of power and how discursive institutional practices are used to maintain power relations by, for example, 'obscuring or mystifying power inequalities' (Willig, 2014). A researcher uses this method to unearth, for example, power relations embedded in narratives with the purpose of either challenging existing relations or maintaining the status quo. Consequently, the researcher often approaches the analysis with the specific agenda of exposing, for example, covert forms of discrimination and prejudice in texts. The best application of critical discourse analysis in research would be in a socio-political context. A researcher may also want to unearth covert attitudes and behaviour described in, for example, propaganda messages.

In discourse analysis the researcher is looking at how meaning is constructed in messages. It is also used to understand the narrative or story that a text may reveal. Discourse analysis is also often used in education and mass communication to assess how messages are constructed and used by people.

When you conduct discourse analysis, it is important that you decide on codes and standardise them, so that the coding within your research material can be applied consistently. Create an easily referable key for your own use when you start coding and stick to it. See the previous section for more detail on the coding process

In the transcription of data a researcher would employ certain conventions used in a specific discipline. For example:

- Capitals are used for emphasis.
- To indicate an overlap of speech — where two participants have been speaking simultaneously — descriptions are written in parentheses (. . .), and transcriptions will be in square brackets, thus: [. . .].
- Utterances in another language, or some convention that the researcher sees happening throughout the speech, can be transcribed in italics, and so on.
- Lines are numbered and usually relate to words uttered as a section of speech or where sentences broke by way of natural pauses.

Figure 16.4 below is an example of how a researcher could code text in discourse analysis. In the transcription of a conversation between Bob and Annie, one can see how the researcher used certain conventions of coding to refer to the rhythm, tone and detail of the conversation for later analysis. In line 2, for instance, Bob and Annie talked simultaneously. Capitals indicate emphasis, and [.] shows a pause in an utterance. Italics here were used to indicate a voice trailing off, getting softer while someone else talked 'over' the softer voice.

(1)	Annie:	I am saying that
(2)	Bob:	No but you are not listening.
	Annie	I am not
(3)	Annie	sure
(4)	Bob	[.] If you let me EXPLAIN [.] properly
(5)	Bob	you might be able to understand *better*
(6)	Annie	I'm done talking [.]

Figure 16.4 An example of a transcription for discourse analysis purposes

Critics of discourse analysis argue that transcribing the spoken word into text, such as the example above, does not yield the necessary depth of interpretation because some inflections and emphasis — and therefore deeper meanings — might get lost in the process.

Conversation analysis

Conversation is an activity in which one person speaks while another listens. A participant changes from the role of speaker to listener, and vice versa, all the time. Conversation analysts have noted that speakers have systems for determining when one person's turn to speak or listen is over and the next person's turn begins. This exchange of turns (or 'floors') is signalled by such linguistic means as intonation, pausing and phrasing. Some people wait for a definite pause before beginning to speak, but others assume that 'winding down' is an invitation to someone else to take the floor. When speakers have different assumptions about how turn exchanges are signalled, they may inadvertently interrupt or feel interrupted. On the other hand, speakers also frequently take the floor even though they know the other speaker has not invited them to do so.

Conversation analysis is sometimes called the study of talk-in-interaction, and it looks for patterns in language (Toerien, 2014). This method highlights subjective ideas and the understanding that people exhibit in their everyday communication. The researcher uses micro-analysis of a certain piece of the text. It is thus not suitable for large amounts of data. The approach can be time-consuming and intensive.

When you plan to use this method it is essential to make either audio or video recordings because they need to be analysed in detail. After the first round of coding has been done, you will narrow your areas of focus to such an extent that you can identify a limited amount of video, such as 30 seconds, on which to concentrate. When working with audio only, these sections might be longer. It is, however, key that these sections represent most of the themes and contexts on which you decided to focus. It is therefore obvious that this method is not suitable for large amounts of text.

When working with audio and video recordings of individuals it is essential to obtain informed consent from your participants. They should be fully aware of what you are using the material for, whether you will publish examples of texts or video recordings and if their identities will be protected.

There are sensitive ethical issues concerning minors. Researchers should always obtain parental consent. Consult your own educational institution's guidelines regarding research ethics and follow the rules carefully. If a researcher errs in this respect, it might render a whole body of research null and void.

Multimodal conversation analysis

Multimodal conversation analysis consists of using a set of communicative modes such as proxemics (the use of space and distance), posture, head movement, gestures, gaze and spoken language as sets of representation to understand the meaning of both implied and overt messages (Norris, 2004). This type of analysis is an outflow of social semiotic analysis methodology specifically concerned with human movement and interaction between parties. This method of analysis attempts to take body language and other modes of expression used as part of a conversation into account.

Multimodal conversation analysis is useful if a research study deals with non-verbal cues as a significant aspect of the data. Sometimes attitudes are communicated more clearly by way of body language and other forms of non-verbal communication than by the spoken word. This technique combines textual analysis with multimodality to gain a more layered understanding of a social phenomenon.

A multimodal approach deals with all kinds of modes that the researcher identifies as being important in the communication process. Sound (voice, ambient sounds or music), the proximity of bodies, body language and the spoken word can be identified and coded as significant factors in a focus group. Other modes that might be analysed in other situations could be colour, the layout of a room, room temperature, and many other visual and non-visual aspects influencing a communication situation.

This method can be very productive if the researcher clearly describes which modes are important for the study and crafts the coding according to what would serve the research study best.

Researchers commonly use the following three aspects for analysis:

1. *Proxemics* is the distance between people in a conversational stance. Here one considers intimacy and attitude. Be mindful that many aspects of proxemics, such as distance, are culturally conditioned (for example, in Western cultures people have a larger personal space than in most African cultures).

2. *Posture* is also culturally determined. Many aspects of body language can be considered here, such as the position and general demeanour of a person's body.

3. *Gaze* involves the organisation (direction) and intensity of looking at people during a conversation.

Semiotics

It is important to note that the following section is an abridged version of a very complicated and involved, yet popular, method of analysing and interpreting text. The reason why we have included semiotics in this chapter is to make you aware of this method, should it suit your study. We advise you to use additional sources that discuss semiotics in more detail should you choose to use it as a data analysis method in your own research. What follows is therefore only a summary of semiotics.

Two dominant models of contemporary semiotics emerged from the theories of the linguist De Saussure (1857–1913), also sometimes referred to as Saussure, and the philosopher Peirce (1931–1958) (Chandler, 2017:3). The term 'semiology' (from the Greek *semeion*, which means 'sign') refers to the Saussurean tradition, whilst 'semiotics' sometimes refers to the Peircean tradition. Nowadays, however, the term 'semiotics' is more likely to be used as an umbrella term to embrace both traditions (Chandler, 2017:3).

One of the broadest definitions of semiotics is that it is concerned with anything that can be considered a sign. Chandler (2017:2) describes semiotics as the study of how meanings are made and 'how reality is represented through signs and sign systems'. Semiotic analysis is hence focused on the construction of socially derived meanings found primarily in text. It is the study of the processes by which meaning is created, transferred and circulated, and includes three principal areas of study: signs, sign systems and codes. This process of creating meaning is also referred to as *signification*. In semiotics the significance that readers attach to the signs within a text is hence emphasised. A semiotic textual analysis involves an attempt to determine and deconstruct the ways in which signs and codes operate within texts (usually popular texts that can be found in the mass media) or genres (Chandler, 2017).

Semiotics involves the study of what is referred to as signs or the arbitrary associations between signs and the things to which they refer — their referents — as used in everyday speech. For example, the letters *c-a-t* make up the sign or symbol 'cat', which refers to a four-legged mammal, which is the referent of the sign. The sign also includes anything which stands for something else and may take the form of words, images, sounds, gestures and objects. An image of a cat is therefore also a sign for a cat. It is generally referred to as text.

Semiotics can be applied to any sign which can be seen as signifying something. What we mean by signification is that all signs have meaning, and people sometimes attach different meanings to the same sign, which is why sharing meaning is so difficult. The Saussurean terms 'signifier', 'referent' and 'signified' are most often used in semiotics.

Chandler (2017) states that semiotics seeks to analyse text as structured wholes and investigate latent and, hence, connotative meanings. Therefore, concepts that relate to semiotics are *denotation* and *connotation*, or the primary and secondary meanings associated with signs and symbols. Denotation is described as the definitional, literal, obvious or common-sense meaning of a sign or symbol (Chandler, 2017). The term 'connotation' is used to refer to the sociocultural and personal ideological and emotional associations of the sign or a person's personal interpretation of the sign.

Since only a summary of semiotic and semiotic textual analysis are provided here, you are advised to identify and consult comprehensive sources should your study include semiotic textual analysis.

Data presentation

By now you have revisited your research problem and question many times during the process of data analysis and interpretation. In this section you are once again required to reflect on your research problem and question. Although you are not recrafting the research question itself, this is your opportunity to answer it and to indicate how you have achieved your goal and solved your research problem by presenting your analysis and interpretation of data. In your presentation, take a moment to remind your reader exactly what the problem was, and how you investigated it. Hence, in your presentation of your data you are revisiting the main research question with a short preview of how you endeavoured to answer it.

When presenting qualitative content analysis results, you should strive for a balance between description and interpretation. Keep in mind that qualitative research is fundamentally interpretive and that the interpretation represents your personal and theoretical understanding of the phenomenon under study. You therefore need to give rich and thick descriptions with verbatim exemplars mined from data to increase the trustworthiness of your findings. You need to organise your information throughout the presentation in terms of the themes and categories that you used in your analysis and interpretation.

In many instances the presentation of your data analysis and interpretation is done concurrently and alongside the actual analysis and interpretation. For example, researchers include quotations and highlighted codes in the text of a research report, dissertation or thesis to illustrate the processes. Although it is common practice to use typical quotations to justify conclusions, you also may want to incorporate other options to display your analysis and interpretation, including matrices and conceptual coding schemes.

Keep in mind that you need to provide a thick description of the analysis and interpretation. Remember that you are showcasing the evidence of how you analysed and interpreted your data. Put in the necessary effort to use academic writing in its finest form.

Accuracy should be an obvious foundation throughout the presentation. The reader needs to know that the report is trustworthy and worth citing. The presentation needs to be open and accessible, using the data as unwavering truth. Hence, present the data as accurately and comprehensively as possible by using rich and thick descriptions.

You can juxtaposition or use contrast to describe your analysis and interpretation in such a way as to create a compelling story of your journey of research. You are telling readers your research story, and you need to convince the audience that it is a true and noteworthy body of research. In order to increase the trustworthiness of your study it is imperative that you describe the method-creation processes in detail.

It is also important to contextualise data analysis and interpretation and present it in a way that people can relate to. By describing the context and background of your study, you are grounding your analysis and interpretation.

Finally, it is important to understand that the trustworthiness of the body of research lies in the way in which the data analysis and interpretation are presented. The researcher needs to maintain an openness and honesty in unpacking the analysis and interpretation of data and should provide the reader with the necessary insight and understanding.

Summary

In this chapter we discussed the nature of qualitative data analysis and interpretation, with the purpose of providing a background against which you can view various techniques. We discussed the iterative nature of analysis and interpretation and explained how difficult it is to present the two processes separately.

We also discussed qualitative data analysis and provided an eight-step process to allow you to conduct qualitative analysis. Coding and different forms of coding were explained, and examples were provided.

Several data analysis methods were discussed, including discourse analysis, conversation analysis, multimodal conversation analysis and semiotics. Lastly, we discussed how you should go about presenting qualitative data analysis and interpretation.

Review the chapter

Answer the questions and complete the tasks to assess whether you understand the content of this chapter:

1. What is the nature of qualitative data analysis and interpretation?
2. Explain the eight steps in conducting qualitative data analysis.
3. What is coding?
4. Explain four different forms of coding.
5. What is discourse analysis?
6. Explain how to conduct discourse analysis.
7. What is conversation analysis?
8. What is multimodal conversation analysis?
9. Define semiotics.

CHAPTER 17

Validity and reliability

Marla Koonin

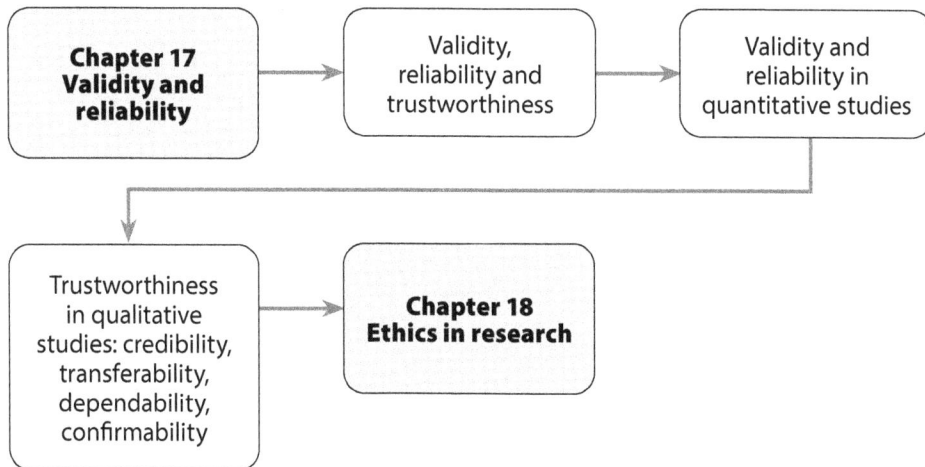

Overview

So far, you have learnt what research is, as well as how to identify a research problem, formulate your research aims and questions, conduct a literature review, select the population and sample, and collect and analyse data. However, none of these processes has any merit if your research design and the research methods you use to collect your data are not reliable and valid.

Reliability and validity in research are much like the way in which human beings develop feelings of trust in certain people. When we trust someone, we also feel that we can rely on that person; we trust that when this person tells us something, it is true. In a similar way, the characteristics that make us trust in the truthfulness of research need to be considered. Therefore, in this chapter you are introduced to reliability and validity, and trustworthiness in relation to research.

It is important to make you aware of the fact that the concepts 'reliability' and 'validity' are most used in quantitative research, relating to the evaluation of the quality of a study. This does not mean that qualitative researchers do not deem validity and reliability important; they just use different terminology to describe the same notions. Instead of referring to validity and reliability, qualitative researchers refer to trustworthiness, which is made up of four criteria, namely credibility, transferability, dependability and confirmability.

Objectives of this chapter

By the end of this chapter, you should be able to demonstrate your understanding of the following:
- the concept of reliability in the context of quantitative research;
- the concept of validity in the context of quantitative research;
- internal and external validity;
- trustworthiness in relation to qualitative research;
- credibility in relation to qualitative research;
- transferability in relation to qualitative research;
- dependability in relation to qualitative research; and
- confirmability in relation to qualitative research.

Validity, reliability and trustworthiness

Think of people in your life whom you consider to be reliable. Who are they? What makes them reliable? Is it because they are people who always do what they say they will do, when they say they will do it? The people we find reliable are generally people who do as they say — if a person says she or he will meet you at your house at 7 am, then you know you can rely on that person to be there. These are people whom you would probably trust to do things for you because they do what they say they will.

In research, we also want to be able to trust the findings of researchers. We want to know that if a different researcher repeats the research, she or he will find similar results. As was mentioned before, the terms 'reliability' and 'validity' are most commonly used in quantitative research. When conducting quantitative research, researchers tend to use research methods that generate measurable, numerical and statistical results. We also often seek causal relationships in quantitative research. Thus, we are looking for the causes of certain effects. We can test and retest whether the same cause, under the same circumstances, causes the same effect. If we conduct an experiment, for example, and we find the same result every time we repeat the experiment, we can be sure that our findings are reliable. IQ tests, for example, are very reliable because you are likely to get a similar IQ score every time you take the test.

In contrast, the purpose of qualitative research is not to find causal relationships or to generalise results to a broader population. Instead, qualitative researchers attempt to provide an in-depth understanding of a phenomenon. Because the aim of qualitative research is not to generalise results, 'reliability' and 'validity' are not useful terms to use within these types of studies. Qualitative researchers therefore prefer to use the concept *'trustworthiness'* to measure reliability and validity within qualitative studies. However, it should also be noted that when qualitative researchers use the terms 'reliability' and 'validity', they apply them differently (Lincoln & Guba, 1985).

Validity and reliability in quantitative studies

Reliability and validity in quantitative research are ensured through, for example, large sample sizes, random sampling and reliable research tools.

Reliability in quantitative research

Reliability is linked to the findings of research. When assessing if a research method or instrument is reliable, you need to ask whether the same results could be produced if the research were to be repeated by a different researcher at a different time using the same method or instrument. Therefore, reliability is about the stability, accuracy and the consistency of a measure (Heale & Twycross, 2015:66; Patten & Newhart, 2018). If other researchers use your data collection instrument, will they obtain the same results? Thus, how stable is your instrument? For example, if you used a survey with a closed-ended questionnaire to determine how many hours per day young adults in Gauteng use social media, another researcher using the exact same questionnaire on a different set of young adults (from the same population) should find similar results to yours. If she or he does find similar results, it means that your research instrument can be considered reliable.

In other words, reliability refers to 'a research instrument that is able to provide similar results when used repeatedly under similar conditions' (Kumar, 2019:346). However, keep in mind the possibility that some sources of error could affect your data collection and, thus, the reliability of your data. This should be considered when analysing the reliability of a research project. An error in this regard could be anything that affects your data. A source of error could be, for example, if people misinterpret a question in your questionnaire or even interpret the same question differently. Reliability is thus not a fixed property of, for example, a questionnaire and will depend on the function of the instrument, the context of the assessment environment and statistical analysis, among others. Three attributes or aspects that are used to measure reliability include:

- *Homogeneity:* the internal consistency of an instrument and how the items of the instruments measure a specific construct;
- *Stability:* the degree to which the same instrument when tested and retested under the same conditions produces the same results; and

- *Equivalence:* the consistency of responses by multiple respondents to an instrument or different forms of an instrument.

Another term used when looking at reliability is '*generalisation*'. Reliability can be seen as the extent to which the results can be generalised and similar results obtained if the research was conducted again. Generalisation is an important concept in quantitative studies, since the aim of quantitative research is often to find universal laws that are applicable in all circumstances (Carminati, 2018; Cheng, Dimoka & Pavlou, 2016).

Imagine you were asked by Food Lover's Market, a South African supermarket chain operating franchised grocery stores and convenience stores, to measure how satisfied their customers are with the service of the cashiers at the check-out counters. You conduct a study on 10 000 Food Lover's Market customers countrywide, using a telephonic survey and asking them four questions. You conduct these telephonic interviews between January and April 2021. When you analyse the results, certain trends emerge about how Food Lover's Market customers feel about the service of the cashiers. If you had to conduct this study on a different set of 10 000 Food Lover's Market customers, in the same period, asking them the exact same questions, you should find similar trends related to customer satisfaction of Food Lover's Market cashiers. The results are thus generalisable.

It is important to know that there are also different types of reliability and different concepts related to reliability, as in the case of qualitative research. As you progress in your own research and move on to more complex and sophisticated research, you will learn about different types of reliability. The purpose of this book is to lay the foundation and explain the primary concepts of research, and we will therefore not explore the different types of reliability in great depth. However, it is important that you know that different types or forms of reliability exist. Table 17.1 briefly summarises the different types and techniques used to measure reliability.

Validity in quantitative research

Validity concerns determining whether a test or instrument (for example, a questionnaire) measured what it was supposed to measure. In other words, validity is the extent to which the instrument that was selected reflects the reality of the constructs that were being measured. A valid instrument thus measures what it claims to measure or was designed to measure. For example, IQ tests are very reliable, but they are often criticised for not being valid. It is arguable whether the questions asked in an IQ test really measure how intelligent a person is or whether they simply measure how good the person is at solving certain problems, ignoring the person's abilities. It is also important to keep in

Table 17.1 Different types of reliability

Type of reliability	What it measures	How it is established	How to improve it
Inter-rater (inter-observer) and inter-coder	A measure of agreement and consistency (terms used are 'replicability', 'repeatability', 'dependability' and 'generalisability') and equivalence	Used to assess the agreement and consistency between independent researchers/observers/coders observing the same phenomenon at the same time. Inter-observer or inter-rater reliability coefficients are used.	• Training of researchers • Well-defined and developed criteria to measure variables • Comprehensive operationalisation of constructs
Test–retest	A measure of stability	Assessed when an instrument is administered using the same participants more than once under similar circumstances, at two different points in time.	• Questionnaire design should consider respondent fatigue and moods • External factors that could influence data collection should be considered
Parallel (or equivalent) forms	A measure of equivalence	Measures the correlation between two equivalent versions of a test across time or one set of questions is divided into two equivalent sets measuring the same construct, knowledge or skill. The two sets of questions are given to the same respondents within a short period of time.	• Ensure that all questions or test items are based on the same theory and formulated to measure the same thing

→

| Split-halves | A measure of homogeneity (internal consistency) within the test itself | One group of respondents is randomly split into two and both groups respond to the test at the same time. Different participants are used, but the same method, tool or instrument is administered. When a researcher correlates the two sets of scores, a split-half reliability coefficient is determined. Researchers can also use Cronbach's alpha, a measure of the internal consistency of a test or scale. | • Eliminate poorly correlated items across an instrument
• Include highly reliable items to scales |

mind that validity is a 'matter of degree; it is appropriate to discuss how valid a test is — not whether it is valid' (Patten & Newhart, 2018:123). Hence, tests and instruments may be partly valid depending on the extent to which they measure a construct.

It is also important to know that there are different forms and types of validity. Firstly, it is important to distinguish between internal and external validity. We discuss these in the sections that follow. Table 17.2 explains some other types and forms of validity that you may encounter in your research.

Table 17.2 Different types of validity

Type of validity	Explanation	Questions to ask
Judgemental validity (based on expert judgements) has two forms: • Content validity • Face validity	*Content validity* assesses the appropriateness of the contents of a test or instrument and if a test or instrument represents the current available knowledge of a construct of interest. *Face validity* assesses how a test or instrument measures what it claims to measure at face value.	Is the test representative of the constructs measured? Does the test measure what it claims to measure at first inspection? Is it well designed? How does the test or instrument represent the construct and the existing domain of a topic of interest? For example, when testing the prevalence of dementia, an instrument should include known and established dimensions and constructs.
Empirical validity (based on data collected and not subjective judgements or theory): predictive or criterion-related validity	Comparisons based on a chosen criterion.	Does the test accurately predict future behaviour? How accurate is the measure or procedure when compared to another?
Construct validity (based on both subjective judgements and empirical data)	Assesses if a measurement tool or instrument represents the construct to be measured. Establishes the overall validity of a method.	Does the test measure the construct it is intended to measure? Is the theoretical construct comparable to the specific measurement or procedure?

Internal validity

Internal validity refers to whether the research method or design will answer your research question. In other words, there must be no errors in the design of your research and your research method must be able to assist you in answering your research question.

Internal validity also speaks to errors in the results that may still emerge, even though certain controls were put in place to prevent this from happening. Unfortunately, there will always be a small margin of error in all research studies, regardless of how meticulous the researcher was.

External validity

External validity focuses on the ability to generalise findings from a specific sample to a larger population. External validity refers to your ability as a researcher to state with confidence that, if the same research method and design you applied to your sample were applied to the rest of the population, you would find the same results. In other words, you can generalise the results from your sample to a broader population. If, for example, you conducted an experiment in a controlled environment such as a laboratory, you should be confident that you will find the same results when you test your respondents outside a controlled environment. Thus, your research should be conducted in such a way that if, for example, children show violent behaviour in a laboratory after exposure to violence on television, it means they would do the same when they are at home. (Note that the example study we have used here has certain ethical implications — see Chapter 18 for more on ethics in research.)

Pilot studies

Quantitative research projects generally use what is termed a 'pilot' study to increase the validity and reliability of a study. A pilot study can also increase the quality of a study by enhancing validity and reliability (Malmqvist, Hellberg, Möllås, Rose & Shevlin, 2019). Pilot studies are sometimes also referred to as feasibility studies. Pilot studies can be seen as mini versions of the research project. They are mostly used to pre-test the measurement instrument and are therefore frequently referred to as pre-tests. In a pilot study you test a small segment of the actual population that you will draw your sample from; however, these respondents are not from your actual sample.

A pilot study can act as a pre-warning system because possible errors or difficulties with your measurement instrument will emerge during a pilot study. You can then modify your measurement instrument based on the feedback and information you gained from your pilot study. A pilot study could, for example, be used to determine whether your respondents understood all the questions in your questionnaire correctly.

Trustworthiness in qualitative studies

Since qualitative researchers do not use numbers as evidence, they use different criteria to determine the trustworthiness, or integrity, of research findings. Keep in mind that the aim of qualitative research is to gain an understanding of a particular phenomenon within a specific context and not to generalise results to a broader population.

It is easier to measure reliability and validity in quantitative research because the research is often based on causal (cause-and-effect) relationships or aspects about a relationship that can be measured. For example, you could enumerate how many students between the ages of 18 and 25 consider tattoos to be fashionable. Through, for example, a survey, you could calculate that 86% of students between the ages of 18 and 25 consider tattoos to be fashionable. However, what you would not be able to determine through quantitative means is an in-depth understanding of why these students think tattoos are fashionable, and what the significance of tattoos is to them. If you repeated the quantitative study using a different sample from the same population, you would be likely to get a similar result. However, repeating a qualitative study to get the same results is not possible — participants' answers are not objectively measurable, since they are unique to each individual's experience.

Even though some qualitative researchers still use the terms 'reliability' and 'validity', the way in which they determine reliability and validity differs from how this is done in quantitative studies. There is a move towards the use of different terminology to indicate validity and reliability in qualitative studies. The overarching term that is used for validity and reliability in qualitative research is *'trustworthiness'*, consisting of the four criteria of credibility, transferability, dependability and confirmability, or the 'goodness or quality criteria' (Guba & Lincoln, 1994:112). Ensuring the trustworthiness of a study is thus an attempt by a researcher to safeguard research rigour and the quality of a qualitative study. We discuss the four criteria of trustworthiness below.

Credibility

Credibility refers to the accuracy with which the researcher interprets the data based on the responses as actual meanings of the research participants, or the 'truth value' of the interpretations (Lincoln & Guba, 1985). Credibility is increased when the researcher spends long periods of time with the participants to understand them better and gain insight into their lived experienced related to a phenomenon. This is also referred to as *prolonged engagement* with participants.

Credibility is also increased by making use of triangulation (Lincoln & Guba, 1985). For example, using methodological triangulation such as in-depth interviews, focus group discussions and reflective field notes to collect the data in one study will ensure credibility. Several researchers may also be used to ensure credibility. Known as *investigator triangulation*, two researchers, for example, will code and interpret data independently and then compare the interpretations (Korstjens & Moser, 2018:122). This process is also referred to by some qualitative researchers as 'inter-coder reliability'. It is used when evaluating the inter-coder reliability (ICR) of a coding frame in the analysis of qualitative data (O'Connor & Joffe, 2020). O'Connor and Joffe (2020:1) concur that the practice is controversial in qualitative research as 'an inappropriate or unnecessary step within the goals of qualitative analysis'. Nonetheless, they argue that it may increase the trustworthiness of a study by improving 'the systematicity, communicability, and transparency of the coding process; promoting reflexivity and dialogue within research teams' (O'Connor & Joffe, 2020).

Korstjens and Moser (2018:122) include data triangulation as a strategy to ensure credibility. For example, by using various data sets such as raw data, codes, concepts and theoretical saturation, the credibility of findings may be enhanced.

Credibility is also increased when your findings are believable from the participants' perspective, referred to as *member checks*. For example, if you do a study on prostitution, your participants must find your description of their lives believable. A researcher may, for example, allow participants to review and verify the authenticity of interview and focus group transcripts, interpretations and findings to determine if they reflect their experiences.

Transferability

Transferability is the applicability or usefulness of a study's findings to the theory and practice of another study in a similar context and delivering similar results. It could thus be compared to the external validity of a quantitative study (Moon, Brewer, Januchowski-Hartley, Adams & Blackman, 2016). In other words, it is the degree to which the analysis and findings can be applied beyond a specific research project (Lincoln & Guba, 1985). Transferability is ensured by the researcher using detailed and thick descriptions in describing the behaviour, experiences and opinions of participants.

Dependability

Dependability refers to the quality of the process of integration that takes place between the data collection method, data analysis and the theory generated from the data (in the case of a grounded theory approach) (Lincoln & Guba, 1985). Dependability is comparable to the consistency and reliability of the research findings of a quantitative study. It relates to how detailed the research procedures of a study are documented and described to allow other researchers to critique, follow and review the process, thus the repeatability of a study. To increase the dependability of a qualitative study the researcher should provide rich and thick descriptions of the research design (methodology and methods), the data collection processes including field notes, memos, the researcher's reflexivity journal, the data analysis process (the coding process and the coding frame or manual), data interpretation and a reflective appraisal of the project.

The richness and depth of descriptions affords *transparency* to a qualitative study and allows determining if appropriate methods were used and sound research practices were followed. The concept of transparency in qualitative research has three dimensions: data, analytic and production transparency (Moravcsik, 2019). *Data transparency* relates to the augmentation and amplification of data to reflect the richness and diversity of the social activities and contexts of qualitative research. Because qualitative research often includes intangible constructs and 'inner truths', *analytic transparency* means that researchers must 'show and tell' how they analyse, interpret and use deductive, inductive or abductive reasoning to arrive at meanings of the lived experiences of participants. *Production transparency* relates to how researchers describe the design and methodological decisions they made during the research process, how robust their methods were and what contextual factors may have influenced their judgements.

Confirmability

Confirmability refers to how well the data collected supports the interpretation of the researcher and the findings of the study. It indicates how well the findings flow from the data. It requires the researcher to describe the research process fully to assist others in scrutinising the research design (Lincoln & Guba, 1985). Other researchers who look at the data must come to similar conclusions as the researcher did. As with establishing credibility, you can improve the confirmability of a study by utilising the processes of methodological, data source, investigator and theoretical triangulation.

Researchers can increase the confirmability and credibility, and hence the rigour of a study, by using a reflexive journal to record and reflect on their biases and preconceptions during the research process. Using a reflexive process, they should question, acknowledge and address the effects that their backgrounds, beliefs and experiences may have on design and methodological choices and data analysis and interpretation. Reflexivity thus includes the iterative examination of a researcher's biases and assumptions regarding aspects of the research process such as methodology, theory, participants and 'self'. This means that reflexivity involves more than simple reflection on the research process and outcomes and should include multiple layers and levels of reflection of the research process. For example, if you are conducting a qualitative study on why students cheat in writing academic assignments, such as contract cheating (paying someone to do an assignment on your behalf) or other forms of academic dishonesty, you must reflect on your own assumptions and bias towards academic dishonesty as a researcher and how these assumptions may affect the research process and the findings of your study. The process of reflexivity is discussed in more detail in Chapter 16.

Table 17.3 A comparison of terminology in qualitative and quantitative research

Qualitative terminology	Quantitative terminology
Credibility	Internal validity
Transferability	External validity
Dependability	Reliability
Confirmability	Objectivity

(Kumar, 2019; Lincoln & Guba, 1985)

In quantitative research, researchers set out to show that their findings are valid. They demonstrate that if the study is repeated, the same results will be obtained. They also attempt to ensure that their measurement instruments measure what they were designed to measure. Similarly, qualitative researchers need to persuade their readers, and the participants, that their findings are trustworthy and contribute to a deeper understanding of phenomena.

In quantitative research, researchers use certain controls—such as randomisation, large sample sizes, controlling intervening variables, and so on — as ways to ensure validity and reliability. Qualitative researchers use the four criteria of trustworthiness to ensure that their research is transparent and sound.

Summary

In this chapter, we have explained what reliability and validity are, and why these concepts are important in a research project. If your research is not reliable and valid, it is not significant. You already learnt in Chapter 1 that research begins with a question or a problem, and that it involves processes of inquiry. All the information collected and presented needs to be valid and reliable. Thus, the conclusions drawn from the data must be valid and the data collection method must be reliable. Every time you make a decision in the research process, ask yourself if you have selected the method or instrument that will produce the most valid and reliable results for your specific problem.

You also need to consider your research approach regarding matters of reliability and validity, since different terminology is used in the different approaches. In other words, when you use a quantitative research approach, you will attempt to establish the reliability and validity of your study, whereas when you use a qualitative research approach, you will use the four criteria of trustworthiness: credibility, transferability, dependability and confirmability.

Review the chapter

Answer the questions and complete the tasks to assess whether you understand the content of this chapter:

1. Explain reliability in your own words.
2. You are a researcher for the National Research Foundation (NRF) and you are training a new group of research interns. How would you describe validity in research to them?
3. You want to design a questionnaire for one of your studies. What will you do to increase the reliability of your instrument?
4. Describe trustworthiness in terms of the following concepts:
   (a) Credibility
   (b) Transferability
   (c) Dependability
   (d) Confirmability
5. How is reflexivity related to trustworthiness?
6. How would you describe transparency in qualitative research?

Ethics in research

Marianne Louw

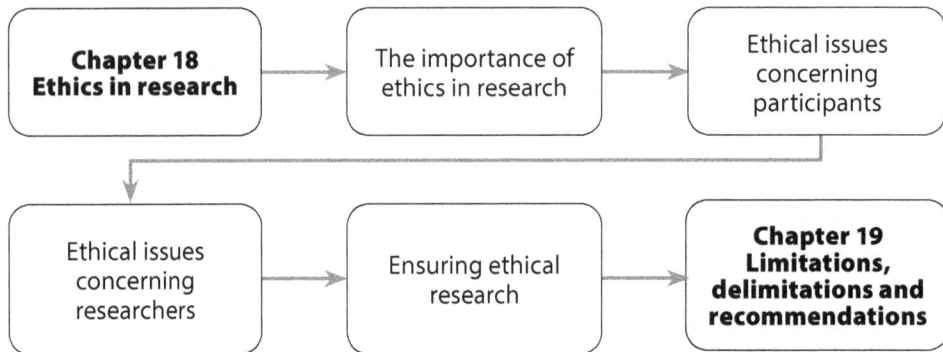

```
┌─────────────────┐      ┌─────────────────┐      ┌─────────────────┐
│   Chapter 18    │ ───▶ │ The importance  │ ───▶ │ Ethical issues  │
│ Ethics in       │      │ of ethics in    │      │ concerning      │
│ research        │      │ research        │      │ participants    │
└─────────────────┘      └─────────────────┘      └─────────────────┘

┌─────────────────┐      ┌─────────────────┐      ┌─────────────────┐
│ Ethical issues  │ ───▶ │ Ensuring ethical│ ───▶ │   Chapter 19    │
│ concerning      │      │ research        │      │   Limitations,  │
│ researchers     │      │                 │      │ delimitations and│
│                 │      │                 │      │ recommendations │
└─────────────────┘      └─────────────────┘      └─────────────────┘
```

Overview

Ethics are a matter of integrity on a personal level, but their implications reach much further than the individual. In this chapter we explain how a lack of ethics in research affects various stakeholders in the research process. A researcher who acts with integrity adheres to ethical principles and professional standards which are essential for practising research in a responsible way. It is a commitment to act in a trustworthy and respectful way, even in the face of adversity. We examine various ethical issues concerning the research participant and the researcher and make suggestions for maintaining high standards as an ethical researcher.

Objectives of this chapter

By the end of this chapter you should be able to demonstrate your understanding of the following:
- what ethics are;
- the importance of ethics in research;
- who the stakeholders are in the research process and results;
- ethical issues that affect the research participant;
- ethical issues concerning the researcher; and
- how to remain ethical as a researcher.

The importance of ethics in research

Your ethics are your moral or professional code of conduct which sets a standard for your attitudes and behaviour. This applies to life in general, in the sense that it is important to be a person of integrity who can be trusted to maintain certain principles. In research, specifically, ethics are crucial because they potentially affect all the stakeholders in research. A stakeholder is someone who has a vested interest (a stake) in something.

Let's look at typical stakeholders in research and their interest in your ethics as a researcher:

- The *participants* in your projects want to trust you and feel safe with you. They do not want to be misled or exploited.
- The *broader public* wants to believe in the value and credibility of your results and their implications for society.
- The local and international *research communities* — in your discipline, as well as in the broader research community — want to rely on you as a credible source, and they want to build their research on reliable evidence. They do not want to be discredited by association.
- The *academic institution* at which you do your research has to maintain its own reputation, which is tainted when its researchers or students behave unethically.
- Any *funding body* (such as your employer or the trustees of a research fund) that invests time, money, or expertise in supporting your research expects results worthy of its investment. If you behave unethically, not only does it taint your results — implying that the funding body has wasted its money — but the funding body's own reputation is also tainted.
- The *community* that directly benefits from your research has a great vested interest in your research. For instance, if you are doing research on the causes of poverty in a particular rural community, the members of that community may benefit from your study (or fail to benefit); therefore you have an ethical obligation to them to conduct your research in a responsible manner.
- *Policy makers* may want to use your research results to create and improve policy. The large number of people affected by policies, especially national policies, increases your ethical burden.
- The *mass media* want to convey newsworthy aspects of your research to their target markets. If your results are skewed due to unethical approaches, a multitude of people are misinformed, and the consequences of your unethical behaviour expand.
- You, the *researcher*, are a stakeholder in your research. Your personal and professional reputation and your current and future employability are linked to your reputation as a researcher.

Ethical issues: concerning participants

There are several important ethical issues that affect the participants in your research, such as:

- informed consent;
- collecting data from participants;
- dealing with sensitive information;
- providing incentives;
- avoiding harm;
- dealing with confidentiality versus anonymity; and
- avoiding deception.

Informed consent

Participants should know that they are taking part in a research study. They should be formally informed of this and should give their consent. They should clearly understand what will be required of them during their participation, whether and how their identities will be protected, and how results will be used. Preferably state this information in writing, have participants sign their consent and keep these documents on record. The challenge is when you are dealing with an illiterate community who cannot read the purpose statement or sign their consent. You will then have to find creative ways of recording this, for instance making an audio recording where participants clearly state their names, the time and date, and their consent.

Remember that children can only participate in research with their legal guardians' consent, as they lack the mental maturity to grasp fully the implications of their participation. The same applies to other people who are similarly vulnerable, such as someone who is mentally handicapped.

Collecting data from participants

In collecting data from participants we need to prioritise their physical and psychological comfort. This implies that we should:

- inform them if and how their identities or sensitive personal information will be protected;
- avoid situations where they need to answer potentially embarrassing questions within the hearing of other people;
- avoid wasting their time through, for instance, poor organisation (making them wait while you are busy with other participants) or overly long questionnaires or interviews;
- train properly any research assistants (who will collect data on your behalf) to communicate effectively with participants and manage the research process sensitively; and

- carefully consider the physical and social context in which we gather data from participants.

Dealing with sensitive information

Some research studies reveal sensitive information about participants. An ethical researcher protects this information as a matter of principle and does not allow his or her personal feelings to interfere. Here are two examples:

- You are doing research on employees' attitudes towards their manager and one employee expresses particularly negative views. When you report on the results to the manager, he or she insists on knowing which employee was so negative. It would be unethical of you to reveal this information.
- You are doing research on intimacy in marriages and a wife admits to having an extramarital affair of which her husband is unaware. You may feel that the husband should know, but you cannot reveal this information if you promised confidentiality to your participants.

Providing incentives

Providing incentives — such as money, food, a possible holiday or a television set — seems like a good idea to get people to participate in your research, but there are ethical implications to this of which you need to be aware. It may distort your results in the following ways:

- It may influence *who* participates in the first place. For instance, you may no longer be able to call your sample random, since it may be that only a particular kind of person is motivated by that incentive to take part in a particular study. This may exclude other segments of the population.

- It may affect *how* participants participate. Despite your assurances to the contrary, participants may believe that they need to respond in certain ways to get the incentive or they may consciously or subconsciously want to please you in return and give you the responses that they think you want.

These disadvantages do not imply that you cannot use incentives. However, generally they should not be large, but rather a token of appreciation. They should also realistically be an incentive to most of your population. For instance, if your incentive is a cigarette lighter, smokers will likely be more interested in the incentive than non-smokers. If you are doing a study on the health of employees working for a particular organisation, having mostly smoking participants will clearly distort your data.

You should also avoid using incentives to get vulnerable people to participate in risky and unethical research. Some researchers have earned a very negative reputation for offering money to poor communities to participate in highly unethical and sometimes even risky research. For example, if you want to test the effects of cocaine on creativity, it would be unethical to offer money to a very poor community — the members of that community may be motivated by their poverty to volunteer for your unethical and illegal research.

Avoiding harm

It stands to reason that researchers should not harm their participants in any way, but in the social sciences this may be more complex than in the natural sciences. For instance, if you are doing a medical study, it seems clear that you cannot give your participants medication that will physically harm them. But in the social science context 'harm' may include things that are more difficult to eliminate, for example:

- causing participants to recall emotionally painful memories;
- asking questions in a group setting that may cause one participant to be embarrassed in front of the others;
- creating situations where a participant's future prospects (for instance, in his or her job) may be harmed; and/or
- conducting a focus group in such a way that some participants feel their contributions are less intelligent, relevant or valuable than those of other participants.

As researchers, we must be sensitive to these issues. Yet we may still want to research a sensitive topic in the hopes of making a useful contribution to society. In such a case we must be very clear in advance — before the participant gives his or her consent to take part in our research — about what the exact nature of our research is and what kinds of sensitive information will likely be explored.

Confidentiality versus anonymity

An important concern for many research participants is the protection of their identity and sensitive information about themselves, for the following reasons:

- The research study may record information about them that can lead to emotional, relational, physical or occupational harm to themselves.
- Some people are not concerned about sensitive information, but want their identities protected as a matter of principle.
- The participants may fear that their contact details will be exploited by the researcher or other parties for marketing purposes.

Confidentiality and anonymity are not synonymous and do not refer to the same concept. When we communicate our intentions and ethical responsibility to participants, we need to distinguish between the two and clearly explain what we are undertaking:

- When we promise participants *anonymity*, we undertake that we will not record their names at any stage of the research process, and that we will not be able to match their identity to their research responses in any way. This is the case where you have a sample of respondents completing a questionnaire that does not ask for their names or any other identifying information and where you do not mark the response in any other identifying way. Afterwards, you will have questionnaires to analyse, but no way of knowing which respondent gave a particular answer.

- When we assure *confidentiality*, we undertake that, even though we will be able to match the participants' identities to their research responses, that information will be known only to the researcher and will be made available to no one else. This is often the case when you conduct in-depth interviews with participants or when you let participants complete a questionnaire where their names are recorded. However, you have to assure your participants that their identities will remain secret and will not be revealed to anyone else through the use of pseudonyms that de-identify them. Alternatively, you could number the participants on a list that you keep confidential and give each participant an anonymous questionnaire with their corresponding number. In this way, other people can look at a completed questionnaire without knowing the identity of the participant, while you can consult your list to find out exactly who it was.

Before you promise participants anonymity or confidentiality, make sure that you can guarantee it. On most anonymous questionnaires we ask participants to provide other details about themselves, such as gender or age, to enable us to interpret the data meaningfully. But if you do so, for example, in a group of employees where there is only one male over 50 years of age, you cannot guarantee anonymity or confidentiality — the male respondent over 50 can clearly be only one person, and so his identity is exposed. Another example would be a questionnaire which, even though it contains no such distinguishing information, is completed by hand by employees and seen by their manager, who might recognise their handwriting.

Also keep in mind that highly educated, literate and mentally able people are much better able to understand the implications of anonymity and confidentiality than are people who do not possess those qualities. As researchers, we are being unethical if we fail to protect our participants (for instance, by not fully informing them or by letting them consent to processes which they clearly do not understand) simply because they do not insist on or know their rights. Exploiting people in any form is always unethical.

Deception

The most common ways of deceiving participants are:
- telling them your research is about one thing when it is really about another; or
- giving them the general purpose of your research, but not telling them what specifically you are looking for.

We should avoid deception as far as possible. However, some studies do require a degree of deception to yield credible results. For instance, you may want to determine whether people remember advertisements with sexual content better than advertisements without sexual content. This means your participants will have to look at different kinds of advertisements. If you alert them to your specific purpose, it may draw their attention to the sexual content. If your results then show greater memory of advertisements with sexual content, it is difficult to discard the influence that your prior communication may have had on your participants' memories.

When you have no choice but to deceive your participants in order to get valid results, keep the following in mind to still maintain ethical standards:

- After you have collected the data, inform participants of how and *why* they have been deceived. The motivation is very important, since most participants will not mind being deceived if the reason makes sense and, especially, if the research contributes to some higher purpose of bettering society. Assure them of the value of their participation and avoid being perceived as having deceived them on a whim.
- Participants must be fully *debriefed* and be given an opportunity to express their thoughts and feelings about the data collection process. Whether it is more appropriate to do this individually or in groups will depend on the particular study.
- Participants must sign an *acknowledgement* that they have been informed of the true purpose of the research, and that they consent to their data being used.

Ethical issues concerning researchers

Apart from ethical issues concerning the research participants, there are several ways in which the researcher's approach to data analysis and data reporting can be unethical, such as:
- falsifying information;
- distorting results;
- allowing bias to influence interpretation or results;
- misusing information; and/or
- using inappropriate research methods.

Falsifying information

Falsifying information is deliberately fabricating or changing data, and it is always unethical. There are several reasons why researchers falsify information, for example:
- to save their reputation or to gain status (if their true results are disappointing or contrary to what they wanted or predicted);
- to keep their funding or to secure additional funding;

- to please employers or to keep their jobs;
- to avoid difficult, boring or time-consuming aspects of data collection and analysis;
- to get a desired outcome (for instance, a human resource officer wants to transfer employees to a different medical fund and has been given permission to do so if the majority of staff agrees, so he falsifies the results of his survey to accomplish his goal); or
- to retain a client (for example, a public relations consultant finds no significant difference in her client's positive media exposure since she was contracted to do their media relations, but she falsifies the information to show a difference).

Let's use the example of a journalist at a daily newspaper who is instructed to do research for an article on people's use of condoms. The journalist is, however, too lazy to collect and analyse information from reputable sources and decides to take a shortcut and make up some facts. The article is published with this false information. Why is this behaviour unethical?

Another example of this could be where a person recruited to a research team decides that interviewing participants is too time-consuming. She completes the remaining questionnaires herself. If this is discovered, she and her participants will have to be replaced. This can have implications for the research study — if, for example, this happened at the last minute, the project may not be completed by the deadline and may lose its funding.

Distorting results

Distorting results is somewhat different from fabricating information. There are often different ways of interpreting or communicating the same results. You are guilty of distorting results (and, thus, unethical behaviour) when you deliberately:
- *emphasise certain aspects* over other aspects of equal significance; and/or
- quote numbers *out of context*, which might distort interpretation.

Researchers may do this to get or retain funding because some funding bodies withdraw their financial support when the findings are not to their liking. Sometimes a researcher will receive seed funding to do some exploratory research to determine whether a particular research topic is worth investigating. If the findings of the exploratory study are significant and promising, more funding is then allocated to the project. However, if it looks like the hypotheses are wrong or like the study is not worth pursuing, the funding is likely to be withdrawn. In situations such as these researchers are often tempted to distort their findings to make it look like a study is actually worth pursuing when it is not, simply because they want to obtain more funding.

Bias

Bias is much more subtle than falsifying or distorting information because researchers themselves may not even be aware of it. Bias in research is the desire or expectation of achieving a particular result. This may influence the research results in the sense of how and where the researcher collects his or her data, and how he or she interprets the data.

For instance, a certain researcher firmly believes in a particular model of marital counselling. She does a qualitative study on the topic, comparing the effectiveness of different approaches. Her results are rather inconclusive, but she really wants to show that her preferred method is more effective. She subsequently selectively perceives and interprets her data, emphasising evidence in support of her desired results and downplaying evidence that points to the contrary.

Misusing information

Any data collected from participants for research purposes may not be used for any other purposes, unless you have obtained participants' permission to do so. For instance, it is unethical to sell participants' contact details or demographic information to marketers.

Let's look at an example of this. While shopping, Nomsa is approached by a man who asks her to fill in a research questionnaire on crime. Feeling that it was an important topic, she agrees. He asks her for her name and contact details so that, as a token of appreciation, she can be entered into a competition to win a prize. Some days later someone else calls to tell her that she has won the prize and that she needs to attend a presentation to claim it. She discovers that the whole exercise had been a marketing ruse and that she never contributed to any worthwhile research project. She decides never to fill in another questionnaire for anyone ever again. Why was the marketing company's behaviour unethical and what further damage did their unethical behaviour potentially cause for the bigger research community?

Using inappropriate research methods

Inappropriate research methods are those that are either:
- *harmful* to participants, for instance making children watch pornography to document their response to it; or

- highly *unsuited* to the researcher's stated purpose or results, for instance measuring and comparing participants' mental intelligence using an unscientific questionnaire that the researcher has developed him or herself.

As researchers, it is our ethical responsibility to protect our participants from harm and to constantly question whether our chosen methods and approaches are the most valid and ethical ways of solving our research problem or answering our research question.

As an example of harm caused to participants during a study, a very interesting example to look at is the Stanford prison experiment. It was conducted in 1971 by Professor Philip Zimbardo and his team at Stanford University in the USA. The aim was to examine people's behavioural responses to opposing roles of authority and powerlessness in a mock prison setting. Zimbardo hypothesised that abusive behaviour in real prison situations was due mainly to guards' and prisoners' personality traits.

Undergraduate male volunteers were recruited and the 24 who were deemed to be the most psychologically stable were selected for the experiment. Half were randomly assigned to be prisoners, and the other half guards. The duration of the experiment was to be two weeks, during which the prisoners had to stay in their cells.

Zimbardo instructed the 'guards' to create a sense of powerlessness in the 'prisoners' by, for instance, taking away their freedom, individuality and privacy, but not to physically harm them. However, both guards and prisoners adapted to their roles beyond the researchers' expectations. Over time, several guards treated the prisoners with increasing psychological and physical cruelty, some exhibiting sadistic traits. Several prisoners were psychologically traumatised (two left the experiment early), yet most accepted the abuse — having, Zimbardo argued, internalised their prisoner role.

Zimbardo stopped the experiment early (after only six days), when Christina Maslach, a graduate psychology student, questioned the ethics of the experiment. Why do you think this experiment is seen as unethical?

Ensuring ethical research

There are a number of ways to make sure that you remain an ethical researcher:
- Draw up your own personal ethical code of conduct as a researcher. This is not necessarily for others' eyes (although you can show it to your research participants to demonstrate your ethical stance); it is more as a reminder to yourself of what you stand for.
- Learn from other researchers' ethical mistakes, whether intended or unintended. For example, by subscribing to Retraction Watch, a blog that reports on scientific studies that have been retracted or removed from

journals and publications due to various ethical concerns, you will become familiar with the unethical behaviour of other researchers and should strive to avoid such behaviour.

• Continue to educate yourself on the topic. Regularly read about or attend workshops on ethics in research. Not only can one become a bit desensitised to ethical issues over time but there may also be new developments or views in the research field. For example, researchers should familiarise themselves on the impact of the Protection of Personal Information (POPI) Act 4 of 2013, which came into effect on 1 July 2021, on data collection, the securing of data and the de-identification of data. If personal information is collected from South African citizens through interviews, focus groups or surveys displaying names and contact information, compliance with the POPI Act is essential. Datasets should be de-identified when using cloud storage, and on-site storage (personal hard drives, external hard drives, campus systems) should be strictly access-controlled by named and designated researchers to prevent the data being harvested and used by third parties without participant, researcher and institutional consent.

• Form a 'partnership' with a fellow researcher (or more than one). Agree to read each other's work and warn each other about any grey areas concerning ethics.

• Ask yourself whether you like to be deceived, and then consider how others would feel if they found out that you deceived them and acted without integrity.

• Consider the harm you are doing to the rest of the research community if you behave in unethical ways.

Summary

Ethics are to a researcher what impartiality is to a judge. It is the cornerstone of research and, without it, the delicate and complex interweave of research falls apart in undesirable ways. What we do as researchers and the quality of work we produce often affects other people and we therefore have a responsibility to the bigger community that we serve to act with honesty and integrity so that everyone can have and maintain confidence in the research process. No one can call him or herself a legitimate researcher if his or her work does not speak of a solid ethical foundation. Research ethics benefit not only the researcher's own reputation and credibility but affect various other stakeholders in the research process.

Figure 18.1 summarises key stakeholders in the research process, ethical issues concerning the participant and the researcher, and how researchers can ensure they behave ethically.

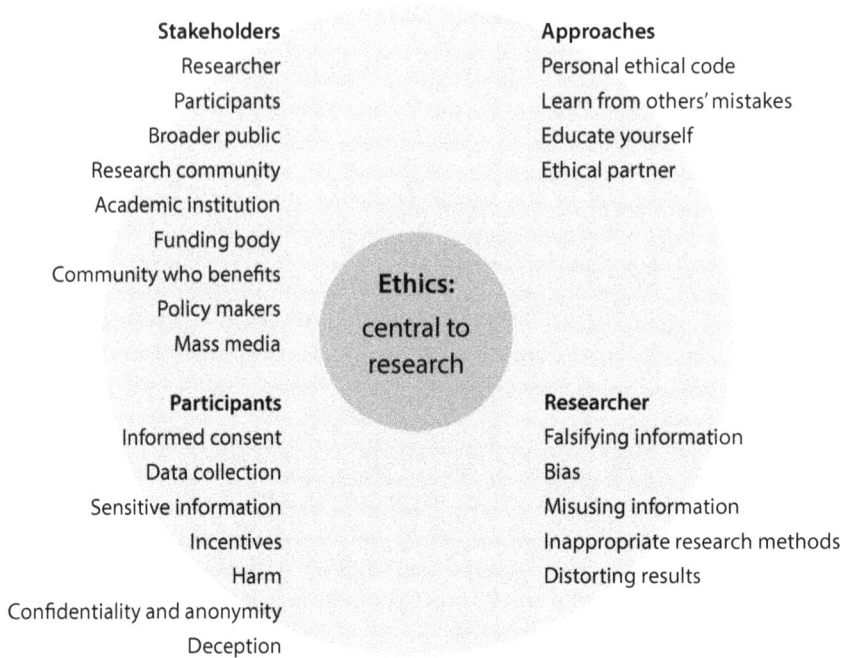

Figure 18.1 Ethics in research

Review the chapter

Complete the following tasks to assess whether you understand the content of this chapter:

1. Define ethics and explain why they are important in research.
2. Discuss some ethical issues that affect the research participant.
3. Discuss some ethical issues concerning the researcher.
4. Describe what researchers can do to maintain their own ethical integrity.

CHAPTER 19

Limitations, delimitations and recommendations

Carla Enslin

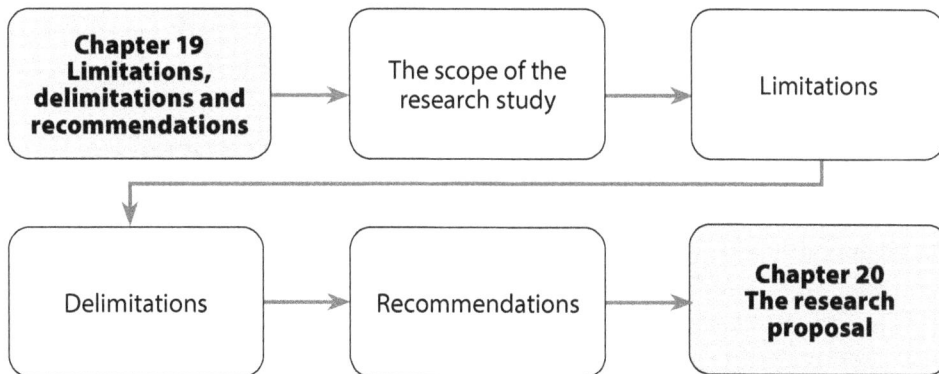

Overview

The limitations, delimitations and recommendations of a research study are usually identified, described and discussed in the concluding chapter or section of a research report, dissertation, thesis or proposal. Every chapter in this book thus far has identified numerous decisions involved in every step of the research process. As you may have gathered by now, every decision has implications, which we refer to as delimitations. Regardless of the careful decisions you make during your research study, there will always be things that you have little or no control over, and those we refer to as limitations.

In this chapter we distinguish between limitations and delimitations and show you how both can be translated into recommendations for further research, to conclude your research study. These also extend the meaning and value of your research and add to the heuristic value 3 of your study. When we refer to the heuristic value of research, we simply mean research's potential to stimulate and encourage further thinking and research. Finally, pointing out the limitations and delimitations of your research shows that you engaged critically with the steps in the research process and that you understand the confines of your findings.

Objectives of this chapter

By the end of this chapter you should be able to demonstrate your understanding of the following:

- the limitations to a research study;
- the delimitations to a research study;
- how to present recommendations for further study;
- how to present recommendations for practice; and
- the interrelatedness of limitations, delimitations and recommendations.

The scope of the research study

As you will recall, a research study is intended to resolve a research problem within a specific domain or scope. Simply put, the scope of a study refers to what is and what is not relevant to your particular study. You therefore need clarity about what exactly your study entails, and you should avoid deviating from this by including irrelevant information. For example, a study to explore people's perceptions of luxury brands that originated in Africa may deal with the problem that luxury brands from developed markets are often perceived to be superior to luxury brands that originate from Africa. The scope of this study is then defined by its focus on luxury brands, and specifically luxury brands from Africa — the aim is to identify the challenges that luxury brands from Africa face in positioning themselves on the continent. Including information on whether income influences the purchasing of luxury brands, in this instance, is irrelevant to your study. Even though income influences whether people are able to afford luxury brands, it falls outside the scope of your study because it will not contribute to an explanation of why luxury brands that originate from Africa are perceived to be inferior to luxury brands from developed markets. This is an important point because it is very easy to get distracted from the real purpose of your study and to include irrelevant information. Always make sure you have clarity about the purpose of your study so that you do not make this common mistake.

Limitations

Limitations can be described as constraints or limits in your research study that are out of your control, such as time, financial resources, access to information, and so on. For example, if you have to complete your research project within a period of three months, there is a limit to the amount of information you can collect within this given period of time. In our example of an exploratory study of luxury brands in Africa you may, for example, encounter *budget limitations* for the local research teams to cover the continent successfully and to bridge language and/or cultural barriers. A limitation may cause the scope of the research to be redefined. The study of luxury brands, for example, may thus be limited to an exploration of markets in southern Africa only.

Consider another example of a research limitation: *accessibility*. For example, a study of the criteria that South African film directors consider when screening South African scripts for acceptance and possible production was limited by the fact that a number of the directors who agreed to in-depth interviews were simply not available during the research period. The production schedules of film directors are not under the researcher's control. Yet, by clearly stating the limitation the research findings were reliably contextualised within the sample of film directors interviewed, and a future researcher will be able to extend the research project by conducting interviews with the film directors that the study was unable to include.

Limitations may also surface due to *shifts in conditions* during the study. Imagine that an extreme incident of cyberbullying makes headlines on global and local news networks during the primary research phase of a study on the subject. It is easy to imagine that the sheer scale of reporting on this incident may influence how people perceive cyberbullying and, consequently, skew the results of the study. By recognising this potential limitation and discussing its possible influence, the conclusions may remain valid and reliable in the context of the data collected.

Clearly identified limitations guide us in the reporting of findings and support the reliability and validity and/or trustworthiness of research findings within the scope of a study. For the researcher, limitations can be constraining or even liberating (for example, by making the study more manageable or offering broad scope for future research and investigation). However, and this is another very important point, they are never a sign of failure. Because a researcher does not have total control over every condition within the scope of a study, it is natural and expected for a research study to encounter limitations. The limitations of your study need to be acknowledged; you need to demonstrate that you have considered them and are aware of ways in which addressing them can contribute to the validity and reliability and/or trustworthiness of your study.

Delimitations

As we said earlier, delimitations result from the very specific and definite choices researchers make when they decide on the scope of a particular research study. All the decisions you make during the different steps in the research process determine, to some degree, the delimitations of your research study. They are often referred to as the parameters that you set. These parameters or borders are essential in order for you to focus on specific concepts, theories, literature, methods, and so forth, so that your research will have a clear direction, focus and emphasis.

Your choice of a purpose for your research study, your research questions, the variables you choose to test, the theoretical perspective you adopt and the population you choose to investigate are all delimiting factors. When you describe the delimitations of your study, you will spell out who the population in your study is and why, what geographic region your study covers, and what field of specialisation you are covering, among other factors you may choose to explicate.

It follows from our discussions on qualitative and quantitative methodologies in previous chapters that each method comes with its own delimitations. It is therefore imperative that you make informed choices during every step of the research process so that you fully understand what you can and cannot achieve through the methods you choose.

Delimitation

- What falls outside the scope of your study?
- Building in parameters
- Assists with focusing your study
- Assits with shared meaning

Figure 19.1 Example of delimitation for research

Delimitations can be applied to any part of the research scope, to any area of the research study or to challenges encountered during the implementation of the research design. These decisions are predominantly made in order to focus and manage a research study and to support the validity and reliability and/or trustworthiness of the results and consequent findings. Consider the following examples:

- *Delimitation from the theoretical framework.* A study focused on the online behaviour of digital natives attempted to explore and clearly define the concept 'digital native' (a term conceived to identify individuals for whom the digital world and its applications are natural, everyday realities). The researcher investigated literature on the online media consumption of this social segment. The delimitation that the researcher purposefully set was that results could not be generalised to make assumptions about the offline media consumption of digital natives. The study was decidedly specific in its focus on the online consumption behaviour of digital natives and its findings were limited to this media channel and sample group.

- *Delimitation from the research design.* A study focused on a comparison between young adolescents who had access to pornography and those who did not, and on whether the young adolescents' exposure to pornography influenced their likelihood to explore online pornography in adulthood. The researchers used a structured quantitative design so that the comparison could take place. The research design did not include a qualitative component, since its aim was to compare the differences in the likelihood to explore online pornography between these groups and not to explain why certain adolescents chose to view pornography and others not.

• *Delimitation from the research method.* A study of consumer responses to month-end sales promotions conducted a large number of surveys to source consumer opinions. Useful results regarding attitudes toward month-end sales promotions were gained. However, because the study did not employ observational research to track and verify actual consumer behaviour, it could not empirically substantiate the qualitative insights that were gained from the study.

How to identify delimitations

Because delimitations result from the decisions made by the researcher they must be noted and declared, and you need to provide robust reasons or justifications on all levels for these choices of inclusion and exclusion. Meticulously noting delimitations throughout the development of the research study limits your chances of overlooking a decision or neglecting the reasoning behind one. Doing this will also mean that your delimitations will be composed by the time the conclusion to the study has to be written.

Studying the theory of research methodology is a useful preparatory step and will help you gain insight into the possible delimitations of the research method or methods you want to use. Let's say you intend to use ethnographic research. You need to point out to your reader why the method you chose is the most appropriate method to help you to solve your research problem or answer your research question. You may find a discussion on qualitative analysis that includes the advantages and disadvantages of using ethnographic research as a research method. You may discover that one of the disadvantages is that the results from ethnographic studies cannot be generalised. This is something you will need to report on and you should be able to justify why this is not a threat to your study.

Recommendations

Bless, Higson-Smith and Sithole (2013) argue that research is mainly relevant if findings have the potential to improve the human condition — a valuable line of reasoning. The purpose of recommendations in the concluding section of a research study is to highlight the validity of the research results, to identify further areas of useful research or to point to omissions and knowledge gaps. The recommendations you make at the end of your research study also demonstrate the insights you have gained through your research and how your findings can be implemented and applied.

How to identify recommendations

The following sections contain some suggestions as to how you can identify recommendations for your study. We explore the first and second levels of critical reflection.

The first level of critical reflection

Recommendations emerge from reflecting on the research findings in the context of research questions and problem statements. The analysis and discussion of research results and findings involve determining which research questions and purposes have been met and which remain unanswered. The following three questions broadly encourage a first level of critical reflection when producing recommendations:
1. Which research questions and goals are satisfactorily dealt with?
2. Which are not satisfactorily dealt with, and why is this the case?
3. Which have not been dealt with at all, and why did this happen?

The research problems and questions that have not been satisfactorily dealt with, the questions that are left unanswered and the problems that are left unsolved present immediate recommendations for further research. This is known as the *heuristic value* of your study, as was mentioned earlier in this chapter. The reasons why these problems and questions have not been dealt with can again present new or additional insights into limitations and delimitations of the study (Adams, Khan, Raeside & White, 2012:55).

The second level of critical reflection

Having determined which research questions have been answered and which remain unanswered, the research purpose is to make sense of research results in order to present an insightful discussion of findings and, importantly, to produce valuable recommendations. A useful method to apply when delving into findings with a view to developing recommendations is to consider the value of the research findings in contributing to theory, guiding future research, informing professional practice or solving a practical problem. Consider the following helpful questions (Bell, Foster & Cone, 2020):
*   Are any of your findings inconsistent with the literature?

- Do any of your findings clarify or resolve contradicting opinions in the literature?
- Do any of your findings change the field's understanding of the concept under investigation?
- Are there results that you did not expect?
- Are there results that you did not expect to be significant but that now seem to be?
- Are any of the unexpected findings the result of specific measures implemented in the process of conducting research?
- Can or should any of your findings be extended to or tested in, for example, other populations or fields of research?
- Could any of your findings lead to changes in the way that professionals currently do things?
- Are there findings that may be of interest to specific role players in the field?
- Are there findings that may be of interest to new role players in the field?
- Are there findings that can be used to solve a practical problem?

Two types of recommendations

There are two distinct types of recommendations: recommendations for further study and recommendations for practical application.

Recommendations for further study

Recommendations for further study generally propose follow-up studies or replication studies. Herein lies the heuristic value of your study. The questions posed under the first and second levels of critical reflection typically lead to further research recommendations.

Findings that are not validated by the literature study may indicate useful avenues for further study. The same applies to research questions that have not been satisfactorily dealt with or that remain unanswered and research problems that have not been solved in full, as we discussed earlier. The failure to answer research questions or solve research problems may also be the result of limitations or delimitations that can be adequately addressed under different conditions or with the use of different methodologies. Using our previous example of the study of young adolescents exposed to pornography, a recommendation for further study may be as follows: 'The findings of the study revealed that young adolescents exposed to pornography tended also to explore online pornography as adults. Future studies on young adolescents' sexual behaviour should include qualitative methods to explore why some adolescents are drawn to pornography and others are not.'

Recommendations for practice

Recommendations for practice are usually based on specific results and findings which prescribe what could or should be done (or done differently) in practice. These recommendations arrive from critical reflection on the questions listed on the previous page. Recommendations for practice will then specifically highlight findings of interest to specific role players in professional fields or propose changes in the way that professionals currently approach a problem or conduct business. For example: 'Research findings suggest that greater depth of insight can be gained into a brand situation if the client (marketing or brand manager) and advertising agency (communication partner) write the communication brief (the document that defines the brand communication challenge) together. It is therefore proposed that the writing of briefs be done jointly, rather than by marketing managers alone, as is the traditional practice.'

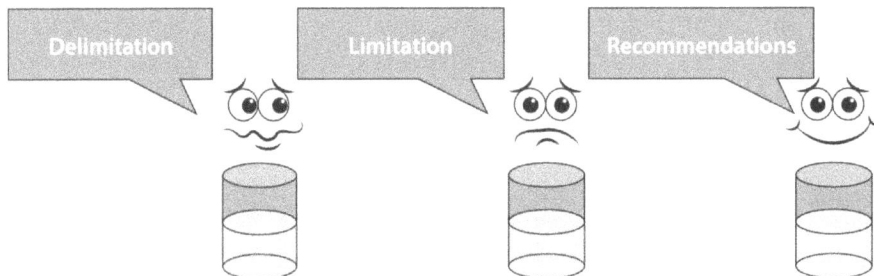

Figure 19.2 Delimitation - Limitation - Recommendation

Summary

The concluding chapter or section of a research study should present insightful discussions of key research findings, including the limitations and delimitations of the study. It is important to understand the difference between limitations and delimitations. Limitations identifies potential weaknesses of a research while delimitations addresses how a study will be narrowed in scope or how it is bounded. The reliability and validity and/or trustworthiness of research findings depend greatly on the researcher's accurate and comprehensive reporting of factors beyond the researcher's control (limitations) as well as factors that decidedly shaped the focus and scope of the study (delimitations).

The concluding chapter or section of a research study should also include a discussion of recommendations and how these recommendations are arrived at. The recommendations should be presented as recommendations for practice and/or recommendations for further study. Of critical consideration is that limitations, delimitations and recommendations are often interrelated and that recommendations require careful reflection. Recommendations carry significant weight because they have the potential to move a field of research forward, contribute to developing theory, guide future research and inform professional practice.

Review the chapter

Answer the questions and complete the tasks to assess your understanding of the content of this chapter:

1. Explain the importance of limitations, delimitations and recommendations in concluding a research study.
2. What are some of the differences between limitations and delimitations? Provide examples to illustrate the difference.
3. What questions can a researcher critically reflect on to identify research recommendations?
4. Name and describe the two types of research recommendations. Provide examples to illustrate the difference.
5. How are research limitations, delimitations and recommendations interrelated?

CHAPTER 20

The Research Proposal

Franzél du Plooy-Cilliers

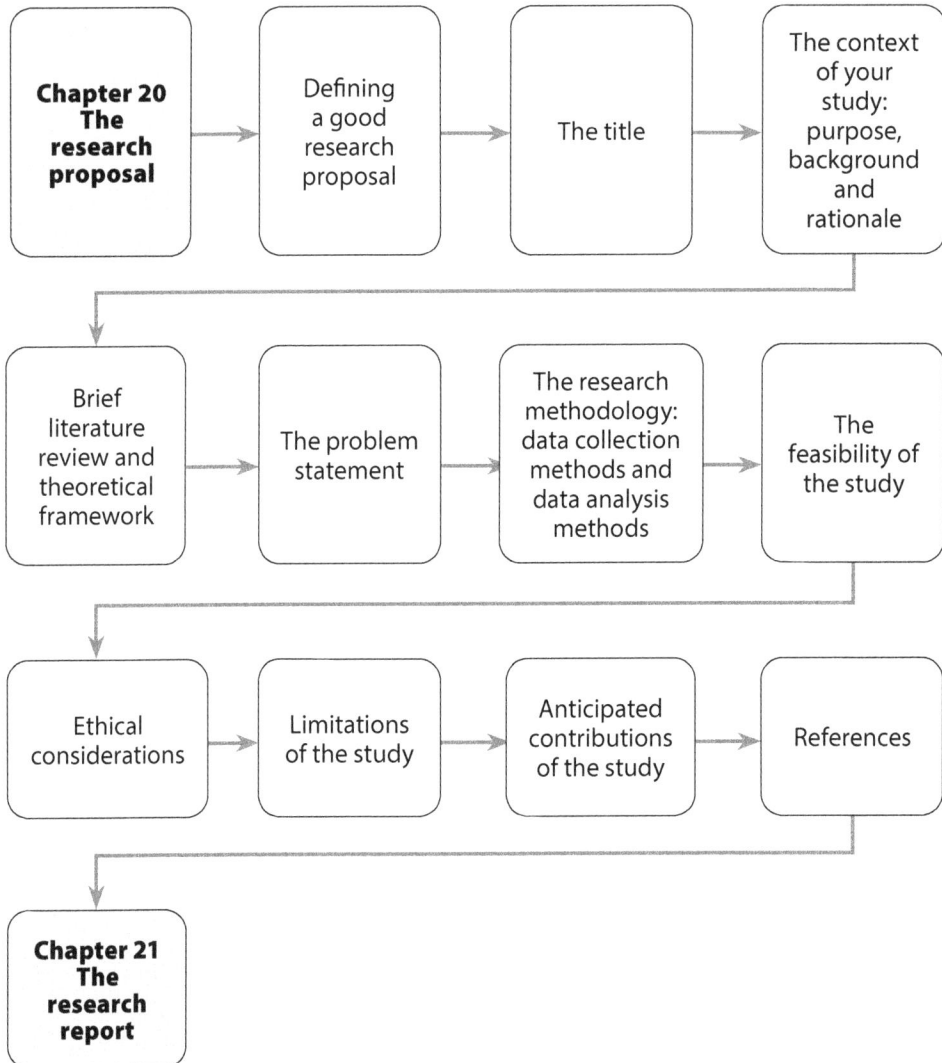

```
┌─────────────┐     ┌─────────────┐     ┌─────────────┐     ┌─────────────┐
│ Chapter 20  │     │  Defining   │     │             │     │ The context │
│    The      │ ──> │  a good     │ ──> │  The title  │ ──> │  of your    │
│  research   │     │  research   │     │             │     │   study:    │
│  proposal   │     │  proposal   │     │             │     │  purpose,   │
│             │     │             │     │             │     │ background  │
│             │     │             │     │             │     │    and      │
│             │     │             │     │             │     │  rationale  │
└─────────────┘     └─────────────┘     └─────────────┘     └─────────────┘
```

Chapter 20 The research proposal → Defining a good research proposal → The title → The context of your study: purpose, background and rationale → Brief literature review and theoretical framework → The problem statement → The research methodology: data collection methods and data analysis methods → The feasibility of the study → Ethical considerations → Limitations of the study → Anticipated contributions of the study → References → Chapter 21 The research report

Overview

Imagine you are able to have your dream house designed and built. What will you need to do before the building of your new house can commence? First, you need to have a plan drawn up by an architect. This plan will provide the builder with specific instructions on how to build your house. Next, you need to know how much building the house will cost, how long it will take the builder to complete it, and so forth. Conducting a proper research study is akin to building a house. Similar to the house, it should also start with a plan. This plan is known as a research proposal.

Research can become an expensive, cumbersome and extremely time-consuming process, especially if you do not have a carefully constructed plan which can guide your study. Without a plan you will be lost. Researchers are often tempted to skip this step in the research process; however, without spending the time to think carefully about what you want to achieve, how you ought to go about achieving it, and how feasible what you want to achieve is, you may run into some serious trouble. Therefore, it is always best to draft a research proposal before starting your research. In fact, it is often a requirement for students who wish to enrol for post-graduate studies or researchers who want to apply for research funding.

Keep in mind, however, that one of the most important reasons why you should write a research proposal before you conduct your research is that it will help you to refine your thinking and to attend to all the details involved in the research process. Moreover, it can be very beneficial to your study to submit a research proposal, as it is usually presented to a committee of experts in research who will evaluate your proposal and provide you with valuable feedback and suggestions on how you can improve or modify your study (Gravetter & Forzano, 2018).

You need to draw on the information in all the other chapters in this book to write your research proposal, as the purpose of this chapter is limited to providing you with a structure for your proposal and some guidelines for writing the proposal.

Objectives of this chapter

By the end of this chapter you should be able to demonstrate your understanding of the following:

- the purpose of a research proposal;
- the factors that should be taken into account when writing a research proposal;
- what should be included in a research proposal;
- structuring a research proposal;
- the writing conventions to consider when writing a research proposal; and
- the factors that need to be considered to determine the feasibility of a study.

Defining a good research proposal

First of all, your research proposal should be a clear and detailed description of all the steps you intend to follow to complete your research project. Your research proposal must provide a cohesive picture, showing how all the pieces of the puzzle fit together for the entire proposed project. In fact, your proposal should be so well written and formulated that someone else should be able to execute your proposed research study without ever having to consult with you. You must therefore attempt to anticipate any questions that could be asked and address them in your proposal. If a section you have written is not clear in your own mind and not clarified in your proposal, it will certainly not be clear to others, so always keep your reader in mind when you put together your proposal.

Remember that everything in your proposal must follow a certain logic. For example, if you want to investigate the 'friends with benefits' phenomenon and gain an in-depth understanding of why people engage in these types of relationships, you cannot propose that you are going to analyse the movie *Friends with Benefits* to determine the answer to this question. Can you see that your unit of analysis (a movie) will not provide you with an answer to your research question (why people form casual sexual relationships with people they consider their friends)? Therefore, if you want to know why people form these types of relationships, you will have to ask them, and so your unit of analysis will have to be individuals. This kind of thinking is required in order to create or draft a good research proposal.

We provide you with some guidelines on what should be included in your research proposal. You should keep in mind that the exact content of your proposal will depend on whether your study utilises a quantitative, qualitative or mixed-methods approach. However, all proposals, regardless of their approach, need to provide information regarding:

- what you propose to study;
- the purpose of the study;
- why it is a topic worth studying;
- the problem you wish to solve through your research;
- the background of the topic, to assist your readers in understanding your topic better;
- your proposed unit of analysis;
- the context of your study;
- what method(s) of sampling you are going to use;
- what method(s) of data collection you are going to use;
- what method(s) of data analysis you are going to use;
- how you will validate your findings;
- what ethical issues you need to consider;
- the feasibility of your study from a resource perspective;
- the possible limitations of your study; and

- the possible contributions to the body of knowledge that your study will make.

Figure 20.1 gives you an overview of all the headings and subheadings that you should include in your proposal. We then discuss each section in greater detail.

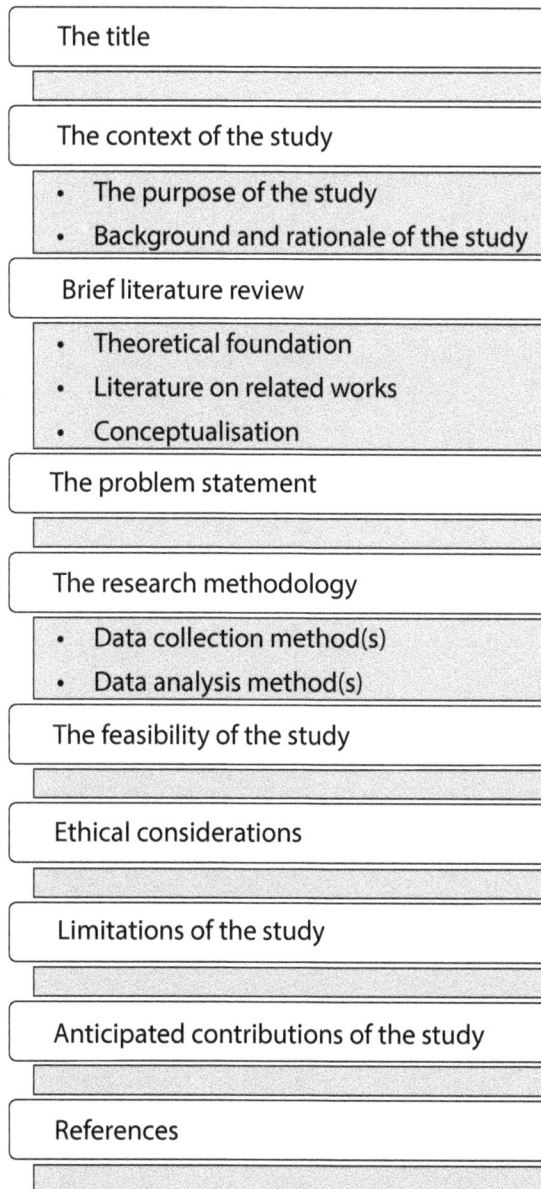

The title

The context of the study

- The purpose of the study
- Background and rationale of the study

Brief literature review

- Theoretical foundation
- Literature on related works
- Conceptualisation

The problem statement

The research methodology

- Data collection method(s)
- Data analysis method(s)

The feasibility of the study

Ethical considerations

Limitations of the study

Anticipated contributions of the study

References

Figure 20.1 The headings and subheadings to be used in a research proposal

The title

The title of your study, which is surprisingly difficult to formulate, should be your first consideration. It should capture the essence of your study, although it should also be as concise as possible — preferably no more than 10 words. It is furthermore important not to use unfamiliar abbreviations in your title.

Something to consider when constructing a title for your study is the nature of your study. You can also use the purpose or even your research methodology (for example, 'A survey of . . .') to assist you in formulating an informative title. Some researchers also like to include words describing what they will be doing in their study, such as 'An analysis of . . .', 'A comparison between . . .', and so on. Most importantly, though, is that you should aim for a title that communicates the importance of your study.

Revise your title a few times to make sure it has impact — remove additional words that may detract from rather than contribute to the meaning in your title. Please note, though, that your title is likely to change a few times. As you gain more insight into your topic and as your thinking around your topic becomes more sophisticated, you are likely to change your title so that it describes your study more accurately. This is a normal part of the research process, so do not get discouraged if it is not perfect for the purpose of your proposal.

The context of the study

Most researchers become deeply engaged with their studies and they do a lot of preliminary or background reading before putting together their proposal. Although your study can only benefit from extensive reading on the topic, keep in mind that the reader of your proposal is likely not to have studied your topic in the same depth as you have and will therefore not have as much background information regarding your topic as you do. For this reason you have to bring your readers into the picture and provide them with enough background information (or context) to understand what you are trying to achieve through your study. Thus, the purpose of contextualising your study is to explain broadly what you want to do and what your main argument (or thesis) is.

The purpose of the study

Without a purpose your study is meaningless. It is therefore important to explain to your reader what the purpose of your study is. The clear articulation of the purpose of your study is also useful in guiding your research. It is very easy to deviate from your original goal and to get lost in information if your study does not have a clearly defined purpose. Your purpose therefore acts as a compass that directs your study in all respects. The purpose of research can also take on one or a combination of various forms, namely (Explorable, 2013):

- to *explore* an area in which little previous work has been done and that is still under-researched;
- to *speculate* about current situations and their future impact and implementation;
- to *describe* certain phenomena or the relationships and links between variables;
- to *explain* why certain relationships, patterns or links occur;
- to gain an *in-depth understanding* of a particular phenomenon;
- to *predict* a likely course of events given particular circumstances; and/or
- to *evaluate* the impact of one thing on something else.

Background and rationale of the study

In the background section you need to build a preliminary picture for your readers and provide them with some context to understand the nature of the research topic. Give a brief overview of the work that has been done in this area, some of the controversies and debates around the issue you want to do your research on, what you intend to add to the debate, and so on. You also need to convince your reader that your research is relevant and worth doing. Tell your reader, for example, how your research could help to solve a practical problem, influence a policy, change the way things work, improve a system, empower people, change lives, and so forth.

A major mistake that researchers make is to confuse the research problem with the rationale. Some also confuse the research purpose and the research problem, or they state the research question as a purpose or problem instead of a question. The rationale of your research problem is the reason for conducting the study. It provides reasons for the need for conducting the said research and is a very important part of your research as it justifies the significance and novelty of your research problem. A research problem is an area of concern, a gap in the existing knowledge, or a deviation from the norm that points to the need for further understanding and investigation. The research problem, in comparison to the rationale, is usually short and assists you in focusing your study.

Let's say, for example, you would like to understand why, despite the funds that are allocated to women to start up new ventures, the rate of start-ups in the country has not improved. The rationale of your study will explain why it is problematic if new ventures started by women fail and why it is important to conduct research on this topic. The research problem, however, is that we currently do not have an in-depth understanding of why these new ventures fail, so research needs to be conducted to fill this gap in our knowledge.

Brief literature review and theoretical framework

A critical, well-synthesised and integrated literature review that demonstrates the need and justification for your study forms a vital part of your proposal. What we mean by a synthesised literature review is that you should integrate information from several sources in such a way that it forms a logical and coherent whole.

The general purpose of a literature review is to gain an understanding of the current state of knowledge about a selected research problem. Your literature review must therefore show gaps in the knowledge or it must point towards certain theoretical and methodological shortcomings, unanswered questions, contradictions, disagreements, and so forth. Moreover, you need to demonstrate what research has already been conducted within your area of interest and what has not been investigated yet. You must also use your literature review to build and support a strong argument (or thesis) that you wish to make through your study.

As part of your literature review you can also refer to your theoretical framework (not to be confused with a conceptual framework). Since theory is based on research, and vice versa, it is essential to understand the dynamic relationship between them. Research provides a coherent body of knowledge to stimulate the development of new theories. However, theories can also generate new research questions and support existing ideas. You therefore need to include a discussion of the existing theories that can contribute to your study.

Your literature should also form the foundation of your conceptual framework, which will allow your reader to understand your research question and choice of methodology better. A proper literature review will further demonstrate to your reader that you are aware of the breadth and diversity of literature that relates to your research question.

Conceptualisation of key terms

One of the key aspects of effective communication is that you must share meaning with your listener or reader. Thus, you need to ensure that when you use certain key terms in your study, others will understand exactly what you mean by that term. You can use authoritative sources to help you with your conceptualisation. Keep in mind, however, that conceptualisation is not merely providing a definition from a dictionary or textbook. You need to be clear and specific and state as exactly as possible how you interpret and are going to use a particular key term. You must then also use these terms consistently throughout your study. We usually do not conceptualise too many terms, only the most important ones. Most of these terms are likely to appear in your title as well and will all be related to the purpose of your study. Other concepts that are not likely to be broadly understood can be defined as you introduce them and do not necessarily have to be conceptualised.

Complicated concepts usually have dimensions and indicators. When we talk about operational definitions, we usually refer to quantitative studies where an operational definition typically specifies how a concept will be measured by making use of dimensions and indicators.

The problem statement

Research is always about finding a solution to a problem or finding an answer to a question. You must therefore formulate a problem statement in your proposal in a clear and concise way. Your problem statement must indicate what the main issues are that you need to address through your investigation. Thus, explain what the problem is, why it is a problem and why it needs to be solved. Your problem must be strongly related to the purpose of your study.

You may also wish to restate your research problem in the form of a question which will help you to address your research problem. Remember that research is about solving problems and answering questions. In the case of quantitative research, you may also need to formulate testable hypotheses linked to your research question in order to solve your research problem. However, we only make use of hypotheses if the study is explanatory. If the study is exploratory or descriptive, we usually make use of sub-questions instead of hypotheses. Both hypotheses and sub-questions should relate directly to the research problem and sub-problems.

In the case of qualitative research we tend to use objectives or goals, and sometimes sub-goals, to help us answer the research question and solve the research problem. When a combination of qualitative and quantitative methods are used in a study, both hypotheses (or sub-questions) and goals can be used in combination.

The research methodology

Two of the most important aspects that you need to discuss under your methodology are the way(s) in which you will collect your data and, once collected, how you will analyse your data. We discuss both these aspects in more detail below.

Although not always required, it is very useful to include a brief discussion about the research paradigm or tradition you are following. The reason for this is that if you do not state, for example, your epistemological and ontological positions clearly, a reader from a different tradition may judge your research unfairly by using the criteria from that tradition. It is also necessary to point out whether you are going to use qualitative, quantitative or mixed-methods to collect your data and these choices must be justified. This too will determine how your study will be judged. Something to take note of is that researchers sometimes also get confused between multi-methods and mixed-methods. Figure 20.2 below should allow you to make this distinction.

The word 'mono' means 'one', so when a researcher only uses one data collection method, it is referred to as a mono-method. Thus, one can use one qualitative or one quantitative research method to collect your data. However, sometimes researchers will make use of more than one data collection method. Thus, if a researcher, for example, uses more than one qualitative research method to collect data, such as a combination of in-depth interviews and focus groups, it is referred to as multi-methods. In the case of multi-methods, the data collection methods are either only qualitative or only quantitative. A mixed-method design is used when quantitative and qualitative data collection methods are mixed. There are different types of mixed-methods designs as well. The most common ones are a convergent parallel design, explanatory sequential design and an exploratory sequential design. In a parallel design the quantitative and qualitative data collection takes place at the same time, whereas in a sequential design, either the quantitative data is collected first, followed by the qualitative data, or vice versa. It will be worth your while to familiarise yourself with these designs should you be interested in making use of a mixed-methods design.

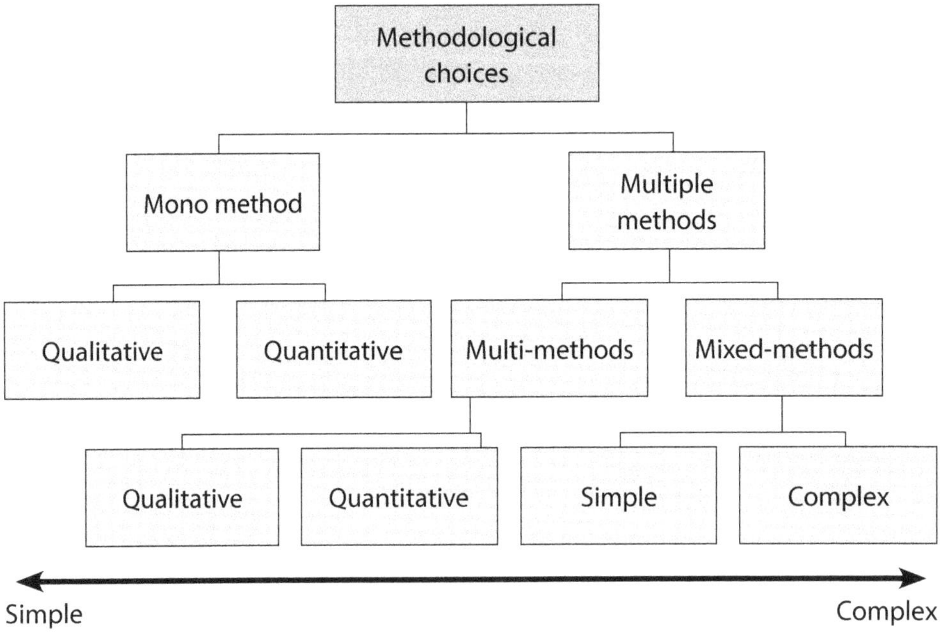

Figure 20.2 Methodological choices

As part of your research methodology you need to explain what sampling method you are going to use and why you have decided on this particular sampling method. It is not enough to merely describe your sampling method. Talk about the pros and cons of the sampling method you have selected and make sure your choice is clearly justified. Where applicable, you should also specify the population to which you want to generalise your results. Moreover, it is useful to specify your unit of analysis, which is usually either individuals, groups, organisations or social artefacts.

In terms of your research design you need to stipulate, for example, whether you will be doing a cross-sectional or longitudinal study, or whether your study will, for example, be grounded theory or action research. Your choice of design should be appropriate for your research problem and research question. Again, do not merely describe the design. Explain why the particular design is appropriate for your study and what the possible limitations of using such a design could be. The next aspect that you can address under your methodology section is whether you will be doing basic research (also referred to as pure research) or applied research or a combination of both:

- *Basic research* is typically used to develop fundamental knowledge and to investigate and develop theories to explain a specific phenomenon. Basic or pure research is not designed to solve problems, but it helps us to think about and perceive phenomena in a particular way.
- *Applied research* investigates practical problems in order to find solutions which can be applied in practice.

Data collection method(s)

There are several methods that can be used to obtain answers to research questions. However, as was mentioned in Chapter 2, your research paradigm will determine the data collection method(s) you will use. You may also recall that quantitative researchers collect numerical data and they therefore depend on data collection methods that will assist them in producing quantifiable results. Qualitative researchers, on the other hand, collect artefacts, stories, phrases, words, images and all kinds of symbols that will assist in creating a deeper understanding of a phenomenon. In addition, researchers using mixed-methods collect both types of data.

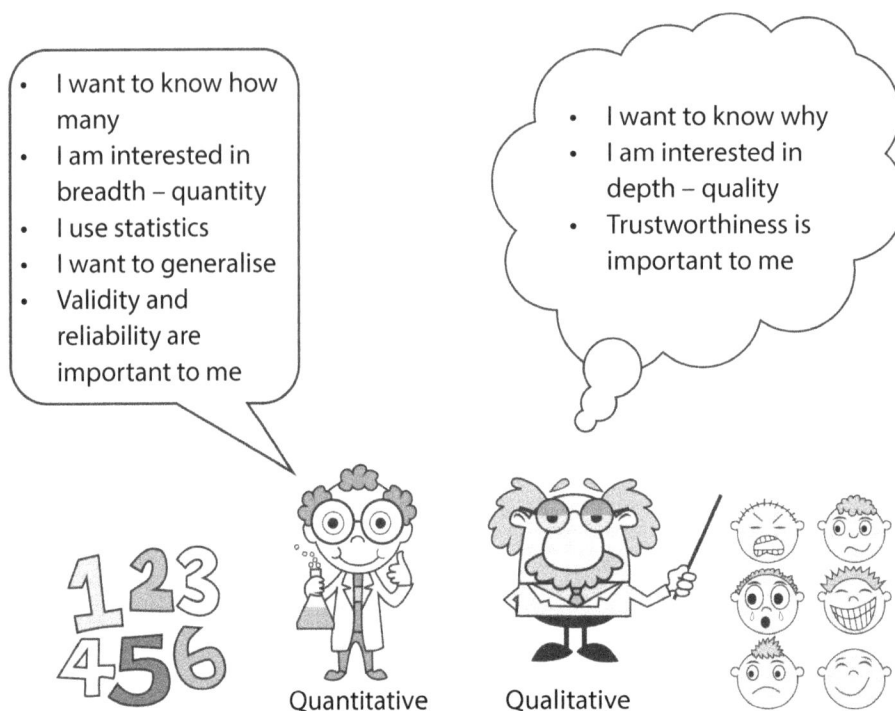

Figure 20.3 Quantitative versus qualitative research

Some typical qualitative data collection methods are:
- in-depth interviews;
- focus groups;
- ethnography and other forms of field research such as participant observation;
- questionnaires consisting of open-ended questions; and
- case studies.

Some typical quantitative data collection methods are:
- experimental designs;
- measurement instruments such as the Likert scale;
- questionnaires consisting of closed-ended questions; and
- correlational studies.

When you collect data you need to ensure that the type of data you are collecting will assist you in answering your research question or solving your research problem. During this stage you should also consider the ethical implications of your research.

In the data collection section of your research proposal you must go into detail about how the data are to be collected. For example, if you are using a survey approach, you should specify your population and sample size. You should also clarify how the questionnaires will be distributed and how they will be collected.

Data analysis method(s)

In your research proposal you also need to demonstrate that you have a good grasp of the method(s) you will use to analyse your data. The data analysis method(s) will depend on the method(s) you used to collect your data and the type of data you have collected. You therefore need to select a data analysis method that will help you to identify the key features and issues under investigation.

Analysis requires that you sift through the data collected and that you sort, select and organise information to give you a better understanding of the phenomenon under study. There are several statistical methods that can be used to analyse numerical and statistical data, such as the Pearson correlation test or the t-test. When the aim is to collect qualitative data, researchers are more likely to use coding and thematic or narrative analysis.

The feasibility of the study

Before you can start any research project you need to be able to convince your reader that your study is indeed doable and that the time and resources that your study will require are realistic and justifiable. In some instances you will be required to submit a budget for your study. Some institutions also require that you provide a timeframe for your study, like a Gantt Chart, where you stipulate by when you will complete what sections of your research. In short, you should demonstrate to your reader that you have thought carefully about all the issues regarding your method and the relationship of these issues to your research objectives.

Ethical considerations

Most institutions require that certain ethical principles be adhered to when researchers conduct their research, especially when their research involves humans and/or animals. Ethics provide us with guidelines in terms of what can be considered acceptable and unacceptable behaviour. It refers to methods, procedures or perspectives that tell us how to act and how to analyse complex problems and issues (Resnik, 2020).

If your unit of analysis is individuals, you need to explain how you will ensure anonymity or, where this is not possible, confidentiality. Informed consent should also be sought; it is important to ensure your reader that participation in your study will under no circumstances be under duress and that all participation will be on a voluntary basis only. Keep in mind that you need to explain how you will uphold ethical principles — merely describing them will not be sufficient.

Limitations of the study

Limitations are any potential problems you foresee for conducting your study. Anything that can possibly threaten the validity or trustworthiness of your study can be considered a limitation. You should also indicate the scope and logistical and resource limitations of your study.

Anticipated contributions of the study

Not all institutions require their students to include a section on the anticipated contributions of the study. Some, in fact, believe that it should be avoided, since it could be seen as a way of pre-empting or predicting the findings. However, it is useful to make sure that you know what kind of a contribution your study is likely to make to the body of knowledge. Be mindful, though, that the anticipated contribution of the study should not pre-empt findings. Thus, say, for example, that your study could make a contribution in terms of influencing a particular policy, but do not make a prediction as to what you think you will find.

References

Ensure that all the sources consulted and referenced in the text are included in the reference list. Do not bullet or number the sources in the reference list and make sure the sources are in alphabetical and chronological order.

You must always use an appropriate referencing system. This is likely to be prescribed by your institution (university or college). You can also refer to the referencing guidelines provided in Chapter 22 of this book. One of the most important aspects of referencing, regardless of the referencing system you are using, is that your referencing style be consistent throughout your entire document. Try also not to use sources that are more than five to ten years old, unless they are seminal sources. Avoid using Wikipedia as a reference because the information presented in Wikipedia is not verifiable and therefore not considered academically sound.

Summary

Your research proposal should answer the questions 'What?', 'Why?', 'Who?', 'When?' and 'How?':

- In terms of what will be researched, you need to include the main purpose of your study, the main problem for which you are seeking a solution and the question for which you are seeking an answer.
- You also need to describe and justify why you are doing the study. You must therefore motivate the importance and relevance of your study. Arguments as to how the proposed study will assist people or the ways in which it will contribute to the body of existing knowledge must be specified.
- You further need to describe who or what is going to be researched. This includes your unit of analysis and defining your population and sampling methods. You may also need to refer to the ethical considerations involved in your study.
- The question 'when'? refers to the time frame of the study.
- Lastly, you need to explain how you are going to conduct your research. In other words, you need to describe the theoretical approaches you are going to review and the research design you are going to apply. Make certain that you motivate the selection of your research methodology. You must therefore explain how you are going to collect your data and how you will analyse it.

Also remember that your research proposal needs to be written in the future tense. The same technical matters that you need to consider in writing a research report (discussed in greater detail in the next chapter) also apply to research proposals. Thus, make sure you use appropriate academic discourse, that your spelling and grammar are correct and that your report is technically edited and looks professional.

Review the chapter

Answer the questions and complete the tasks to assess whether you understand the content of this chapter:

1. What would you say are the benefits of constructing a research proposal before you commence with your research study?
2. List all the aspects that you need to address in a research proposal.
3. Explain the key information that should be included in a research proposal.
4. Critically evaluate the importance of stating a clear purpose in your research proposal.
5. Explain the link between the research approach, data collection and data analysis methods.

→

6. A researcher wants to conduct a study to determine whether there is a correlation between smoking marijuana and academic performance.
    (a)   What do you think the research problem in this situation is?
    (b)   What will the research question for this study be?
    (c)   What kind of an approach will this researcher use?
    (d)   What are some of the ethical issues this researcher will have to consider?

CHAPTER 21

The research report

Lorette Jacobs

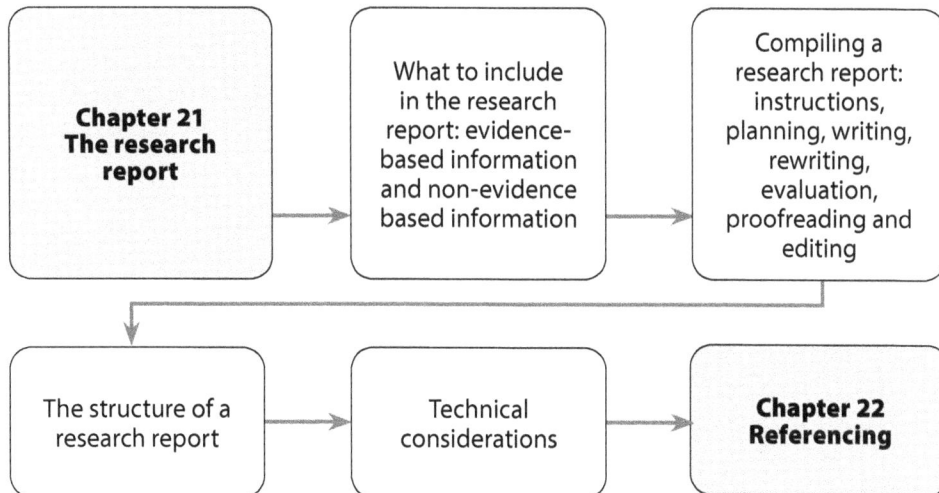

Chapter 21 The research report	What to include in the research report: evidence-based information and non-evidence based information	Compiling a research report: instructions, planning, writing, rewriting, evaluation, proofreading and editing
The structure of a research report	Technical considerations	**Chapter 22 Referencing**

Overview

Welman, Kruger and Mitchell (2005) state that if a researcher takes the trouble to carry out a research project, the findings thereof should be released to expand scientific knowledge. Such research findings can be presented in a variety of formats, such as a research essay, report, dissertation, thesis or even a journal article. The focus of this chapter is on assisting you to compile a research report. A research report is a well-researched, clearly written, logical, balanced, objective, impartial and concise document that presents research conclusions in an uncomplicated and clear manner (Fox & Bayat, 2007:150). Even though this chapter will focus specifically on the scope and content of research reports, it is important to note that this information can also be applied when writing research essays, dissertations and theses.

In general, the research report aims to report research findings to others. It is used to answer questions such as:

- What was the research problem?
- How was the problem investigated?
- What has been found?
- What are the implications and the meaning of the findings in terms of the problem originally posed?

Writing up the research findings is usually the last step in the research process and, for many researchers, the most difficult one. This is because a badly written research document will spoil all the hard work that went into the research project. Alternatively, a well-structured and organised research report will give the reader the opportunity to appreciate the hard work involved in the compilation of a research report (Caprette, 2000). This chapter will therefore provide you with details related to the information and evidence to include in a research report, the process to follow to write a report and a proposed structure that can be followed to present research information.

Objectives of this chapter

By the end of this chapter you should be able to demonstrate your understanding of the following:
- the use of various types of information to present the content of a research report;
- the process to follow to write a research report;
- how to structure the contents of the research report; and
- the technical issues to consider when compiling the research report.

What to include in the research report

Before we investigate the process to be followed to write a research report, or even look at the structure in which content is to be presented, it is important that we focus our attention on the information to be included in each section, as provided in the previous chapters of this book. The aim of this section is to emphasise the importance of ensuring that you include the most applicable and relevant information. Machet, Olen, and Behrens (2017) refer to two categories of information that can be used to compile the research report. A summary of these is presented in Figure 21.1.

Using evidence-based information

As indicated in Figure 21.1, evidence-based information consists of definitions, evidence and inferences. Researchers often use definitions to ensure that readers know that a specific term is used to denote only one meaning and to avoid confusion with other terms. The first step to define a term is to use a comprehensive and reputable dictionary. If you are defining a word in a particular discipline, such as psychology, physics or business management, you will need to use a subject dictionary rather than a general dictionary. The reason is that a term may have specific meanings within that discipline which are different from the way the term is used in everyday language.

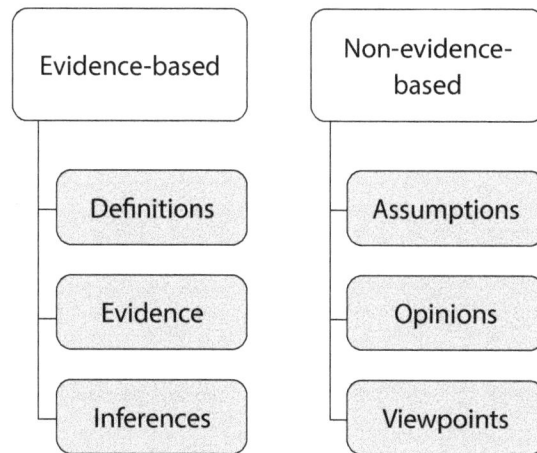

Figure 21.1 Categories of information

Evidence-based information obtained from authoritative sources such as encyclopaedias, textbooks, journal articles, newspapers and government publications is used to provide sufficient evidence in the research report so that few people will dispute the validity and reliability of its information. You learnt about validity and reliability in Chapter 17 of this book. You should therefore now be able to determine when information is valid and reliable. To refresh your memory: validity requires using the best available evidence to ensure that the data presented in the research report are as accurate as possible. Reliability is the extent to which we can rely on the source of the data to be trustworthy and authentic (Pierce, 2008:83). Figure 21.2 illustrates in a more practical way what is meant by validity and reliability.

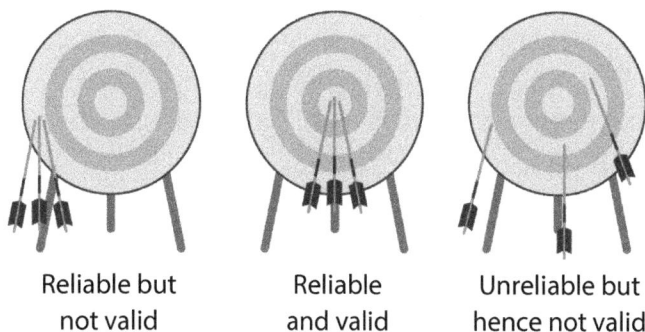

| Reliable but not valid | Reliable and valid | Unreliable but hence not valid |

Figure 21.2 Validity versus reliability

The third type of evidence-based information that can be used in a research report is known as inference. Machet et al (2017) state that inferences can be defined as conclusions based on known facts. An inference is therefore an educated guess that we use to explain something. We draw inferences by reasoning from or interpreting available evidence. Linked to this, Mouton (2001:114) divides inference information into three types:

1. *Deductive inference* involves drawing conclusions from statements. Conclusions in a deductive argument can be derived from theories and models. Phrases that usually indicate that deductive reasoning is being used include 'on the basis of the aforementioned', 'hence', 'thus', 'therefore', 'this leads to . . .', and so on.

2. *Inductive inference* involves the generalisation of observations from samples or case studies to the population studied in the research. Any form of statistical interpretation in which you generalise from a sample to the general population is a form of inductive inference.

3. *Retroductive inference* provides an interpretation in order to explain a phenomenon. On the basis of an observation we create an explanation that would explain the observed event. For example, if observations have been made about certain trends related to romantic feelings between men and women that were not predicted by a theory, the researcher may propose possible explanations for the phenomenon. Whether this explanation is credible is left to the reader, in some sense, and to further research.

Using non-evidence-based information

When compiling your research report, you often have to deal with assumptions, opinions and viewpoints which are not based on scientific evidence. It is sometimes very difficult to differentiate between evidence-based and non-evidence-based information or to decide whether non-evidence-based information should be considered for inclusion in your research report.

When you include *assumptions* in your research report you take for granted a belief, value or idea that is commonly applied in society. One example may be stereotypes, such as that all highly intelligent people are socially awkward. These assumptions may lead to faulty reasoning. They should therefore be identified and critically examined to determine their validity, based on evidence-based scientific information from authoritative sources.

Similarly, opinions and viewpoints should be compared to evidence-based information to determine their validity. An *opinion* is a belief based on substantiation of some kind. For an opinion to be convincing, it should be based on factual evidence or extensive research. Reasonable opinions should be well supported and based on reliable evidence. Irresponsible opinions are often based on insufficient evidence or feelings and beliefs (Machet et al, 2017). Opinions based on substantiated and reliable scientific evidence may be used in research reports to emphasise a point or present an argument.

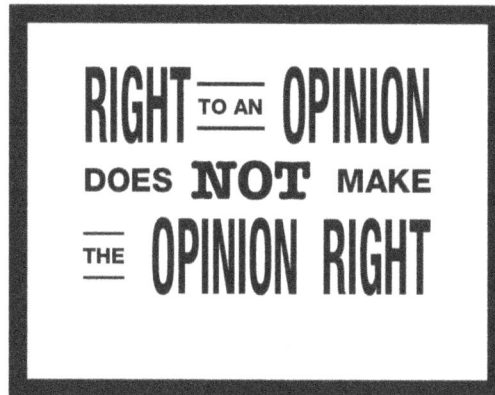

Figure 21.3 Opinion versus viewpoint

Viewpoints are often used to persuade the reader to accept or acknowledge a topic from the point of view of the author. Many forms of writing are used specifically to persuade the reader to view something in the same way as it is viewed by the author. An author may even omit certain evidence in order to persuade the reader of her or his point of view. It is therefore important to apply a critical eye when you read sources where an author wants to promote a specific viewpoint. When reading critically, Machet et al (2017) propose that we determine whether a topic is presented from only one viewpoint and whether the authors are using emotive language to persuade the reader of their viewpoint. As with opinions, only viewpoints that can be verified by other authoritative sources should be used in the research report.

Compiling a research report

When you embark on a project, regardless of what type, there is always some kind of process (steps) that you need to follow to ensure that the project is completed successfully. Similarly, you should follow a process when writing your research report. If you do not follow a process, chances are that you will struggle to complete the report and that the end result will not comply with set academic standards.

Authors such as Caprette (2000), Mouton (2001:122–123), Brown (2005), Fox and Bayat (2007:15) and RMIT University's Study and Learning Centre (2007) propose a number of steps to follow when compiling a research report. A six-step process based on the information from these sources is presented in Figure 21.4. A brief description of each step follows.

Figure 21.4 Steps in the research report writing process

Be clear about the instructions

Before starting to write the research report, ensure that you have a clear understanding of what is expected from the report. Read over the requirements provided for the report several times. Make sure that you thoroughly understand what is meant by keywords that may impact on the content to be included in your research report, such as 'describe', 'classify', 'compare' and 'analyse'. For example, if the instructions state that there must be some comparison to various theories related to the topic, ensure that such a comparison is included. If the report only states that you should write about a topic, it is implied that you should present arguments for and against the topic, supported by scientific literature as well as qualitative and/or quantitative research data.

Planning the structure

Once you have identified the topic and conducted some preliminary research, you might want to start writing about the topic. Resist that urge! Before you begin, think about the structure that you will follow to present the information. Fox and Bayat (2007:151) state that before a report is written, it should be planned thoroughly. This will save time and promotes clarity. In the following section we provide you with detail on the structure a research report should follow. To assist with planning, you can make use of a mind map to structure your report. To do this, take a piece of paper and write the topic in the middle of the page. Draw a circle or square around the topic and branches that point away from the centre. Each branch symbolises a new idea related to the topic. Each branch can also have sub-branches that symbolise ideas or thoughts related to that idea. Use colours, images and icons to assist you in creating this structure. Once the structure is in place, you can start writing the first draft of your research report. See Figure 21.5 for an example of a mind map.

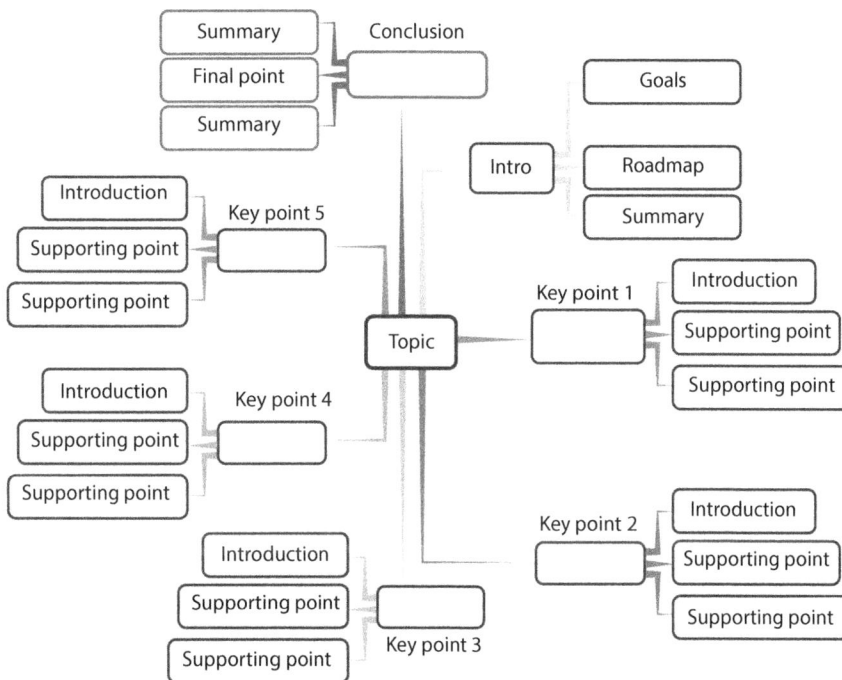

Figure 21.5 Example of a mind map

Writing the first draft

It is important to remember that you cannot start writing the research report until you have done a thorough literature review and collected the data, using one or more types of data collection method.

When writing the first draft of the report you need to continuously keep the purpose of the report, as well as your intended target audience, in mind (Machet et al, 2017). You should aim to present ideas coherently and logically.

It is important to note that writing does not normally progress in an orderly manner. Your initial structure may change as you work through the content and you develop new ideas or perspectives on the topic. It is therefore important to give yourself sufficient time for writing. In the first draft, concentrate on what you want to communicate. Focus on the content. The first draft is the one you write for yourself — the one that helps you to find out what you want to say and to get those ideas on paper. You could approach the process as follows:

1.   One way to get started with the first draft is to *brainstorm* ideas around the content to be included in the report, and to decide which information you want to include where. Identify all information that you think should be included in the report. Write your ideas down in the form of a list or mind map.

2.   Once all the ideas have been written down, *evaluate* and *sort* them according to the structure of your research paper. This will help you to organise the content.

3.   Based on the list or mind map, you can now *write* about all the information that was collected for the research. The most important thing about writing the first draft is to write down everything you want to say.

4.   Once all information is on paper you can start to *reorganise* and polish what you have written.

Rewriting the first draft

It is important to note that the first draft is not, and can never be, the final draft. Revising the first draft will provide you with an opportunity to check if your ideas are presented in a logical order. Also, any unnecessary information can be deleted. You may write various other drafts before you get to the final draft that you will submit. As you work on improving the drafts, you should pay more attention to the structure of the content, the logical flow of information, as well as grammar, spelling and layout.

At this point it may be valuable to provide you with some information on paragraph structuring, as many writers struggle with this. It is important to remember that sentences form the building blocks of paragraphs. A paragraph is a set of sentences all dealing with the same general idea, and linked together in a logical, flowing sequence. You must lead your reader from one idea to the next — you cannot just introduce a new idea without preparing your reader for what is to follow.

Each paragraph should deal with a single subject; the sentences need to be relevant to the subject and connected in a logical manner. Each paragraph should start with a topic sentence which tells you what the subject of the paragraph is. The topic sentence contains the main idea(s) of that particular paragraph. Other sentences in the paragraph explore the main idea(s) and may include evidence, illustrations, definitions or explanations. When a new point is to be discussed you should start a new paragraph. Remember that you should also build an argument throughout. Figure 21.6 illustrates in a practical manner how to construct an argument.

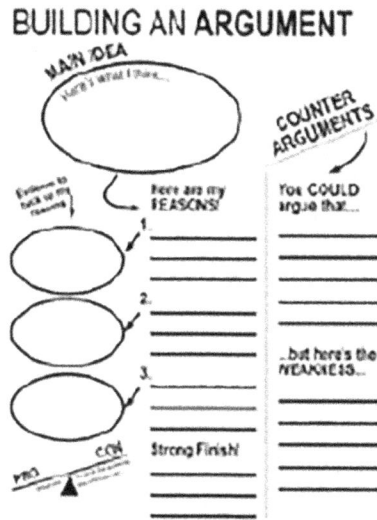

BUILDING AN ARGUMENT

Figure 21.6 Building an academic argument

Evaluating the content

All good writers evaluate what they have written in order to improve their work. Evaluation involves cutting, sifting, rearranging and polishing in order to make the report more effective for your target audience. Evaluating your content provides you with an opportunity to find out if you need more information, if you need to make new connections or consolidate and restructure the information included in the draft. As part of the evaluation process, you also need to analyse your draft by looking at broad features such as paragraph structure and the logical order in which you present the information.

Proofreading the report

Proofreading is not the same as evaluating your draft. During evaluation, you assess the logical flow and inclusion of evidence in the report. Proofreading requires fixing typographic errors as well as looking for spelling, grammar, formatting and spacing problems. Before proofreading the final report that you want to submit, put it away for a few days so that you give yourself the opportunity to read the report afresh (Brown, 2005).

When proofreading you can use a spellchecker to identify spelling errors or incorrect sentence constructions. However, keep in mind that the spellchecker will not identify all the mistakes in your writing. You need to look out for spelling mistakes that the spellchecker cannot identify, such as using 'bare' when you meant to say 'bear'. We therefore recommend that you also read the content aloud from beginning to end. This will help you catch omitted or repeated words and awkward sentence construction. It may even help to get someone to read the report aloud to you whilst you listen. Some word processing applications also have a 'read aloud' function that you can use to determine whether your writing is flowing and your argument logical.

Editing the report

Editing the report requires a final read and making required alterations to ensure that the structure is logical and coherent, and that grammar, spelling and punctuation are correct. Because many South African writers are second- and even third-language English users, it may be necessary to get the research report edited by a professional editor to ensure that all grammatical errors are fixed. Poor spelling and incorrect grammar detract from the work and may annoy the reader. They also create a negative impression about the quality of your work. In fact, some may even question the trustworthiness of your research because research requires you to be precise in your reporting, so attention to detail is very important.

The structure of a research report

In step two of the process to follow when compiling a research report (see Figure 21.4), we proposed that you plan the structure of your research report. Planning the structure is important, as this will assist you to organise information in a logical manner which will communicate the main idea of the report effectively. The structure of your research report may be similar to the outline of the research proposal that you used to implement the research project.

Mouton (2001:120) proposes that the research report provide information related to key areas, namely the theoretical background, research methodology followed to investigate the research problem, methods of analysing the results, and so on. Kumar (2019) suggests that this information be presented in the overall introduction, body and conclusion of the research report, as well as in a section on your findings and an interpretation of your findings.

The first sections of the report set the scene by informing the reader what the report aims to achieve. The middle part delivers the detail of the message and develops the arguments supported by the research findings. The conclusion follows logically from the main body of the report and should guide the reader to a series of recommendations. Structuring the outline of the report requires that you identify headings and subheadings to show different sections. Figure 21.7 provides an outline of proposed headings that should ideally be included in a well-structured research report.

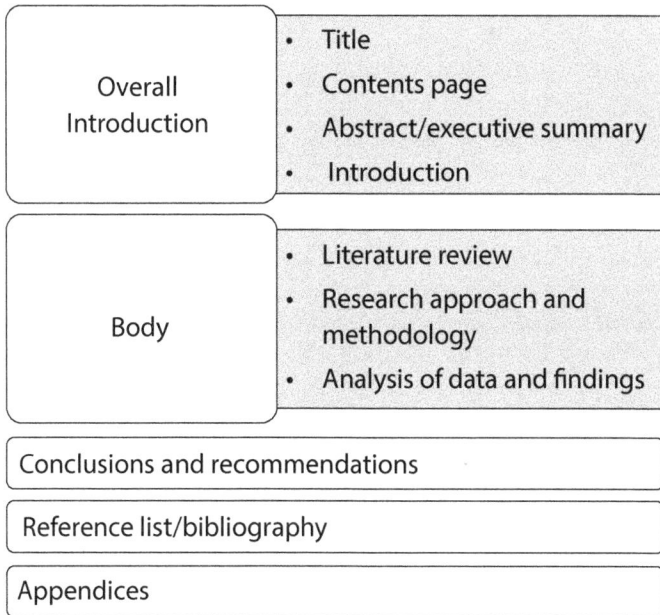

Overall Introduction	• Title
	• Contents page
	• Abstract/executive summary
	• Introduction

Body	• Literature review
	• Research approach and methodology
	• Analysis of data and findings

Conclusions and recommendations

Reference list/bibliography

Appendices

Figure 21.7 The basic structure of a research report

It is important to note that these headings provide the basis or framework with which a research report should comply. You may, however, want to add additional headings or subheadings to ensure that all relevant information is presented. Brief descriptions of the main content to include in your research report follow.

Overall introduction

As indicated in Figure 21.7, there are a number of key components that make up the overall introduction. The purpose of this overall introduction is to provide the reader with a clear overview of the scope and purpose of the research report.

Title page

The title of the report, as well as the name of the author and the date on which the report was written or finalised, should be displayed on the title page. The title of the research report should concisely and unambiguously reflect the exact topic of the project, for example: 'The relationship between gaming and aggressive behaviour in children.'

Selecting the title is important. It must be clear and concise, and it must accurately inform the reader of the aim of the report. The title (preferably no more than 10 words) should provide a description of the study. Remember that your reader will initially see the title and nothing else. The title should therefore spark interest and entice the reader to continue reading. A subtitle (if needed) may be included as a clearer description of and supplement to the main title (Fox & Bayat, 2007:151).

Contents page

The contents page follows the title page and informs the reader of the organisation of the report. It lists the sections that lead progressively and logically to the conclusion and enables readers to find their way. A contents page should include all the headings and subheadings used during the compilation of the report. Machet et al (2017) state that headings are usually numbered using Arabic numerals (1, 2, 3) whilst subheadings are indicated using the main number plus a decimal point (1.1, 1.2, 1.3). Using more than third-level headings in your contents page is usually not a good idea because your content page is likely to become too cluttered.

Abstract or executive summary

The abstract or executive summary is a very important part of the report as it is used by readers to determine whether they want to read the content of the report. Its main purpose is to provide readers with an overview of the whole report before they consider each section in detail. It therefore provides brief information on:

- the research problem;
- how the problem was investigated;
- what the main findings are; and
- what the implications are of the meanings of the findings.

The length of the abstract or executive summary depends on the length of the report. A short report needs only two to four paragraphs, while a long and complex report could require more than one page. Because it is such a condensed version of the paper, it may require several drafts before you succeed in capturing the essence of the report.

It is important to note that the abstract or executive summary is written only after the whole report has been completed and it is usually written in the past tense, as it provides an overview of the research that has already been completed. Also remember that writing up research is not the same as creative writing — the main findings are communicated upfront so that the reader knows what to expect.

Introduction

The introduction is usually the first section (or, in the case of dissertations and theses, the first chapter) of the research report. It provides information on:
- the reason for writing the report;
- the methodological research approach followed;
- the purpose and scope of the research approach; and
- the structure of the rest of the report.

After reading the introduction the reader should have a thorough understanding of what the study involved and what it aimed to achieve. At the same time the introduction should allow someone who is not an expert on the topic to understand the basic motivation or rationale for the study.

When writing the introduction try to create interest by, for example, beginning with a controversial statement and building a general description of the purpose and scope of the research around this statement. Machet et al (2017) and Howitt and Cramer (2020) propose that, in order to provide a comprehensive overview of the content included in the research paper, the introduction should include the following:
- an outline of the topic being discussed and an introduction to the main issues and problematic aspects of the topic — past works on the topic are referred to in this general description;
- an indication of the direction of the research report, where you explain what you intend achieving with the research and the line of arguments followed, as well as the perspectives from which you will investigate the problem;
- a summary of the research approach and methodology followed during the research and the main objectives of the research; and
- an explanation of the order in which the research information will be presented to provide your reader with a 'roadmap' of the rest of the paper.

The main body of the research paper

The aim of the main body of the research paper is to provide detailed information on the research through discussions, explanations, analyses, illustrations, supporting evidence, examples, comparisons, and so forth. It is important to note that information included in the body of the report should be confined to evidence-based information only. As indicated in Figure 21.7, the body of the report can be divided into a variety of sections, namely the literature review, the research approach, the analysis of the data and the findings.

Literature review

The literature review and theoretical framework are used to present key concepts, ideas, theories, and models related to the research topic. It contains detail on literature published on the topic. One or more sections of the body can be allocated to the presentation of information on a research topic. See also Chapter 8 for more information on how to write a literature review.

Research approach and methodology

Following the section(s) of the literature review is the research approach. Fox and Bayat (2007:153) state that this section should detail:
- the methodological approach used (qualitative, quantitative or mixed-methods);
- the reasons for choosing certain methodologies over others;
- the design followed; and
- the techniques and tools that were used to obtain and analyse the data.

Analysis of data and findings

This section of the research report should present the research results and discuss these results. Qualitative data, quantitative data or a combination of both types of data may be presented in this section, depending on the research approach applied. Data can, for example, be reported in the form of tables and diagrams with supporting narrative descriptions.

Qualitative data are usually presented in the form of a narrative, interspersed with verbatim quotes to illustrate or support the points being made. Supportive or supplementary information can be presented in flowcharts and spider diagrams to enhance the presentation of qualitative data. Key findings of qualitative or mixed-methods should be identified and evidence should be arranged in such a way as to convince the reader of the validity or trustworthiness of results (Fox & Bayat, 2007:153). Also keep in mind that direct quotes from participants serve as evidence in qualitative data in the same way that statistics are used in quantitative research.

Quantitative data can be presented in the form of diagrams, tables, and charts. This type of data always includes statistical data as supporting evidence for any conclusions drawn. Note that in research that relies heavily on statistical information, tables are an effective way of presenting the data to show patterns, which in turn can be used to make certain predictions. Tables should be kept simple and each table should be labelled with a heading that clearly states what the table represents. Similarly, bar and pie charts are extremely versatile in presenting information in interesting and versatile ways. As with tables, it is important that charts and diagrams be labelled and that explanations be given to clarify the meaning of the information included in these tools. It is therefore important that you explain the significance of the statistical findings and that you 'translate' them into useful information that all readers will be able to follow and understand. This implies that you must not merely present your statistical findings, you also need to interpret these findings and explain their meaning for your reader.

Conclusions and recommendations

The final section of the research report presents conclusions and recommendations. The conclusions and recommendations section states the implications of the research findings and links the findings to broader issues and recommendations. It includes information related to the interpretation of the results based on literature or theory. The conclusions and recommendations section is used to discuss the most important points related to the analysis of the research findings and to merge final arguments.

This section concludes with an investigation into suggestions for how the problem could be resolved. By stating how a particular problem or situation can be resolved or clarified you will find that the recommendations flow naturally from the conclusions. State significant results clearly and present recommendations regarding the implementation of findings. Details on further research to be conducted based on the findings and recommendations are also presented in this section (Mouton, 2001).

Reference list/bibliography

All sources referred to in the text or appendices should be acknowledged in the reference list or bibliography. It is also important that you understand the difference between a reference list and a bibliography. A reference list is a complete list of all the sources that were referenced in the text. A bibliography is similar to a reference list, but it also includes additional sources that were consulted and that were not referenced or cited in the main text of the report. Including a reference list or bibliography is essential for various reasons:
- Referencing helps you to avoid plagiarism, which is a serious offence.
- It is academic courtesy to acknowledge that your information came from a particular source.

- The reference list or bibliography offers substantiation for what you are saying, as sources may be used to support your views. They thus serve as evidence to support the arguments that you are making.
- The reference list or bibliography enables anyone reading the research report to go and check the original source if they wish to do so.

More detail on how to use in-text referencing, as well as how to compile a reference list or bibliography, is provided in the following chapter.

Appendix

The appendix (plural appendices) serves as a reference section for the research report and provides additional information which may further substantiate information included in the report. Appendices may include details about statistical data, graphs, tables, questionnaires, ethical clearance certificates, and so on. They may also contain further information and provide further analytical data to clarify various statements and/or assumptions made by the researcher. Attention should be drawn to the appendices at points in the text where the information included in appendices is relevant.

Technical considerations

A well-written and well-structured research report will have a positive effect on how the reader receives the content. It is therefore very important that attention be given to technical detail such as the language of the report, the format, academic style and tone. To assist you, the final section of this chapter provides you with information on key technical aspects to consider. The information included here is not comprehensive, however, and we recommend that you use a style guide when compiling your research paper. Key technical aspects that you should take note of include the following:

- Reports should be written in language that is easy to understand. Sentences are meant to convey meaning. Some writers mistakenly believe that scientific writing means writing long and complex sentences which include a lot of jargon and convoluted arguments. A piece of writing does not have to be complex in order for it to be academic. Writing can be simple without being simplistic. Sentences and paragraphs should therefore be kept short, simple, clear and understandable.
- The past tense is usually used when writing the research report because the research has already been done. However, the present tense is always used in the literature review, even if the author that is being referenced is no longer alive.

- The active voice should preferably be used where possible. For example, rather say: 'An assistant interviewed the respondent' instead of 'The respondents were interviewed by an assistant.' It is, however, acceptable to use the passive voice in order to avoid using the first person. For example, instead of saying: 'I interviewed seven participants to determine whether ...', you can say: 'Seven participants were interviewed to determine whether ...'.

- Clichés and jargon should be avoided where possible. If the meaning of a word or concept is not clear or common knowledge, you need to define and explain it as you introduce it.

- The full term or name of an abbreviation or acronym should be used the first time it occurs in the text and the abbreviation or acronym should be given in parentheses. After that the abbreviation or acronym may be used on its own.

- Be sparing with the use of personal pronouns ('we', 'I', 'our', 'me', and so on). Frequent use of personal pronouns can make your writing sound anecdotal, that is, based on opinion instead of evidence. Another potential problem with using personal pronouns such as 'we' is that it is not precise and some readers may not identify with the group you are referring to as 'we'. For example, if you say: 'As South Africans we need to be mindful of past injustices', you may alienate readers who are not South Africans. It is therefore better to be specific and simply say: 'South Africans need to be mindful of past injustices.'

- Keep sentences relatively short. Sentences that are too long usually result in poor sentence construction or inaccurate punctuation. Be concise and to the point. Try not to use more than 20 words per sentence. Do not add clause after clause after clause. If there are too many clauses in a sentence, it is best to break it up into separate sentences.

- Avoid slang, informal or colloquial vocabulary as well as emotive, flowery and subjective language. The only time you can use this type of language is when it forms part of a direct quote. Please note that, in academic discourse, the evidence must speak for itself. As Dinwall (in Gomm 2004:320) puts it, 'research is about presenting evidence and arguments and allowing readers to decide whether to believe it or not.' Your reader must be convinced by the soundness of your arguments, not by flowery, emotive and other subjective language. Keep in mind that you are not writing a novel and therefore creative writing should only be used if it forms part of a direct quote.

- Avoid the use of contractions (such as 'don't', 'can't' or 'won't'). Contractions form part of informal writing, which is not academically acceptable.

- Repetition of content should not occur in a research report. If you find yourself repeating large chunks of material, it means you have not planned the content of your sections properly. The exception to this rule is the abstract, which should contain only information reported elsewhere. You should not include any 'new' information in your abstract.

- Structure your work logically and move ideas sensibly from one sentence or paragraph to the next. Make sure you link paragraphs and explain to your reader when you are moving on to a different idea. Do not confuse your readers by jumping from topic to topic without guiding them. It is also important that you do not make your reader do the thinking on your behalf. Point out and be explicit about connections and conclusions and do not assume your readers will draw the same conclusion as you.
- Provide additional supporting details, examples and information where something may be confusing or unclear, especially to explain difficult constructs, theories, or jargon.
- Do not leave ideas unfinished. If the meaning of what you said is not obvious, you need to elaborate on the idea and make the meaning clear. Make sure you follow all the points you make through to the end and reach a logical and evidence-based conclusion.

Summary

In a way, writing a report is the most crucial step in the research process, as it communicates the findings of the research to the intended audience. A badly written report can spoil all the hard work you have put into the research study. Before you start writing the research report, develop an outline of the different sections and their content. Sections should be written around the main themes of the study. The write-up should therefore integrate the rationale for studying the topic, the literature review, the findings, conclusions, and recommendations.

Review the chapter

Answer the following questions and complete the tasks to assess whether you understand the content of this chapter:

1. What are the different types of inferences that can be used to draw conclusions in a research report?
2. What process will you follow to compile a research report? What additional steps can be added to this process that may further assist you to compile a quality research report?
3. What key information should be included in the introduction of a research report?
4. What type of information should be included in the research approach, findings and analysis sections of the body of the research report?

→

---

5. How would you say the research findings, conclusions and recommendations of a research report are linked?
6. What are some of the key technical considerations to ensure that you write a quality research report?

CHAPTER 22

Referencing

Lorette Jacobs

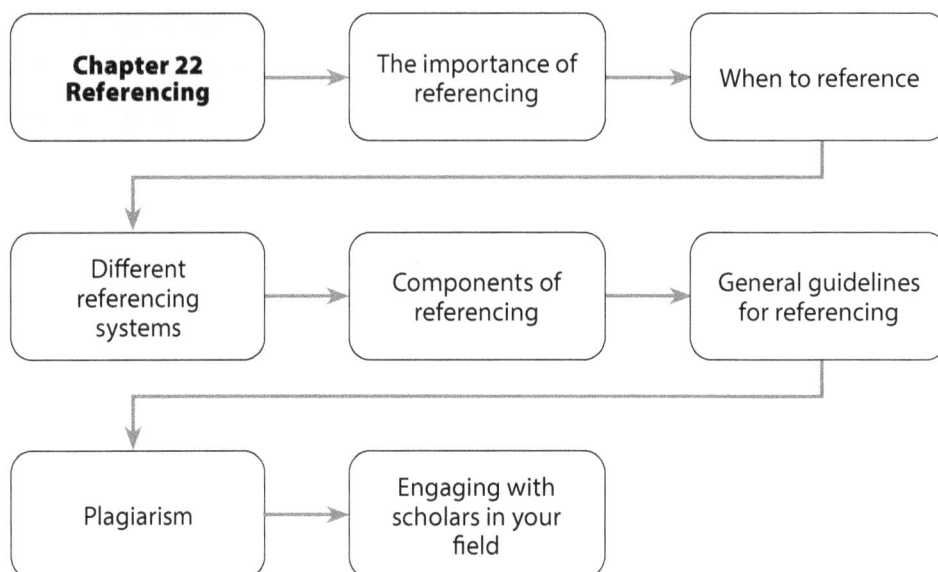

```
┌─────────────────┐      ┌─────────────────┐      ┌─────────────────┐
│  Chapter 22     │ ───▶ │ The importance of│ ───▶ │ When to reference│
│  Referencing    │      │   referencing    │      │                 │
└─────────────────┘      └─────────────────┘      └─────────────────┘

┌─────────────────┐      ┌─────────────────┐      ┌─────────────────┐
│   Different      │ ───▶ │  Components of   │ ───▶ │ General guidelines│
│   referencing    │      │   referencing    │      │  for referencing │
│   systems        │      │                 │      │                 │
└─────────────────┘      └─────────────────┘      └─────────────────┘

┌─────────────────┐      ┌─────────────────┐
│   Plagiarism     │ ───▶ │ Engaging with   │
│                 │      │ scholars in your │
│                 │      │     field       │
└─────────────────┘      └─────────────────┘
```

Overview

You will have realised by now that most academic assignments or tasks require referencing and, in spite of there being many resources to consult, students still find it challenging. This need not be the case, as we show you in this chapter. While there are many technical aspects to referencing that you have to familiarise yourself with, such as the requirements of different academic journals, the referencing you need to do at undergraduate or honours level is pretty standard.

It is most likely that you have submitted some assessments to SafeAssign or TurnitIn, so you know why good knowledge of referencing as well as plagiarism is essential. Referencing not only means that you acknowledge the thoughts and ideas of the people who wrote them but that you have also studied the subject and can provide evidence for your arguments and opinions.

In this chapter we introduce you to different referencing systems and different kinds of referencing. We also give you some guidelines on where to find good sources and how to engage with key scholars in your field. We show you how a good bibliography or reference list can add credibility and substance to your work.

Objectives of this chapter

By the end of this chapter you should be able to demonstrate your understanding of the following:

- the need for referencing;
- which sources need to be referenced;
- various referencing systems;
- how in-text referencing should be done;
- engaging with key scholars and knowing who the seminal sources are in your field;
- how to compile a reference list or bibliography; and
- plagiarism.

The importance of referencing

Most people think the only function of referencing is to acknowledge the ideas of other authors. However, there are a number of other reasons why referencing is crucial. When you engage with a research topic you need to know the context of that topic and how it has been addressed in your field of study. For example, if you want to research how people responded to the publication of the national strategic plan to address gender-based violence (GBV), you will need to understand the background. If you are a communications scholar, it is unlikely that you will find any information on this subject in communications journals. This means that you will have to find articles written by experts in GBV and then find key sources on stakeholders and their responses to social issues, for example. Showing that you consulted relevant and expert sources on your topic gives credibility to your arguments. Demonstrating that you have done your homework will add authenticity and validity to your arguments and will provide testimony of your academic integrity.

The inclusion of recent or current sources in your list of references shows that your reading and research are up to date. However, sometimes it is also necessary to include the work of seminal sources. For example, the work of sources such as Talcott Parsons, Niklas Luhmann, Jürgen Habermas and Shannon and Weaver goes back many decades, but it is still being referenced. Referencing also provides other researchers with an opportunity to identify and access related sources that they could possibly use in their own work. Nobody can read all the material in a field or discipline, so by introducing the work of sources that you may find interesting to your field, you can guide scholars who share your field of interest to consider points of view other than those historically covered in that field.

When to reference

When is it important to reference? Whenever you use the direct words or particular information you need to reference the source. More specifically, referencing has to be done when you:

- paraphrase the work of someone else (even though it is in your own words, it must still be acknowledged);
- summarise ideas in your own words;
- quote someone else's ideas by using that person's exact words; or
- copy or adapt a diagram, table, image or any other visual material from a source.

You do not need to include a reference when the information you give in your research document is:

- common knowledge;
- your own views and opinions; or
- your own conclusions based on data obtained through your own research.

Different referencing systems

There are multiple referencing systems that are used in different fields and different kinds of publications in the same field. You have probably heard of at least two, the American Psychological Association (APA) and Harvard styles. There are others that are used in specific fields such as Vancouver, Modern Language Association (MLA), Chicago, which you will see when you do searches in Google Scholar, as illustrated in the image below.

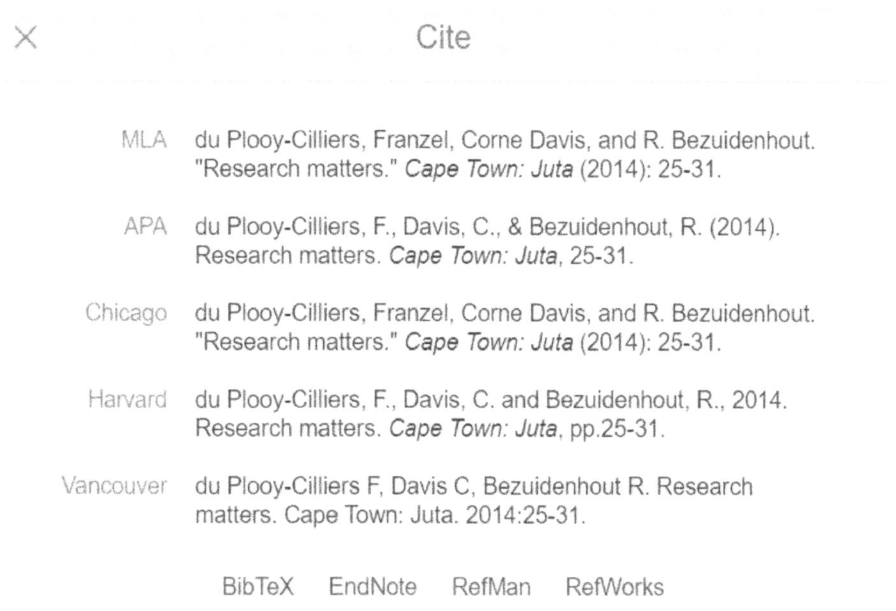

Figure 22.1 Example of referencing system

The *Harvard system* — and variations thereof — is the most widely used. This system provides the surname of the author(s), date of publication and page number(s) of the source. Even though it is the most used system, there are many variations in its application. It is consequently impossible to provide you with a fixed referencing system. You will need to refer to the reference guide of the institution where you study to ensure that your referencing complies with its variation of the Harvard system.

The *APA system* is used in psychology and related disciplines. It involves name and date references similar to the Harvard system. Differences between the Harvard and the APA systems are the use of punctuation in the reference list and bibliography, as well as the use of page and issue numbers.

You will also see links to different referencing software, namely BibTex, EndNote, RefMan and RefWorks, that you can subscribe to online. Then there is Mendeley, which has become popular over the past few years. These applications have different functionalities, but in essence they allow you to upload the sources you are working with and to have citations generated automatically, while also compiling a reference list or bibliography. You may also collaborate in a particular research project with other researchers, who can then share the folder in the application you are using for referencing so that they can also use or add sources. Be careful when using automatic referencing software because there are different versions of these referencing systems. You must make sure that you use the one prescribed by your faculty, as indicated by your lecturer. Without referring to specific referencing systems, you should still take note of some of the general components of referencing.

Components of referencing

Referencing sources that you consulted and/or used when compiling your research document consists of two components, namely in-text referencing and the compilation of a reference list or bibliography at the end of the research document. Let's examine each of these components in more detail.

In-text referencing

Referencing in the text is important to guide your reader to where the ideas or facts you are stating come from. You will have seen many examples of in-text referencing throughout this book. Familiarise yourself with the version of in-text referencing your lecturer or faculty prescribes. You will see that different methods use commas, full stops and ways of page numbering differently. Once you have figured it out, it is not difficult to abide by the prescribed method.

The reference list or bibliography

The reference list or bibliography provides full bibliographic details for all the sources referred to in the research document. Each source referenced in the research document must have a matching entry in the reference list.

Researchers often do not know whether or not to compile a reference list or a bibliography to refer to the sources consulted during the completion of a research document. Generally, a source list is a list in alphabetical order, compiled in accordance with the prescribed method for your subject, that contains all the sources you have referred to in your document. A bibliography typically refers to a list in alphabetical order of all the material you have worked with in your project, even though they may not all appear as references in your text.

General guidelines for referencing

Keep in mind that besides acknowledging the sources of the information, your readers should be able to find the sources should they wish to verify what you are saying or want to read it themselves. Students typically use three kinds of sources: books, journal articles or websites/Internet. Familiarise yourself with the referencing system or format required by your lecturer or supervisor and make sure that you pay careful attention to where full stops, commas and italics go in that system or style. It may seem insignificant to you, but it matters that you do this correctly. Also pay attention to whether you use 'p', 'pg' or just a ',' to reference page numbers. The small things really count in referencing.

Going back to finding sources cited, a system called digital object identifier (DOI) was developed more recently to identify electronic documents published via databases. This system is similar to the concept of the ISBN (International Standard Book Number) allocated to printed material. Where the DOI of an electronic source is available, it should be included in the reference list or bibliography (Burger, 2010). For example: Muldoon, K. 2012. Analysis of mathematical skills and ability across Grade 3 pupils. *Developmental Psychology*. 13(1): 141–155. Available from Advanced Online Publication. DOI: 10/1002/a0028430.

(Database name)

(The DOI number refers to the database as well as the location of the source in the database.)

These general guidelines should give you a clear understanding of the kinds of things to look out for when you reference sources. Another key challenge students experience is with the concept of plagiarism, which we explain next.

Plagiarism

Before we conclude this chapter, it is important to focus our attention on the issue of plagiarism. If you do not acknowledge the sources that you have consulted or the authors whose ideas you are using in your research document, you run the risk of plagiarising ideas or content. Plagiarism is the act of stealing another person's intellectual property. This happens when you reproduce someone else's written or spoken words or ideas and present them as your own. Plagiarism is, simply put, fraud. P.org (2021) defines plagiarism as:

- presenting another person's work as your own;
- taking someone else's words or ideas and copying them without acknowledging the author;
- using a direct quotation but not putting the words in quotation marks;
- not referencing a source correctly;
- paraphrasing (for example, by replacing words and retaining the sentence structure of the source material) and not acknowledging the source; and/or
- basing the greater part of your work on copied words and/or ideas. This is plagiarism even if you acknowledge the source.

Plagiarism results in severe consequences for those who commit it, particularly when they are caught and discredited within the academic community. Also, if you plagiarise, you never really learn the skill of writing — you will therefore always feel that your own work is inferior to that of others.

To avoid plagiarism, you must *reference all sources* consulted. Referencing sources allows you to give credit to the original author(s) and it adds value and credibility to your work. When readers can see which sources, and how many, you have consulted, your research has a stronger research base and people will respect you for the amount of work and effort that you have put into your research.

Engaging with scholars in your field

There are many platforms for scholarly engagements in different fields. Some require formal registration and payment of membership fees, such as the European Group for Organisation Studies (EGOS). Lecturers and academics are usually members of such organisations, where they engage with leading theorists and scholars. However, there are two other platforms that students can join free of charge, namely Researchgate.net and Academisa.edu. You can register on these platforms to find who the leading scholars in your field are. Researchers and scholars often upload their publications or projects on which they are working, onto these platforms. You can also send them messages or ask them to send you work that they have not uploaded for copyright or other reasons. You can see key scholars' networks and what material they work with or how they apply their work in their field. These are great platforms to find sources that you may not notice in the library or in online searches.

Summary

Thorough research relies on the consultation of a variety of sources to obtain information on past research, historical occurrences, trends, arguments, developments in a discipline and even projections. For the credibility of your own research it is important that you consult sources and use existing information to support your own viewpoints and findings. However, you must acknowledge ideas and quotations from other sources to avoid plagiarism.

If you apply your referencing skills correctly, it will contribute significantly to your academic integrity. It will also enhance the quality of your work, help you to achieve higher marks and deepen your knowledge of your particular field of study.

Review the chapter

Answer the questions and complete the tasks to assess whether you understand the content of this chapter:

1. What reasons can be given for referencing academic work?
2. Discuss different types of referencing systems that can be used to reference sources.
3. What is the difference between a reference list and bibliography?
4. Why is it important to include the URL in the reference to an online source?
5. Define plagiarism in your own words. Provide an example to illustrate.
6. Discuss some of the acts that can be described as forms of plagiarism.

Bibliography

Adams, J, Khan, HTA, Raeside, R & White, D. 2012. *Research methods for graduate business and social science students*. New Delhi: Sage.

Adams, KA & Lawrence, EK. 2018. *Research methods, statistics, and applications*. 2nd ed. New Dehli: Sage.

Adams, TE, Jones, SH & Ellis, C. 2015 *Autoethnography*. New York: Oxford University Press.

Adelman, C. 1993. Kurt Lewin and the origins of action research. *Educational Action Research*. 1(1): 7–24. Published online: 11 August 2006. Available at: http://www.tandfonline.com/doi/pdf/10.1080/0965079930010102 [Accessed: 3 September 2013].

Allen, M. 2017 (ed). *The SAGE encyclopedia of communication research methods*. Thousand Oaks: Sage.

Ary, D, Jacobs, LC, Sorensen, C & Walker, D. 2017. *Introduction to research in education*. 10th ed. Belmont: Cengage Learning.

Ashlee, AA, Zamora, B & Karikari, SN. 2017. We are woke: A collaborative critical autoethnography of three 'womxn' of color graduate students in higher education. *International Journal of Multicultural Education*. 19(1): 89–104.

Atmowardoyo, H. 2018. Research methods in TEFL studies: Descriptive research, case study, error analysis, and R & D. *Journal of Language Teaching and Research*. 9(1): 197–204.

Babbie, ER. 2002. *The basics of social research*. 6th ed. Belmont: Cengage Learning.

Babbie, E. 2015. *Observing ourselves. Essays in social research*. 2nd ed. United States of America: Waveland.

Babbie, E. 2017. *The basics of social research*. 7th ed. United States of America: Cengage Learning.

Babbie, E. 2021. *The practice of social research*. 15th ed. Boston: Cengage Learning.

Bailey, KD. 1997. System entropy analysis. *Kybernetes*. 26(6/7): 74–68.

Bell, DJ, Foster, SF & Cone, JD. 2020. *Dissertations and theses from start to finish: Psychology and related fields.* 3rd ed. Washington DC: American Psychological Association.

Berger, PL. & Luckmann, T. 1966. *The social construction of reality.* Harmondsworth, Middlesex: Penguin Books.

Bhandari, P. 2020. *A guide to operationalization.* Available at: https://www.scribbr.com/methodology/operationalization/ [Accessed: 17 December 2020].

Blaikie, N. 2007. *Approaches to social enquiry. Advancing knowledge.* 2nd ed. Cambridge: Polity Press.

Blaikie, N. 2009. *Designing social research.* Cambridge: Polity Press.

Blaikie, N & Priest, J. 2019. *Designing social research: The logic of anticipation.* 3rd ed. Cambridge: Polity Press.

Bless, C, Higson-Smith, C & Sithole, SL. 2013. *Fundamentals of social research methods: An African perspective.* 5th ed. Cape Town: Juta.

Bradley, N. 2013. *Marketing research: Tools and techniques.* 3rd ed. Oxford: Oxford University Press.

Braun, V & Clarke, V. 2019. Reflecting on reflexive thematic analysis. *Qualitative Research in Sport, Exercise and Health.* 11(4): 589–597.

Brown, CK. 2005. *7 steps to writing a great research paper.* Available at: http://www.back2college.com/writingresearchpaper.htm [Accessed: 6 September 2012].

Bryman, A. 2012. *Social science research.* 4th ed. New York: Oxford University Press.

Bryman, A. 2016. *Social science research.* 5th ed. New York: Oxford University Press.

Burger, M. 2010. *Bibliographic style and reference techniques.* Pretoria: University of South Africa.

Burkholder, GJ, Cox, KA, Crawford, LM & Hitchcock, JH. 2020. *Research design and methods. An applied guide for the scholar-practitioner.* Los Angeles: Sage.

Caprette, DR. 2000. *How to write a research report.* Available at: http://dwb4.unl.edu/Chem/CHEM869K/CHEM869KLinks/www.ruf.rice.edu/~bioslabs/tools/report/reportform.html [Accessed: 5 September 2013].

Carminati, L. 2018. Generalizability in qualitative research: A tale of two traditions. *Qualitative Health Research.* 28(13): 2094–2101.

Chandler, D. 2017. *Semiotics. The basics.* 3rd ed. New York: Routledge.

Cheng, Z, Dimoka, A & Pavlou, P. 2016. Context may be king, but generalizability is the emperor! *Journal of Information Technology.* 31: 257–264.

Clarke, JJ. 1994. *Jung and Eastern thought. A dialogue with the Orient.* London: Routledge.

Clarke, V & Braun, V. 2014. Thematic analysis. In Michalos, AC (ed). *Encyclopedia of quality of life and well-being research*. Dordrecht: Springer.

Cohen, L, Manion, K & Morrison, K. 2018. *Research methods in education*. 8th ed. London: Routledge.

Coombs, C. 2017. Coherence and transparency: Some advice for qualitative researchers. *Production*. 27: 1–8.

Craig, DV. 2009. *Action research essentials*. San Francisco: Jossey-Bass.

Cresswell, JW & Cresswell, JD. 2018. *Research design: Qualitative, quantitative and mixed methods approaches*. 5th ed. Thousand Oaks, CA: Sage.

Creswell, JW & Poth, CN. 2018. *Qualitative inquiry and research design. Choosing among five approaches*. 4th ed. Los Angeles: Sage.

Dainton, M & Zelley, ED. 2019. *Applying communication theory for professional life: A practical introduction*. 4th ed. Los Angeles: Sage.

DeCarlo, M. 2018. *Scientific enquiry in social work*. Roanoke, VA: Open Social Work Education. file:///C:/Users/27810/Downloads/Scientific%20 inquiry%20in%20social%20work%20(printPDF).pdf

Denzin, KD & Lincon, YS. 2018. *The Sage handbook of qualitative research*. 5th ed. Thousand Oaks, CA: Sage.

Drisko, JW. & Maschi, T. 2016. *Content analysis*. New York: Oxford University Press.

Du Plooy, GM. 2006. *Communication research*. Cape Town: Juta.

Du Plooy-Cilliers, F. 2003. Paradigms and paradoxes: Shifting management thinking. In Verwey, S & du Plooy-Cilliers, F (eds). *Strategic organizational communication: Paradigms and paradoxes*. Johannesburg: Heinemann.

Edmonds, WA & Kennedy, TD. 2017. *An applied guide to research designs. Quantitative, qualitative and mixed methods*. 2nd ed. New York: Sage.

Erlingsson, C & Brysiewicz, P. 2017. A hands-on guide to doing content analysis. *African Journal of Emergency Medicine*. 7: 93–99.

Explorable. 2013. *Research basics*. Available at: http://explorable.com/research-basics. [Accessed: 12 March 2013].

Feldman, J. 2016. The simplicity principle in perception and cognition. *WIREs (Wiley Interdisciplinary Reviews) Cognitive Science*. 7(5): 330–340. https:// www.ncbi.nlm.nih.gov/pmc/articles/PMC5125387/

Fox, W & Bayat, MS. 2007. *A guide to managing research*. Cape Town: Juta.

Frauley, J. 2017. Synoptic vision: Metatheory, conceptualisation, and critical realism. *Canadian Journal of Sociology/Cahiers Canadiens De Sociologie*. 42(3): 293–324.

Fried, EI. 2020. Theories and models: What they are, what they are for, and what they are about. *Psychological Inquiry*. 31(4): 336–344.

Geertz, C. 1973. *The interpretation of cultures*. New York: Basic Books, Inc.

Gibbs, P. 1996. *What is Occam's razor?* Available at: http://math.ucr.edu/home/ baez/physics/General/occam.html [Accessed: 12 October 2013].

Glaser, BG & Strauss, AL. 1967. *The discovery of grounded theory: Strategies for qualitative research.* Piscataway, New Jersey: Aldine Transaction.

Gravetter, FJ & Forzano, LB. 2018. *Research methods for the behavioural sciences.* 6th ed. Belmont: Cengage.

Gray, DE. 2014. *Doing research in the real world.* 2nd ed. London: Sage.

Guba, EG & Lincoln, YS. 1994. Competing paradigms in qualitative research. In Denzin, NK & Lincoln, YS (eds). 2018. *The Sage handbook of qualitative research.* Thousand Oaks, CA: Sage, pp 105–117.

Hall, R. 2020. *Mixing methods in social research.* Los Angeles: Sage.

Hammond, M & Wellington, J. 2021. *Research methods: The key concepts.* 2nd ed. London: Routledge Taylor & Francis.

Heale, R, & Twycross, A. 2015. Validity and reliability in quantitative studies. *Evidence Based Nursing.* 18 (3): 66–67.

Howitt, D & Cramer, D. 2020. *Introduction to research methods in Psychology.* 6th ed. Harlow: Pearson.

Kennedy, BL & Thornberg, R. 2018. Deduction, induction and abduction. In Flick, U (ed). 2018. *The SAGE handbook of qualitative data analysis.* Thousand Oaks: Sage.

Kivunja, C. 2018. Distinguishing between theory, theoretical framework, and conceptual framework: A systematic review of lessons from the field. *International Journal of Higher Education.* 7(6): 44–53.

Korstjens, I & Moser, A. 2018. Practical guidance to qualitative research. Part 4: Trustworthiness and publishing. *European Journal of General Practice,* 24(1): 120–124.

Koshy, E, Koshy, V & Waterman, H. 2011. *Action research in healthcare.* London: Sage.

Kühl, S. 2020. Groups, organizations, families and movements: The sociology of social systems between interaction and society. *Systems Research and Behavior Science.* 37: 496–515. file:///C:/Users/27810/Downloads/Groups_organizations_families_and_movements_The_so.pdf

Kumar, R. 2019. *Research methodology: A step-by-step guide for beginners.* 5th ed. London: Sage.

Lawton G. 2020. How do we leave lockdown? *New Scientist.* 246: 10–12. https://doi.org/10.1016/S0262-4079(20)30706-5

Leavy, P. 2017. *Research design. Quantitative, qualitative, mixed methods, arts-based, and community-based participatory research approaches.* New York: The Guilford Press.

Leedy, PD & Ormrod, JE. 2015. *Practical research. Planning and design.* 11th ed. Boston: Pearson.

Leedy, PD & Ormrod, JE. 2019. *Practical research. Planning and design.* 12th ed. Boston: Pearson.

Littlejohn, SW & Foss, KA. 2009. *Encyclopedia of Communication Theory.* Thousand Oaks, CA: Sage.

Littlejohn, SW, Foss, KA & Oetzel, JG. 2017. *Theories of human communication.* 11th ed. Illinois: Waveland Press, Inc.

Luhmann, N. 1981. The improbability of communication. *International Social Science Journal,* XXXIII(1): 122–132.

Luhmann, N. 1996. *Social systems.* Stanford: Stanford University Press.

Luhmann, N. 1998. Globalization or world society? How to conceive of modern society. *International Review of Sociology.* 7(1): 67–79.

Luhmann, N. 2002. *Theories of distinction: Redescribing the descriptions of modernity.* California: Stanford University Press.

Luhmann, N. 2012. *Theory of society.* Vol 1. Stanford: Stanford University Press.

Machet, MP, Olen, SII & Behrens, SJ. 2017. *Mastering information skills for the 21st century.* Pretoria: Unisa Press.

Macnamara, J. 2018. Content analysis. In Napoli, P (ed). *Mediated communication.* 2018. Boston: de Gruyter Mouton.

Malmqvist, J, Hellberg, K, Möllås, G, Rose, R & Shevlin, M. 2019. Conducting the pilot study: A neglected part of the research process? Methodological findings supporting the importance of piloting in qualitative research studies. *International Journal of Qualitative Methods.* 18: 1–11.

Maree, K (ed). 2019. *First steps in research.* 3rd ed. Pretoria: Van Schaik.

McCaig, C & Dahlberg, L. 2010. *Practical research and evaluation: A start-to-finish guide for practitioners.* London: Sage.

McKoon, G & Ratcliff, R. 1995. The minimalist hypothesis: Directions for research. In Weaver III, CA, Mannes, S & Fletcher, CR (eds). *Discourse comprehension: Essays in honor of Walter Kintsch.* Lawrence Erlbaum Associates, Inc, pp 97–116.

McNiff, J. 2017. *All you need to know about action research.* London: Sage.

Moon, K, Brewer, TD, Januchowski-Hartley, SR, Adams, VM & Blackman, DA. 2016. A guideline to improve qualitative social science publishing in ecology and conservation journals. *Ecology and Society.* 21(3): 17.

Moravcsik, A. 2019. Transparency in qualitative research. *SAGE Research Methods Foundations.* London: Sage.

Mouton, J. 2001. *How to succeed in your Master's and Doctoral studies: A South African guide and resource book.* Pretoria: Van Schaik.

Neuendorf, KA. 2002. *The content analysis guidebook.* Thousand Oaks, CA: Sage.

Neuman, WL. 2014. *Social research methods: Qualitative and quantitative approaches.* 7th ed. Harlow: Pearson Education Limited.

Nilsen, P. 2015. Making sense of implementation theories, models and frameworks. *Implementation Science.* 10: 1–13.

Norris, S. 2004. *Analyzing multimodal interaction*. New York: Routledge.

O'Connor, C & Joffe, H. 2020. Intercoder reliability in qualitative research: Debates and practical guidelines. *International Journal of Qualitative Methods*. 19: 1–13.

Onen, D. 2016. Appropriate conceptualisation: The foundation of any solid quantitative research. *The Electronic Journal of Business Research Methods*. 14(1): 28–38. Available online at www.ejbrm.com.

Passey, D. 2020. Theories, theoretical and conceptual frameworks, models and constructs: Limiting research outcomes through misconceptions and misunderstandings. *Studies in Technology Enhanced Learning*. 1(1): 1–20. https://implementationscience.biomedcentral.com/articles/10.1186/s13012-015-0242-0

Patten, ML & Newhart, M. 2018. *Understanding research methods: An overview of the essentials*. 10th ed. New York: Routledge.

Pierce, R. 2008. *Research methods in politics: A practical guide*. London: Sage.

P.org (PlagiarismdotOrg). 2021. *What is Plagiarism?* Available at: http://www.plagiarism.org/plagiarism-101/what-is-plagiarism. [Accessed: 9 July 2021].

Pouchera, ZA, Tamminen, KA, Caron, JG & Sweet, SN. 2020. Thinking through and designing qualitative research studies: A focused mapping review of 30 years of qualitative research in Sport Psychology. *International Review of Sport and Exercise Psychology*. 13(1): 163–186.

Radiopaedia. nd. *Fracture healing*. Available at: http://radiopaedia.org/articles/fracture-healing [Accessed: 9 December 2013].

Resnik, DB. 2020. *What is ethics in research & why is it important?* Available at: https://www.niehs.nih.gov/research/resources/bioethics/whatis/index.cfm [Accessed: 2 August 2021].

RMIT Study and Learning Centre. 2007. *Writing a research report*. Available at: https://www.dlsweb.rmit.edu.au/lsu/content/2_assessmenttasks/assess_pdf/ research_report.pdf [Accessed: 5 September 2013].

Saldaña, J. 2014. Coding and analysis strategies. In Leavy, P (ed). 2014. *The Oxford handbook of qualitative research*. New York: Oxford University Press.

Saldaña, J. 2016. *The coding manual for qualitative researchers*. 3rd ed. Los Angeles: Sage.

Salganik, MJ. 2018. *Bit by bit. Social research in the digital age*. Princeton New Jersey: Princeton University Press.

Saunders, MNK, Lewis, P & Thornhill, A. 2019. *Research methods for business students*. 8th ed. Harlow: Pearson.

Saxe, JG. 1873. *The poems of John Godfrey Saxe*. Complete edition from the Library of Congress. Originally published in Boston: James R Osgood and Company. Available at: http://ia600406.us.archive.org/32/items/poemsofjohngodfr00saxe/poemsofjohngodfr00saxe.pdf [Accessed: 12 October 2013].

Scheidel, TM. 1972. *Speech communication and human interaction.* Glenview, Ill: Scott and Foresman.

Schreier, M. 2014. Qualitative content analysis. In Flick, U (ed). 2014. *The SAGE handbook of qualitative data analysis.* Thousand Oaks: Sage.

Serpa, S & Ferreira, CM. 2019. Micro, meso and macro levels of social analysis. *International Journal of Social Science Studies.* 7(3): 120–124.

Strauss, AL. 1987. *Qualitative analysis for social scientists.* New York: Sage.

Strauss, AL & Corbin, J. 1990. *Grounded theory in practice.* New York: Sage.

Stringer, ET. 2013. *Action research in Education.* 4th ed. New York: Sage.

Toerien, M. 2014. Conversations and conversation analysis. In Flick, U (ed). 2014. *The SAGE handbook of qualitative data analysis.* Thousand Oaks: Sage.

Toulmin, S. 1964. The complexity of scientific choice: A stocktaking. *Minerva.* 2(3): 343–359.

Tracy, SJ. 2020. *Qualitative research methods: Collecting evidence, crafting analysis, communicating impact.* 2nd ed. New York: Wiley Blackwell.

Trent, A & Cho, J. 2014. Interpretation strategies: Appropriate concepts. In Leavy, P (ed). 2014. *The Oxford handbook of qualitative research.* New York: Oxford University Press.

Walliman, N. 2018. *Research methods: The basics.* 2nd ed. London and New York: Routledge Taylor & Francis.

Welman, C, Kruger, F & Mitchell, B. 2005. *Research methodology.* 3rd ed. Cape Town: Oxford University Press.

Willig, C. 2014. Discourses and discourse analysis. In Flick, U (ed). 2014. *The SAGE handbook of qualitative data analysis.* Thousand Oaks: Sage.

Yin, RK. 2016. *Qualitative research from start to finish.* 2nd ed. New York: The Guilford Press.

Yin, RK. 2018. *Case study research and applications: Design and methods.* 6th ed. Thousand Oakes: Sage.

ZAM. 2013. *Whisper (wow).* Available at: http://wow.allakhazam.com/wiki/whisper_(wow) [Accessed: 21 November 2013].

Zhang, Y & Wildemuth, BM. 2009. Qualitative analysis of content. In Wildemuth, BM (ed) 2009. *Applications of social research methods to questions in Information and Library Science.* Westport, CT: Libraries Unlimited.

Index

Note: Page numbers in *italics* refer to Figures or Tables.

www.ingramcontent.com/pod-product-compliance
Lightning Source LLC
Chambersburg PA
CBHW061219270326
41926CB00032B/4771